LUTHER'S EARLIEST
OPPONENTS

LUTHER'S EARLIEST OPPONENTS

Catholic Controversialists, 1518–1525

DAVID V. N. BAGCHI

FORTRESS PRESS   MINNEAPOLIS

LUTHER'S EARLIEST OPPONENTS
Catholic Controversialists, 1518–1525

All Scripture quotations are from the New Revised Standard Version Bible, copyright © 1989 by the Division of Christian Education of the National Council of the Churches of Christ in the United States of America.

Interior design by Publisher's WorkGroup

Cover design by Jim Gerhard

Cover art: Title page to *Die Luterische Strebkatz* (P. Schöffer, Worms, 1524)

Library of Congress Cataloging-in-Publication Data

Bagchi, David V. N., 1959–
    Luther's earliest opponents : Catholic controversialists,
    1518–1525 / David V.N. Bagchi.
        p.   cm.
    Revision of thesis (D. Phil.)—University of Oxford.
    Includes bibliographical references and index.
    ISBN 0-8006-2517-X (alk. paper)
    1. Luther, Martin, 1483–1546—Adversaries.   2. Pamphleteers—
Europe—History—16th century.   3. Church—Authority—History of
doctrines—16th century.   4. Catholic Church—Doctrines—History—
Modern period, 1500–   5. Reformation.   I. Title.
BR355.P36B34   1991
270.6—dc20   91-34266
                                                                  CIP

The paper used in this publication meets the minimum requirements of American National Standard for Information Sciences—Permanence of Paper for Printed Library Materials, ANSI Z329.48–1984.   ∞™

Manufactured in the U.S.A.   AF 1–2517

95   94   93   92   91   1   2   3   4   5   6   7   8   9   10

For my father,
Jitendra Chandra Bagchi,
and in memory of my mother,
Eileen Bagchi

CONTENTS

ACKNOWLEDGMENTS

Many debts of gratitude have been incurred in the making of this book. Although I can never repay them, I gladly take the opportunity of acknowledging some of them here.

This book originated as a thesis for the degree of Doctor of Philosophy at the University of Oxford under the supervision of the late Dr. Garry Bennett. My thanks are due to him, and to Dr. John Platt, who stepped in at short notice to escort a nervous doctorand through the final stage of examination; to Dr. Alister McGrath, for sage advice and practical support; to Dr. Peter Newman Brooks, a foster-*Doktorvater* of apparently inexhaustible patience and enthusiasm; to Professor Mark Edwards, not the least of whose kindnesses was to bring my manuscript to the attention of Fortress Press; and to Professor Pierre Fraenkel, whose gracious assistance I have shamelessly exploited. To work in the field of Reformation studies is itself a privilege. To have benefited from the generosity of scholars such as these makes it a privilege twice over.

By far my greatest debt is to my wife, Fiona, who has acted throughout as supervisor, critic, and colleague. This book would not have been possible without her.

David V. N. Bagchi
The University of Hull

ABBREVIATIONS

ARC	G. Pfeilschifter, ed., *Acta reformationis catholicae ecclesiam Germaniae concernantia saeculi XVI.* Vol. 1, *1520 bis 1532* (Regensburg: F. Pustet, 1959).
ARG	*Archiv für Reformationsgeschichte*
BHR	*Bibliothèque d'Humanisme et Renaissance*
Briefmappe	J. Greving, ed., *Briefmappe: Erstes Stück.* RST 21/22 (Münster-Westfalen: Aschendorff, 1912)
CC	Corpus Catholicorum: Werke katholischer Schriftsteller in Zeitalter der Glaubensspaltung
CHR	*Catholic Historical Review*
CICan	E. Friedberg, ed., *Corpus iuris canonici,* vol. 1, *Decretum magistri Gratiani;* vol. 2, *Decretalium collectiones* (Leipzig: Bernhard Tauchnitz, 1879–1881)
COD	J. Alberigo et al., eds., *Conciliorum Oecumenicorum Decreta,* 3d ed. (Bologna: Istituto per le scienza religiose, 1973)
CR	Corpus Reformatorum
CSEL	*Corpus Scriptorum Ecclesiasticorum Latinorum*
CT	*Concilium Tridentinum: Diariorum, actorum, epistularum, tractatuum nova collectio* (Freiburg im Breisgau, 1901–)
CWM	*The Complete Works of Sir Thomas More* (New Haven and London: Yale University Press, 1963–)
DS	H. Denzinger and A. Schönmetzer, eds., *Enchiridion symbolorum definitionum et declarationum de rebus fidei et morum,* 36th ed. (Barcelona, Freiburg im Breisgau, and Rome: Herder, 1976)
DTC	*Dictionnaire de théologie catholique*
EEJ	L. Pastor, ed., *Erläuterungen und Ergänzungen zu Janssens Geschichte des deutschen Volkes* (Freiburg im Breisgau, 1898–1905)
Flug.	H.-J. Köhler et al., eds., *Flugschriften des frühen 16. Jahrhunderts* (Zug and Leiden: Inter-Documentation, 1978–87)

FStud	*Franziskanische Studien*
Gess	F. Gess, ed., *Akten und Briefe zur Kirchenpolitik Herzog Georgs von Sachsen*, 2 vols. (Leipzig: Königlich Sächsische Kommission für Geschichte, 1905–7)
HJ	*Historisches Jahrbuch*
KLK	Katholisches Leben und Kämpfen ("und Kirchenreform" after 1966) im Zeitalter der Glaubensspaltung
Lauchert	F. Lauchert, *Die italienische Literarischen Gegner Luthers*, EEJ 8 (Freiburg im Breisgau, 1912)
LJ	*Luther-Jahrbuch* (Leipzig and Göttingen: Vandenhoeck & Ruprecht, 1919–)
L. Lemmens	*Pater Augustin von Alveld: Ein Franziskaner aus den ersten Jahren der Glaubensspaltung in Deutschland*, EEJ 1, iv (Freiburg im Breisgau, 1899)
Löscher	V. E. Löscher, ed., *Vollständige Reformations-acta und -documenta*, 3 vols. (Leipzig, 1723–27)
LThK	*Lexikon für Theologie und Kirche*, 11 vols., 2d ed. (Freiburg im Breisgau: Herder, 1957–67)
LW	J. Pelikan and H. T. Lehmann, eds., *Luther's Works* (Philadelphia: Fortress Press; St. Louis: Concordia Publishing House, 1955–86)
MPL	J.-P. Migne, ed., *Patrologiae cursus completus. Series Latina* (Paris: Garnier, 1844–62)
MRL	P. Balan, ed., *Monumenta reformationis Lutheranae ex tabulariis S. Sedis secretis 1521–1525* (Regensburg, New York, and Cincinnati: F. Pustet, 1883–84)
Op. Lat.	*Tomus primus (-quartus) omnium operum Reverendi Patris D. Martini Lutheri* (Jena, 1564)
Pijper	F. Pijper, ed., *Bibliotheca Reformatoria Neerlandica: Geschriften uit den Tijd der Hervorming in de Nederlanden I: De oudste Roomsche bestrijders van Luther* (The Hague, 1905)
RST	Reformationsgeschichtliche Studien und Texte
SCJ	*Sixteenth Century Journal*
StAusg	H.-U. Delius et al., eds., *Martin Luther Studienausgabe*, 5 vols. (Berlin: Evangelische Verlaganstalt, 1979–)
StTh	*Studia theologica*
SVR	Schriften des Vereins für Reformationsgeschichte

WA	*D. Martin Luthers Werke: Kritische Gesamtausgabe* (Weimar: Böhlau, 1883–1983)
Walch	J. G. Walch, ed., *D. Martin Luthers Sämtliche Schriften*, 24 vols. (Halle, 1739–50)
WA Br	*D. Martin Luthers Werke: Kritische Gesamtausgabe: Briefwechsel* (Weimar: Böhlau, 1930)
WA Tr	*D. Martin Luthers Werke: Kritische Gesamtausgabe: Tischreden* (Weimar: Böhlau, 1912–21)
ZHT	*Zeitschrift für historische Theologie*
ZKG	*Zeitschrift für Kirchengeschichte*
ZKTh	*Zeitschrift für katholische Theologie*

THE SIGNIFICANCE OF
THE CATHOLIC RESPONSE

The initial success of the Reformation is often attributed in part to a natural alliance of Protestantism and print.[1] An early exponent of this view was Martin Luther himself, who hailed the printing press as God's most signal act of grace in the furtherance of the gospel.[2] An ideology that maintains the external clarity of Scripture and the priesthood of all believers (so this argument runs) must accept with alacrity the egalitarian implications of the open book—open, that is, to anyone who can read or who knows someone who can. The argument may oversimplify, but it helps to account for the flood of pamphlets that accompanied the Reformation in its early years.

There is, however, a respect in which the argument appears flawed. It implies that an ideology of the closed Bible and of the priesthood of some believers (the very Roman Church that Luther attacked) would reject the press. It seems that this was far from being the case. According to the standard bibliography, the literary defenders of the old faith are to be numbered in their hundreds, their books and pamphlets in their thousands.[3] Indeed, the surprising claim has been made that, if Luther's writings are excluded from the equation, Catholics actually outpublished Protestants in the sixteenth century, even in the period before Trent.[4]

Therefore, there is a prima facie case for challenging the conven-

---

1. See, e.g., R. Wohlfeil, *Einführung in die Geschichte der deutschen Reformation*, 132.
2. Cited in A. G. Dickens, *The German Nation and Martin Luther*, 109.
3. Klaiber's catalogue of sixteenth-century Catholic controversialists and reformers lists 355 authors and 3,456 titles. This impressive tally excludes the entire corpora of such prolific figures as Canisius, Cochlaeus, Eck, Ellenbog, Erasmus, Loyola, and More, on the grounds that their writings have already been adequately catalogued. The figure of 3,456 titles also excludes, of course, reprintings and later editions. See W. Klaiber, ed., *Katholische Kontroverstheologen und Reformer des 16. Jahrhunderts: Ein Werkverzeichnis*. As the title suggests, her inventory is not confined to controversial writers.
4. R. A. Crofts, "Printing, Reform and the Catholic Reformation in Germany (1521–1545)," 381. M. U. Edwards, Jr., takes issue with Crofts's statement in "Statistics on Sixteenth-Century Printing," in *The Process of Change in Early Modern Europe: Essays in Honor of Miriam Usher Chrisman*.

tional theory of an exclusive alliance of print and Protestantism. How radically it will have to be reformulated will depend on a closer analysis of the nature and extent of the Catholic use of the press at the time of the Reformation—an analysis that in turn should result in an explanation of this use, a general theory of the relationship between print and Catholicism. This book, a study of some 180 works by fifty-seven Catholic controversialists active against Luther between 1518 and 1525, is offered as a contribution to such a task. It is not primarily an account of individual controversialists, although it does contain brief introductions where biography is important for elucidating motive. Nor is it intended as a systematic presentation of their theology, although it will be largely concerned with identifying their characteristic theological emphases. Its purpose is to discover whether the medium they used, the message they intended, and their motives in writing (or, more simply, the literary and theological aspects of their work) can be related, and, if they can, whether this relationship can be explained.

The effort is worth making. Since the early years of this century much work has been done in publishing and analyzing the writings of the sixteenth-century Catholic controversialists.[5] However, it is fair to say that few of its results have filtered into the mainstream of Reformation studies.[6] The reason for this neglect is not hard to find. The

---

5. "Catholic controversialists" ("katholische Kontroverstheologen" in the German literature) is the term most frequently used by modern scholars. They referred to themselves most typically as *docti* ("the learned"), which would be a rather meaningless designation for us to use. Luther's *Romanistae* is helpful, but his *papistae* is probably best avoided for fear of confusing them with "papalists," which by no means all his conservative opponents were. I have therefore preferred the designations "Catholic controversialist" and "Romanist." I do not intend to suggest by their use that the writers had any greater claim to catholicity than Luther or that they were Roman Catholic in the post-Tridentine, confessional sense of that term.

6. More than a century ago, the Protestant historian W. Walther could complain that "our knowledge of the Reformation suffers from a one-sidedness, a degree of uncertainty, while we are incomparably better acquainted with the reformers and their colleagues than with their opponents" (Walther's review of H. Wedewer's *Johannes Dietenberger*, in *Historische Zeitschrift* 63 [1889], 311). His words have been invoked as a justification for controversialist studies by Roman Catholic historians N. Paulus, *Die deutschen Dominikaner im Kampfe gegen Luther (1518–63)*, v; and R. Bäumer, "Vorgeschichte der bibliographischen Erfassung von Schriften katholischer Kontroverstheologen und Reformer des 16. Jahrhunderts," in W. Klaiber, ed., *Katholische Kontroverstheologen*, xviii. As recently as 1978 the leading Protestant controversialist scholar could conclude that Reformation history had ignored the Roman polemicists, with Protestants taking the reformers' verdict for granted and Catholics such as J. Lortz dismissing them as at best "negative correctives" (P. Fraenkel, "An der Grenze von Luthers Einfluss: Aversion gegen Umwertung," 22).

controversialists seem to be marginal figures. For the theologian, their writings lack both the creative force of the magisterial and radical reformers and the dogmatic significance of Trent. For the historian, they add little to our understanding of the people, the ideas, or the events of the sixteenth century. The general scholarly verdict upon them is that they were failures both as writers and as theologians. A fairer appreciation of the constraints under which the controversialists worked (which in turn explain the "failure" of their writings), especially in the context of the interplay of ideas and new forms of communication,[7] will enable all students of the Reformation to look at the controversialists in their own terms and with a degree of historical sympathy. That mainstream Reformation scholarship may be more disposed to such a reevaluation now than in the past is perhaps indicated by the recent burgeoning of English-language (particularly American) controversialist studies.[8]

The value of the Catholic controversialists for Reformation scholarship in general is not, however, exhausted by an evaluation of them in their own terms. They wrote against a particular man and his ideas, ostensibly on behalf of their ecclesiastical establishment, and it is valid to take account of this wider context also. Since the beginning of the "Luther renaissance" in 1883, scholars have sought to explain in detail what the reformer thought and how he came to think it. This worthwhile enterprise has nevertheless obscured equally important questions: How was Luther perceived by others? and What effect did these perceptions have? The reaction of the ecclesiastical establishment is particularly important, because the legal process against Luther was

7. M. U. Edwards, Jr., has suggested that the Catholic controversialists can adequately be understood only in the context of the "structural constraints" that accompanied the attempt of the first major established ideological institution to resist the appeal of a mass medium ("Catholic Controversial Literature, 1518–1555: Some Statistics," 204).

8. Relevant English-language publications since 1985 (restricted to those dealing with pre-1525 Catholic controversialist writings) include, in addition to the articles by Crofts and Edwards already cited, D.V.N. Bagchi, "'Eyn mercklich underscheyd': Catholic Reactions to Luther's Doctrine of the Priesthood of All Believers, 1520–25," 155–65; M. U. Edwards, Jr., "*Lutherschmähung*? Catholics on Luther's Responsibility for the Peasants' War," 461–80; J. M. Headley, "The Reformation as Crisis in the Understanding of Tradition," 5–22; S. Ickert, "Defending and Defining the *ordo salutis*: Jakob van Hoogstraten vs. Martin Luther," 81–97; idem, "Catholic Controversialist Theology and *sola scriptura*: The Case of Jakob van Hoogstraten," 13–33; G. F. Lytle, "John Wyclif, Martin Luther and Edward Powell: Heresy and the Oxford Theology Faculty at the Beginning of the Reformation," 465–79; R.A.W. Rex, "The English Campaign against Luther in the 1520s"; idem, "The Polemical Theologian"; J. D. Tracy, "Two Erasmuses, Two Luthers: Erasmus' Strategy in Defense of *De libero arbitrio*."

the formal cause of his break with Rome. It is well known that the bull *Exsurge Domine* simply listed those of Luther's propositions that were deemed to be variously heretical, scandalous, offensive, and so on. No attempt was made to indicate the degree of error attached to each proposition or to explain the reasons for its condemnation. The work of the Catholic controversialists is the best indication we have of the grounds for Roman opposition to Luther. To that extent at least, the controversialists, far from being of only marginal interest to Reformation studies, are vital for a full understanding of why the Reformation happened at all.

Such an assertion, of course, raises a number of questions. To what extent did the controversialists reflect the views of the Catholic establishment? What part did they and their writings play in the legal process? To what extent did they agree among themselves on the nature of the threat posed by Luther? This book will also address these questions. The material cause of Luther's break, his theological estrangement from the Roman Church, was, of course, a much more complicated affair. Nonetheless, the influence of the Catholic controversialists must be reckoned with even here, for the reformer himself maintained throughout his life that they contributed in no small measure to his own intellectual development. At the conclusion of this book, therefore, I shall also be concerned with the question of how Luther responded to the controversialists and how they might have affected his theological career.

Roman Catholic Perspectives

It is not surprising that study of the Catholic controversialists has been dominated by Roman Catholic scholars, for whom the controversialists represent almost the sole example of "Catholic" intellectual activity in the Reformation period before Trent.[9] Scholarly interest in them dates from the 1830s, when German Catholicism, between the Enlightenment and the *Kulturkampf*, was slowly regaining its confidence.

---

9. For useful reviews of earlier literature on this subject, see H. Jedin, "Die Erforschung der kirchlichen Reformationsgeschichte seit 1876: Leistungen und Aufgaben der deutschen Katholiken," reprinted with R. Bäumer's supplementary review, "Die Erforschung der kirchlichen Reformationsgeschichte seit 1931: Reformation, katholische Reform und Gegenreformation in der neueren katholischen Reformationsgeschichtsschreibung in Deutschland." See also R. Bäumer, "Vorgeschichte der bibliographischen Erfassung von Schriften katholischer Kontroverstheologen und Reformer des 16. Jahrhunderts," vii–xxiii.

J. A. Möhler's assessment of pre- and post-Tridentine doctrines, Hugo Lämmer's well-documented study of the controversialists' theology, and J. Janssen's history of the German people all date from this time.[10] After the silence of the *Kulturkampf*, research on the Catholic controversialists was resumed by two men. The first, Nikolaus Paulus, was able to publish many of his findings in the *Historisches Jahrbuch*, founded in 1880 by the Roman Catholic *Görresgesellschaft*. The second, Josef Greving, wrote a number of monographs (notably on Eck's early theological development) and also founded two series, Reformationsgeschichtliche Studien und Texte (Münster-Westfalen: Aschendorff, 1906–) and Corpus Catholicorum: Werke katholischer Schriftsteller im Zeitalter der Glaubensspaltung (Münster-Westfalen: Aschendorff, 1919–). These publications, which specialize in critical editions and detailed studies, were joined in 1926 by the more discursive Katholisches Leben und Kämpfen ("und Kirchenreform" after 1966) im Zeitalter der Glaubensspaltung. By the 1930s, therefore, scholarly scrutiny of the controversialists was an established feature of Reformation history writing. But to what end?

The renewal of German Roman Catholic self-confidence brought in its wake a renewed interest in those whom Roman Catholics hailed as their sixteenth-century predecessors. This, however, raised a problem of reconciling honest historical criticism of writers whose lives and works were rarely attractive with confessional loyalty to the very teachings, mutatis mutandis, the latter had defended. For example, when the editor of the *Historisches Jahrbuch* first received Paulus's manuscripts, he thought he was dealing with a Protestant author. The dilemma was resolved at first by recognizing not only the inadequacy but also the heroism of those who defended medieval doctrines in the face of hostility from below and apathy from above.[11] During this time, however, another solution to the Roman Catholic historian's dilemma was being developed—the theory of *Unklarheit*. The supposition of a widespread theological vagueness pervading the church at the close of the Middle Ages, which both spawned the Reformation

---

10. J. A. Möhler, *Symbolik oder Darstellung der dogmatischen Gegensätze der Katholiken und Protestanten nach ihren öffentlichen Bekenntnisschriften* (Mainz, 1832), Eng. trans. *Symbolism or Doctrinal Differences between Catholics and Protestants*, trans. J. S. Robertson (London, 1906); H. Lämmer, *Die vortridentinisch-katholische Theologie des Reformationszeitalters aus den Quellen dargestellt*; J. Janssen, *Geschichte des deutschen Volkes seit dem Ausgang des Mittelalters*, 8 vols. (Freiburg im Breisgau, 1876–91).

11. N. Paulus, *Die deutschen Dominikaner im Kämpfe gegen Luther (1518–63)*, vi.

and hindered an authentically "Catholic" reaction to it, is usually associated with one book, Joseph Lortz's *Die Reformation in Deutschland* (1939–40). But it had much deeper roots. The idea had already been expressed by Hubert Jedin,[12] and Etienne Gilson's theory of a decline in medieval theology from Aquinas's reasoned faith to Ockham's fideism and skepticism owes much to Hartmann Grisar's and Heinrich Denifle's earlier vilification of an uncatholic nominalism. The problem with the theory of *Unklarheit* is that it is open to the charge of being essentially anachronistic, because it applies to pre-Tridentine theology criteria drawn from post-Tridentine (or even post–Vatican I) orthodoxy. One can detect confusion over what is correct doctrine only if one already has an idea of what correct doctrine is. Correct doctrine, in the opinions of all the above-mentioned historians and theologians, was to be found in the writings of Thomas Aquinas: his was the truth from which late medieval theology declined; his was the truth rediscovered by the fathers at Trent, which resolved the doctrinal confusion of the previous two centuries. The use of Thomism as a standard owes much to Pope Leo XIII's adoption of Aquinas as the "official" theologian of the Roman Catholic Church in 1879, and it is noteworthy that the *Unklarheit* theory and its variants cannot be shown to have predated this adoption.[13] Nevertheless, it must be said that the introduction of the Council of Trent into the debate had, from our point of view, at least one beneficial consequence. By finding within the sixteenth century an alternative standard of Catholic orthodoxy, in comparison with which other contemporary writers could be shown to be more or less correct, Roman Catholics were now less likely to treat the works of the Romanists as in some sense definitive. The *Unklarheit* theory therefore had a liberating and not wholly baleful effect on postwar Roman Catholic scholarship.

This theory of doctrinal confusion is today almost universally accepted by Roman Catholic historians, especially by those who write about the Catholic controversialists. Their assessment of these authors' positive achievement, on the other hand, now seems to be divided. There is a minimalist position, of which Lortz is the best representative. In a perceptive essay published in 1968, he addressed the question of how a modern Catholic was to regard these writers who had

12. See Bäumer, "Erforschung," 119.
13. See the papal encyclical *Aeterni Patris* (*DS*, 3139–40).

anathematized churches that Vatican II had since declared to be under the direction of the Holy Spirit.[14] The most that can be said of them, he argued, was that they distinguished what was then seen as truth and error and kept Catholic truth alive through dangerous times; but their lasting contribution was to be found in the quality of their spirituality and of their personal, pastoral ministry. Lortz's pupil, Erwin Iserloh of the University of Mainz, continued this line of interpretation, pointing out that the high moral earnestness of some was not matched by their theological acumen and that the academic prowess of others lacked religious depth.[15]

The maximalist position is represented by Remigius Bäumer of the University of Freiburg, who credits the controversialists not only with having penetrated the *Unklarheit* but even with influencing to no small extent the decrees of Trent.[16] Bäumer is probably most famous for upsetting the Roman Catholic consensus on Luther established by Lortz. In a book published to coincide with Pope John Paul II's visit to the German Federal Republic in 1980, he vilified the reformer and his motives in a manner reminiscent to some of the polemic of eighty years before.[17] For our purposes, he serves to show that when a Roman Catholic scholar stresses the controversialists' doctrinal significance apart from Trent, he or she is also obliged to defend and justify them personally, as Bäumer's laudatory biography of Cochlaeus demonstrates. Lortz and Bäumer represent two extremes. The American John Dolan occupies the middle ground. He agreed that many of the Romanists, such as Cochlaeus or the early Johannes Eck, were reactionaries whose impact on the Reformation period was at best negligible and at worst exacerbatory. But he also pointed to those whom he

14. J. Lortz, "Wert und Grenzen der katholischen Kontroverstheologie in der ersten Hälfte des 16. Jahrhunderts," 14.

15. E. Iserloh, *Der Kampf um die Messe in den ersten Jahren der Auseinandersetzung mit Luther*, 33, 57; idem, *Johannes Eck 1486-1543: Scholastiker, Humanist, Kontroverstheologe*, 80. See also J. Lortz and E. Iserloh, *Kleine Reformationsgeschichte: Ursachen, Verlauf, Wirkung*, 126–41.

16. See, e.g., Bäumer, "Lehramt und Theologie in der Sicht katholischer Theologen des 16. Jahrhunderts," 60; and idem, *Johannes Cochlaeus (1479–1552): Leben und Werk im Dienst der katholischen Reform*, passim.

17. Bäumer, "Das Zeitalter der Glaubensspaltung," in B. Kötting, ed., *Kleine deutsche Kirchengeschichte* (Freiburg, Basel, Vienna, 1980). For Bäumer's notoriety, see P. Manns, "Katholische Lutherforschung in der Krise?" in P. Manns, ed., *Zur Lage der Lutherforschung Heute*, Institut für europäische Geschichte Mainz (Wiesbaden: Franz Steiner Verlag, 1982), esp. 110–28; and G. Wiedermann, "Cochlaeus as a Polemicist," esp. 204f.

called the "theologians of mediation," such as Gaspar Contarini, Johannes Gropper, Julius Pflug, Michael Helding, and Georg Witzel, who, though distrusted by both sides, refrained from mere abuse of their opponents and concentrated instead on developing a biblically based presentation of the faith through catechisms, sermons, hymns, and enchiridia, with the double aim of edifying Catholics and converting Protestants.[18]

Protestant Treatments

Understandably perhaps, Protestant scholarship has largely passed over the Catholic controversialists as an object of serious inquiry. The first and, to my knowledge, only full-scale appreciation of their work by a Protestant writer was Lämmer's theological anthology of 1858.[19] This was, however, the exception to prove the rule—shortly after the appearance of the book its author was received into the Roman Catholic Church. At the turn of the century, Walther Friedensburg edited a number of the Romanists' letters held in the Vatican archives, but these have remained a source without any accompanying analysis. The most significant recent treatment has been that of Jaroslav Pelikan,[20] who admirably attempts to encapsulate the teachings of the pre-Tridentine Romanists in the space of a few pages, but almost inevitably tends to blur any sense of historical development or of differences between the writers. Even if we ignore the overtly polemical treatments, we see that the controversialists have been dealt with by Protestants only in order that Luther and his allies could shine more brightly by comparison.[21] In this reading, their inability to comprehend the level on which Luther's theological arguments were being forged was matched only by their readiness to abuse him, and their inability to

18. See J. P. Dolan, "The Catholic Literary Opponents of Luther and the Reformation."

19. H. Lämmer, *Die vortridentinisch-katholische Theologie des Reformationszeitalters aus den Quellen dargestellt.*

20. See "Roman Catholic Particularity" and "The Gospel and the Catholic Church," in J. Pelikan, *Reformation and Dogma of the Church, 1300–1600.*

21. Despite the fact that they are works of first-class historical scholarship still unsurpassed in their respective fields, the monographs of T. Wiedemann on Eck (*Dr Johann Eck, Professor der Theologie an der Universität Ingolstadt—eine Monographie*); M. Spahn on Cochlaeus (*Johannes Cochläus: Ein Lebensbild aus der Zeit der Kirchenspaltung*); W. Kawerau on Murner (*Thomas Murner und die Kirche des Mittelalters*; idem, *Thomas Murner und die deutsche Reformation*); and G. Kawerau on Emser (*Hieronymus Emser: Ein Lebensbild aus der Reformationsgeschichte*) started from the assumption that the controversialists were mistaken, and this assumption dominated their assessments.

stage a literary counterattack of equal quantity and quality brought its own reward.[22] No more positive appreciation than this has been made by Protestants; while some Roman Catholics have felt obliged, in the interests of ecumenism, to apologize for the controversialists, ecumenically minded Protestant historians of the Reformation have thought it best to ignore them altogether.

Consensus on the
Controversialists' Failure

Excluding the minority opinion of Bäumer, the view of modern scholarship is that the Catholic controversial effort was a movement that failed. On the one hand, the writers failed to communicate their ideas to the reformers and to the general public. On the other hand, they lacked a sound theological basis for their arguments. The reasons frequently given for their failure to communicate effectively may be summarized as follows: (1) they lacked coordination and leadership;[23] (2) widespread anti-curialism did not provide the best conditions for a sympathetic reception of their message;[24] (3) the German bishops were too apathetic to support them;[25] and (4) the moderate controversialists, who had the best chance of converting Protestants, were treated with grave suspicion by both sides, and their pleas for conciliation were drowned out by their more militant colleagues.[26] The theological failure of these writers has also been put down to a number of possible causes. They were unable to think "biblically"[27] or "pastorally,"[28] and therefore to comprehend the message of the Reformation. They tragically underestimated the strength of their opponents' positions and were overconfident in their own.[29] Their polemic was too vicious.[30] They relied excessively on the early fathers and lacked any doctrine of doctrinal development that would have helped them explain the accretions in practice and belief of the medieval church.[31] They were

---

22. See, e.g., Dickens, *German Nation*, 121.
23. Lortz, "Wert und Grenzen," 31.
24. Lortz and Iserloh, *Reformationsgeschichte*, 127; Dolan, "Catholic Literary Opponents," 193.
25. Lortz and Iserloh, *Reformationsgeschichte*, 141.
26. Dolan, "Catholic Literary Opponents," 206.
27. Lortz, "Wert und Grenzen," 22.
28. J. Wicks, "Roman Reactions to Luther: The First Year (1518)," 548.
29. Lortz, "Wert und Grenzen," 20.
30. Ibid., 21f.
31. Ibid., 23.

too ready to contradict the reformers on the basis of established authorities rather than engaging with the issues with any seriousness.[32] The demand of polemical writing for an instant answer conflicted with the demands of theology, which is a more reflective process.[33] Widespread *Unklarheit* disguised the true, revolutionary nature of Luther's teachings until it was too late,[34] and in certain respects (notably in its teaching on the mass) late medieval theology had not prepared conservative scholars for the type of attacks they were to face from the reformers.[35]

In addition to these two classes of explanation, there is a third, which purports to explain both the controversialists' theological failure and their inability to communicate to their readership. First, it is argued, their preferred literary method was to refute their opponents sentence by sentence. This meant that they were always reacting and could never wrest the initiative from the reformers.[36] Second, their automatic reaction was simply to negate, to reply to Luther in detail before they could appreciate the totality of his teaching or before they had read him at all.[37] They were too ready simply to deny Luther's arguments without giving reasons for their disagreement.[38] They signally failed to admit that any guilt lay with the Roman Church.[39] They were too concerned with justifying themselves personally.[40] They were too "scholastic" in their method, even when claiming to be humanists, and the genuine humanists among them were only secondarily theologians.[41]

Prospectus

The majority verdict of those who have studied the Catholic controversialists is that they failed, both as theologians and as writers.

32. Wiedermann, "Cochlaeus as a Polemicist," 201; R. G. Cole, "The Reformation Pamphlet and Communication Processes," 139.

33. Iserloh, *Kampf um die Messe*, 58.

34. Dolan, "Catholic Literary Opponents," 191.

35. Iserloh, *Kampf um die Messe*, 58.

36. J. Lortz, *The Reformation in Germany* 2:189; idem, "Wert und Grenzen," 18; E. Iserloh, *Katholische Theologen der Reformationszeit* 1:1, 8, 39.

37. Lortz, "Wert und Grenzen," 19; Wiedermann, "Cochlaeus as a Polemicist," 200.

38. Lortz, "Wert und Grenzen," 19.

39. Lortz, *Reformation in Germany* 2:193.

40. Wiedermann, "Cochlaeus as a Polemicist," 199.

41. Dolan, "Catholic Literary Opponents," 194; Wiedermann, "Cochlaeus as a Polemicist," 199.

The argument of this book is that by identifying the nature of the relationship between the theological and literary characteristics of their writings—between message and medium—this apparent failure becomes understandable. With some notable exceptions, the Catholic polemicists were not attempting to do the same thing as Luther and his colleagues, and they therefore cannot be dismissed as failures by comparison.

Those who claim to have identified the shortcomings of past scholarship should be at least as conscious of the beams in their own eyes. Let me try to forestall two criticisms that could immediately be made of this book. First, the treatment of message is disproportionate to that of medium. Most of the chapters deal with the theological concerns of the controversialists, and do so in an occasional and unsystematic way. Second, the scope of the survey itself is limited, both in its concentration on writings against Luther and in its restriction to the years 1518 to 1525. It seems arbitrary to end a study of anti-Lutheran pamphlets in 1525. This used to be a convenient terminus for studies of Luther, on the assumption perhaps that the reformer's best work was behind him when he clashed with Erasmus and the peasants, or perhaps in the misogynistic belief that he went downhill after marriage. But Luther continued for another two decades to write works of immense quality and quantity, many of which brought forth replies—and replies to replies—from his Catholic opponents.[42]

I believe that both of these aspects can be justified. Choosing a method by which to elucidate the literary and theological characteristics of a diverse body of literature presents a problem. To study the highly intricate arguments of these pamphlets in a strictly chronological way would be confusing, tedious, and repetitive, even over the relatively short period selected. But to analyze the points of controversy according to a thematic framework would give the impression of a theological coherence that did not in fact exist. Such an approach would also forfeit any chance of identifying the development of Luther's and the controversialists' positions. Fortunately, however, the controversy of these years had a pattern, a rhythm of its own, which

42. For the standard account of Luther's later, but still extraordinarily prolific, polemical career, see M. U. Edwards, Jr., *Luther's Last Battles: Politics and Polemics 1531–46*. Also significant for the reclamation of the post-1525 Luther are H. Bornkamm, *Luther in Mid-Career, 1521–1530* (Philadelphia: Fortress Press, 1983); and *Leben und Werk Martin Luthers von 1526 bis 1546*, ed. H. Junghans, 2 vols. (Berlin, 1983).

allows us to take a thematic approach without doing too much violence to the chronology. The year 1518 was taken up with the debate initiated by the Ninety-five Theses and reheated by Luther's Latin and German clarifications. This is the subject of chapter 1. The following year saw a greatly increased number of pamphlets, this time on the subject of the proceedings of the Leipzig disputation, the subject of chapter 3. The year 1520 witnessed a fierce exchange on the main topic debated at Leipzig, papal primacy (chapter 2), and the initial reactions to the first of Luther's revolutionary manifestos, *To the Christian Nobility*, which in turn dominated the debate in 1521 (chapter 4). *The Babylonian Captivity of the Church* (1520) attracted a growing number of refutations, which reached a peak in 1525. These are considered in chapter 5. Between 1523 and 1530, works against Luther either tended to deal with two or more of his doctrines or were concerned with such secondary matters as the invocation of the saints, monastic vows, and clerical celibacy (chapter 6).

There is a definite pattern here, in which subjects increase in importance, reach a peak, and then fall away again, only to be immediately overlapped and replaced by a new subject. Of course, this pattern was imposed by Luther himself, who in these years broke radical doctrinal ground with practically every new publication. The Romanist response was always instant, but took time to gather and lose momentum because of the number of writers involved (and to some extent geography—Italians were still replying to the indulgence theses in 1522!). Each year or couple of years is thus dominated by a different subject, and it is possible to take a thematic approach chapter by chapter in a more or less intelligible theological order without thereby sacrificing chronological sense.

Having decided upon a method, the structure of the individual theological chapters presents less of a problem. A brief summary of the publication by Luther that precipitated the debate being considered is followed by an account of the Catholic replies, their authors and their backgrounds, and the circumstances of production. There follows a discussion of the general themes involved in the debate, of the similarities and differences between the controversialists' presentations, and of the manner in which they treated the sources available to them. This approach offers the best way of allowing the controversialists to speak for themselves. It would have been possible, for instance, to have begun each chapter by outlining the theological problems that confronted anyone who wished to refute Luther's criticisms. Such a briefing would certainly provide a coherent introduction to an investigation of the controversialists' response, but it would also put the cart before the horse. An example of this is Iserloh's *Der Kampf um die Messe*. After summarizing Luther's objections to the sacrifice of the mass, and before embarking on an author-by-author survey of the controversialists' replies, he quotes Aquinas's teaching that the sacrifice of the altar is not a second Calvary and suggests that the controversialists' task was to reproduce this teaching.[43] The difficulty with such an approach is that the only indication we have of the theological problems facing those who wished to refute Luther is, of course, given by the works of the controversialists themselves. Unless we let them speak for themselves as far as possible, we run the danger of subjecting them to alien criteria.

Content analysis along such lines is bound to be long-winded. The consideration of such formal and quantifiable matters as the backgrounds and prolificity of authors and choice of literary styles, on the other hand, lends itself to the economy of statistical expression. Only half of chapter 7, therefore, is devoted to the literary characteristics of the Catholic response, with the remaining half devoted to a summary of the controversialists' expressed aims in writing and of their self-imposed ideological constraints. Similarly, only chapter 8 is concerned with setting the controversialists in a historical (as opposed to a theological or literary) context, by elucidating the nature of their relationship with establishment Catholicism. Although the evidence for this relationship is as fascinating as it is profuse, it was important to restrict its use in order to prevent the context from overshadowing the text. This investigation is therefore unbalanced in its attention to message, medium, and motive—but justifiably so, I think.

Concluding the investigation as early as 1525 can also be justified. First, overall literary production dropped dramatically and permanently after the Peasants' War, as the publicists' aims of propaganda and agitation became equally suspect on both sides; therefore, the earlier period was quantitatively the most important phase of the pamphlet war. Second, it has been suggested that the year 1525 represents

43. Iserloh, *Kampf um die Messe*, 13.

a decisive turning point for the character of the Catholic response.[44] Third, 1525 marked the logical conclusion of the initial phase of the controversialists' work, which was concerned predominantly with Luther's supposed anti-authoritarianism, and particularly with the charge that his religious rebellion necessarily entailed social revolution. With the outbreak of the peasants' revolt came the clearest vindication of this charge, and little remained to be said. Fourth, an automatic limitation is imposed by our decision to study only those pamphlets and books directed specifically against Luther. Although this category accounts for most Catholic polemic written up to about 1525, anti-Lutheran works thereafter became a less significant part of overall Catholic publication as attention was turned to other areas, especially to south Germany and Switzerland, in the hope of meeting with more success on a less established front. From this time even pamphlets bearing the words "against Luther" or "against the Lutherans" on the title page would actually contain predominantly anti-Zwinglian or anti-radical polemic. Finally, the horizon of our study is justified inasmuch as these early years were more significant in terms of the effectiveness of the Catholic literary response. The middle of the third decade of the sixteenth century was by no means the end of the Reformation or even the end of Luther, but it was the end of the beginning. The late Gordon Rupp wrote of this juncture:

> In 1525 it did not really matter any more whether in fact Luther was inconsistent, whether he contradicted himself, whether indeed he were an unconscionable liar, whether an argument was fallacious or a citation inaccurate. Intricate polemic of this kind, notably from Eck and Cochlaeus, was to follow Luther all his days. But such writing could do nothing to halt the Reformation.[45]

44. H. Jedin, "Die geschichtliche Bedeutung der katholische Kontroversliteratur im Zeitalter der Glaubensspaltung," 78–80, argued that between 1518 and 1525 Catholic authors were largely concerned with marking out the boundaries between Catholic and "Lutheran" belief; between 1526 and 1545 they were occupied, on the one hand, with "trench warfare"—numerous isolated controversies—and, on the other, with confessional handbooks for the confirmation of the faithful.

45. E. G. Rupp, "The Battle of the Books: The Ferment of Ideas and the Beginning of the Reformation," 18–19.

PART ONE

AUTHORITY IN THE CHURCH, 1518–1519

1

THE INDULGENCE
CONTROVERSY

The earliest written refutations of Luther appeared as a result of the publication of the Ninety-five Theses, the famous criticism of certain aspects of the theory and practice of indulgences, which he wrote in October 1517. At first sight, these initial responses do not seem to be a particularly promising starting point for our study. Few in number and largely the work of Dominicans, they were unrepresentative of the wider variety of theological traditions that would ultimately be brought to bear upon the reformer. Moreover, they were concerned only with Luther's first, tentative steps toward what would become a radical break with Rome, at a time when, we might suppose, the implications of his writings were still unclear to him and even more unclear to others. Nevertheless, a study of this phase of the Catholic literary response is essential, because in spite of the limitations of the indulgence controversy, this period witnessed the formulation of all the major arguments controversialists were to use against Luther over the next seven years. For this reason, a study of these first exchanges provides a clue to understanding the Catholic controversial literature as a whole.

By the beginning of the sixteenth century, indulgences had become an important part of religious life in Europe. They had achieved greater popularity with each extension of their application, so that isolated protests from Peter Abelard, the Cathars, and a few others were insufficient to unsettle either the Curia, which became ever more financially dependent on income derived from indulgences, or the people, who grasped at the assurance they gave. An indulgence had come to mean a concession, granted under special circumstances, for penitential good works to be commuted to some other good work such as visiting a particular shrine or giving alms for a particular cause. It was awarded to a penitent after he or she had performed the first two parts of the sacrament of penance (*contritio* and *confessio*, which remove the *culpa*, or blameworthiness, of a sin) as a substitute for the third (*satisfactio*, which discharges the *poena*, or punishment due for sin). This commutation was brought about, according to the papal bull *Unigenitus* of 1343, when the pope, by the power of the keys, applied an appropriate share of the treasury of merits that had been earned by Christ and the saints.[1]

In 1476, Pope Sixtus IV sanctioned the application of indulgences to souls in purgatory, on the analogy that their suffering was satisfaction for sins left undischarged on earth. In this case, the treasury of merits was also applied analogously, by means of the pope's intercession rather than by the power of the keys.[2] But in spite of the fact that this so-called holy commerce had reached significant proportions (significant enough, for example, to constitute a monetary drain on some German territories),[3] the theory of indulgences had not been fully worked out. Practice had far outrun theological reflection, and the scope for theological confusion and misunderstanding was enormous.

Theologians were not happy about this state of affairs. In the autumn of 1517, Cardinal Cajetan prepared for Cardinal Medici a memorandum to show how much need there was for the tighter definition of indulgences. The following May the theology faculty at the Sorbonne criticized the idea that the release of a soul from purgatory could be related in any mechanical way to the payment of money: "if this is preached," the faculty warned, "it should be revoked for the sake of troubled consciences."[4]

Against this background Luther tried in October 1517 to initiate an academic debate on the nature and extent of indulgences. He had already preached on the subject on at least four occasions in the preceding twelve months and had gone so far as to complain to the German primate about the instructions recently issued to indulgence preachers.[5] Now he evidently felt that it was the academic community's turn to mark out more precisely the extent of the validity of indulgences. Using the freedom allowed him in a university disputation on a matter that the Church had not formally defined, and "out of

1. Clement VI, *Unigenitus Dei Filius*, 27 January 1343 (*DS*, 1025).
2. Sixtus IV, *Salvator noster*, 3 August 1476 (*DS*, 1398).
3. See M. Brecht, *Martin Luther: His Road to Reformation, 1483–1521*, 178.
4. See H. A. Oberman, *Werden und Wertung der Reformation: Vom Wegestreit zum Glaubenskampf*, Spätscholastik und Reformation 2 (Tübingen: J.C.B. Mohr [Paul Siebeck], 1977), 192 n. 90.
5. See Luther's sermons of 26 July 1516, 4 January, 24 February, and March 1517 (*WA* 1:424.1–10, 30–34; 1:509.35–510.8; 1:141.11–38; 9:133). See also Luther to Archbishop Albrecht, 31 October 1517 (*WA Br* 1:110–12).

an earnest desire for the truth,"[6] Luther began by questioning the twin pillars upon which indulgence theory rested. The value of the sacrament of penance was doubtful, he argued in the first four theses, and it could not be proved that purgatory lay within papal jurisdiction (theses five to twenty-nine). The people should be encouraged to trust not in remissions of temporal punishments but in God, who remits the greater matter, guilt (theses thirty to thirty-eight); in any case, indulgences are inferior to true contrition and to works of mercy for their own sake (theses thirty-nine to forty-seven), and the pope would surely object if he knew that the opposite was being preached (theses forty-eight to fifty-five). The treasure of the church, that is, the gospel of God's grace, must not be confused with the treasure of indulgences (theses fifty-six to sixty-eight). The excessive claims of indulgence preachers (theses sixty-nine to eighty) could only distress conscientious Christians (theses eighty-one to ninety). Such false preaching must be replaced by the true papal teaching that Christians should choose to endure suffering; suffering is not a punishment, but the proper following of Christ (theses ninety-one to ninety-five).

Luther's theses on indulgences differed little in content from the independent reappraisals being conducted by Cajetan and the Sorbonne. Yet the theses led to his being accused of heresy for attempting to diminish the power of the pope. This in itself seems odd, because our summary has shown that wherever the pope was mentioned it was as the defender of true indulgence preaching against the false. Of course, it would be naive to suggest that Luther could criticize the theory and practice of indulgences without in some way touching upon the question of papal jurisdiction. The pope alone could commute penance as possessor of the keys or as intercessor on behalf of the dead, although lower officials could grant papal indulgences by obtaining a special license. In the Ninety-five Theses, therefore, Luther restricted the pope's power in three ways: (1) he denied that the pope could remit any *punishments* other than those expressly prescribed in canon law; (2) he denied that the pope could remit any *guilt* at all but only declare it remitted by God; and (3) he denied that the pope could remit any punishments in purgatory but only intercede with God for their removal. Such restrictions of papal power were not, however,

6. These are the opening words of the introduction to the Ninety-five Theses (*WA* 1:233.1, *LW* 31:25).

without good precedents: they might indeed be regarded as a valid exposition of the relevant bulls. In any case, they are not the main theme of the Ninety-five Theses. Certainly, Luther's other writings from this period would not indicate that he was inordinately concerned with questions of papal power and supremacy. As late as the following July, his colleague at the University of Wittenberg, Andreas Bodenstein von Carlstadt, could demonstrate in his own theses the compatibility of a critical attitude toward indulgences with loyalty to the pope's preeminent position as doctrinal authority, as had Cajetan and the University of Paris before him.[7] Yet the Catholics who answered Luther in the year 1518 all attempted to prove that he had offended against the pope's majesty. The questions that will concern us in this chapter will be how and why they did this.

Reactions to the Ninety-five Theses

The campaign against Luther between 1517 and 1521 was two-pronged. On the one hand were the written or printed refutations, intended to be read by Luther, his supporters, and the general reading public. On the other was the so-called trial of Luther—the lengthy legal proceedings that culminated in the temporal enforcement of his spiritual excommunication after the Diet of Worms. The relationship between propaganda and the legal process will be referred to at various points throughout this story; however, the two were never so closely related as they were in the first year of Luther's revolt, when three of his four literary opponents (Konrad Wimpina, Johannes Tetzel, and Sylvester Prierias) were also key prosecution figures.

Archbishop Albrecht of Mainz, the primate of Germany whom Luther had approached, sent his copy of the Ninety-five Theses to Rome, and on 3 February Rome spoke. Pope Leo X wrote to Gabriele della Volta, the vicar-general of the Eremitical Order of St. Augustine to which Luther belonged, ordering him to silence the German priest who was propounding novelties. This relatively mild form of discipline proved ineffective. In addition to his extended Latin *Explanations* on indulgences and his sermon *On Indulgence and Grace*, Luther now published a provocative sermon on the subject of excommunication. To make matters more difficult, his prince, the Elector Frederick, seemed determined to protect him.

---

7. Andreas Bodenstein von Carlstadt, *Apologeticae conclusiones*, in Löscher 2:78–102.

The case against Luther had to be stepped up. The pope's procurator-fiscal, Mario de Perusco, accordingly instituted formal proceedings under a *processus ordinarius* for suspicion of heresy. The new charge was investigated by Leo's chief lawyer, Girolamo Ghinucci, and his chief theologian, Sylvester Mazzolini of Prierio, both Dominicans. Mazzolini, better known as Prierias, was at the age of sixty-two at the peak of his career. After a variety of teaching and administrative posts, during which he published commentaries on the schoolmen and a handbook for the confessional, he had been appointed in 1515 to the office of Master of the Sacred Palace and censor and inquisitor for the city of Rome. His considered opinion on Luther's theses was published as the *Dialogue against the Arrogant Theses of Martin Luther Concerning the Power of the Pope*.

The case against Luther was escalated further when, in August, Emperor Maximilian wrote to Leo accusing Luther of obstinate heresy. A complaint at this level was sufficient to institute a *processus summarius*: Luther was faced with the simple choice of recanting or being condemned. For this purpose Luther was interviewed by the papal legate at the Diet of Augsburg, Tommaso Cardinal de Vio. Known as Cajetan after his birthplace, Gaeta, he was also a Dominican. Indeed, he had been voted general of the order in 1508 and raised to the cardinalate in 1517 when Leo, fearing another attempt on his life, secured a power base by packing the College of Cardinals with his own appointees. Cajetan was perhaps the most famous theologian of his day. His literary labors included biblical commentaries, work on Aristotle, a penitential compendium, and a refutation of conciliarism. His commentary on Aquinas's *Summa theologiae* was reprinted as late as 1882 under the auspices of Pope Leo XIII. Cajetan published nothing against Luther at this time, but his reflections on the interview at Augsburg provided the basis for the bull *Cum postquam* of November 1518.[8] In keeping with Cajetan's fair and sensitive spirit, this bull vindicated many of Luther's original criticisms of indulgences, but by now the Wittenberger's position had so developed and the case against him was so advanced that the bulls of excommunication and their temporal enforcement, although delayed, were inevitable.[9]

The intervention of Prierias and Cajetan marked an advanced

8. *Cum postquam*, 9 November 1518 (*DS*, 1447–49).
9. *Exsurge Domine*, 15 June 1520 (*DS*, 1451–92).

stage in the process against Luther. Before that point had been reached, the initial allegations had to be made and substantiated. It is generally assumed that the charge of heresy was first laid against Luther by Hermann Rab, the provincial of the Saxon Dominicans, when he was in Rome at the end of May 1518. It is possible—although by no means certain—that he took with him evidence in support of his claim, including the writings of two members of his own province. On 20 January a disputation had taken place at the University of Frankfurt-on-Oder, in which one hundred and six theses attacking the Ninety-five Theses were defended by the indulgence commissioner for the diocese of Brandenburg, Tetzel, the reports of whose preaching had so upset Luther. They had been drawn up by Konrad Koch, a Frankfurt professor better known as Wimpina. Tetzel entered the lists under his own colors later that year. His *Refutation* of Luther's sermon *On Indulgence and Grace* and the fifty theses he defended for his doctorate at Frankfurt in April 1518 are usually dismissed by modern commentators as attempts simply to justify himself and his involvement in the indulgence trade. But there is more to it than that. Apart from the customary obligation he bore as a Dominican to root out heresy, Tetzel held the office of inquisitor of heretical depravity for the province of Saxony, granted by Cajetan around 1509. Because it was explicitly in this official role that Tetzel published against Luther, his participation was a more serious matter than mere literary revenge.

Johannes Eck was the only scholar who wrote against Luther at this time without an eye to his legal condemnation. Eck was a professor of theology at the University of Ingolstadt and moved in much the same circles as Luther. Through their common friend Christoph Scheurl, the Nuremberg humanist, Eck obtained a copy of the Ninety-five Theses and proceeded to sketch a refutation on grounds he believed would be acceptable to humanists.[10] These annotations, or "obelisks," were not published but circulated privately within the network of German humanism. Eck's work therefore differs from that of his colleagues at this stage in being both avowedly non-scholastic and unconnected with the public process against Luther. Eck's intentions, however, were soon to change dramatically.

---

10. Eck promised that, with the exception of his criticism of the first thesis, he would not counter Luther "scholastically" (*WA* 1:281.18–20, 283.23f.).

The Case against
the Ninety-five Theses

To regard the writings of Luther's opponents in 1518 as simply academic refutations would be a mistake. They were, in every case except Eck's, attempts to secure Luther's condemnation. Nonetheless, these writings were theological works that provide the only clue we have to the detailed grounds on which Luther was first arraigned. Wimpina, Tetzel, and Prierias were Dominicans and Thomists, and we would expect their refutations of the Ninety-five Theses to be essentially the same. Eck, who attempted to reply to the theses in a non-scholastic way, might be expected to have diverged from his colleagues in a number of ways. What we find in fact is that, with regard to those areas that they believed Luther was in error over indulgences, all four theologians differed consistently and, at times, dramatically, on the basis of four quite different sets of conclusions.

Eck took particular exception to Luther's attempt to drive a wedge between God's requirements and those of canon law. Luther's thirty-sixth thesis stated that God unconditionally remits both the guilt of sin, the graver matter, and its punishment, the lighter matter. A theological commonplace since at least the time of Anselm was that a sin was an offense against divine honor for which God must be compensated. Christ's death compensates vicariously for the sin with which each human being is born, but further compensation must be paid by the individual—on earth or in purgatory, in punishments or in painful good works—for sins committed after baptism, the precise amount of compensation being codified in the penitential canons. Eck saw as Luther's fundamental errors, first, his denial of the need for post-baptismal reparation by human effort[11] and, second, his suggestion that penances imposed by the priest bear no relation to the penalties imposed by God.[12] Eck's counter-theses therefore emphasized the consonance of the human and divine systems of justice and laid great store by those mechanisms that connect the two: the power of the keys, the treasury of the church, the sacrament of penance, and the communion of saints. He did not think it necessary to give a full

11. Johannes Eck's *Adnotationes* (*Obelisci*) are printed with Luther's reply, *Asterisci* (Asterisks) in *WA* 1:281–314. The reference here is to *Obelisci* 14 (*WA* 1:298.14–17).
12. Eck, *Obelisci* 2 (*WA* 1:283.25–29), 10 (*WA* 294.36–38), 15 (*WA* 299.33–39), and 27 (*WA* 312.6–8).

rationale of his theological position, confidently counting any doubt on the matter "a dissemination of the Bohemian virus," insofar as it would undermine the church's sacramental system.

A desire to defend the integrity of the sacramental system also characterized Wimpina's response. With Eck, he stated that divine mercy was prevented by divine justice from forgiving anyone anything without due compensation;[13] also with Eck, he held that this compensation must be the third part of the sacrament of penance, satisfaction.[14] But Wimpina was concerned, even more than Eck was, to defend the sacrament of penance as a whole, not just part of it. (In line with this concern, much of his argument was reinforced by reference to Lombard's fourth book of *Sentences*, the leading textbook of sacramental theology.) For example, when Luther maintained that Jesus's command to repentance referred to an inward, lifelong state, Wimpina had no hesitation in replying that the dominical injunction referred unambiguously to the sacrament of penance: "Our Lord Jesus Christ, who desired to bind all men to the sacraments of the New Covenant after his passion and ascension, desired also, by this most plain saying, to teach all men these sacraments before his passion."[15]

It was true that Luther had added, in his third thesis, the qualification that this inward penitence was nothing without outward mortifications of the flesh. But even this qualification did not placate Wimpina, for whom neither intention nor works had any standing before God outside the system God had provided, namely, the sacrament itself.[16] Luther had held that the priest did not himself absolve guilt but simply declared that it had already been absolved by God. Wimpina reminded him that Christian sacraments confer the grace they signify by virtue of their being performed, and so the priest truly does absolve guilt.[17]

In Eck's opinion, then, Luther's error lay in denying the validity of the penitential canons. For Wimpina, it was that he had denied the validity of penance itself. Faced with the new problems raised by

13. Wimpina, *106 Theses* (20 January 1518), in Löscher 1:504–14. The reference here is to thesis 5 (Löscher 1:505): "Such satisfaction (since God will not allow a crime to go unavenged) is made by a punishment or by something equivalent in divine acceptation."
14. Ibid., thesis 6 (Löscher 1:505).
15. Ibid., theses 1 and 2 (Löscher 1:505).
16. Ibid., thesis 4 (Löscher 1:505).
17. Ibid., thesis 19 (Löscher 1:506).

Luther, Wimpina's method was to appeal to contemporary sacramental practice. He was unable to grasp Luther's approach, and it is not fanciful to attribute this basic lack of understanding to the differences between the two theological schools that the antagonists may have represented. According to the *via antiqua*, the tradition best represented by Thomas Aquinas, God's dealings with the human race are totally predictable. God acts, and always will act, *de potentia ordinata*, in the ways laid down in Scripture and by tradition, working within the sacramental system of the church to the reward of virtue and the punishment of vice. Alongside this view of God grew another, represented by William of Ockham, and known by contrast as the *via moderna*. According to the latter view, God was perceived as being completely free to do as God pleases, short of acting contrary to God's nature. Although God's *potentia absoluta* (as this freedom was called) was originally conceived of as no more than a logical but unrealized possibility, by the sixteenth century the modernist Gabriel Biel was teaching that God can and does act according to a sovereign illimitability. It could be argued that Luther, who had been educated at the modernist-influenced University of Erfurt and who knew Biel by heart, was objecting to indulgences because they presumed that God's action always followed upon ecclesiastical action. If this is the case, then Wimpina's use of the technical term *potentia ordinata* and his assertion that "nothing which has not been ordained by heaven can be pleasing to heaven"[18] explain why he continually appealed to existing sacramental practice in his reply to Luther's theses.

Prierias believed that the cause of Luther's error was to be sought elsewhere. The first two controversialists had been at pains to underline the validity *sub specie aeternitatis* of the canonical penances, seeing a direct correspondence between them and God's punishments. Prierias took the opposite course of emphasizing that no one could be sure of satisfying God even if that person had satisfied the priest. He based this on an argument first put forward by Aquinas.[19] When the priest has absolved a penitent and when the penitent has executed the penance allotted, there must still be, Aquinas reasoned, a residual amount of satisfaction left unpaid in the eyes of God. If this were not

18. Ibid., after thesis 106 (Löscher 1:514).
19. See, e.g., P. Mandonnet, ed., *S. Thomae Aquinatis scriptum super quarto iibrum sententiarum* (Paris: P. Lethielleux, 1947), dist. 20, art. 2 (p. 1021).

the case, the penitent who had completely satisfied the priest would have satisfied God as completely, and, dying in that state, would go straight to heaven. To believe that would be heresy. For Prierias, therefore, the discrepancy between priestly and divine requirements on the one hand necessitated purgatory as a place where the soul may receive its inevitable but unknown amount of excess punishment, and on the other rendered pardons attractive as insurance against such punishment.

The first reactions to Luther's indulgence theses show that there was complete agreement only in a belief that Luther was in error. Wimpina accused Luther of raging insanely; Eck accused him of disseminating the condemned doctrines of the Hussite Bohemians; and Prierias accused him of being both mad and wrong. Yet, despite the gravity of the charges, they could not agree on precisely where his fault with regard to indulgences lay. This is hardly surprising, because they were fishing in the same theological waters whose murkiness had so alarmed not only the Wittenberger but also Cardinal Cajetan and the theologians of Paris. They had very little official guidance on the question of indulgences. *Unigenitus* and *Salvator noster*, which were in any case not definitions of dogma,[20] had served only to raise questions not satisfactorily addressed until the publication of *Cum postquam*. Indeed, the late medieval doctrine of indulgences provided Lortz with his most convincing evidence of a vagueness that he believed pervaded contemporary theology. The controversialists' difficulties in identifying the nature of Luther's error were compounded by the curt, allusive, and paradoxical style of Luther's theses, the intention of which was as much to provoke debate as to propose his own interpretation. In short, Luther's opponents could detect the scent of heresy in the Ninety-five Theses, but they could not flush it out.

Considering the controversialists' disarray on indulgences, it was all the more significant that with regard to the question of papal power they were in agreement. As noted previously, Luther had attempted to restrict the pope's jurisdiction in three basic areas: the remission of extracanonical penance, guilt, and purgatorial punishment. Against the first restriction, the controversialists appealed to Aquinas's opinion that even penalties imposed by God can be remitted by the pope

20. This point was made by N. Paulus, *Geschichte des Ablasses im Mittelalter* (Paderborn: Schöningh, 1923) 3:88.

through the power of the keys.[21] In the second case, the majority of them maintained the performative and not merely declaratory nature of the papal remission of guilt on the basis of the scholastic adage that Christian sacraments convey the grace they signify.[22] Against Luther's third objection, Eck explained that the *Salvator noster* clause "by means of intercession" did not diminish but rather expounded and magnified the pope's method of applying indulgences to the church expectant; in the same way, Prierias and Wimpina supposed that pardons could still be effectively applied to souls in purgatory even without the direct use of the power of the keys.[23]

So the Catholic response to the Ninety-five Theses, although confused on the question of indulgences, was virtually agreed on the secondary issue of papal jurisdiction. Impressive as this consensus may have been, it was only a consensus of opinion. Invoking the authority of medieval scholars—even those as eminent as Lombard or Aquinas—was ineffective against Luther, who, with the status and academic immunity of a disputant, believed he was at liberty to debate any matter on which no binding dogmatic decision had been made. Yet Luther's opponents were convinced that he had to be silenced, because not only was he in error but, by the widespread publication of his theses, he was leading many simpler souls into danger with him. His silence could be achieved by the institution of heresy proceedings, and for this to be successful his work had to be demonstrated as contrary to revealed truth. But for the most part Luther had been careful to argue from Scripture and the fathers in areas where a variety of opinions was still possible. It was for this reason that Tetzel and Prierias introduced into the indulgence debate the question of the status and authority of the pope, not in his administrative capacity as possessor of the keys or of the treasury of the saints but as the defender of the church's rule of faith.

This question was introduced most clearly in the methodological preconditions, or *fundamenta*, with which Prierias prefaced his first

---

21. Wimpina, thesis 45 (Löscher 1:508); Eck, *Obelisci* 10 (*WA* 1:294); Prierias, *Dialogus* (Löscher 2:21).

22. Hugh of St.-Victor, *De sacramentis Christianae fidei* 2, pars 6, qu. 3 (*MPL* 176:448). Adopted by Peter Lombard, *Sententiarum libri quatuor* 4, dist. 1 (*MPL* 192:839–41). See Wimpina's theses 21–28 (Löscher 1:506–7); and Eck, *Obelisci* 2 (*WA* 1:286.6f.).

23. One inspiration for these glosses seems to have been Gabriel Biel. See H. A. Oberman and W. J. Courtenay, eds., *Gabrielis Biel Canonis misse expositio* (Wiesbaden: F. Steiner, 1965), 2:403–5. See also Eck, *Obelisci* 12 (*WA* 1:296.17–20); Wimpina's thesis 33 (Löscher 1:508); and Prierias, *Dialogus* (Löscher 2:22–23).

work. Significantly, it was entitled "On the Power of the Pope," and the premises themselves began not with indulgences or sacramental penance but with the nature of the church.

> The universal Church is, in its being [*essentialiter*], the calling together for divine worship of all who believe in Christ. But the universal Church is, in its power [*virtualiter*], the Roman Church, which is the head of all churches, and the Supreme Pontiff. The Roman Church is representatively the College of Cardinals but, in its power, is the Supreme Pontiff, who is head of the Church, though in a different way from Christ.[24]

The second *fundamentum* was the inerrancy of a pope in his ex officio pronouncements and of a general council duly convoked. The third was the heretical character of anyone who did not submit to the rule of faith of the Roman Church and pontiff, which has greater authority even than Holy Scripture. The fourth *fundamentum* concluded:

> The Roman Church can decide on faith and custom as much by deeds as by words. And there is no difference between them save that words are more convenient for this purpose than are deeds. Custom attains the force of law. Consequently, as he is a heretic who dissents from the authority of Scripture, so also is he a heretic who dissents from the teaching and practice of the Church in respect of faith and morals.

> *Corollary*
> Whosoever says of indulgences that the Roman Church cannot do what it has *de facto* already done is a heretic.[25]

This corollary is therefore the keynote of the *Dialogus*: the rule of faith, the protection of which had been entrusted to the supreme pontiff, included not just the written deposits of Scripture and tradition, but also the practices that the church had adopted.

Prierias's position raised an important question of whether these practices need to be tested by the usual standards of orthodoxy or whether they should be deemed acceptable merely because they fell under the aegis of the pope.[26] It is not unfair to accuse Prierias of deliberate ambiguity on this point. His first line of defense was to

24. Prierias, *Dialogus* (Löscher 2:14–15).
25. Ibid. (Löscher 2:15).
26. Such an extreme position did find its representatives in late medieval ecclesiological thought. See B. Gogan, *The Common Corps of Christendom: Ecclesiological Themes in the Writings of Sir Thomas More*, 61, 335–37.

refuse to believe that any preacher could have said such things;[27] the next was to remind Luther that he should have followed the monastic principle of brotherly correction by cautioning the offenders privately, not in public propositions;[28] finally, he attempted to defend the very sayings he had initially declared himself unable to believe.[29] Whatever may have been his intention, the effect of Prierias's *fundamenta* was to interpret any criticism of ecclesiastical practice, however well-argued theologically, as an unjustifiable and indeed heretical diminution of papal majesty.

The same tactic was adopted by Tetzel in his *Subscriptas positiones*, which reached Luther three months before Prierias's *Dialogus*.[30] These fifty theses, which Tetzel defended for his doctorate, were designed as a series of tests of orthodoxy by which "whosoever may be judged heretical, schismatic, pertinacious, contumacious, erroneous, seditious, blasphemous, scandalous, temerarious, and injurious may be instantly and clearly recognized."[31]

In spite of its wide aim and the fact that it named no one, there can be little doubt that the series was aimed at Luther. The theses are each introduced with the refrain "Christians are to be taught that," the phrase used to introduce some of the ninety-five theses. Moreover, Tetzel's final two theses condemn errors concerning indulgences and sacramental penance, and other theses make oblique reference to Luther's publishing activities and the protection he enjoyed from the Elector Frederick.[32] The disputation as a whole was explicitly intended to accompany Tetzel's refutation of Luther's *Sermon on Indulgence and Grace*.[33] In a manner very similar to Prierias's, Tetzel sought to establish the pope's supreme dogmatic position in the church as a guarantee of the rule of faith. The pope derives his authority directly from God and is therefore superior to the church in general and to an ecumenical council in particular. He alone can interpret Scripture correctly and is inerrant in matters of faith, so that whoever detracts from

27. Prierias, *Dialogus* (Löscher 2:29, 35).
28. Ibid. (Löscher 2:29).
29. Ibid. (Löscher 2:35).
30. Johannes Tetzel, *Subscriptas positiones* (Löscher 1:517–22). Luther received these theses on 4 June 1518 (*WA Br* 1:181.14). Assuming a delay of about a month before they reached Wittenberg, they must have been printed in late April or early May.
31. Ibid. (Löscher 1:517).
32. Ibid., theses 44, 47–50 (Löscher 1:521–22).
33. This intention had been expressed in the twentieth and final article of Johannes Tetzel's *Vorlegung* of April 1518 (Löscher 1:502).

the honor of the pope is guilty of blasphemy.[34] The pope can make authoritative statements of that in which the rule of Catholic truth consists. It is a universally binding body of doctrine that contains but exceeds both in authority and in scope the Bible and fathers.[35] It includes, but is not limited to, all the judgments of the Apostolic See. "Christians should be taught," asserted Tetzel, "that those who deny any Catholic truth which is published among the faithful, with which they are conversant as being Catholic and which has been publicly preached as such by preachers of the word of God, should be considered obstinate in their error."[36] In a manner reminiscent of Prierias, Tetzel seemed to be promoting the Augustinian notion, which he first employed in the *Refutation*, that "the customs of the people of God should be regarded as law" and stating that anything a priest might preach as Catholic would thereby become Catholic.[37]

Thus the question of papal power came to dominate the indulgence debate through the tactics of certain of the Catholic controversialists. They did this neither solely nor even mainly because Luther's theses challenged the pontiff's power of the keys or the contents of the treasury with which he was supposed to have been endowed, but because the theses queried a practice of the church. It mattered less to Tetzel and Prierias that the practice was orthodox than that it enjoyed papal patronage and that, in attacking the practice, Luther was attacking the patron.

34. Ibid., theses 1–11 (Löscher 1:518).
35. Ibid., theses 14–18 (Löscher 1:519).
36. Ibid., thesis 39 (Löscher 1:521).
37. H. A. Oberman, "Wittenbergs Zweifrontenkrieg gegen Prierias und Eck: Hintergrund und Entscheidungen des Jahres 1518," analyzes admirably the four *fundamenta* and concludes that in the *Dialogus* Luther was confronted with the triumphalist ecclesiology of Italian money- and power-politics a full sixty days before his interview with Cajetan at Augsburg and was led to reject papal and ecclesiastical infallibility long before Leipzig. Oberman's treatment is, however, deficient in two respects. First, for the purposes of his article, Oberman concentrated on the first two *fundamenta*, which deal with papal infallibility and its relationship to conciliar infallibility. It must, however, be remembered that this was only the first half of Prierias's argument: the Roman Church's and the pontiff's rule of faith is infallible, and that rule of faith can be made to include deeds as well as words (in this case, the practice of indulgences in addition to the theory). In many ways this second pair of *fundamenta*, together with the "corollary," sets out a far more straitening and authoritarian ecclesiology than do the examples Oberman cites, for it permits the acceptance even of abuses as articles of faith. Second, Oberman correctly points out that the *Dialogus* anticipates both Augsburg and Leipzig. But the *Dialogus* was itself anticipated by Tetzel's *Subscriptas positiones*, which enunciated the same authoritarian ecclesiology. Luther was therefore introduced to these arguments not two but five months before his interview with the papal legate.

The Underlying Objections

One of the difficulties facing the student of the indulgence controversy is the thesis-by-thesis approach adopted by the opponents of the Ninety-five Theses. This approach gave equal and indifferent weight to each of the many varied points made by Luther, and it is therefore not easy to identify the basis of the controversialists' objections. The most discursive parts of the literature, where this slavish following is abandoned, are Tetzel's *Subscriptas positiones* and the introduction to Prierias's *Dialogus*. Here, as we have seen, the theory is developed that indulgences, as part of the *regula fidei*, fall under the protection of the pope and are therefore beyond theological discussion. But this argument was developed primarily in order to secure Luther's silence: it was a symptom of their opposition to his indulgence teaching, rather than its cause.

The question remains, Why did the controversialists think Luther's teaching objectionable? The usual explanations adduced are the lucrativeness of the indulgence trade and the readiness of existing rivals—academic, religious, and political—to find bones of contention: the orders of Dominic and Augustine; the Universities of Wittenberg and Frankfurt-on-Oder; the houses of Saxony and Brandenburg. All these explanations may be valid in varying degrees, but we are primarily interested in theological motivations, and the work of the Catholic controversialists provides us with the best way of determining why the Ninety-five Theses appeared so revolutionary to contemporaries. It is clear not only from their explicit statements, but also from their asides, that the controversialists considered Luther's threat to be most serious in three areas in particular: his rejection of the authority of scholastic theologians, his emphasis upon religious assurance, and his apparently positive attitude toward the common people. The objections were to be developed and extended in the course of the controversy with Luther over the ensuing years; but it is of interest to examine how they were formulated at the very beginning of the campaign.

The Status of Scholastic Theology

In questioning indulgences, Luther felt his own position secure for two reasons. He believed that he enjoyed the academic immunity of one who disputed a matter that the church had not yet defined. And he knew that he was not bound to accept any argument based solely on the authority of medieval schoolmen. As he wrote: "I have asserted nothing, but have disputed and have tried to do so in a Catholic way. I desire, not that my proposition be accepted as certain, but only that the opinion of scholastics need not be accepted as certain."[38] By the time he had formulated his one hundred theses of September 1517, Luther had already convinced himself that scholastic theology, insofar as it accommodated itself to the methods of pagan philosophy, diverged radically from the church's traditional sources of Holy Scripture, the ancient fathers, and canon law. When he came to explain the Ninety-five Theses for the benefit of the academic community in the *Explanations* and promised to prove his case from these so-called "ecclesiastical" authorities, he also reserved the right to reject any "scholastic opinions held without proof."[39] In his popular exposition of the theses, Luther was more direct: "On these points I have no doubts, for they are well enough grounded in Scripture. And you should have no doubts about them either. Let the scholastic doctors be scholastic. Even put together, their opinions can't prove so much as a single sermon."[40]

Luther's rejection of scholastic theology was a serious matter in the eyes of his opponents. Prierias had suspended work on his commentary on Aquinas's *Summa theologiae* in order to refute Luther, and although he later excused his reliance on the Angelic Doctor on the grounds that he was merely essaying a coherent alternative to the Ninety-five Theses, he soon moved on to the offensive and compared the praise bestowed on Aquinas by Pope Innocent VIII and upon Aristotle by Boethius with the condemnation rightly received by two of Luther's own authorities, Jean Gerson and Panormitanus. The scholastic authorities were of such importance in the church, claimed Prierias, that if Luther denied them he would himself be denied and condemned.[41] Tetzel's threat was even more direct. The scholastic doctors were, he stated, numbered in their thousands, and many were to

38. Luther, *Asterisci* (WA 1:294, 302).
39. Luther, *Explanations of the Ninety-five Theses* (WA 1:529–628, esp. 530.4–12; LW 31:(77)83–252, esp. 83).
40. Luther, *Ein Sermon von den Ablass und Gnade*. The quotation is from the nineteenth article (WA 1:246.27–30).
41. Prierias, *Replica F. Sylvestri Prieratis, sacri Palatii Apostolici Magistri, ad Martinum Luther Ordinis Eremitarum*, printed with Luther's answer in WA 2:50–56. The reference is to WA 2:54.9–11.

be accounted among the saints in heaven. The last man to reject them was John Huss, and he ended his opposition at the stake.[42]

This raises a question. Why did Luther's rejection of the medieval schoolmen's teaching on indulgences merit so bitter a reaction from the controversialists when his much more stinging criticism of scholastic theology in the previous month had (so far as we know) gone unchallenged? One obvious answer is that the September theses were written for the limited audience present at a degree promotion whereas the October theses had been intended for a public debate. This is not the complete story, because an original broadsheet of the *Disputation against Scholastic Theology,* discovered in 1983 at the Herzog August Bibliothek, Wolfenbüttel, shows that Luther had a number of copies printed by Grünenberg for circulation. He would take the same action a few weeks later with the Ninety-five Theses.[43] Therefore, Luther himself gave equal publicity to both sets of theses. The only difference between the two was that those of October were pirated by other printers and translated into German. It was this fact, and the consequent fear that the public might lose its reverence for the schoolmen, which so alarmed the traditionalists and impelled them into vehement controversy. As Tetzel wrote:

> Though the erring may despise them, the holy Roman Church and sacred Christendom unanimously maintain that the holy scholastic doctors are able, by means of their true and life-giving doctrine, to substantiate not "one sermon" but the holy Christian Faith against heretics on Christian grounds. Luther's erroneous article will encourage many people to despise the might and authority of his Papal Holiness and of the holy Roman See. They will neglect the work of sacramental satisfaction. They will never now believe the preachers and doctors. Everyone will interpret

42. Tetzel, *Vorlegung* (Löscher 1:485). For evidence that in spite of their partisan attitude toward Aquinas, the "veritable Thomist phalanx" of Wimpina, Tetzel, Prierias, and Cajetan frequently misrepresented their master in this controversy, see D. R. Janz, *Luther on Thomas Aquinas: The Angelic Doctor in the Thought of the Reformer,* Veröffentlichungen des Instituts für europäische Geschichte Mainz 140 (Stuttgart: Franz Steiner Verlag, 1989), 32–45.

43. The text of *Disputatio contra scholasticam theologiam* can be found in WA 1:224–28, LW 31:9–16, and in J. Atkinson, ed., *Luther: Early Theological Works,* Library of Christian Classics 16 (London: SCM Press, 1962), 266–73. The broadsheet discovered at Wolfenbüttel had been pasted into a copy of Adam Petri's Basel (1520) collection of Luther's works.

Scripture as takes his fancy. And all sacred Christendom must come into great spiritual danger when each individual believes what pleases him most.[44]

Tetzel's dire warning anticipated by some months Prierias's similar diagnosis of Luther's position:

You think that your teaching should be imposed upon the whole world and that the monuments of antiquity should be torn down merely because you interpret Scripture without making scholastic distinctions, as if Scripture contained no equivocal or analogous passages.[45]

The Romanists argued that the "ecclesiastical" sources of doctrine (Scripture, the fathers, and canon law) were incomprehensible unless interpreted, and that the interpretation provided by the schoolmen was not idle, pagan speculation but part of Christian revelation itself—a fact confirmed by the personal sanctity of many of the scholastic fathers. In the Romanists' opinion, the ecclesiastical sources and the scholastic commentaries, taken together, constituted a consensus of authority, which Tetzel called the rule of Catholic truth, Prierias the rule of faith, and Cajetan the mind of the church.[46] Even Eck, who had promised that his comments on the theses would not be "scholastic," cited a spectrum of authorities ranging from Ecclesiastes to Lombard, Aquinas, Duns Scotus, and the church's *lex orandi*. Modern Roman Catholic scholars have been almost as scandalized as Luther himself by this confusion of text with interpretation, of dogma with private opinion: Paulus remarked that Cajetan had broken with precedent in elevating the papal bull *Unigenitus* to the status of a binding decision, and Iserloh criticized Wimpina's theses for presuming to declare what was and what was not dogma before a definition had been reached.[47]

Luther's claim to the privileges of a disputant and his refusal to accept scholastic theology as a final authority were therefore not recognized by his opponents of 1518. They did not regard the disputation as an opportunity for exploring the question of indulgences. Wimpina saw it as a way of publicly declaring established points, while Tetzel

44. Tetzel, *Vorlegung*, thirteenth article (Löscher 1:495).
45. Prierias, *Replica* (WA 2:52.22–24).
46. J. Wicks, "Roman Reactions to Luther," 543, 551.
47. Paulus, *Geschichte des Ablasses im Mittelalter* 3:88; E. Iserloh, *The Theses Were Not Posted*, 46.

held it heretical to air any doubts at all in debate.[48] They did not think indulgences a matter undecided, because in their opinion the church had come to a decision, if not de jure then at least de facto. It was incomprehensible to them that anyone should dismiss as "scholastic opinions" the teachings of men whose learning, sanctity, and numbers proved their divine inspiration.

The Issue of Religious Assurance

The second issue on which the Romanists thought it vital to oppose Luther was the question of religious assurance. The most dramatic instance of this clash occurred in October 1518, when Cajetan accused Luther of trying to "build a new Church" with his insistence on the absolute confidence one may have in Christ's promise of forgiveness. Yet even before he met Cajetan, Luther had faced several attacks on this very issue. What, then, was so objectionable about his views on certainty? Part of the problem was that, in the Ninety-five Theses, Luther was judging indulgences by a highly personal standard: his "theology of the cross." It was a theology centered in the themes of election, grace, and Christ's redemptive suffering, and concerned not only with salvation but also with revelation: just as God saves only through the cross, so God is revealed only through the cross, not only taking the initiative but doing so in a way contrary to human expectations. Over the following six months Luther was to develop the theology of the cross as an explicit alternative to scholasticism ("the theology of glory"), but in October 1517 he was still applying it to a practical pastoral and homiletic problem.

The theology of the cross showed Luther that indulgences were wanting for the simple reason that neither in purgatory nor on earth can people actually know for certain that they have received the benefits indulgences were said to convey. People who are about to die or who are in purgatory, he explained in the Ninety-five Theses, are fearful precisely because they have no absolute certainty of their ultimate salvation, and it is hard to see how they can be made more certain merely by the purchase of indulgences on their behalf on earth. In fact, remission of punishments for souls in purgatory is far less assured than for the living, because remission for the living is activated by the power of the keys, while remission for souls in purgatory is (according

48. Tetzel, *Subscriptas positiones*, thesis 50 (Löscher 1:522).

to the bull *Salvator noster*) by means of intercession and so is dependent on the will of God alone. Indulgences for the living are uncertain enough—if plenary remission of punishments can be granted to anyone, it must be to those whose contrition is perfect. Few can attain to such perfection; therefore, the majority of people who are sold indulgences do not actually receive them.[49] The theology of the cross also showed Luther that indulgences are wanting soteriologically: they are useless insofar as they offer only remission of the punishment for sin when the cross of Christ has already wrought for the penitent complete forgiveness of the sin itself; rather, they are worse than useless, because they encourage people to avoid suffering and works of mortification that Christians should rather welcome as opportunities for bearing their own crosses.

The majority of the controversialists rejected what was to them a gloomy picture. They maintained that one could have more confidence in the system of indulgences than Luther would allow. First, Wimpina and Eck recalled the distinction that Lombard and Hugh of St.-Victor had made that the sacraments of the New Testament, unlike those of the Old, convey the grace they signify. Second, they linked Christ's promise to Peter that whatever he should loose on earth would be loosed in heaven (Matt. 16:19) as proof that the pope is empowered to grant indulgences. To Luther's objection that this "power of the keys" does not extend beyond the church militant, Wimpina replied that the pope's jurisdiction in purgatory was nevertheless "a sort of" power of the keys (*sub specie clavis*); and Eck replied that the intercession described in *Salvator noster* made the pope's jurisdiction more, not less, certain. The fourth ground of assurance they put forward was that one may be reasonably, or "conjecturally," certain, so far as human disability permits, that one's contrition is sufficient and that one has received divine remission. Tetzel, Wimpina, and Cajetan held that this "conjectural certainty" (the term was given currency by Nicholas of Lyra and was increasingly influential from the fourteenth century on) could be increased by following the procedure laid down by the

---

49. Luther was here displaying a negative attitude to false assurance and a positive attitude to one realistically based. Lortz's judgment that "the theses on indulgences are an expression of Luther's theology of the uncertainty of salvation, of his theology of the cross" concentrates on the former at the expense of the latter (Lortz, *Reformation in Germany* 1:230).

church, for instance in the penitential canons, but could never be absolute. Eck, on the other hand, held the recommended procedure to be so reliable that priest and penitent could be absolutely certain.[50] A minority view was expressed by Prierias, who accepted the force of Luther's major premise that indulgences were based on a set of uncertainties, although for quite different reasons. There was no guarantee, he argued, that God's remission followed automatically upon the priest's absolution. But, as we have seen, Prierias actually considered that this uncertainty made indulgences all the more attractive as an insurance policy.

Why could the controversialists not accept Luther's views on assurance? One answer is that they did not understand the theology of the cross that lay behind the Ninety-five Theses. Luther himself realized this and claimed to be encouraged. It confirmed for him that here was a spirituality too deep, too Christian to be recognized by pagan scholasticism. Noting that Eck had failed to comment on his fourteenth to twentieth theses (which propose that it is possible to experience purgatory and hell even in this life), Luther commented:

> It was only right that Eck should have left these theses intact, for they are too profound to be ensnared in any way by scholastic opinions and too full of the experience of this saying: "He brings down to Hell and raises up again" [1 Sam. 2:6].[51]

And referring to Eck's assertion that souls in purgatory are assured of their ultimate salvation, he asked:

> How do they know for certain? Because Eck says so. He is ignorant of the theology of the cross if he believes they can be certain they are saved merely because they are "friends of God" and absolved in body.[52]

Luther showed himself equally aware that his theology had isolated him from his opponents when he wrote his *Response* to Prierias, in which he forgave the Italian's inability to understand that a Christian can grieve even when joyful and rejoice even when sad on the

50. Eck, *Obelisci* 15 (*WA* 1:299).
51. Luther, *Asterisci* (*WA* 1:289).
52. Ibid. (*WA* 1:290–91).

grounds that such an insight derives not from scholastic theology but is of a quite different temper.[53]

Another answer is that the controversialists did not understand what Luther meant by "contrition," sorrow over sin motivated by love for God. This was partly Luther's own fault, because in almost the same breath he used the word in opposite senses. The thirtieth thesis of the ninety-five theses reads, "No-one can be sure of the reality of his own contrition, much less of receiving plenary forgiveness,"[54] whereas the thirty-sixth thesis reads, "Any Christian whatsoever who is truly repentant has as his due plenary remission of punishment and guilt even without letters of indulgence."[55] He later elaborated in the *Explanations* that in the thirtieth thesis he was using the word in the conventional sense of an act we perform, an emotion we produce from our natural resources, while in the thirty-sixth thesis he was using the idea in his own specialized sense of something inspired in us by God.[56] So when Luther spoke of confidence in having our sins forgiven, the controversialists took him to mean that Christians can be so genuinely, perfectly, and unfeignedly sorry that God cannot withhold from them immediate forgiveness, and this struck them as a doctrine both untrue and presumptuous. In fact, this confidence or faith was for Luther based not on our tears but in Christ's blood, and for this insight he was chiefly indebted to Johannes von Staupitz.[57] Staupitz's views were

---

53. Luther, *Responsio ad Prieratus dialogum* (Löscher 2:395). It is relevant at this point to ask why the controversialists did not understand Luther's theology of the cross. Perhaps the most obvious explanation is that they had not shared his personal experiences. When, e.g., Johannes Cochlaeus came across the passage in the *Resolutiones* in which Luther gives the testimony of "a man I knew" who had suffered the pains of eternal torment in this life (*WA* 1:557.33–558.18, *LW* 31:129f.), he commented that such a man must have been possessed by the devil (*Uff CLIIII Artikeln*, Hi^v). Although it is generally recognized that Luther's debt to mysticism is not a simple case of "influence" (the most recent summary can be found in A. E. McGrath, *Luther's Theology of the Cross: Martin Luther's Theological Breakthrough* [Oxford: Basil Blackwell, 1985], 171 n. 69), the controversialists' apparent ignorance of mystical writers with whom Luther was well-acquainted might also have contributed to their incomprehension of the *theologia crucis*. Eck could sneer at "one Tauler—whoever he may have been" (*WA Br* 1:295.10–11), while Ambrosius Catharinus could call Tauler "some nameless and secret author" (*Apologia*, 237). Catharinus also made fun of Luther's appeal to obscure German mystics when he came to refute a later treatise: "Now as to your Babylonia—may I ask who it is that supports you? Perhaps it's that Tauler of yours, or one of the other extremely well-known authors whose books you keep hidden away at home!" (*Excusatio*, 22).

54. *WA* 1:234.35f., *LW* 31:28.

55. *WA* 1:235.7f., *LW* 31:28.

56. Luther, *Explanations*, conclusion 30 (*WA* 1:586.23–587.2, *LW* 31:178f.).

57. Dedicatory letter to Staupitz, 30 May 1518 (*WA* 1:525–27).

unpublished and unknown beyond a few choice spirits among the Augustinians and in Nuremberg. The only other likely influence that may have predisposed anyone to the same ways of thought was Duns Scotus, who taught a "fiduciary certainty" (*certitudo fidei*) in the objective efficacy of the sacraments of baptism and penance.[58] Luther's view of grace certainly shows many similarities with Scotus's, and it may be that he was also indebted in some way to Scotus's doctrine of faith. What we do know is that none of Luther's opponents of 1518 had been trained exclusively in the *via moderna*. Indeed, Prierias had devoted a book to the condemnation of Scotism in 1514.[59] Eck had been trained in both the *viae* but showed no familiarity with the idea of fiduciary certainty.

A third answer is that Luther was suspect because he so emphasized the importance of contrition. However contrition was defined, it was still motivated by a pure love for God, and in itself it deserved God's reward without requiring further compensations or satisfactions. Luther's thirty-ninth thesis pointed out the difficulty of preaching both the bounty of indulgences and the need for true contrition.[60] Prierias agreed: "If anyone is so tortured with contrition that he discharges the guilt of all his sins, then the pope remits no punishment."[61] In other words, contrition had to be present before God could remit sins, and yet if it were present it rendered unnecessary or at least relatively unimportant the sacerdotal and sacramental system of the church so far as penance was concerned.[62] This meant that Luther was using the Ninety-five Theses to probe an already sensitive area. Eck and Prierias attempted to harmonize contrition and indulgences by making the first refer only to the guilt of a sin and the second only to its satisfaction.[63] Prierias attempted to reinstate the importance of the sacerdotal system by arguing that very few people are ever really contrite but that they do have in their attrition an imperfect contrition that the

---

58. E.g., H. Jedin, *A History of the Council of Trent* 2:252.

59. Prierias, *Malleus in falsas assumptiones Scoti in primo Sententiarum libro* (Bologna: B. Hector, 1514).

60. *WA* 1:235.14f., *LW* 31:28.

61. Löscher 2:37.

62. Even Roman Catholic theologians have conceded that this was a sensitive area. Dolan writes: "Especially urgent for Luther, as for the late medieval theologians, was the question of why there are sacraments if faith already justifies" ("Catholic Literary Opponents," 32).

63. Eck, *Obelisci* 19 (*WA* 1:303); Prierias, *Dialogus* (Löscher 2:26).

pope can commute to full contrition through his power of the keys.[64] It is not surprising that Luther could not accept the validity of these defenses, because they fell into his category of "scholastic opinions held without proof." It is perhaps surprising that his own solution to the problem of reconciling contrition with a role for the priest was to make the priest more important.[65] But his conservatism was apparent only in the *Explanations*; the damage had been done by the radical-sounding Ninety-five Theses. Luther's emphasis on contrition was seen to relativize the significance of the church's ritual, and all his opponents would have agreed with Eck that his purpose was to "disseminate the Bohemian virus."[66]

The Attitude toward the Common People

The third area in which the Romanists believed that Luther presented a threat in 1518 was in his positive attitude toward the common people. It is quite true that (despite the form of the Ninety-five Theses) Luther did not think of indulgences as some abstract theological conundrum to be puzzled over in a university lecture hall. To him it was a problem because it misled ordinary, poor, uneducated Christians into a false security of salvation and a false conception of God. In sermons delivered at Allhallowtide in 1515 and 1516, Luther provided for such people what was in his opinion a more Christian interpretation of indulgences.[67]

Although he showed immense personal courage in thus casting a critical eye at the Wittenberg collection of relics to which the elector was so devoted, he realized that a local protest was not enough. The entire theory and practice of indulgences stood in need of reexamination if the people were to be helped. The preaching of the jubilee indulgence for the building of St. Peter's Basilica provided the opportunity for that review. His concern for the people is clear from his letter to Archbishop Albrecht of October 1517 requesting the withdrawal of the instructions to the Mainz and Magdeburg preachers.

> I am not criticizing the preachers' sermons (which I have not heard) but I grieve over the false constructions the people may

64. Prierias, *Dialogus* (Löscher 2:24–25).
65. Luther did this by making contrition (in the sense of "faith") dependent on the word of promise spoken by the priest in absolution, not vice versa.
66. Eck, *Obelisci* 18, 22 (WA 1:94–99).
67. See, e.g., WA 1:94–99.

put on them, namely, these wretched souls believe themselves certain of their salvation if they purchase letters of indulgence.[68]

It is evident also from the ninety-five theses themselves. Nine times he asks that "Christians should be taught" the correct doctrine—"Christians" here being used in the common medieval sense of "laity."[69] Eight times he quotes the sort of questions conscientious lay people might ask on hearing the indulgence preaching currently employed.[70] Luther was criticized at the time and has been since for ascribing his own thoughts to others. That these were authentic complaints can indeed be doubted, but it is safe to assume that he was making intelligent guesses as to the problems likely to trouble sensitive Christians.[71] He was taking seriously not only the downward flow of correct or incorrect teaching but also the upward flow of popular response, at least in the confusion that misleading information can create. His request was that these questions be answered by rational argument and not silenced by authority.[72]

In one sense, Luther's opponents shared his concern that the common people were being misled by incorrect preaching, for in their turn they described Luther's published propositions as liable to lead many souls into heresy and therefore into danger of eternal punishment.[73] Tetzel even took the step of publishing a vernacular refutation of Luther's 1518 *Sermon on Indulgence and Grace* to counter the Wittenberger at a popular level. But they could not share Luther's view that the people's objections were to be taken seriously. To Wimpina, the "conscientious questionings of the laity" were nothing more than the "trifling arguments of little old women."[74] And while he and Eck thought that these arguments could be answered by reason,[75] Tetzel and Prierias defended the church's (that is, the hierarchy's) right to use naked authority to silence opposition from among Christians.[76]

68. *WA Br* 1:111.16–20.
69. Theses 42, 43, 45–51 (*WA* 1:235.20–23, 26–41; *LW* 31:29f.).
70. Theses 81–90 (*WA* 1:237–38, *LW* 31:32).
71. Prierias, *Dialogus* (Löscher 2:35).
72. Thesis 90 (*WA* 1:238.9–11).
73. E.g., Wimpina, theses 72–76, 79, 102, 103 (Löscher 1:510, 511, 513); Tetzel, *Subscriptas positiones*, theses 32, 36 (Löscher 1:520, 521).
74. After Wimpina's thesis 106 (Löscher 1:514).
75. After Wimpina's thesis 106 (Löscher 1:514); Eck, *Obelisci* 30 (*WA* 1:313).
76. "The Roman Church, which is included in the Roman pontificate, has as its supreme head in both temporal and spiritual power the pope. And, through the secular arm (as the laws decree) it has the power to restrain those who, after first embracing the faith, subsequently err" (Prierias, *Dialogus* 90 [Löscher 2:38]).

Prierias had a low view of "rustics" who, he thought, would never confess their crimes but for the sacrament of penance and would never do good works without the incentive of indulgences;[77] and it is helpful to recall the controversial view that the confessional was used as a means of social control.[78] Certainly, Luther's theses were seen to shake the people's confidence in the church, with the result that the church's influence over them might be weakened. For Eck, the theses were so conducive to "tumult" and "sedition" that the clergy could "scarcely be defended from the insults, let alone the swords, of the prattling laity."[79]

The Romanists, therefore, displayed an attitude toward the people that revealed not simply disdain of social inferiors but also a deep fear of a potential source of violent revolution. For a religious and a priest to take the complaints of lay people seriously and on this basis to criticize a practice of the church (in the medieval sense of the "clergy") was to commit class treason. It is well known that in years to come Luther was to use inflammatory language urging the laity to "reform" the cardinals with cold steel; it is not so well known that his Catholic opponents first put these words into his mouth. In accordance with their abhorrence of Luther's apparent betrayal, Wimpina, Eck, and Prierias were agreed that, if he felt he had discovered an abuse, he should not have stated this publicly but should have followed instead the "rule of brotherly correction" by privately admonishing the offenders.[80] The replies of all three were in Latin and Eck's was not even published. This shows that they were striving to limit the potential audience of the controversy and to keep it within the bounds of brotherly correction—in other words, to close ranks on the subject.

The fact that the Romanists could not share Luther's positive attitude toward ordinary Christians also explains their antipathy to his rejection of scholastic theology and of the traditional grounds for assurance—the other two areas in which they felt his threat most acutely. His pugnacious *Disputation against Scholastic Theology* of September

---

77. Prierias, *Dialogus* (Löscher 2:34).
78. T. N. Tentler, "The *Summa* for Confessors as an Instrument of Social Control," in C. Trinkaus and H. A. Oberman, eds., *The Pursuit of Holiness in Late Medieval and Renaissance Religion* (Leiden: E. J. Brill, 1974), 103–25.
79. Eck, *Obelisci* 29 (*WA* 1:312–13).
80. Wimpina, thesis 102 (Löscher 1:513); Eck, *Obelisci* 26 (*WA* 1:311); Prierias, *Dialogus* (Löscher 2:29, 35).

1517 passed without comment. It was only when this attack became associated with a practical problem of concern to the common people and was translated into the vernacular (with or without his consent) that it became, in the eyes of those who wrote against him, dangerous: a theologian was teaching the people that scholasticism, from which the late medieval church drew so much of its inspiration, was not to be trusted. Indeed, Luther even expressed the view privately to Eck that those who perpetuate the doctrines of the schoolmen

> have created nothing else than a tyranny in that the theology they turn out in those neologisms of theirs is not understood by the people. The indulgence racket is thus so obscured that they do not understand themselves the extent of its validity. All that matters to them is that the people must not be allowed to know it or to ask about it from us, just in case our income should diminish.[81]

Similarly, it was only when Luther began publicly to replace "parchment and sealing-wax" certainty with "death and hell" certainty that he became dangerous: a priest was teaching the people that the church's means of grace (or at least one of them) was not to be trusted.

The Bastion of the Papacy

Luther's critique of indulgences was considered so revolutionary by his objectors, not primarily because he had thereby called into question the papal plenitude of power but because he had rejected scholastic theology, had declared at least one of the church's widely acknowledged means of grace unreliable, and had adopted a positive attitude toward the laity—and because he had done this not within the confines of the lecture hall or as one brother-priest to another but publicly. Yet Luther could not be silenced or prevented from so undermining the hierarchy because he had said nothing formally heretical. No official dogma had yet been formulated. Although they could cite weighty authorities against him, the Romanists were aware of this basic aspect of dogmatic etiquette.

Tetzel, Prierias, and (to a lesser extent) Cajetan set about declaring Luther a heretic on the charge of offending the pope's majesty, on the grounds that to question any indulgence preaching was to question the authority of its sponsor, the pope. This use of the papal office as a bastion against reform was intolerable to Luther, who was now

81. Luther, *Asterisci* (WA 1:313).

forced to turn his attention to the question of the pope's authority in the church to see whether it was, after all, a valid expression of God's will and could therefore be regarded, as the Romanists claimed, as a divinely instituted guarantee of the church's teaching.

2

THE DIVINE RIGHT
CONTROVERSY

The second phase of the Catholic literary response can be said to cover the period from mid-1519 to mid-1520 and to have been dominated by the question of the divine right of the papacy.[1] This phase saw the continued participation of some of the veterans of the indulgence debate, but also the emergence of many new writers representative of a wider range of theological traditions.

This proliferation of the controversial effort is problematic in two respects. It is by no means clear why a man whose case was pending at Rome and whose utterances might reasonably have been considered sub judice should have become the target of a literary free-for-all. Nor is it immediately obvious why this larger and more diverse second phase of the controversialists' campaign should have manifested a greater degree of unanimity than the smaller and more uniform reaction to the indulgence theses. In order to resolve these difficulties, it is important to look at the case Luther presented against the papacy in 1519, as well as the context of the Catholic replies to it, before examining the main features of the Catholic response on the question as a whole.

Luther's Thirteenth Proposition

Throughout the year 1518, Luther's literary opponents had concerned themselves with demonstrating the connection between indulgences

---

1. For the general background to Luther's critique of the papacy and the Catholic response, see esp. O. Starck, "Luthers Stellung zur Institution des Papsttums von 1520 bis 1546 unter besonderer Berücksichtigung des 'ius humanum,' " (Ph.D. diss., Münster, 1930); L. Buisson, *Potestas und caritas: Die päpstliche Gewalt im Spätmittelalter* (Cologne: Böhlau, 1958); K. W. Norr, *Kirche und Konzil bei Nicolaus de Tudeschis (Panormitanus)*, Forschungen zur kirchlichen Rechtsgeschichte und zum Kirchenrecht 4 (Cologne: Böhlau, 1964); O. de la Brosse, *Le pape et le concile: La comparaison de leurs pouvoirs à la veille de la Réforme* (Paris: Editions du Cerf, 1965); F. Rickers, "Das Petrusbild Luthers: Ein Beitrag zu seiner Auseinandersetzung mit dem Papsttum" (Ph.D. diss., Heidelberg, 1967); P. Fraenkel, "John Eck's Enchiridion of 1525 and Luther's Earliest Arguments against Papal Primacy," 110–63; R. Bäumer, *Martin Luther und der Papst*. Of particular value for seeing the controversy of 1519–20 in the context of Luther's wider engagement with the papacy is S. H. Hendrix, *Luther and the Papacy: Stages in a Reformation Conflict*.

and the power of the pope, with the result that his criticism of the practice had earned him a formal accusation of injuring the pope's majesty. To Luther, it seemed as if vested interests within the Curia were deliberately magnifying the pope's power so that anything might be defended in its name. After his interview with Cajetan at Augsburg, he wrote:

> I worship and follow the Roman Church in all things. I resist only those who in the name of the Roman Church strive to erect a Babylon among us; they desire that whatever they think up, so long as they can move their tongues to pronounce the words "Roman Church," be immediately and unreservedly received as the opinion of the Roman Church, as if Holy Scripture were not supreme.[2]

At the end of 1518, therefore, Luther was attempting to reconcile respect for the papacy with detestation of the abuses he considered to have been introduced and perpetuated in its name. He was given the opportunity to pursue this double aim in more detail in the middle of the following year. Referring to a remark Luther had made in the course of his *Explanations* on indulgences, Eck added an extra proposition to the twelve he had already drawn up for debate with Karlstadt at Leipzig: "We deny that the Roman Church was not superior to the other churches before Pope Sylvester's time. Rather, we have always acknowledged the possessor of the most blessed Peter's faith and throne as Peter's successor and Christ's vicar-general."[3] Luther replied to Eck with a set of counter-theses, including his own thirteenth proposition: "That the Roman Church is superior to all others is proved by the exceedingly feeble decrees of the Roman pontiffs which have appeared in the last four hundred years. Against them stand the history of the previous eleven hundred years, the text of divine Scripture, and the decree of the Council of Nicaea, the most sacred of all councils."[4]

It was to defend the meaning of this thesis in public, before engaging with Eck at Leipzig, that Luther wrote his *Explanation of His Thirteenth Proposition Concerning the Power of the Pope*.[5] In it he claimed

---

2. Luther, *Acta Augustana* (WA 2:22.23–27).
3. Johannes Eck, *Contra novam doctrinam scheda disputatoria* (Löscher 3:211).
4. Luther, *Disputatio et excusatio adversus criminationes D. J. Eccii*. (WA 2:161.35–38).
5. WA 2:183–240.

to be as concerned as anyone to uphold the dignity of the pope; but if papal primacy were to be defended adequately, the belief in its establishment by God must be abandoned. Of course, Roman primacy could still be seen as in accordance with God's will, because the pope is de facto head of the church and the powers that be are ordained of God[6]— but this could be the only sound reason for accepting papal supremacy. The texts of Scripture and canon law commonly put forward in its defense were not unequivocal. The rock of Matt. 16:18, upon which Christ intended to found his church, most probably refers to the confession of faith exemplified by Peter in the preceding dialogue, not to Peter himself; and the "keys of the kingdom of heaven" were promised to all the disciples, not to Peter alone, as is evident from the parallel key sayings of Matt. 18:18 and John 20:23. Similarly, Christ's instruction to "tend my sheep" (*pasce oves meas*, John 21:15-17) would have been demanded of all the disciples, since Peter could scarcely have been expected to serve the whole church by himself, and history shows that the apostle to the circumcised shared his ministry with others. Furthermore, the Lord's use of the word "tend" suggests that Peter's primacy was meant to be one of love and self-sacrifice, not of power. As for those decretals most commonly cited, they are variously blasphemous, unspiritual, counterfeit, contradictory, or based on a misunderstanding of biblical passages.[7]

Arguments from history and reason, Luther continued, provide no firmer support for papal primacy as the sole option for the church than those from Scripture and canon law. The Greek, Russian, African, and Asian churches have never accepted the superiority of Rome, and it would be impious to suggest that they were not truly Christian. The letters of such fathers as Augustine, Jerome, Gregory, and Bernard, which set limits to the pope's power, far outweigh both in numbers and in antiquity the dubious decretals cited in its favor. Finally, he objected, the argument from natural law that sees monarchy as the

---

6. *WA* 2:185–87.

7. The decrees Luther criticized were: *De libellis* (dist. 20 c. 1, Leo IV ad Britt. episc., *CICan* 1:65), for putting human statutes on a par with the gospel; *Inferior sedes* (dist. 21 c. 4, Nicolas ad Constantin. episc., *CICan* 1:70), for making the pope God and the bishops his creatures; the pseudo-Isidorian *Cleros et clericos* (dist. 21 c. 1, *CICan* 1:67–69) and Anicetus's *Primae sedis episcopus* (dist. 99 c. 3, *CICan* 1:350f.), on account of their mutual contradiction; and *Ita Dominus noster* (dist. 19 c. 8, Leo I ad episc. Vienn. ep. 87, *CICan* 1:62), for misinterpreting Scripture. He also cited a "Pelagius dis. xxi," which we take to be a misreading for Gelasius, *Quamvis universae* (dist. 21 c. 3, *CICan* 1:70).

best model for church government runs counter to the Lord's own teaching on true greatness: "but it shall not be so amongst you."[8]

In this treatise, which dates from the period when he was still expressing his disapproval of the papacy in moderate terms, Luther was attempting to distinguish between two ways of defending Roman primacy. The right way, he thought, was to accept it as an institution tolerated by God's permissive will (*de voluntate Dei*); the wrong way was to claim its establishment by divine law (*de iure divino*). To modern eyes this may seem a fine distinction,[9] but the trenchant opposition it met from Luther's contemporaries suggests that it was considered a significant step toward total rejection of the papacy.

The initial literary campaign against Luther had been part of a legal process involving German plaintiffs (Wimpina and Tetzel) and an Italian judge (Prierias). By the time the campaign had entered its second phase, after the publication of Luther's *Explanation of the Thirteenth Proposition*, it had become separated from the judicial proceedings that were now being pursued through the offices of the papal nuncio Miltitz. Nevertheless, the controversy was still firmly rooted in the countries originally involved, with five Italian writers joining Prierias, and Eck, Augustinus von Alveld, and Thomas Murner replacing the Frankfurt Dominicans.

The first reaction to Luther's treatise was published in March 1520. This was Prierias's three-volume work, entitled, without undue modesty, *Martin Luther's Erroneous Arguments Named, Exposed, Rejected, and Most Utterly Ground to Pieces.*[10] The third volume was in fact an index to the previous two volumes, which Prierias entitled the *Epitome of His Response*—"for an index it is indeed rather long," he admitted, "but for an epitome, it is very short"—and which Luther reprinted with marginal comments and a foreword and afterword in June of that year. The purpose of *Erroneous Arguments* was to prove that "the Church Militant is the monarchical and hierarchical kingdom of Christ, and that the Roman high priest has primacy over it by divine authority,

---

8. *WA* 2:225–35.

9. The statement *Authority in the Church II* of the first Anglican–Roman Catholic International Commission is, e.g., prepared to overlook it. See the Anglican–Roman Catholic International Commission, *The Final Report* (London: SPCK/CTS, 1982), 87.

10. Prierias, *Errata et argumenta Martini Luteris recitata, detecta, repulsa et copiosissima trita;* and *Epitoma responsionis ad Martinum Lutherum.*

and is the supreme arbiter and sole infallible judge in questions of faith and morals."[11]

In December, another Italian joined the literary fray. Ambrosius Catharinus Politus, a year Luther's junior, had been a lecturer in civil law and chief advocate of the Consistory; but in 1517 he entered the religious life as a Dominican and began to teach himself theology. His *Apology* was at once a refutation of Luther's works up to 1519 and a public appeal to the emperor to intervene in the case.[12] Although it is a wide-ranging work, dealing in five books with the reformer's opinions on a number of subjects, more than half of it was concerned with the pope. Book Two was directed against *Explanation of the Thirteenth Proposition* and took the form of an imaginary dialogue between Origen, Jerome, Augustine, Chrysostom, Ambrose, Gregory the Great, and Bernard of Clairvaux, as they exchanged their views on the interpretation of the Petrine texts. Needless to say, none was shown to favor Luther's exegesis.[13] Book Three dealt with the infallibility of the papal *magisterium* (teaching office), its consequent superiority to that of a general council, and the ability of the church, through the pope, to dispense indulgences.

A more specific treatise was the primatial defense published the following March by Cardinal Cajetan, who at Augsburg had already faced Luther in person on the questions of faith, indulgences, and the power of the pope.[14] Although it did not mention Luther by name, it followed closely the structure of his *Explanation of the Thirteenth Proposition*. Luther's interpretation of the two key Petrine texts was criticized on grounds of grammar and tradition, and this criticism takes up the greater part of the book. Luther's historical arguments were countered by Cajetan's contention that councils and the saints of antiquity were themselves legitimated by St. Peter and his successors and so could not in turn be used to demonstrate or counter the validity of Petrine-Roman primacy. This work was remarkably calm and objective and was free from the abuse that Catharinus, for instance, thought

11. *WA* 6:330.16–18.
12. Catharinus, *Apologia*.
13. This section of the *Apologia* was reprinted at Dresden in 1525 by Hieronymus Emser as *Contra Martinum Lutherum super his verbis: Tu es Petrus*.
14. Cajetan, *De divina institutione Pontificatus Romani Pontificis super totam ecclesiam a Christo in Petro*.

so necessary. But for such a careful scholar it was also a comparatively short work, and in his dedication to Pope Leo he felt obliged to apologize for such a "little lucubration . . . for the cruder sort of people."[15]

In June of 1521, another Italian refutation of *Explanation of the Thirteenth Proposition* was published, this time by Cristoforo Marcello, archbishop of Corfu. He divided his *Authority of the High Pontiff and Related Matters* into two sections.[16] The first was a straightforward point-by-point rebuttal, with particular emphasis on the question of the original identity of bishop and presbyter. The second dealt with indulgences and scholastic theology, matters which Marcello, with Prierias and Tetzel before him, deemed pertinent to pontifical authority.

The last Italian to enter the lists against Luther's treatise on the papacy was a Franciscan, Thomas Illyricus, a hell-fire preacher whose comminations had alienated many in his adopted town of Lyons. But it was not solely at the laity that he directed his zeal. In introductory letters to *A Defense of Papal Status* of January 1523, he urged both the pope and secular authorities to reform the church from within as well as to guard against heresy from without.[17] Such reform-mindedness may also have affected his ecclesiology: certainly he shared with the German Franciscans a certain reluctance to attribute absolute power to the pope.

In his homeland, Luther was answered first and foremost by Alveld, a Franciscan observant at Leipzig who had been specially commissioned by Bishop Adolf of Merseburg and the papal nuncio Miltitz to refute the Wittenberger's position on papal primacy. It is worth considering Alveld's work in more detail, not least because of all his opponents on this point, Luther deemed only Alveld deserving of a reply. Alveld's first pamphlet, *The Apostolic See*, was arranged according to seven arguments, or "swords," as he called them, in defense of the divine institution of the Apostolic See.[18] The first, reason, indicated

---

15. Cajetan, *De divina institutione*, 1.
16. Cristoforo Marcello, *De authoritate summi pontificis et his quae ad illam pertinent: Adversus impia Martini Lutherii dogmata.*
17. Thomas Illyricus, *Libellus de potestate summi pontificis editus a Fratre Thoma Illyrico, minorita verbi dei precone famatissimo & apostolico: qui intitulatur Clipeus status papalis.*
18. Augustinus von Alveld, *Super apostolica sede, an videlicet divino sit iure nec ne, anque pontifex qui Papa dici caeptus est, iure divino in ea ipsa praesideat, non parum laudanda ex sacro Bibliorum canone declaratur.*

that every earthly institution requires an earthly head. The second, Scripture, showed that Peter's pontificate was adumbrated by the Aaronite high priesthood. The third, "true knowledge," required that no source be ignored in the search for truth: many authorities supported papal primacy, but Luther, like the Sadducees of Jesus' day, accepted only those authorities with which he agreed. The fourth sword, piety, prompted all true Christians to confess that many popes have been godly men and that Christ could hardly have suffered his bride to live in error over this doctrine for so many centuries. The fifth sword, "sound understanding," clarified the apparently anti-primatial passages cited by Luther from the Scriptures. The sixth sword, "plain and simple wisdom," dealt with the problem of ecclesiastical abuses: abuses, Alveld argued, were inevitable in human society, and it was therefore an indication of God's will that the Roman see had survived them. Alveld's final argument was a tendentious comparison of Luther's character with his own.

Within a few days of completing this pamphlet, Alveld began work on a second, *A Very Fruitful and Useful Little Book*.[19] It was not simply a translation of *The Apostolic See*, but an entirely rewritten work with a much more popular slant. It set out to answer the question, How do we recognize the true church of Christ? The seven swords of the Latin work become seven signs that Peter's sheepfold is alone authentic. Only in this church, Alveld argued, were miracles performed; this church alone had preserved intact the Scriptures and doctrines handed down from the apostles, the seven sacraments, and obedience to Christ's commands to Peter. All other communions and religions, he continued, were vitiated morally and doctrinally and were of more recent date, and the repeated failure of schemes for unity was a reflection of the purity and inviolability of Peter's see. The most interesting part of the treatise was the concluding section, in which popular objections to the Catholic faith were answered. How can the pope "feed" me, people ask, if he can't even see me? Through the sacraments, was Alveld's answer. Why must I give him so much money? Who needs money, asks Alveld in return, who has the sacraments? Is it not true that the Curia is immoral? Yes, but you must "do as they say and not as they do." Do they not say that our eyes have

19. Alveld, *Eyn gar fruchtbar und nutzbarlich buchleyn von dem Babstlichen stul: und von sant Peter: und von den / warhafftigen scheflein Christi sein / die Christus unser herr Petro befolen hat in sein hute und regirung.*

now at last been opened? So were Adam's and Eve's. And are not cardinals a recent invention? They seem to be—if you judge the matter by outward appearances and not by truth and reason.

Luther felt compelled to write against this "ape-like" book because, in the vernacular, he feared, it would poison the minds of the poor laity, and his reply, *The Papacy,* appeared in June 1520. In it he was able to refine his critique of the papacy further and to make two demands: that sincere Christians were not to be slandered as heretics merely because they dwelt outside Roman unity, and that the pope was to remain obedient to Scripture and thus to Christ.[20] Alveld answered immediately that he was as concerned as anyone to see the abuses of the Curia remedied, but could not see what any outsider could do to effect reform. The end of the year witnessed the entry into the debate of another Franciscan, the Strasbourgeois humanist Murner, with a short work also directed against *The Papacy.* Here Murner gave the stock Romanist objections a new twist by declaring Luther's arguments against papal primacy liable to cause sedition.[21] Eck's written contribution to the debate had appeared in May 1520.[22] (He had given a verbal answer at Leipzig the year before.) His 384-folio treatise, *The Primacy of Peter against Luther,* was divided into three volumes, reflecting the three divisions of Luther's tract, though of course treating the evidence at much greater length. In Book One he attempted to establish the divine right on the basis of Matt. 16:18, John 21:15, and ten other Gospel passages illustrative of Peter's pre-eminence. In Book Two he presented the evidence of more than fifty fathers, popes, and councils. Book Three was devoted to the difference between *ius* and *voluntas,* the status of the non-Roman churches, and the relation of the episcopacy to the presbyterate.

The primacy debate was now all but exhausted as the more productive controversialists turned their attention elsewhere. The vicar-general of the diocese of Constance, Johannes Fabri, published a comprehensive tome in the tradition of Eck's *Primacy,* entitled *The Work against Luther's Dogmas* (1522), reprinted in 1524 as *Hammer of Lutheran Heresy.*[23] At the end of 1523, an Englishman, Edward Powell,

---

20. Luther, *Von dem Papstthum* (*WA* 6:322.1–22, *LW* 39:101f.).
21. Thomas Murner, *Von dem babstentum, das ist von der höchsten Obrigkeit des christlichen Glaubens.*
22. Johannes Eck, *De primatu Petri adversus Lutherum libri tres.*
23. *Johannes Fabri Constantiensis in spiritualibus vicarii opus adversus nova quaedam et a christiana religione prorsus aliena dogmata Martini Lutheri.*

canon of Salisbury, challenged Luther in a volume that answered both his *Explanation of the Thirteenth Proposition* and his *Babylonian Captivity.*[24] Two years later, Jakob Latomus of the University of Louvain published a set of propositions *On the Primacy of the Roman Pontiff against Luther.*[25] These latecomers added little to the arguments of their predecessors, but their continuing interest in the divine right question even after it had been overtaken by events indicates at least their own order of priorities.

The Defense of the Divine Right

The Catholic controversialists who tilted against Luther's *Explanation of the Thirteenth Proposition* were therefore much more numerous and representative of a wider range of backgrounds than those who engaged in the indulgence controversy. In part, this was due to the fact that Luther's *Explanation of the Thirteenth Proposition* had considerably more structure and coherence than his indulgence theses. These qualities were mirrored in turn by those refutations that kept closely to the form of Luther's original and even lent them a certain outward uniformity. The similarities, however, were more than merely formal. There was considerable unanimity between them in the detailed arguments they deployed against Luther's treatise. A number began their defenses with almost identical condemnations of the public questioning of papal power as a potentially seditious act. As Eck wrote: "What else do they seem to do who seek to abolish the ministerial head, or assert that it was not established by divine right, than prepare and strew the way with heresies, schisms, rebellions, dissensions, and contentions?"[26]

The divine institution of the papacy, they all argued, was clear from Christ's double promise to Peter at Caesarea Philippi, that on him the church would be founded and that he would possess the keys of the kingdom of heaven. This was supported by the most natural, grammatical meaning of the text, and by the early fathers' interpretation of it: "Tu es *Petrus*, et super hanc *petram* aedificabo ecclesiam

---

24. Edward Powell, *Propugnaculum summi sacerdotii evangelici, ac septenarii sacramentorum, editum per virum eruditum, sacrarumque literatum professorem Edoardum Pouelum, adversus Martinum Lutherum fratrem famosum et Wiclefistam insignem.*

25. Jakob Latomus, *De primatu romani pontificis adversus Lutherum.*

26. Eck, *De primatu Petri* 1:1. Cf. Murner, *Von dem babstentum,* Aiiff.; Latomus, *De primatu romani,* 59ᵛ.

meam."[27] Such an interpretation was, they believed, entirely consistent with the other passages in the Gospels that witnessed to Peter's precedence over his fellow disciples: the payment of Jesus' and Peter's tribute with the same coin, which Augustine understood as a prophecy of Peter's vicariate; Peter's question, "We have left all to follow you—what then shall we have?" which he asked not on his own account (he had already received the very keys of heaven) but in his capacity as spokesman of the apostles; and Christ's prayer that Peter's faith not fail, which occurs after an argument over which of the apostles was greatest—"Wyl ye not see how Christ was the mouthe of Peter towards almighty God . . . and contrary wyse was not Peter the mouthe of Christ when he to the true waye converted dyd conferme his brethren?"[28] Luther's criticism of this interpretation of Matt. 16:18 was based on the fact that the power of binding and loosing is elsewhere (Matt. 18:18; John 20:23) given to the disciples in general, not to Peter alone. The controversialists answered variously that Matthew 16 and 18 refer to different powers of the keys,[29] which are "similar but not identical"—a difference that Cajetan, Powell, and Catharinus expressed as the distinction between full *potestas* and mere *facultas*, *usus*, or *actus potestatis*[30]—or else that the power was the same but had been given to Peter in a primary sense and to the other apostles in a secondary sense.[31]

The other classic proof-text of Petrine primacy was the risen Christ's injunction "Feed my sheep" (John 21:15ff.). The controversialists readily disposed of Luther's objection that *pascere* implies feeding with the pure Word of God in self-sacrificial service and not domination: the shepherd's job, they replied, inevitably involves coercing his flock, and the Old Testament often describes kings as tending their subjects.[32] Marcello argued that Christian people could

27. Alveld, *Super apostolicae sede,* Div–Eii^v; Cajetan, *De divina institutione,* 3–15; Catharinus, *Apologia,* 95–96; Latomus, *De primatu romani,* 62^v; Eck, *De primatu Petri* 1:4–9; Murner, *Von dem babstentum,* Biv^v–Eii.

28. John Fisher, *Sermon* (1521), 316–17. See also Catharinus, *Apologia,* 96; Eck, *De primatu Petri* 1:47–50; Illyricus, *Clipeus status papalis,* Cvii–Hvii; Marcello, *De authoritate,* 8^v–9; Powell, *Propugnaculum,* 14–16.

29. Marcello, *De authoritate,* 13.

30. Cajetan, *De divina institutione,* 33; Catharinus, *Apologia,* 130; Powell, *Propugnaculum,* 19^v–20.

31. Eck, *De primatu Petri* 1:8; Marcello, *De authoritate,* 12.

32. Alveld, *Super apostolicae sede,* Fiv^{v}f.; Cajetan, *De divina institutione,* 55–56; Eck, *De primatu Petri* 1:33; Hieronymus Emser, *Assertio,* 716; Latomus, *De primatu romani,* 63^v.

be fed in this way as much by deeds as by words, and that it was more dignified for Peter's successors to tend their flocks by setting an example of sound government than by an itinerant preaching ministry.[33] Against Luther's contention that Peter's ministry was simply one among many, the controversialists argued that the subsidiary ministries of the other disciples no more detracted from Peter's sole rule than the representatives of a king might diminish his monarchy.[34] Luther had argued that, as the commission to "Feed my sheep" had followed the question "Do you love me?" a pope who by his actions proved his lack of love for Christ would forfeit the authority committed to him. To Cajetan, such an argument was redolent of Wycliffe's perfectionism: "Had Peter fallen from charity, he would not have forfeited the office of pastor, but only the right use of the same. For it is not the office which depends on charity, but correct use, as is plain enough to Catholic doctors and contradicted only by heretics."[35] Murner made the same point more succinctly: "In this you say nothing more than that he is a bad pastor, not that he is no pastor."[36]

To prove Petrine primacy *iure divino* was not, however, to prove papal primacy *iure divino*, for neither Matt. 16:18 nor John 21:15ff. say anything of successors. The Romanists, therefore, had to present a convincing case for connecting the two. A time-honored way of doing this was by reference to the tradition that Peter had spent twenty-five years as bishop of Rome and had been martyred there, and that therefore his primacy was inherited by his successors in the Roman See. In *Explanation of the Thirteenth Proposition*, Luther doubted that Peter could have been in Rome for such a length of time, considering the evidence of the New Testament; for him, this effectively settled the question of succession. Two years later, Luther came across a pamphlet written by the minor Bohemian nobleman Ulrichus Velenus that denied that Peter had ever been in Rome at all. Luther does not himself seem to have been convinced by Velenus, because he continued to question only the length and not the fact of Peter's stay, but he now began to suggest that Peter's total absence from Rome could in principle be proved

---

33. Marcello, *De authoritate*, 20.
34. Ibid., 18ᵛ.
35. Cajetan, *De divina institutione*, 56.
36. Murner, *Von dem babstentum*, Fiiᵛ. Cf. Catharinus, *Apologia*, 159: "If he does not love, then he does not tend or at least does not tend well. But he does not thereby lose his authority to tend or cease to be a pastor."

from Scripture, and that therefore the pope's claim to spiritual descent from Peter could be historically disproved.[37]

This aspect of Luther's case against the papacy did not generally attract the Romanists' attention. Cochlaeus, it is true, was alarmed by Luther's suggestion (in *Auff das . . . buch Bocks Emszers zu Leypczick Antwort*) that Peter had not been in Rome for twenty-five years, or even that he had not been there at all: such an argument, he warned Aleander and the pope, destroyed "the very foundation-stone of our cause."[38] He penned a detailed refutation of Luther's case, which was translated and published by Dietenberger in 1524 as *Whether St. Peter Was Ever in Rome*, and under his own name brought out a reply to Velenus the following year.[39] Fisher had already published a slightly more pedantic reply to Velenus in 1521. Such interest was nevertheless exceptional and it is fair to say that the historicity of Peter's sojourn in Rome did not figure largely in the controversialists' defense of the papacy. This lack of interest must be partly due to the fact that it did not figure largely in Luther's own case, in which it was simply one reason among many for not elevating Roman primacy to the status of a dogma. But the chief reason must be that the controversialists saw that establishing the case for a universal primate and vicar of Christ was far more important than discussing where his see should be

37. A. J. Lamping, in his otherwise excellent study, *Ulrichus Velenus and His Treatise against the Papacy*, mistakenly dates Luther's interest in calculating the length of Peter's sojourn in Rome from his acquaintance with Velenus's *Petrum Romam non venisse*. While it is true that "no questions had even been raised about the length of Peter's stay in Rome in the disputation at Leipzig in 1519" (p. 139), Luther had raised precisely that question in the treatise *Explanation of the Thirteenth Proposition*, published just before the debate. Because he dates Luther's denial of the twenty-five years to a time after he had read Velenus in 1521, Lamping is obliged to dismiss Murner's reference to the question in *Von dem babstentum* (1520) with the rather odd statement: "If any polemics were intended at all in this case, then they must have been directed against the Waldensians"! He also seems unaware of the even earlier reference to Luther's denial made by Prierias at the end of 1519, in *Errata* 1:3, i.

Lamping also makes too hard and fast a distinction between Luther's questioning the *length* and his not questioning the *fact* of Peter's residence (p. 148): while strictly speaking Luther denied only the former, he did raise doubts about the latter, and in his opinion the papacy was undermined as much by the one as by the other. See, e.g., Luther's *Answer to the Hyperchristian Book of the Goat Emser* (*LW* 39:204–5): "They have established the papacy on Peter's being in Rome, and although this question is not an article of faith, I come to the conclusion that it is unnecessary to consider the pope either the pope or the heir to St. Peter's see until they verify with Scripture that Peter was in Rome." Note that Luther is here referring only to the fact and not to the length of Peter's stay.

38. Cochlaeus to Leo X, 19 June 1521 (*ZKG* 18 [1898], 116).

39. Cochlaeus, *De Petro et Roma adversus Velenum Lutheranum libri quatuor*.

located. Prierias, Catharinus, Latomus, and Cajetan were at pains to point out that Peter would have been the church's primate even had he not died in Rome.

> Had Peter remained until his death in the see of Antioch (which he had formerly occupied), Peter's successor would have been the Antiochene rather than the Roman pontiff. And had Peter quitted Rome not only as a place but as a see, and had located his see elsewhere, the Roman pontiff would not have succeeded Peter— any more than the Antiochene pontiff would have succeeded Peter who in leaving Antioch had changed not only places but sees. It is therefore clear that it is not by the institution of the gospel that the pontiff of Rome should succeed Peter.[40]

If the controversialists did not specifically argue for the inheritance of Peter's primacy through the succession of the Roman see, how did they understand the continuance of papal primacy? Cajetan maintained that, as the church received the keys *in persona capitis* (Peter), so the church retained them *in persona capitis* (the pope).[41] The similar view was championed by Eck that the keys were given to Peter as the one "who wears the face of the Church [*persona ecclesiae*], by which much that is said of him pertains also to his successors."[42] Such an argument, however, finds the continuity between Peter and his heirs in the church, and seems to support the very claim the controversialists had so vehemently opposed, namely, that Christ had made his promise of the keys to the whole church and not to Peter alone. Luther had set his trap quite deliberately. The Romanists' solution was to admit that the church possessed the keys after a manner of speaking, but that its possession was strictly incidental to Peter's: "It was not the Church that originally received the keys but Peter," says Eck; Marcello that "the other apostles received the keys secondarily not primarily"; Powell that Peter's reception was "in a singular and peculiar mode."[43] Catharinus summed up the argument thus:

---

40. Cajetan, *De divina institutione*, 79. Cf. Prierias, *Errata* 1:3, ii; Catharinus, *Apologia*, 127–28, 186; Latomus, *De primatu romani*, 63: "The centre, as it were, of the Catholic Church was the place where Peter was when he was alive in the flesh, and he had his authority wherever he was, whether in Jerusalem or Judaea or Samaria, or afterwards Antioch and finally Rome. It was not necessarily bound to a particular earthly city."
41. Cajetan, *De divina institutione*, 46.
42. Eck, *De primatu Petri* 1:9.
43. Eck, *De primatu Petri* 1:8; Marcello, *De authoritate*, 12; Powell, *Propugnaculum*, 19ᵛ–20. Cf. Cajetan, *De divina institutione*, 16–25; and Catharinus, *Apologia*, 99.

> Through Peter therefore the rest of the Church confesses its own
> faith. Through Peter it receives the keys. Peter is here accepted by
> the Lord as a mediator by virtue of his reply, and he will be
> equally accepted as a mediator by the rest of the Church, that
> through him it might receive the keys. This is the sacrament and
> mystery of this passage, which if anyone will not accept, let him
> rightly be anathema.[44]

This cannot, however, be regarded as a successful resolution of the
problem, because if the church had the keys only insofar as Peter had
them, once Peter died that ownership would revert from the church
back to God. Perhaps it was with this illogicality in mind that Prierias
and Cajetan offered supplementary proof: the very magnitude of the
office granted to Peter was sufficient of itself to merit perpetuation
through others after his death.[45]

One way of understanding such a perpetual office was by
analogy with the Aaronite high priesthood of the former dispensation.
Alveld, Eck, and Powell justified the analogy by the similarities in the
careers of Aaron and Peter: men who were called by God and prepared for office, who fell from grace for a season that they might rule
their own subjects more compassionately, who performed miracles,
and who even took life in order to demonstrate their authority.[46]
Alternatively, the pontificate could be seen as a monarchy. Prierias,
Marcello, Eck, and Murner argued that monarchy was the most
appropriate means by which the Supreme Deity might conduct affairs
on earth, particularly in spiritual matters, and a continuous succession
of papal monarchs was therefore required.

> Natural reason seems to support an ecclesiastical monarchy. In
> Book III of *Politics* and Book VII of *Metaphysics*, Aristotle com-
> mends the singularity of the principate, and all pagan philoso-
> phers agree with him. Nor is it surprising that the whole world
> should have come to share the same opinion; for God himself, the
> creator and governor of all things, is such a prince who rules the
> universe. Why then should the Christian commonwealth [*Christi
> respublica*] not also depend on one head, which increases harmony,
> order, and morality?[47]

44. Catharinus, *Apologia*, 124.
45. Prierias, *Errata* 1:4, iii, p. xviii^v; Cajetan, *De divina institutione*, 73.
46. Alveld, *Super apostolicae sede*, Ci^{v}f.; Eck, *De primatu Petri* 2:27; Powell, *Propugnaculum*, 9–13.
47. Marcello, *De authoritate*, 7^v. Cf. Prierias, *Errata* 1:2, iii, pp. iv–v; Eck, *De primatu
Petri* 2:27; Murner, *Von dem babstentum*, Aii^v; Joannes Modestus, *Oratio*, Aiii^v; Powell,
Propugnaculum, 8ff.

It was not enough, however, for the controversialists to demonstrate that Peter was chief of the apostles, or that he alone had been given the power of the keys, or that he could be succeeded, or even that his primacy and power could be transmitted to his successors. Luther's explanation of the thirteenth proposition "on the power of the pope" had also called into question the nature and extent of this power, and its defenders were obliged to answer his critique in these areas too. The pope's plenitude of power, of course, was believed to reside primarily in the power of the keys. But as Luther had shown, Christ had given this power to the other apostles as well. So the controversialists' first statement concerning the power of the keys was that it comprised both an extraordinary power given to the apostles, which, like the apostolate itself, died with them, and an ordinary power given to Peter, which would continue as long as the dispensation under which it was issued. When given to Peter, this command became an ordinary power; however, when given to the other apostles, it was simply a commission or instruction. It was given to Peter both in his own right and for his successors, but to the others only in respect of their own persons.[48] The ordinary power was generally further divided into the *potestas iurisdictionis* (the creation and enforcement of laws), the *potestas ordinis* (the ordination of clergy), and the *potestas magisterialis* (the definition of faith and morals).[49]

While the controversialists were thus agreed on the *areas* of papal power, it is possible to detect differences of emphasis with respect to the *extent* of that power. A Dominican such as Prierias could attempt to justify papal absolutism. He asserted that the pope's jurisdictional power was absolute not only in the Roman Church but even in churches outside Rome and over non-Christians;[50] that his ordinative power was absolute, so that even a bishop's ordinating power was derived from him and not, for instance, from the apostles;[51] and that,

48. Caspar Schatzgeyer, *Warhafftige Erklerung,* Iiii^v. Cf. Eck, *De primatu Petri* 3:43; Cajetan, *De divina institutione,* 73.
49. These were the distinctions generally adopted by the controversialists, although Cajetan was characteristically precise in further subdividing jurisdictional power into *potestas iudicaria, potestas gubernativa, potestas clavium in purgatorio,* and *potestas imperativa* (Cajetan, *De divina institutione,* 51–52).
50. Prierias, *Errata* 1:5 (pp. xxiv^v–xxvii^v) and 1:7 (pp. xxx^v–xxxvii). Prierias also asserted the pope's absolute power over temporal affairs, in accordance with the bull *Unam sanctam* ("prout iura decernunt"). See Prierias, *Dialogus* (Löscher 2:38).
51. Prierias, *Errata* 1:5 (pp. xxiv^v–xxvii^v); Marcello, *De authoritate,* 71–73^v; Eck, *De primatu Petri* 3:43.

with respect to his teaching office, the pope was the "sole arbiter and infallible judge of the truth in matters regarding faith and morals."[52] Another Dominican, Cajetan, in company with Eck, Latomus, and Marcello, supported Prierias's papalism. The absolute jurisdictional and ordinative authority of the papacy was, they agreed, undiminished by an individual pope's lack of integrity: "One little woman can be greater and more perfect than the pope; but with respect to jurisdictional power, a sinful pope is greater than many righteous people."[53]

Similarly, a pope's personal infidelity in no way affected the magisterial infallibility in matters of faith and morals he possessed by virtue of his office.[54] A problem for the papalists was the Council of Constance, which had decreed the superiority of a council to a pope. Latomus's solution was, on the one hand, to declare the decree invalid (on the grounds that it had been passed while only one of the three rival papal parties was present, so that the council had been improperly constituted) and, on the other hand, to concede it a limited validity that lasted only until the election of Martin V.[55]

Romanist apologists representative of the Franciscan order were rather more guarded in their descriptions of the extent of papal power. Alveld was prepared to attribute infallibility to the church as a whole, but not to the pope, and pointedly left the question of papal superiority over a council to a future "sacred council," even though he could not have been unaware of Lateran V's decision on the matter. Was he perhaps questioning the independence of the Lateran council?[56] Illyricus also departed from the papalist line in according bishops an ordinating power in their own right and in refusing to accept that the official pronouncements of a heretical pope could be preserved from error.[57] Murner was no less determined that the question of papal superiority to a council should remain open: "We should take the middle course, upholding the power of the pope while not setting aside the rights of ordinary Christians."[58] Even these criticisms of papal

---

52. Prierias, *Epitoma* (WA 6:330.16–18).
53. Latomus, *De primatu romani*, 82ᵛ. Cf. Cajetan, *De divina institutione*, 54–56; Marcello, *De authoritate*, 74ᵛ–81.
54. Cajetan, *De divina institutione*, 83–85; Eck, *De primatu Petri* 1:18.
55. Latomus, *De primatu romani*, 81.
56. Alveld, *Super apostolicae sede*, Giiiᵛ.
57. Illyricus, *Clipeus status papalis* (Lauchert, 245, 247).
58. Thomas Murner, *An den Grossmechtigsten und Durchlüchtigsten adel Tütscher nation*, Eivᵛ.

superiority seem mild in comparison with the outright denial made by the former Franciscan provincial Caspar Schatzgeyer. In his otherwise comprehensive review of the Luther controversy in the *Scrutinium* of 1522, he had avoided the question of the papacy altogether. When he finally came to discuss it in 1525, two years before his death, he adopted Luther's interpretation that the "rock" of Matt. 16:18 was not Peter himself but his confession of faith.[59] (This contrasts strongly with the stock papalist objection that even lay men and women would in that case have the power of the keys.)[60] And he agreed with Luther that papal primacy implied service, not dominion.[61] He even went so far as to imply the superiority of a council to a pope.

> And what of the power or authority of a council? From whom does it derive and how great is it? I answer: the authority of a council is undoubtedly from God, not only because all authority is from God, but also because a council is constituted in its own right for the supernatural purpose of saving souls. It has therefore a supernatural authority. It contains the fulness of the authority of Christ, as much and more than he bequeathed to his bride the Church on earth. It also includes the papal apostolic power and authority, for even the pope, the successor of Peter, is a member of this said Church. As he is the under-head of this Church, therefore, [the Church] may punish and reform all members without exception. For Christ left all his authority to the ministers of his Church. It thus follows that all power is given primarily to the Church.[62]

The differences between the representatives of the orders of St. Dominic and St. Francis are to be explained, of course, by the Franciscans' historic distrust of the papacy and the Dominicans' historic devotion to it. It is, however, possible to overemphasize their disagreement in the context of the debate with Luther. In his *Explanation of the Thirteenth Proposition* he had denied the divine institution of the papacy, and on this point the friars were agreed. Most importantly, we

---

59. Schatzgeyer, *Warhafftige Erklerung*, Hi.
60. "If anyone who has a correct faith has the Church's keys, then any layman or woman can have them" (Latomus, *De primatu romani*, 62); "You say, 'Whosoever receives a revelation thereby receives the keys from Christ.' If what you say is right, Mary Magdalene and many other holy women have been given the keys indiscriminately" (Catharinus, *Apologia*, 134).
61. Schatzgeyer, *Warhafftige Erklerung*, Gi.
62. Ibid., Mi.

can say that at no point did any Franciscan controversialist question the pope's jurisdictional primacy.

Thus the Romanists answered Luther's queries on the origin, nature, and extent of papal power. But the consideration that prompted his original comment on Roman primacy—setting in motion the process of events leading to *Explanation of the Thirteenth Proposition* and Leipzig—and that he continued to find the most compelling was the status of the African, Greek, Russian, and Asian churches: if Rome is sovereign by God's decree, then submission to it is necessary for salvation, and thousands of otherwise devout Christians (to say nothing of saints and martyrs of the early church who died before the creation of the Roman see) must of necessity languish in hell.[63] The Romanists were not moved by such considerations. Latomus explained how the early Christians, such as St. Stephen, were innocent of heresy and schism, but how the non-Roman churches enjoyed no such exemption.

> He does not immediately become a heretic who, like a thief or adulterer, transgresses God's commandments, but only if he persistently thinks contrary to the faith or the Scriptures. In this way a man who does not obey the Roman Pontiff, when or where such obedience is not enjoined, does not sin. And he who, after due warning, refuses his obedience, sins, but is not a heretic except he believe that the Pontiff is not to be obeyed as the successor of Peter and vicar of Christ. Therefore, whosoever in these terms refuses obedience falls into schism and heresy: but perish the thought that the entire early church and all its martyrs were in this way outside obedience to the Roman Pontiff for up to four hundred years.[64]

Although Prierias believed that the pope's jurisdiction extended to other churches, he accounted their non-recognition of this fact as heresy.[65] Alveld maintained that only the church that has Peter for its head is Christ's true sheepfold.[66] The Greek, Russian, and Bohemian churches should be classed with Islam, he asserted, so far are they

---

63. "If the Roman Pontiff is vicar-general of the whole Church by divine precept, it inevitably follows that they are sinners, no, they are heretics, who were not under him. But in that case the entire primitive Church, at least for the first four hundred years, together with all its martyrs and saints, were heretics," (Luther, *Explanation of the Thirteenth Proposition* [WA 2:183.16-19]).

64. Latomus, *De primatu romani*, 74.

65. Prierias, *Errata* 1:5 (pp. xxiv^v–xxvii^v).

66. Alveld, *Super apostolica sede* (Lemmens 33).

from being authentically Christian.[67] Citing twenty-six fathers and councils, Eck argued that the African, Greek, and Asian churches all at one time recognized Roman primacy and that they became heretical at the moment they seceded.[68]

Luther's original concern with extreme assertions of papal power had been with the abuses they could be employed to defend. Serious as such abuses were, they were unlikely to be spiritually lethal. But the same assertions also declared many Christians beyond the pale of salvation. As the controversy wore on, this aspect of the doctrine increasingly disturbed Luther. The Romanists were unanimous in their answer to Luther: members of those churches that refused to recognize the primacy of the Roman see were in error, and while they persisted in this error they would indeed be damned.

For Catharinus, there was historical evidence to show that those who refused Rome obedience were cut off from the source of Christian life.

> Shall we then consult experience? Where are almost all the Asian churches? Gone. Why? (Let Germany hear this, let the world understand why these churches are no more.) Because they separated themselves from their head, and strayed from their shepherd, and were encouraged to seek equality with their mother the Roman Church. . . . Where are the churches of the Greeks and Armenians? They have perished. Why? For the same reason. Bohemia, Germany, Saxony! Who has so bewitched you that you do not see this?[69]

Papal Authority over All Councils

The Romanists' responses to Luther's first treatise on the papacy were considerably more uniform than were their contributions to the indulgence controversy. It is true that the Franciscan controversialists were wary of accepting any notion of the pope's magisterial infallibility and therefore refused to consider the conciliarist question settled. But what reservations they quietly expressed (and they had no qualms about attributing to the pope supreme jurisdictional power) were lost in the chorus of papalist authors led by, but not restricted to, the Domini-

---

67. Alveld, *Super apostolica sede* (Lemmens 34).
68. Eck, *De primatu Petri* 3:8–20.
69. Catharinus, *Apologia*, 222–23.

cans. Iserloh's remark that Eck's *Primacy of Peter* identified the *magisterium* as decisive for the controversy holds true for almost all the defenders of the divine right.[70]

But why was there such unanimity? The answer, I think, lies in the existence of clear precedents. The question of the pope's relationship to the rest of the church had been raised in a dramatic manner in the first half of the previous century. The Western Schism, which had witnessed the simultaneous reign of no fewer than three rival popes, had been brought to an end by the Council of Constance in 1417. The pope it elected, Martin V, was himself a conciliarist. However, his successor, Eugenius IV, was not, and on his accession he immediately attempted to suspend the council at Basel inherited from his predecessor. Basel successfully retaliated in 1433 by reaffirming Constance's decree *Sacrosancta*, which had declared the superiority of an ecumenical council to a pope.[71] It was against this turbulent background that a number of defenses of papalism were written. Notable among them was Juan de Torquemada's *Summa de ecclesia* (1453), which achieved considerable currency in its time and seventy years later provided the intellectual basis of many of the replies to Luther.[72] The controversialists also had from Lateran V a second, more recent and more authoritative argument. Just two-and-a-half years before the publication of Luther's *Explanation of the Thirteenth Proposition*, the council's decree *Pastor aeternus* had determined that "only the pope reigning at the time, who has authority over all councils, has the complete right and power to appoint, transfer, and dissolve councils."[73]

It appears that the extent of agreement among the Catholic polemicists was largely dependent on the existence of a clear precedent. Until the publication of *Cum postquam*, Catholic contributions to the indulgences debate had differed from one another; afterwards, they were noticeably more consistent. Contributions to the divine right debate, on the other hand, showed many similarities with one another from the outset. This confirms, by extension, Lortz's theory of an *Unklarheit* in doctrine that adversely affected the controversialists' task:

---

70. Iserloh, *Johannes Eck 1486–1543*, 48.

71. Council of Constance, *sessio* XII (29 May 1415), *COD* 416.14–417.6.

72. See Jedin, *History of the Council of Trent* 1:26–8. Examples are Catharinus's *Apologia* and Thomas Rhadinus's *Oratio*.

73. Council of Lateran V *sessio* XI (19 December 1516), *COD* 640.1–645.27, esp. 642.19–22.

where there was greater clarity, their task was correspondingly easier. In fact, we can say that they took this dependence on precedent to an extreme. Despite some Franciscan reserve on the matter, the controversialists could legitimately appeal to the magisterial and jurisdictional superiority of the pope to a council, on the basis of the Lateran decree *Pastor aeternus*. They could even attempt to defend the pope's magisterial and jurisdictional infallibility on the authority of Torquemada and other anti-conciliarist writers of the fifteenth century.

Strictly speaking, however, none of these arguments answered Luther's criticism. The *ius divinum* of the papacy as such had never been the subject of an official pronouncement—and indeed would not be until Vatican I's decree *Pastor aeternus*.[74] The controversialists therefore chose to base their defense on areas that had been officially defined or unofficially (but nonetheless thoroughly) discussed, such as the pope's right to summon councils, even though this tactic put them at a remove from the original point at issue. The attractiveness of authoritative statements for the controversialists confirms the tendency we saw at work in the indulgence controversy. Luther deliberately refrained from making any statements in the Ninety-five Theses that could be considered heretical. His opponents therefore set about relating his thoughts on the dogmatically obscure subject of indulgences to the less assailable and more serious matter of papal power. In response, Luther sought to conduct an attack on papal power from the gray area of the *ius divinum* question. In turn, the controversialists tried to relate his position to the recently decreed superiority of popes to councils.

When Luther would next address the question of councils, it would be in the form of a demonstrably illegal appeal to the Christian nobility of Germany to convoke one. The ground upon which Luther could maneuver was rapidly diminishing. The dogmatism of his enemies was forcing him into open revolt.

74. *DS*, 3058.

PART TWO

AUTHORITY IN DOCTRINE
AND SOCIETY,
1519–1520

3

THE AFTERMATH OF THE
LEIPZIG DISPUTATION

An irony of the early Catholic campaign against Luther was that his indulgence theses of October 1517 were instantly condemned from a number of quarters, while his much more radical attack on scholastic theology of the previous month went unnoticed. Nevertheless, it was inevitable that his rejection of the theological sources upon which his opponents based so much of their case would eventually attract their full attention. The opportunity presented itself in the wake of the Leipzig disputation of 1519. Prospective pamphleteers were forbidden, by an injunction against unauthorized accounts, to discuss in detail the theological questions raised in the course of the debate. Controversialists were consequently obliged to comment in general terms on the disputants themselves, their styles of argument, and the different methods they chose to adopt. Therefore, it was in the months following Leipzig that the implications of Luther's rejection of established doctrinal authorities, and of his gradual development of an alternative based on Scripture alone, were first discussed at length.

First Reactions to Leipzig

The Romanists' response to Leipzig formed a considerably less coherent body of literature than their contributions to the other controversies of the period, partly because the subject matter itself was of a different order, and partly because it deteriorated into a literary feud between self-appointed champions of the Universities of Leipzig and Wittenberg. The Leipzig disputation prompted five separate pamphlet battles comprising some twenty-seven publications.[1] The first involved Joannes Rubeus and Johannes Cellarius of Leipzig and Johannes Montanus of Wittenberg, who debated amid a good deal of personal

---

1. For the proceedings of the disputation itself, see esp. J. K. Seidermann, *Die Leipziger Disputation im Jahre 1519* (Dresden and Leipzig, 1843); R. Albert, "Aus welchem Grunde disputirte Johann Eck gegen Luther in Leipzig 1519?"; O. Seitz, *Der authentische Text der Leipziger Disputation*; and K.-V. Selge, "Die Leipziger Disputation zwischen Luther und Eck."

abuse whether Leipzigers had shown favor to Eck and whether the University of Leipzig was committed to embracing the study of "fine letters."[2] A far shorter and better-humored controversy involved Eck and Philipp Melanchthon, who had been present at the debate with the Wittenberg retinue and who had sent a report of it to Johannes Oecolampadius at Basel. The chief bone of contention was whether Melanchthon's report had been in breach of the ban on prejudgments of the outcome of the disputation.[3] Luther himself was engaged in three of the post-Leipzig exchanges, with Alveld on the specific question of papal primacy, with Duke Georg's secretary Hieronymus Emser,[4] and with Eck himself, continuing in print the debate they had been obliged to adjourn at the Pleissenburg.[5]

These exchanges had much in common with the literary duels between humanists and scholastics that proliferated in Germany at the end of the fifteenth century and the beginning of the sixteenth—not least their prolixity. It would be tedious and repetitive to describe these exchanges in detail, but a fair impression of the part played by

2. The exchange consisted of the following pamphlets: Johannes Rubeus, *Solutiones ac Responsa Wit. Doctorum in publica Disputatione Lipsica contra fulmina Eckiana parum profatura, tumorque adventus & humilitas eorum recessus, per Jo. Ru. Longi. comparata*; Johannes Montanus, *Encomium Rubii Longipolli apud Lipsim, in errores quos pueriliter comisit adversus Wittenbergenses Nemo dictavit*; Johannes Cellarius, *Ad Volphangum Fabricium Capitonem, Theologiae Doctorem et Concionatorem Basiliensem, Joannis Cellarii Gnostopolitani, Lipsiae Hebraicae linguae Professoris, de vera et constanti serie Theologica Disputationis Lipsiacae, Epistola*; Johannes Rubeus, *Neu Buchlein von der löblichen Disputation, öffentlich gehalten vor Fürsten und Herren, für Hochgelahrten und für Ungelahrten, in der werthen hochgepreiseten Stadt Leipzig* (1519, untraceable; see Löscher 3:272); Johannes Cellarius, *Nullus Lipsiensis respondet Nemini Wittenbergensi*; Johannes Montanus, *Excusatio Neminis adversus Nullum* (1519); Johannes Cellarius, *Responsio Nullius ad excusationem Neminis* (1519); idem, *Elogium famosissimi viri Neminis* (untraceable; see Löscher 3:804); idem, *Iudicium de Martino Luthero*. Cellarius also took issue with Peter Suavenius's privately circulated account of the disputation in his untraceable *Responsio ironica ad Suavenii epistolam*, which was followed by Suavenius's *Epistola cum apologia I. Cellario missa*, and ultimately by Cellarius's *Seria responsio ad apologiam Suavenii*.

3. See Melanchthon to Oecomlampadius, 21 July 1519; Johannes Eck, *Excusatio Eckii ad ea, quae falso sibi Phil. Melanchton Grammaticus Wittenb. super Theologica Disputatione Lipsica adscripsit*; Philipp Melanchthon, *Defensio Philippi Melanchthonis, contra Johannem Eckium, Theologiae Professorem*.

4. Hieronymus Emser, *De disputatione Lipsicensi, quantum ad Boemos obiter deflexa est*; idem, *A venatione Luteriana Aegocerotis Assertio*; Luther, *Ad Aegocerotem Emserianum M. Lutheri Additio*.

5. Johannes Eck, *Expurgatio Joan. Eckii Theologi. Ingoldstadien. adversus criminationes F. Martini Luther Vuittenbergen. ordinis heremitarum*; idem, *Joannis Eckii pro Hieronymo Emser contra malesanem Luteri venationem responsio*; Luther, *Ad Iohannem Eccium Martini Lutheri epistola super Expurgatione Ecciana*; Andreas Bodenstein von Carlstadt, *Epistola adversus ineptam et ridiculam inventionem J. Eckii* (1519); Johannes Eck, *Contra M. Ludderi obtusum propugnatorem Andream Carlstadium* (December 1519).

Catholic loyalists can be gained from the initial contributions of a representative sample of writers. Because this stage of the Reformation controversy is often characterized as a period in which humanists were, by and large, favorable to Luther and scholastics were, by and large, unfavorable, it would seem useful to select writers representative of both movements.[6]

Rubeus's report of the Leipzig disputation is in many ways the least competent, but it does illustrate how a scholastic reacted to the event. Rubeus, a Frenchman studying at Leipzig, dedicated his report to Conrad von Thüngen, prince-bishop of Würzburg, and had it published on 13 August 1519. The full title, *The Inadequate Responses and Answers to Eck's Thunderbolts Made by the Wittenberg Doctors at Leipzig, and Their Boastful Arrival Contrasted with Their Ignominious Departure,* gives a fair indication of its content, which takes the form of a series of tendentious comparisons between Eck, on the one hand, and Luther and Carlstadt, on the other. The latter, we are told, arrogantly rejected scholastic evidence and attempted to interpret Scripture according to their own geniuses, whereas Eck defended the historic faith of the church.[7] While the doctors from Wittenberg did not understand scholastic theologians as well as they did Scripture and ecclesiastical authorities, Eck was learned enough to be able to quote from both sources in support of his arguments.[8] In fact, Luther and Carlstadt scorned all appeal to the schoolmen and had Eck not accepted this restriction for the sake of argument, they would have claimed the victory.[9] All their arguments were intended to incite the masses. Their opponent, although surrounded by a hostile audience, kept his temper and still managed to construct invincible arguments with his fine memory and ability; and he, unlike Luther and Carlstadt, was able openly to celebrate communion.[10] This series of comparisons is interspersed with actual accounts of the individual exchanges, in which Rubeus's partiality is further aired. Rhetorically he asks, "Who does

---

6. This is the generally accepted view represented in popular accounts of the history of the period. See, e.g., R. H. Bainton, *Here I Stand: A Life of Martin Luther* (Nashville: Abingdon Press, 1950), 93; A. G. Dickens, *Martin Luther and the Reformation* (London: Hodder & Stoughton, 1967), 44; J. M. Kittelson, *Luther the Reformer* (Minneapolis: Augsburg Pub. House, 1986), 136.
7. Rubeus, *Solutiones* (Löscher 3:252–53).
8. Ibid., 254–61.
9. Ibid., 261–63.
10. Ibid., 265–66, 270.

not believe that the pope is head of the Church by divine right? Who believes that a good work is God's alone, with no human contribution?" and so on. Likewise, he recorded the replies of the Wittenberg theologians so tersely as to make them sound worthless.[11]

Rubeus's pamphlet was marred by grammatical slips, which did not escape the notice of such contemporaries as Montanus, Cellarius, and even Emser, and which earned him the role of Eck's assistant in the anonymous satire *Eck Polished Off*.[12] He also had the gift of unintentional humor. In describing the Wittenbergers' sullen departure from the disputation, Rubeus compared them with the pharisees of John 8:9 who silently slipped away from the adulteress (that is, Eck!) whom they came to stone. And in defending the Ingolstadter from unkind remarks about his loud voice, Rubeus mounted a spirited and ingenious defense of the importance of bovinity in Christian history, neglecting neither the traditional iconography of Saint Luke nor the legendary girth of Aquinas.

It should be said in Rubeus's defense that, forbidden by the rules of debate from assessing the arguments until an official verdict had been reached (a stipulation of which he was aware),[13] he was obliged to express his own opinions only indirectly. In other words, he was allowed to do no more than ask rhetorical questions and reduce unacceptable conclusions to absurdity. This may also explain why Rubeus was overridingly concerned with questions of method. The whole problem stemmed, in Rubeus's opinion, from the Wittenbergers' rejection of *sancta philosophia*: "Woe to him who rejects philosophy, for it provides the weapons with which to confute the unlearned. All human sciences are ancillary to divine theology and support it. How ineffective will be the arguments of the man who lacks philosophy!"[14]

For Rubeus, scholastic authorities were not merely legitimate, they were the only means of presenting a reasoned account of the Christian faith. The author sniffily remarked that he was not surprised to hear that the staff at Wittenberg, no less than the students, frequently came to blows. With Rubeus's *Inadequate Responses*, therefore, we have

11. Ibid., 268.
12. See Montanus, *Encomium* (Löscher 3:786, 790), Cellarius, *Nullus respondet* (Löscher 3:800–801); Emser, *De disputatione Lipsicensi* (CC 4:35). See also *Eccius Dedolatus: A Reformation Satire*, ed. T. W. Best (Lexington: University of Kentucky Press, 1971).
13. Rubeus, *Solutiones* (Löscher 3:254).
14. Ibid., 262.

some idea of how scholastics viewed the Leipzig debate. Having arrogantly abandoned holy teachers and holy philosophy and having decided to interpret Scripture according to their own minority methods, Luther and Carlstadt had not only thrown away any chance they might have had of making their views appear reasonable but had also cut themselves off from the historic faith of the church.

Emser's report illustrates the humanist reaction to the disputation. Emser studied law and theology at Tübingen and Basel before transferring in 1504 to Erfurt, where Luther attended his lectures. He later moved to Leipzig to become a university lecturer and secretary and chaplain to Duke Georg. His account of the Leipzig disputation was published in the form of a letter to Jan Zak, the administrator of the Catholic Church in Prague. This was an isolated community, greatly outnumbered by the neighboring Hussite Bohemians. In Emser's opinion, the belief that Luther had at Leipzig defended the condemned articles of Huss would have raised the Hussites' morale and dispirited the Catholic Bohemians. He therefore published *The Leipzig Disputation: Did It Support the Bohemians?* in which he showed that Luther, far from lending his weight to the heterodox cause, actually condemned its secession from the Apostolic See on the grounds that schism can never be excused.[15] Emser conceded that Luther did remark that friendly persuasion had never been tried on the Hussites and, as Eck objected in the debate, such a charge was simply not true.[16] In any case, continued Emser, a patient can sometimes only be saved by drastic surgery.[17] Therefore, it seems that this pamphlet was directed not against Luther, who was presented in a favorable light, so much as against allegations about his religious proclivities. Emser passed off Eck's accusation of Bohemianism as a joke and defended Luther's description of the condemned articles of Huss as "most Christian and evangelical" (or "most Catholic," as Emser has it) on the grounds that it is the peculiar mischief of heretics to mix truth with falsehood. He also pointed to the fact that even when Luther denied the divine institution of the papacy, he was in no way obstinate. Emser took issue with Luther on only one point: if the papacy is not ordained by God, then Christianity is no better than any other hierarchically ordered religion.

15. Emser, *De disputatione Lipsicensi* (CC 4:32, 33).
16. Ibid., 33–34.
17. Ibid., 34.

Emser's account of events at Leipzig was presented in typically humanist language and style. The letter's recipient finds himself likened to Christ, Hercules, St. Paul, and Noah before he can turn the first page. The letter ends with a Sapphic ode on the Leipzig disputation, which gives the author the opportunity to express his dislike of the very idea of a public debate "more likely to produce heat than light."[18] If Christ is the author of peace, Emser asked, carefully fostering that sense of studied detachment characteristic of many sixteenth-century humanists, why does one theological school fight another?[19] However, Leipzig was disdained by the canonist not merely because it was yet another manifestation of scholastic *Wegestreit*, but because it also allowed the common people to pass their judgment on sacred matters before a final decision was made by the appointed judges.[20] This was why *The Leipzig Disputation* was not intended by Emser as an account as such: too many had already been written, he protested, to the great confusion of the Christian faith.[21]

Cellarius's letter to Wolfgang Capito is perhaps the most ambivalent of the Catholic pamphlets of this period. It demonstrates many humanistic traits, and yet Cellarius's very next work was a staunch defense of Aristotelianism.[22] Similarly, the letter to Capito was a favorable account of Eck's conduct at the disputation, and yet Cellarius was soon to transfer from the University of Leipzig, where he was professor of Hebrew, to that of Wittenberg and to embrace Luther's cause. The author's humanistic tendencies are evident in a number of places throughout the letter: he praises Capito (also at that time an opponent of Luther) for his achievements in the three sacred languages and for "an uncommon love of virtue";[23] like Emser, he expresses his contempt for the disputation and the preliminary exchanges by the use of battle imagery;[24] he compares Eck's rhetorical ability with that of Demosthenes;[25] he mentions with approval the opening and closing orations by Simon Pistorius and Johannes Langius Lembergius, both

---

18. Ibid., 33: "Contentionis quam edificationis plus prae se tulerit."
19. Ibid., 40. Battle imagery is used to describe the disputation five times in the five stanzas of the ode.
20. Ibid., 41.
21. Ibid., 35.
22. Cellarius, *Nullus respondet*.
23. Cellarius, *Ad Capitonem* (Löscher 3:225).
24. Ibid., 225.
25. Ibid., 226.

famed for their love of eloquence;[26] and finally he sends through Capito his greetings to two other famous Basel humanists, Oecolampadius and Beatus Rhenanus.[27]

When he came to relate the arguments in detail, Cellarius clearly strove for impartiality—we can see this particularly in that he ended almost every report of an exchange with the words, "But a decision on this must be left to the judges," or a similar formula. He had, however, selected his material in such a way as to show a slight bias in Eck's favor. For example, he records Luther's suggestion that the mendicant orders be abolished; the only other contemporary to mention this was Eck, when writing privately to support his own case and put Luther in a bad light.[28] Again, in connection with Carlstadt's thesis that in every good work the just man sins, Cellarius recorded Eck's bitter question, "Did then St. Laurence sin when he was on the grill, or St. Peter on the cross?" Alone of all the reporters, Cellarius notes this remark.[29] Nevertheless, in other respects Cellarius achieved his aim of sending Capito a reliable description of the events, in contrast with those writers who were interested only "in lust for victory or in spreading gossip." What bias there is toward Eck is certainly not pronounced.

Scholastics and Humanists

The point is frequently made that around the time of Leipzig Luther was supported by humanists and reviled by scholastics. Superficially, this view has much to commend it. It certainly explains the reactions of Rubeus and Eck.[30] It also accounts for the impassioned defenses of "holy philosophy" that appeared in contemporary anti-Lutheran literature not related specifically to the proceedings at Leipzig. Archbishop

---

26. Ibid., 226, 230.
27. Ibid., 231.
28. Ibid., 228. See also Eck to Hochstraten, 24 July 1519.
29. Cellarius, *Ad Capitonem*, 230.
30. Like Luther and Carlstadt, Eck wrote no public report of the debate immediately, in deference to the agreement authorizing the official version alone, and that only after Paris had reached a decision. He did, however, write privately to Jakob Hochstraten, the great adversary of the Hebraist Reuchlin (24 July 1519, in Löscher 3:222–24). His intention was to encourage Hochstraten to use his influence to expedite the Sorbonne's decision. In this letter Eck tried to associate in Hochstraten's mind the cases of Luther and Reuchlin, describing the Wittenberg movement as only one of a series of errors, including the affair of the Jewish books, which *grammatici* had introduced into the church (Löscher 3:223). Eck was only confirming Hochstraten's own conviction, which he had clearly set forth in the dedication to Pope Leo X of his *Destructio cabalae seu cabalisticae perfidiae* (WA 2:384–85), that Luther was in Reuchlin's intellectual debt.

Marcello, for example, concluded his long treatise on pontifical authority and indulgences with a chapter on the Christian edification to be derived from classical philosophy.

> Why, Martin, have you invented this distinction [*distinctio*] between the "theology of glory" and the "theology of the cross," who are yourself wholly foreign to scholastic theology? Why do you declare your intention of "painting Aristotle in his true colors, time permitting," who are not worthy so much as to read Aristotle, let alone be numbered among the theologians whom you despise, distort, and denounce as "Aristotelian"? Are you holier than Thomas? More blessed than Bonaventure? More sacred than so many holy pontiffs and outstanding men? Wiser than Augustine, the wisest of all? For these same men wished us to read the teachings of the philosophers, and taught us to discern in their books truth from falsehood, light from darkness, pure gold from baser metals, for the increase of Catholic piety, for the example of good and virtuous living, to the glory and dignity of the Christian republic.[31]

Prierias had similarly identified the source of all Luther's errors as his rejection of Aristotle and thus of Aquinas.[32] This seems in fact to have been a particular concern of the Italian controversialists, which Catharinus, Thomas Rhadinus, and Isidorus de Isolanis also shared,[33] so that the alignment of scholasticism with the forces of tradition and of humanism with the movement for religious reform certainly holds true for Luther's reception in Italy in these early years.[34]

Attractive as the equation is between humanism and the Reformation, it is also clear that some humanists, such as Emser, remained staunch Romanists. The situation is further complicated by the existence of not a few of Luther's opponents who, like Cellarius, combined in themselves the study of "holy philosophy" and "fine letters." While Cellarius might be considered too equivocal a witness in view of his later desertion to Wittenberg, Luther's staunchest opponents, Eck and Cochlaeus, both answer to the description of scholastic humanists. Eck had made it a point of honor to leave no major area of intellectual endeavor unmastered. He could boast the unusual distinction of a training in both the realist and nominalist schools, and yet was consid-

---

31. Marcello, *De authoritate* 2:ii, 19.
32. Prierias, *Replica* (WA 2:53.24–54.14).
33. Catharinus, *Apologia* 1:5, 7; Isidorus de Isolanis ("Cremoniensis"), *Revocatio*, Aiii^v.
34. See E. Gleason, "Sixteenth-Century Italian Interpretations of Luther."

ered a leading humanist and could at one time or another number among his friends Beatus Rhenanus, Sebastian Brant, Johannes Geiler von Kaisersberg, Jakob Wimpheling, and Willibald Pirckheimer.[35] With a mixture of self-mockery and self-congratulation, he could say of himself in 1512, "I should be thought of as a bat, for I am neither a mouse nor a bird."[36] Eck's desire to be recognized as a humanist and not just the "sophist" he had been painted by Luther became apparent in the course of the controversy that followed Leipzig, where in his defense of Emser he twice accused Luther of "keeping more to the branches than to the roots" of Christian theology.[37] (This was the mortal humanist insult of obscurantism: when Emser presented his own qualifications as a humanist in the debate with Luther, he declared that he, for one, preferred to drink "from the source rather than from the stream.")[38] Eck's brand of scholastic humanism meant that in the same year as he commiserated with Jakob Hochstraten about the grammarians who had allowed errors to flood into the church, he also entertained the latter's archenemy, Johannes Reuchlin, as an honored guest in Ingolstadt.[39]

Cochlaeus, who was yet to enter the lists against Luther, was just as much a humanist as Eck, and like Eck had strong scholastic leanings as well. In an important preface to a pamphlet published at the end of 1522, Cochlaeus addressed himself to "the youth of Germany who study fine letters." Here he tried to dispel rumors that he was an obscurantist. From an early age, he claimed, he had resolved always to seek the sources, not commentaries. It was not he but Luther who criticized the universities, who insulted Erasmus, and who had misled the brilliant young Melanchthon. Now even Melanchthon had forfeited respect and had proved his open heresy by disputing the decision of the Sorbonne theologians. Would that he had remained with Aristotle![40] Here the typically humanist slogan "back to the sources" is unexpectedly combined with a typically scholastic view of what those sources might be. One is reminded of Cellarius's scholastic-humanist defense of Leipzig philosophy: it is better to drink from the source

35. Iserloh, *Johannes Eck 1486–1543*, 8–12, 18–20.
36. Cited in ibid., 14.
37. Eck, *Responsio pro Emser*, Bi[v], iv.
38. Emser, *Assertio*, 712.
39. Iserloh, *Johannes Eck 1486–1543*, 19.
40. Cochlaeus, *De gratia sacramentorum* 1:Ai[v]–ii[v].

than from the stream; and Aristotle is our source in matters of philosophy.[41]

The existence of scholastic humanists among the Catholic controversialists should come as no surprise. It has long been recognized that scholasticism and humanism were not two irreconcilable philosophies each struggling for supremacy over the other,[42] so that J. H. Overfield is able to describe one author—the Catholic controversialist Conrad Wimpina—as "one of those half-humanist, half-scholastic hybrids, so common in late fifteenth-century Germany."[43] No reason has yet been offered for this hybridity. It might be that humanism denotes a method (*bonae literae; eloquentia*), whereas scholasticism denotes a subject matter (*sancta philosophia*), so that it was quite possible for the two to be combined. But in some respects humanism had its own program, and certainly scholasticism had its own method; in any case, the two were never combined south of the Alps as they were in the north.

The phenomena we know as scholasticism and humanism were highly complex. The terms themselves clearly represent a good deal of the picture. (I shall be using the three categories of scholastic, humanist, and scholastic humanist to classify Romanist attitudes to publicity.) But it is equally clear that many nuances are lost by the rigid application of these terms. The situation with regard to the pamphlet war between Luther and the Romanists is even more complicated, because it suited the interests of certain protagonists to portray it as a clash between these two parties. It is therefore possible that our understanding could be helped by the adoption of a different terminology. Humanists were not usually known by that name—their detractors were more likely to call them *poetae* or *graeculi*, while they themselves preferred some such term as *literati*—and "scholastic" was a term of abuse used extensively by Luther, for example, in his campaign for university reform.

The opposite of a scholastic was not in Luther's vocabulary a humanist but an "ecclesiastic." In normal use this meant a clergyman, but Luther used it before and during the Leipzig disputation to indi-

41. Cellarius, *Nullus respondet*, 802.
42. P. O. Kristeller, *Renaissance Thought: The Classic, Scholastic and Humanist Strains* (New York: Harper & Row, 1961); and C. H. Nauert, "The Clash of Humanists and Scholastics."
43. J. H. Overfield, *Humanism and Scholasticism in Late Medieval Germany*, 174.

cate one who subscribed predominantly or exclusively to those theological authorities that were canonical or officially approved by the church.[44] His intention was to distinguish legitimate theological authorities from illegitimate, "scholastic" ones; to distinguish text from commentary, or (in terms of a metaphor that Luther did not seem to use) the source from the stream.

What were these ecclesiastical or canonical authorities? Naturally, they included the canon of Scripture and the early fathers by whom this canon had been established. Surprisingly early in the debate, in his reply to Prierias of August 1518, Luther was obliged to appeal to Augustine's distinction between the doctrinally binding books of the canon and the extra-canonical books that were to be considered only edifying.[45] It also included canon law, comprising the canons and decrees of the ecumenical councils, and the papal decretals. Again and again during the year 1518, Luther listed the authorities on the basis of which he proposed to conduct his case: Scripture, the fathers, canon law, and reason (by which he meant common sense arguments rather than elaborate speculation based on Aristotelian philosophy).[46] All these were *probationes*, proofs. On the other hand, he refused to accept teachings derived only from the schoolmen (who to his mind included Albert the Great, Aquinas, and Scotus, but not Bernard), which were mere *opiniones*.

Although Luther was the only sixteenth-century theologian to my knowledge to have employed the term "ecclesiasticism" so extensively—indeed, to have used it to describe his own program of university reform—other writers did use it in Luther's sense, and there is a possibility that the term was in much wider circulation.[47]

44. Luther, *Asterisci* (*WA* 1:309.22f.) It was in his *Asterisci* of 1518 against Eck that Luther used the word most intensively. The refrain "non scholastice sed ecclesiastice" appears on almost every page of the Weimar edition of the work (*WA* 1:284.26, 285.34, 286.4, 287.10, 288.1f. and 18f., 289.17, 290.1, 292.4 and 9, 293.8, 298.27, 303.2, 306.19, 309.2f., 310.28, 312.11, 313.18f.).

45. Luther, *Responsio ad Prieratis dialogum*, 390. Augustine, *Epistula* 82, chap. 1, para. 3 (*CSEL* 34:3541).

46. This list occurs, e.g., in Luther's *Resolutiones* (*WA* 1:529.33–530.3), *Asterisci* (*WA* 1:308.13f.), and *Responsio ad Prieratis dialogum* (*WA* 1:647.22–25). I am grateful to Professor Fraenkel for pointing out that the division of authorities between the categories of Scripture, the fathers, and reason (the last being further divisible into law, philosophy, and history) was itself a scholastic distinction.

47. Eck had used the word once in his *Obelisci* (*WA* 1:313.1), in its traditional sense of "churchman," but after Leipzig he used it in Luther's sense, even claiming that it was he and not the reformer who could more accurately be described as an ecclesias-

Consensus and Custom

The pamphlet war that ensued after Leipzig demonstrates that the traditional view of the differences between the two camps has been shaped to a large degree by the propaganda of the pamphleteers themselves. It suited the purposes of humanist Lutherans such as Melanchthon, Montanus, and Peter Mosellanus to depict Leipzig as a battle royal between *literati* and obscurantists.[48] Such an interpretation seemed to be confirmed by Rubeus's and Eck's strictures against the "school teachers" (*grammatici*).[49] But the picture is considerably complicated by the number of humanists who opposed Luther, by the fact that Luther himself regarded Leipzig as the battlefield of "ecclesiasticism"—not humanism—and scholasticism, and by the existence of scholastic humanists, who seem to be more numerous and unexceptional than has hitherto been supposed. The anti-Lutheran caucus in the months after Leipzig was clearly one that cut across straightforward affiliations to *sancta philosophia* or to *bonae literae*. Was there a decisive difference of method between Luther and his opponents that manifested itself in the literary debates after Leipzig?

What distinguished Luther's approach to theology from his opponents' was his reductionism, his adoption of a methodological razor that prevented the multiplication of authoritative theological sources beyond necessity. He insisted on a distinction between the canonical and apocryphal books of the Bible, which was by no means universally recognized. Luther's predilection for particular books within even that restricted canon soon became obvious, so that Catharinus, Fabri, and Eustachius van Sichem could speak sarcastically of his

---

tic (*Expurgatio*, Aivᵛ, Biiiᵛ). Rubeus's frequent recourse to the word, in the context of a report on the Leipzig disputation, most probably suggests that he had adopted Luther's own vocabulary rather than that it was in current use independently of Wittenberg reform circles (*Solutiones*, 252, 255–57, 259, 263, 264). Its employment by Alveld suggests the contrary. In the introduction to *Super apostolicae sede* (1520), he promised: "I shall construct a true and genuine truth, on the basis not of the holy fathers (either the ecclesiastics or the so-called [*ut vocant*] scholastics) but rather of these letters" (Aiᵛ). The position of "ut vocant" with "scholastici" rather than with "ecclesiastici" implies that the former phrase was less familiar to him than the latter. It might, however, just as easily denote the use of an offensive as an unfamiliar word. We must therefore conclude that the use of "ecclesiasticus" in Luther's sense by Eck, Rubeus, and Alveld in itself neither proves nor disproves that it was the reformer's own invention.

48. Melanchthon to Oecolampadius, 218; Montanus, *Encomium*, passim, esp. 786, 792; Mosellanus to Julius Pflüg, 8 December 1519 (Löscher 3:242–51), 244, 249.

49. Rubeus, *Solutiones*, 262; Eck to Hochstraten, 223; Eck, *Excusatio*, 592.

"Pauline Christianity."[50] Within the corpus of canon law, Luther denied a place to the so-called *extravagantes*, one of which contradicted his interpretation of indulgences; eventually he would reject canon law in its entirety. Even his reliance on the fathers would become conditional upon their consonance with Scripture.

This reductionist or "analytic" approach stands in marked contrast with the "synthetic" approach of the Catholic controversialists—scholastic, humanist, and scholastic humanist alike.[51] They held to a principle that Fraenkel has aptly characterized as "the more, the better."[52] They were utterly baffled by the grounds on which Luther made qualitative distinctions between theological authorities. Why honor the apostolic fathers responsible for the Scriptures but not the later fathers, or the later fathers but not the schoolmen? Why respect the written teaching of the church but not its practice? There was, they insisted, a quantitative as well as a qualitative dimension to truth. In his correspondence on the eve of the Leipzig disputation, Eck referred to Luther's singularity: "But I should prefer that you change your mind altogether and excel in obedience to the Apostolic See, and listen to Leo X, the vicar of Christ, and not go after singularity, but rather agree with the common opinion [*consensus*] of the doctors, for it is certain that Christ would not have allowed the Church to remain in error (as you call it) for four hundred years."[53] This approach also manifested itself in terms of a crude but effective question repeatedly put to Luther by the controversialists. Who was more likely to be mistaken, an upstart monk from the academic backwaters of Christendom or the almost innumerable saintly doctors and learned saints of the past? In the words of Erasmus,

---

50. Catharinus, *Apologia*, 36; Johannes Fabri, *Malleus*, 24; Eustachius Sichem, *Confutatio*, 286.

51. C. Augustijn, "Die Stellung der Humanisten zur Glaubensspaltung 1518–1530," has suggested that "biblical humanists" remained loyal to Rome—or at least refrained from siding with Luther—throughout the early years of the Reformation. This would seem to contradict my argument that the Catholics' distinctive approach over against Luther was to create a consensus out of all doctrinal authorities and not to elevate one (i.e., Scripture) above the rest. In fact, Augustijn based his case exclusively on the example of Erasmus, and Erasmus, as we shall see presently, firmly supported the "consensus" approach.

52. P. Fraenkel, "An der Grenze vor Luthers Einfluss," 26.

53. Eck to Luther, 19 February 1519 (*WA Br* 1:343). Cf. to Caspar and Zinngiesser, 14 March 1519 (*WA Br* 1:320–22).

> Let him keep continually before his eyes that numerous body of
> extremely learned men, who have found approval [consensus]
> through many centuries down to our own day, whom he should
> commend not only on account of their wonderful knowledge of
> Holy Scriptures, but also for their godly living.[54]

Similarly, Henry VIII writes:

> Not only did God take these men up to heaven; he also required
> that they be venerated on earth and honoured by men, and that
> he himself should be honoured through them. Of these I shall
> name just one, that most erudite man and most holy saint Thomas
> Aquinas, whom I commemorate all the more freely because Luther
> calls the holiness of that man impiety, and everywhere blasphemes
> with unclean lips a man whom all Christians revere.[55]

The assumption behind all this, of course, was that the truth of a
doctrine was directly related to the numbers, the antiquity, the sanctity,
and the erudition of those who upheld it. It was a potent argument,
not least because of its emotiveness, and Luther admitted that of all
the arguments deployed against him by the controversialists, it was
the one that caused him the most soul-searching.[56]

The primary purpose of the fourfold appeal to antiquity, numbers, sanctity, and erudition was to discredit Luther's apparently singular and novel opinions; but an important secondary function was

---

54. Erasmus, *Diatribe*, Aiv^v; cf. Aviii^v.

55. Henry VIII, *Assertio*, Ciii^vf. See also Tetzel, *Vorlegung*, 484; Paulus Bachmann, *Czuerrettung*, Biii; Fabri, *Malleus*, 23; Thomas More, *Rossaeus*, 52; Fisher, *Sermon*, 320; idem, *Confutatio* 272, 291; Emser, *Assertio*, 710.

56. Luther, *The Misuse of the Mass* (LW 36:134): "How often did my heart quail, punish me and reproach me with its single strongest argument: Are you the only wise man? Can it be that all the others are in error and have erred for so long a time? What if you are mistaken and lead so many people into error who might all be eternally damned? Finally, Christ with his clear, unmistakable Word strengthened and confirmed me, so that my heart no longer quails, but resists the arguments of the papists, as a stony shore resists the waves, and laughs at their threats and storms!" Luther's first reaction seems to have been to appeal to St Paul's warning of Gal. 1:8: "Even if an angel from heaven should preach to you a gospel contrary to that which we preached, let him be accursed." This quotation appears very frequently in Luther's works from 1518 to 1520, and I believe it was employed by the reformer as an antidote to the Romanist appeal to the personal sanctity of the theologians they cited. From 1521, Luther attacked their appeal more aggressively. The mark of the saint, he argued, is that he knows he is a sinner and totally dependent on God: St. Bernard's last words were "I have led a damnable life." They knew better than anyone that their sanctity was from God, so it cannot be appealed to as an authority independent of God (Luther, *The Misuse of the Mass*, 186). In the same work, he dismissed another supposed aid to credibility: "It is indeed a fine premise which one bases on size and numbers rather than on the clear, pure Word of God" (ibid., 178–79).

the support it gave to the notion of including the schoolmen in the canon of the church's theological authorities. However, the controversialists soon realized the shortcomings of this argument. The appeal to antiquity proved nothing, for the authorities to which Luther most frequently referred, especially Paul and Augustine, were as old if not older than those cited against him.[57] It was also clear that heretics had often been among the most learned of teachers, and that the appeal to erudition was therefore invalid.[58] Numbers could not in themselves constitute a guarantee of truth, as Luther's growing popularity demonstrated.[59] It became apparent, therefore, that the consensus approach required a more sophisticated defense, and this would be provided between 1521 and 1523 by King Henry and Bishop Fisher: the king on the basis of the corporate nature of the church ("If you attribute so much importance to the member, why not much more to the body as a whole?"),[60] the bishop on the basis of the continual guidance of the church by the Holy Spirit (today's church is no different from the church of the past "to which Christ sent his Spirit, who will teach it all truth, and with which he will remain forever").[61] It would be unfair to regard these successive arguments as signs of a change of mind on the part of the controversialists. Rather, they are different facets of the same argument from consensus that unfolded gradually as Luther criticized it with ever greater precision.

It is impossible to say with certainty what the historical background to the controversialists' synthetic approach is, but I would tentatively suggest two possible sources for it. The first lies in the scholastic method itself. A typical *modus loquendi theologicus* was the so-called comparison, in which a theologian would take two apparently contradictory data or opinions and attempt to harmonize them: this method was enshrined in the *sic et non* of Lombard's books of *Sentences* (the basic theological textbooks of the schools) and in Aquinas's *Summa theologiae*. It was a perfectly logical method, inasmuch as it was believed that the data of revelation were true and that

57. This point was appreciated by Henry VIII when he wrote, "For the Spirit blows when, as well as where, it wills" (*Assertio septem sacramentorum*, Eiv).

58. Fisher, *Sermon*, 340.

59. "The majority always prefers evil" (Eustachius Sichem, *Brevis elucidatio*, Aiv). Simon Blich reminded his readers of the parable of the sower to prove that only a small number ever follows the truth (*Verderbe*, Di^v).

60. Henry, *Assertio*, Oiii.

61. Fisher, *Confutatio*, 273.

truth could never ultimately contradict itself. Scholastic theologians extended this method beyond the realm of revelation and applied it to the opinions of the commentators, with the result that the same attributes of truthfulness and noncontradiction were effectively extended to these theologians of the past. It would not be surprising, therefore, if the opponents of Luther who had been trained in the schools also proceeded from these prior assumptions.

This suggestion is made only tentatively. It should be remembered, first, that Luther himself was scholastically trained but evidently did not subscribe to the synthetic method; and second, that many Catholic humanists were synthesists but were, of course, not necessarily practicing adherents of scholastic methods. Even if we exclude Luther from the reckoning as an exception, the synthetic humanists still cause a problem for this suggestion (unless we make the not unreasonable assumption that the scholastic method was by now an integral part of all theology), and some other hypothesis is needed to explain their support of the consensus. I believe that this can be found in the high regard that the synthetic humanists—together with the scholastics and scholastic humanists—had for "custom." *Mos* and *consuetudo* were portmanteau words, embracing local and universal observances and *leges orandi*. Their importance had been guaranteed by the opening canons of Gratian's *Decretum*, which had declared them second only to divine law and the law of reason. The controversialists returned repeatedly to Augustine's dictum (which was also part of canon law) that "the custom of the people of God has the force of law."[62] The surprising thing about custom, at least as understood by the controversialists, is that it did not have to be old: it simply had to be "received." It is true that *consuetudo* was sometimes preceded by the adjective *longa* in the literature, but long usage was seen as a bonus. It was entirely consistent with this understanding of custom for Tetzel and Prierias to argue that whatever is said to be Catholic (by someone with authority to speak on behalf of the church, for example

---

62. "You see that laws and uses in matters catholic have obligatory force" (Lambertus Campester, *Heptacolon*, Cii^v); "In many cases, use alone puts Christians under obligation. Use supported by Scripture will therefore put Christians under obligation of compulsory observance" (ibid., Hiv); "In those matters in which Holy Scripture gives us no certain guidance, the custom of the people of God and the practice of earlier generations are to be regarded as law" (Johannes Eck, *Enchiridion*, 77). For similar statements, see Johannes Eck, *Enchiridion*, 149, 151; Cochlaeus, *Wideford* Aiv^{v}f.; Prierias, *Dialogus*, 15.

a preacher) thereby becomes Catholic.[63] This was also the understanding of the arch-humanist Sir Thomas More; one of his modern editors has argued that such a view allowed him to regard even recent abuses as "customary."[64]

Antiquity was considered a much less important attribute of custom than its having been received because custom was believed to exercise in canon law precisely the same role as precedent did in civil law. "If custom has the force of law in civil cases," asks Eck, "why not in the observances of the Church?"[65] More, the civil lawyer, went further: "The custom of the Christian people in matters of sacraments and of faith has the force of a more powerful law than has any custom of any people whatever in civil matters, since the latter relies only on human agreement, while the former is promised and prospers by divine inspiration."[66] This precedential function of custom was, I think, paradigmatic for the Catholic controversialists' understanding of doctrine. In the same way as they believed what was was therefore right, they also believed that what was taught was therefore true.

Luther's Threats to
Doctrinal Authority

This survey of the Romanist literature that followed Leipzig has shown that both the scholastic-versus-humanist interpretation, put forward by Lutheran humanists and Romanist scholastics, and the scholastic-versus-ecclesiastic interpretation, preferred by Luther and used by Eck, Rubeus, and Alveld, are inadequate as explanations of the difference in theological method between the reformer and his opponents. The essential distinction was rather between the analytic approach adopted by Luther and the synthetic approach adopted by all Catholic controversialists, scholastic and humanist alike. What did this methodological difference imply for the controversialists, and what danger did they think Luther's alternative approach posed? It appears from

63. Tetzel, *Subscriptas positiones*, 521; Prierias, *Dialogus*, 15.
64. "By making his ultimate authority the action of the Holy Spirit as it inheres in the contemporary faith, institutions and practices of the church, More committed himself in principle to the defense of everything" (J. M. Headley, *CWM* 5:ii, p. 736). "This emphasis upon the sanction of the Holy Spirit has the effect of placing a protective mantle indiscriminately over all the present practices and beliefs of the church, regardless of their origins. More comes dangerously close to saying that what is, is right" (p. 737).
65. Eck, *Enchiridion*, 149.
66. More, *Rossaeus*, 414.

the post-Leipzig literature that the controversialists identified two threats to their conception of authority implicit in Luther's method. First, in making a sharp distinction between divine and human words and in locating the word of God primarily in the Scriptures, he denied the divine guidance of the totality of the church's doctrines and therefore taught that obedience to the church's teaching authority was unnecessary. Second, in wishing to submit the outcome of the Leipzig disputation to the verdict of laity, he had granted it a say in the making of doctrine; this, they believed, could produce only doctrinal anarchy.

The Romanists' belief that Luther's Scripture principle constituted a threat to authority was not peculiar to this phase of the literary controversy. Tetzel had identified the problem as early as May 1518, when he warned that the reformer's preference for biblical over scholastic evidence would "encourage many to despise the might and authority of his holiness the Pope and of the holy Roman see. . . . Now they will never believe the preachers and doctors, but everyone will interpret Scripture as he pleases."[67] It remained a stock objection up to 1525 and beyond.

By contrast, their conviction that Luther had accorded the laity a place in determining dogma arose for the first time in relation to Leipzig. Rubeus had criticized the men from Wittenberg for playing to the gallery during the disputation.[68] This was, however, a predictable accusation under the circumstances, and one that Eck himself did not escape.[69] A less routine and more serious criticism came from Emser, who maintained that an important part of Luther's early critique of the papacy—his distinction between an innocent pontiff and a scheming Curia—had been borrowed directly from ideas current in the courts of princes: "so great is your inadequacy in matters theological that you are obliged to go cap in hand even to lay people for your theology."[70]

But the most sustained criticism of Luther on this point arose out of incidents that took place before the debate proper. During the preliminary negotiations, Luther made two demands. First, he insisted on the presence of scribes, which he hoped would deter Eck from the use

67. Tetzel, *Vorlegung*, art. 13 (Löscher 1:495).
68. Rubeus, *Solutiones*, 267, 269.
69. See, e.g., Mosellanus to Pflug, 8 December 1519 (Löscher 3:247f.).
70. Emser, *Assertio*, 711.

of momentarily dazzling rhetoric. Second, he demanded that the verbatim report be published to allow readers to make up their own minds on the pros and cons on each side, because he did not wish his case condemned by the official judges most likely to be appointed, Rome itself or scholastic theology faculties. To Eck, these demands were highly unsatisfactory. The general public, he averred, is ignorant, malicious, and easily swayed by passions. The majority is always likely to be wrong, and its judgment cannot be relied on as a means of suppressing heresy. Competent judges are always to be found among the educated minority.[71] For these reasons, Eck considered it far more than a breach of disputatory protocol that Melanchthon and Luther had published unauthorized versions of the debate:[72] the invitation to the unlearned to judge the matter for themselves, which these publications implied, was a departure from the accepted procedure for determining the true teaching of the church.[73] Eck's concern for the confusion that might result from Leipzig and from the literature it engendered is thus far removed from the disdain of public contest affected by the humanists. But whereas peace-loving humanists were long inured to bombarding each other with pamphlets, the normally combative Eck (veteran of two public disputations) now stopped short of total pamphlet war, being obliged to defend himself publicly without thereby assigning the public the role of judge. In chapter 7 we shall see how Eck and his colleagues resolved this dilemma.

Eck's belief that Luther intended "the people" as such to rise up and judge his cause was, of course, an oversimplification, encouraged both by the ambiguity of the reformer's statements and by the controversialists' need to embarrass him as acutely as possible. It is

---

71. Eck, *Expurgatio*, Bii[v]f.

72. Luther to Spalatin, 20 July 1519 (*WA Br* 1:420–24); Melanchthon to Oecolampadius, 21 July 1519.

73. Selge, "Die Leipziger Disputation zwischen Luther und Eck," has argued that these preliminary negotiations encapsulated the essential differences between the two main protagonists. Eck accepted the institutional ecclesiology of the late Middle Ages, which held that the monarchical-hierarchical model was the best possible for the church militant, since it reflected the preexistent order of heaven: Eck's court of appeal in this highly structured church was therefore to specialist theologians. Luther, on the other hand, defended the noninstitutional ecclesiology of the late Middle Ages (seen especially in the mystics), which saw the church not as a material entity but as a community bound only by love (pp. 29–31). Selge's analysis is not absolute (in Luther's opinion—especially after the encounter with the Zwickau prophets—membership of the community did not of itself entitle one to the full exercise of theological freedom) but is, I think, extremely valuable.

true that Luther spoke of the proceedings of the Leipzig disputation being exposed to "the light of day" and submitted to "the judgment of the world."[74] But what did he mean? Clearly, he was referring to those who could read Latin. (He never published a German version of the debate; and, while there is evidence that pamphlets were read aloud in sixteenth-century Germany, this practice would almost certainly have been limited to vernacular sermonic material and would not have extended to disputation accounts.) The impression that "the light of day" meant for Luther the scrutiny exclusively or primarily of the educated classes is confirmed by another of his demands made during the discussions preliminary to the debate. He stipulated that if a university were to decide the outcome, the decision should involve physicians or civil lawyers in addition to professional theologians.[75] In other words, Luther believed that his *rationes* would be understood by any educated person, provided that that education had not been of a traditional scholastic or canonist nature.[76]

74. Luther to Spalatin, 20 July 1519 (*WA Br* 1:421.3); Luther, *Super expurgatione Ecciana* (*WA* 2:705.4).
75. See Luther's hastily scribbled memorandum, sent through his legal adviser Pflug, to Duke Georg, 15 July 1519 (Gess 1:93 n. 1): "This is the reason why I have chosen [to have appointed as judges] the university as a whole and not the theology faculty alone. First, because, by God's grace, through many good books the young people have become rather more knowledgeable than the old, who are still steeped in their own books. Second, because this topic can be regarded as counter to the interests of those who became theologians before now. Third, because in these times God has so ordered matters that things are no longer necessarily what they seem. Those who are supposed to be theologians are not theologians, the learned are fools, the spirituals worldly, and so on. Fourth, because in his disputation Dr Eck has taken such care to heap odium and disparagement upon me and my position, and to make himself and his cause so favourable, that it will be read to his advantage, especially by the other theologians, because the issue appears to be against their interests."
76. Luther's appeal to the people as his judges—and his implied attribution to them of the right and power to determine doctrine—has been excellently treated by H. Junghans in his essay, "Der Laie als Richter im Glaubensstreit der Reformationszeit." Junghans shows how Luther's popular works between 1518 and 1520 were concerned with teaching the people and with dispelling misconceptions about his real positions (pp. 45–48). But at the end of 1520, in *Grund und Ursach*, he finally made an appeal to all laypeople as judges of his case (p. 49). Junghans identifies as the turning point in this development as the treatise *To the Christian Nobility* of July 1520, when Luther made an appeal to a limited section of the laity (pp. 50–51). I believe that Luther's appeals to the *educated* laity at the time of the Leipzig debate twelve months earlier also constitute a turning point in this scheme. In fact, this was in many ways a more significant step even than the appeal to the judgment of secular authorities; whereas the latter had been an established part of the church's doctrine-making for centuries (as the controversialists were at pains to point out), the former marked the transition between judgment by the spiritual estate and judgment by the "lower laity," insofar as it extended a university verdict on a theological matter beyond the bounds of the theology faculty.

To the controversialists, this was a nonsensical distinction. In their view, one was either a theologically educated priest or an uneducated layperson. Therefore, the class of people for which the controversialists reserved their severest censure was the educated laity, although they made an honorable exception in the cases of Henry VIII and Georg of Saxony! In a description of how the Lutheran plague had spread to all sections of German society, Cochlaeus wrote: "Also in Luther's school are those awkward folk, the half-learned, striped laity, such as notaries, advocates, counsels, and businessmen, together with the rest of those who can read books in Latin or German and who therefore consider themselves somewhat more knowledgeable than the common laity."[77] These are the men, Cochlaeus continued, whose pretensions Luther tickled by saying that the doctors of the church had all got it wrong while *they* were the competent interpreters of Scripture. The phrase "striped laity" was also used by Johannes Dietenberger in his 1524 pamphlet *The Layman*. In this dialogue, a layman asks his father-confessor for advice about the religious controversy. The priest replies that he will give the man his answer only in the presence of "an unbiased, intelligent, clever, and properly appointed judge." The layman (supposedly a Lutheran sympathizer) balks at such a suggestion: neither judge nor judgment is needed, only his own obedience to the priest's life-giving word. "One must ask and seek the law from the mouth of a priest, who is an angel and an emissary of God, not from the striped laity."[78] The father-confessor applauds this answer, and confirms its rightness in even more pointed terms: "In these new circumstances, you should not follow the easygoing Karsthanses, the knights or the prattling poets, but obey priests, who know the Scriptures and fear God, as God has commanded."[79]

These remarks explain why the controversialists oversimplified Luther's desire to expose the proceedings at Leipzig to the light of day: unlike Luther, they saw "the people" as an undifferentiated mass and made no distinction between the more and less educated or the

---

77. Cochlaeus, *Christliche vermanung*, Fiv.

78. Johannes Dietenberger, *Der leye*, Biii^v f. Latomus also referred sneeringly to the "semi-learned" (*De primatu romani*, 59^v). In 1521, a robust pamphlet was published in Switzerland against an unnamed monk who had preached about the "striped laity," those who read books in Latin and German but did not really understand them. See *Der gestryfft Schwitzer Baur: Diss büchlin hat gemacht ein Baur auss dem Entlibüch / Wem es nit gefall der küss im die brüch*, esp. Ai^v. N.p., [1521].

79. Dietenberger, *Der leye*, Bi^v.

more and less sincere. They laughed off lay people with pretensions to learning as a contradiction in terms. To expose Leipzig to public scrutiny was in their view tantamount to Luther's submitting his case to the judgment of Karsthans.[80]

"He Allows No One to Judge Him"

It was inevitable that questions of methodology would become the subject of heated debate between Luther and the Catholic controversialists. Such questions were raised early in the controversy, notably by Tetzel, and were also addressed later with a great degree of precision, notably by Henry and Fisher. However, it was in the wake of the Leipzig disputation that the methodological question became a topic widely adopted by the controversialists. In retrospect it is easy to see that the main problem faced by the controversialists in answering Luther's method was that it was still in the process of being developed. As soon as it became a straightforward *sola scriptura* approach, the controversialists could object straightforwardly that such had been the argument of heretics through the centuries. But until then, the canon of authorities to which Luther declared himself willing to submit remained a puzzle to the controversialists. Their bewilderment was expressed by Emser toward the end of 1519:

> He sets himself up as a judge, but he allows no one to judge him. Canon law and the decretals he calls "cold." Even deified Fathers he calls mere men (and, of course, he won't accept the traditions of men). If I defeat him with the gospels, he will simply say I haven't understood him properly. Yet he himself says that no-one can speak of God without sinning. Is he therefore without sin?"[81]

One of the tactics the controversialists adopted in response was to take Luther's analytic approach to its logical conclusion and, for example, to credit him with a Scripture principle even before he had actually adopted one.[82] As we shall see in chapter 6, to the controver-

---

80. Karsthans ("Jack Hoe") was the medieval German personification of the simple agricultural worker, whose closest relative in English literature is Piers Plowman. Anonymous pamphleteers (including Vadian and Bucer?) conscripted him to the Reformation cause to demonstrate popular support for Luther—and against such Catholics as Murner—in the early 1520s.

81. Emser, *Assertio*, 697. Marlianus was similarly puzzled: "You will not listen to the philosophers, or admit the decrees of the fathers, or accept the sacred institutions of the councils. But you use the gospels as if you owned them" (*Oratio*, Aiv^v).

82. Tetzel, *Vorlegung*, art. 13 (Löscher 1:495).

sialists' mind Scripture was not its own interpreter; it did not have its own innate sense. To submit only to Scripture was the same as submitting to no authority at all, except the figments of one's own imagining. To speak of Luther's threat to "doctrinal authority," then, is to speak of the threat that the controversialists supposed him to constitute to the different theological authorities as, one by one, he dispensed with the definitive status of the schoolmen, custom, and the pontifical and conciliar decrees of canon law. But it is also, on another level, to speak of the anti-authoritarianism his attitude to doctrine seemed to entail: by rejecting the idea of a Spirit-led consensus and by distinguishing between the word of God and merely human words, Luther encouraged his followers to believe that the church itself was fallible; and by encouraging the people to judge his performance at Leipzig, he opened the way for private (or rather, public) judgment to usher in doctrinal anarchy. How close doctrinal anarchy was to social anarchy was a question that would concern the controversialists in the next stage of their campaign.

4

APPEALS TO THE
CHRISTIAN NOBILITY

The phase of the pamphlet war inaugurated by Luther's appeal to the Christian nobility of the German nation of 1520 was of a quite different order from the exchanges of the preceding years. The controversialists, many of whom were professional theologians, had hitherto been engaged in a theological debate with Luther. While the theological foundations of Luther's appeal to the nobility were unmistakable, it presented nonetheless a challenge to Rome that went further than the abstract treatment of matters of doctrine and helped to associate explicitly Luther's cause with other great contemporary movements, particularly German nationalism. In spite of the immense interest Luther's appeal aroused, the controversialists courageously rose to this challenge, and it is worth examining in some detail the methods they adopted.

Luther's Appeal and
Romanist Reaction

By the summer of 1520, Luther had become convinced of the futility of expecting any reform of the church directed by the higher clergy. His interview with Cajetan toward the end of 1518 and his growing disillusionment with canon law during 1519 led him to believe that too many interests were vested in preserving the status quo. In July 1520 he appealed to the holy Roman emperor and the German aristocracy to convene, on their own authority, a "really free general council in German lands."[1] The purpose of the appeal was "to set to thinking those with the ability and the inclination to help the German nation to be free again after the wretched, heathenish, and unchristian rule of the pope."[2] To this end Luther refuted one by one the defensive walls

1. Luther, *Der allerdurchleuchtigsten, Grossmechtigsten Keyserlichen Maiestet, und Christlichen Adel deutscher Nation, etlicher stuck Christliches stands besserung belangend* (*WA* 6:404–69) = *To the Christian Nobility of the German Nation Concerning the Reform of the Christian Estate* (*LW* 44:[115],123–217).
2. *WA* 6:431.15–18, *LW* 44:161.

erected by the papacy against reform: the superiority of the spiritual estate to the temporal; the exclusive right of the pope, as "the spiritual man," to interpret Scripture; and his equally exclusive right to summon a council.[3] Especially in want of reform, Luther continued, were the many frauds, permitted by canon law, by which "Roman avarice" was allowed to extort money from Germany.[4] But there were also a number of other suggestions (twenty-seven in all, ranging from schemes for union with the Hussites to sumptuary laws) that in his opinion a council should implement.[5] *To the Christian Nobility* was an immensely important document because it attempted to ally Luther's cause with two great contemporary forces: anti-Italian feeling, with its incipient German nationalism, and the desire of territorial princes for greater control over ecclesiastical affairs in their realms. Both aspirations were regularly aired through the so-called grievances of the German nation at imperial diets. Luther's propaganda coup was to combine in the latter part of *To the Christian Nobility* his own demands for ecclesiastical reform with these traditional social and economic complaints against the Curia on the basis of the theological convictions about the nature of the church set out in the first half of the pamphlet. Something of the author's success can be measured by the fact that its first edition of four thousand copies sold out within a week.

As in the divine right controversy, Luther found opponents among the theologians of both Germany and Italy and, as in that controversy, the German response was led by Eck. From a Dominican convent in Leipzig where he was hiding in fear for his life after publicizing *Exsurge Domine*, Eck broadcast his vernacular *Defense of the Sacred Council of Constance, Holy Christendom, His Imperial Highness Sigmund, and the German Nobility.*[6] His primary objective was to demonstrate Luther's inconsistency in appealing to the nobility to con-

---

3. WA 6:406–15, LW 44:126–39. For the influences upon and development of Luther's understanding of 1 Cor. 2:15 ("The spiritual man judges all things, but is himself judged by no one"), see S. E. Ozment, *Homo Spiritualis: A Comparative Study of the Anthropology of Johannes Tauler, Jean Gerson and Martin Luther (1509–1516) in the Context of Their Theological Thought* (Leiden: E. J. Brill, 1969); and W. Rochler, *Martin Luther und die Reformation als Laienbewegung*, esp. 39–52.

4. WA 6:415–27, LW 44:139–56.

5. WA 6:427–68, LW 44:156–217.

6. Johannes Eck, *Des heiligen concilii tzu Costentz, der heylgen Christenheit und hochlöblichen keyssers Sigmunds und auch des teutzschen adels entschüldigung, das in bruder Martin Luder mit unwarheit auffgelegt, sie haben Johannem Huss und Hieronymum von Prag wider babstlich, christlich, keyserlich geleidt und eydt vorbrandt.*

voke a reforming council and at the same time reviling the achievements of the one council—that of Constance—in which the higher
laity did participate. Eck also dealt with the charge that the burning of
Huss at the German council was a violation of promises of safe conduct made by the emperor.

Another veteran pamphleteer to re-enter the lists was Emser.[7]
While Luther had addressed himself to the aristocracy, Emser's was a
warning for "the whole German nation," which, if it continued to
heed the new doctrines, would suffer God's wrath on the day of judgment that was now imminent.[8] The reformation proposed by Luther,
Emser revealed, was in reality deformation.[9] For Emser, Luther's remedy was murder; he would cut off the patient's head (by denying
papal primacy) and set the members of the body at variance with each
other (by rejecting social distinctions).[10] Before joining the battle, Emser
paraded his "weapons." First, he claimed to possess the sword of
Holy Scripture. Luther, he admitted, had tried to wield this himself,
but had neglected to remove the scabbard; that was to say, he had
interpreted Scripture according to the letter and not the Spirit.[11] Second, he claimed the lance of long usage, which explains and augments
Scripture. Its customs, such as invoking St. John as a protection against
poison, were established for the greater glory of God and for our
sanctification.[12] His third weapon was a dagger—the patristic exegesis
of Scripture. Reason, explained Emser, is our noblest part, which, when
joined with contemplation of God as in the writings of the fathers, is
alone capable of penetrating the secrets of divinity.[13] The *Refutation*
followed the tripartite plan of *To the Christian Nobility.* After rebuilding
the three walls ("the walls of Jerusalem," not of Jericho) and denying
the need for reform in the areas specified by Luther ("My dear Germans, the Pope's arrogance is not so great that we should become
schismatics"), the author dealt with those recommendations of the
reformer he considered heretical. Emser was not totally opposed to

7. Hieronymus Emser, *Wider das unchristliche Buch Martini Luthers Augustiners an
den Teutschen Adel ausgangen Vorlegung Hieronymi Emser an gemeyne Hochlöbliche Teutsche
Nation.*
    8. Emser, *Vorlegung,* Ai^v–Aiv, Siii^v–Siv.
    9. Ibid., Rii.
    10. Ibid., Biii^v–Ci^v.
    11. Ibid., Aiv–Bi.
    12. Ibid., Bif.
    13. Ibid., Biif.

reform but thought there was no need to murder the baby just because its bathwater was dirty.

In Murner's opinion, too, a reform of the church in Germany was necessary.[14] But he believed it could best be achieved not by a council (as both Luther and Emser thought) but by a formal presentation of grievances to Charles V, who would in turn petition the pope. In the course of three books, Murner repeated the view that the public discussion of controversial issues would serve only to scandalize the laity and so foment insurrection.[15] Luther, he claimed, was all too aware of this and intended, like some latter-day Catiline, to overturn society and usher in the heresy of Huss under the pretext of a genuine need for reform.[16]

The German protagonists had, in their addresses to the German nation, adopted the form of an open letter. By contrast, the Italians who answered Luther used a forensic style, the *oratio* or speech for the prosecution, casting themselves as prosecutors and Charles and the German nobility as judges. The first such *oratio* was written by Thomas Rhadinus Tedescus, a professor of philosophy and theology at Rome and a keen Thomist who had even cast Aquinas's horoscope.[17] In 1521, he succeeded Prierias as master of the Sacred Palace. Rhadinus, who could boast German descent, began his appeal by lamenting the shame Luther had brought upon the fatherland by "re-forming" it to its previous heathenism.[18] The princes, he continued, were not to believe that Luther alone was right and the testimony of numerous school-authors wrong,[19] for there was in Luther's contempt for pope and tradition a strong anti-authoritarian element, which it was in the princes' own interests to extinguish while it was still possible.[20]

A second Italian oration was written by Joannes Antonius

14. Murner, *Tütscher nation*.

15. Ibid., Biii. While Murner's *Eine christliche und briederliche ermanung* and *Von dem babstentum* were both primarily directed at other targets, their content was to some extent determined by the need to refute Luther's appeal to the German nobility. His *Tütscher nation* was a reply proper.

16. Murner, *Tütscher nation*, Aii, Aiiif, Fi^v.

17. *Thome Rhadini Todeschi Placentini ord. pre. ad illustriss. et invictiss. Principes et populos Germanie in Martinum Lutherum Wittenbergensem or. here. Nationis gloriam violantem: Oratio.* For details of Rhadinus's life and works, see F. Lauchert, *Die italienischen literarischen Gegner Luther*, 117–18; R. Stupperich, "Melanchthon und Radini," esp. 340–45.

18. Rhadinus, *Oratio* Aii^v–iv^v.

19. Ibid., Bii^v–Eii^v.

20. Ibid., Fii, Iif.

Modestus, who had moved to Rome after holding various appointments at the Universities of Vienna and Bologna. His thirty-page treatise appealed to the new emperor to punish the German heretic, for he believed that where kindness and reason had failed, only the stake could succeed.[21] Action, he urged, had to be taken quickly, for civil disobedience would soon raise its head, the inexorable consequence of ecclesiastical disobedience.[22]

A third oration was penned by the Milanese-born Aloysius Marlianus, bishop of Tuy in Galicia and court physician to Charles and his predecessor Maximilian, in which he attributed Luther's success to the anti-Italian, anticlerical, and antitheological character of German humanism.[23] He pointed to Luther's apparent inconsistency in accepting the priest's power to transform bread into God while denying the relatively simple matter of the pope's jurisdiction over souls in purgatory; or in being prepared to obey an unworthy secular prince while advocating sanctions against the Roman pontiff, whom only God may judge. The abolition of confession, he argued, would have the worst moral consequences, and a state that allowed religious crimes to go unpunished would suffer divine chastisement. Furthermore, it was impossible for Luther to attack the pope and not thereby attack the emperor, for the latter's authority was derived from the former. Nonetheless, the bishop held out hope for the erring friar. Circumstances had forced him to go further in his statements than he had originally intended, and there was yet time for him to retract them.[24]

These, then, were the Catholic pamphlets directed exclusively against Luther's *To the Christian Nobility*. In addition, it was referred to in the course of other works not expressly concerned with it, such as Catharinus's *Apology* and the so-called Cremonian author's *Revocation*.[25] The idea of an appeal to the German nation was revived in 1524–25 by Cochlaeus, who had read and disliked *To the Christian Nobility* when it

---

21. Joannes Antonius Modestus, *Oratio ad Carolem Caesarem contra Martinum Lutherum*.

22. Ibid., Aiii.

23. Aloysius Marlianus's *Oratio ad Carolem Caesarem* went through at least four editions, apparently quite rapidly, but none except the (last ?) Leipzig edition carries a date of publication (1522). However, we know from Aleander's correspondence that Marlianus was working on it in December 1520. See Lauchert, *Italienischen Gegner*, 223.

24. Marlianus, *Oratio*, esp. Aiii.

25. Cremoniensis, *Revocatio Martini Lutherii Augustiniani ad sanctam sedem*.

was first published, but who had been unable to participate in the earlier exchanges through difficulties in getting his work published. His companion pieces *Paraclesis* and *A Pious Exhortation* were written as appeals to Germany from the personified Rome.[26] Composed originally during Adrian VI's pontificate to celebrate the accession of a German pope, the two pamphlets reminded Germany of her debt to her glorious past, her debt to her equally glorious future, and above all her debt to Rome, her mother in the faith. By the time these two publications came off the press, however, events had overtaken them. The Peasants' War was now raging, and the Catholic controversialists Emser, Cochlaeus, Sylvius, Johannes Fundling, and Hieronymus Dungersheim lost no time in reminding the public that their predictions of violent revolution had at last come true—predictions which had been made on the basis of such inflammatory treatises as *To the Christian Nobility*.[27]

26. Johannes Cochlaeus, *Ad semper victricem Germaniam, Iohannis Cochlei paraclesis; ut pristinae constantiae fidei & virtutis memor, insolentissima Lutheranorum factione ab dictata in errores se abduci non patratur;* idem., *Pia exhortatio Romae ad Germaniam, suam in fide Christi filiam, per Johannem Cochleum,* translated as *Ein Christliche vermanung der heyligen stat Rom an das Teütschlandt yr Tochter im Christlichen glauben. Durch Johannem Cochleum. Verteütscht durch Doctor Johannem Dietenberger* (Tübingen: U. Morhart, 1524). (Because of publishing delays, Cochlaeus's original appeared after Dietenberger's translation.) A similar but less academic contribution was the anonymous (by "J.H.F.") *Warnung und ermanung der Christelichen Kirchen zw Germanien irer Dochter* (1526), which I have not taken into account.

27. Hieronymus Emser, *Auff Luthers grewel wider die heiligen Stillmess. Antwort. Item wie / wo / und mit wolchen worten Luther yhn seyn buchern tzur auffrur ermandt / geschriben und getriben hat;* Johannes Cochlaeus, *Adversus latrocinantes et raptorias Cohortes Rusticorum. Mar. Lutherus. Responsio Cochlaei Vuendelstini. Cathalogus tumultuum & praeliorum in superiore Germania nuper gestorum. CXXXII articuli excerpti ex seditioso et impio libro Martini Lutheri contra ecclesiasticos. Responsio brevis Iohannis Cochlaei ad singulos;* Petrus Sylvius, *Eyn Missive ader Sendbrieff an die Christliche Versammlunge und ssonderlich and die oberkeit Deutzscher Nation zu wegern den unthergang irer herschafft / und das iemmerlich verterbnis der Christenheit / Eym iden so durch tzeitlichen und ewigen friden / seyn leib und tzele sucht zu bewaren nutzlich und itzt nothafftig tzu erfarn und zu lesen;* Johannes Fundling, *Anzaigung zwayer falschen zungen des Luthers wie er mit der ainen die paurn verfüret / mit dem andern sy verdammet hat / durch Admiratum den Wunderer, genant Johann Fundling;* Hieronymus von Dungersheim, *Multilocus de concitata seditione ex dictis Lutheri p. d. Hie. q. supp. in futurorum cautelam, recollectus.* Luther's appeal to the Christian nobility was cited at this time most notably in Emser, *Stillmess,* Bi, Bii^v, Ci; Dungersheim, *Multiloquus,* 16, 23; Sylvius, *Deutzscher Nation,* Aiii.

On German Catholic literature relating to Luther's supposed role in bringing about the revolt, see M. U. Edwards, Jr., "*Lutherschmähung*? Catholics on Luther's Responsibility for the Peasants' War."

The Romanist Counter-Appeal

The controversialists who decided to write against *To the Christian Nobility* were in a difficult position. Luther had identified himself with the movements for ecclesiastical reform and against curial intervention in Germany. It must therefore have seemed that anyone who opposed him stood for the continuance of abuses and subjugation to Italy. Indeed, had the controversialists simply adopted their usual tactic of refuting Luther in detailed open letters, they might well have embroiled themselves in a tedious and unattractive defense of the Curia's record. But because they imitated in many cases the genre Luther used, an appeal to the emperor, they were able to present an aggressive case for the prosecution against Luther.

We can examine this case in more detail by considering their response to the two issues with which *To the Christian Nobility* was concerned—secular authority and anti-Italianism. First, as Luther's call for a lay-convoked council could be interpreted as an appeal to princely self-interest, so the Romanists attempted to demonstrate the importance to secular rule of suppressing a man and a movement that had already proven themselves thoroughly anti-authoritarian in spiritual matters. Moreover, they reminded the aristocracy that the general council convoked by the German laity that Luther had demanded had already taken place, and when the Council of Constance met, it condemned in the person of Huss the very doctrines Luther wanted them to endorse. Second, as Luther had attempted to use nationalist and anti-Italian sentiment against the Roman Church, so its defenders in turn questioned Luther's credentials as a patriot: they reminded their readers that Luther's doctrines had been borrowed from foreigners—Wycliffe and Huss—and that he treacherously encompassed the dissolution of his country's bonds with Rome, which by virtue of the Holy Roman Empire had guaranteed Germany's domination of the world.

The Catholic Appeal to the Nobility

The Romanist argument that Luther's opposition to spiritual authority also threatened secular authority was established in two ways. The Italian authors Marlianus and Modestus maintained that, since the emperor derived his power from the pope, any diminution of the latter's majesty necessarily affected the former's. "He brands even Your Imperial Highness with a not inconsiderable mark of ignominy.

For whosoever opposes the Pontiff opposes Caesar, whose chief responsibilities are not only to revere and respect the Pontiff, but also to ensure the strict observance of all that touches his power."[28]

Nevertheless, this was not an argument generally employed by the controversialists. Their more usual approach was to argue that all authority, whether ecclesiastical or civil, is essentially the same. The Italian Rhadinus reminded his readers that Luther had already denied Peter and his successors the right to guide his flock, determine the truth, and settle disputes. Rhadinus believed this to be a dangerous precedent. "He will eventually withdraw from every prince the right to exercise judgment, pass sentences, enforce settlements, or promulgate laws, and will contend that all things pertain to all people. And he will come to reject punishment, and will free everyone from the rule of law, and the evil and wicked from fear of the same, and will give them the very worst kind of liberty."[29]

The Germans Emser and Murner were more alarmed at the consequences for secular authority of Luther's doctrine of the universal priesthood. On the basis of St. Peter's description of the church as a royal priesthood, Luther had predicated the priesthood of all believers. Since the apostle goes on to describe the church as a holy kingdom, does this imply, they wondered, "the kingship of all subjects"?[30] Luther had argued that the special priesthood was merely the holding of a public office (*ampt*), which implied no distinction of status (*stand*) from any other Christian. But, objected Murner,

> It follows from this that neither is there any estate of the nobility, but a lord is simply chosen to exercise an authority, and if he lays aside this office, he becomes again the peasant or citizen he had been before assuming the office. But I know well enough that Luther's assertion that there is no noble estate will displease the aristocracy as much as the spiritual estate is annoyed by the suggestion that everyone is a priest or priestess.[31]

28. Modestus, *Oratio*, Aiii. Lauchert summarized Marlianus's position thus: "The Germans have obtained the empire from the pope; whosoever now attacks the pope's authority casts doubt upon the legal basis of the empire; the papacy and empire are so interdependent that they stand or fall together" (*Italienischen Gegner*, 229).

29. Rhadinus, *Oratio*, Ii. Cf. Kilian Leib, *Endschafft und frucht*, Bif.

30. Murner, *Tütscher nation*, Ciii^v; Emser, *Vorlegung*, Ciii.

31. Murner, *Tütscher nation*, Dif. Emser also balked at the suggestion of an "official" distinction only between priests and lay people: "For a real distinction exists between the spiritual and the secular, not only in respect of office, but also in respect of status. The office is consequent upon the status, not the status upon the office" (*Vorlegung*, Ciii).

The controversialists' belief in the basic continuity of all forms of authority was founded on their conviction that order, which brings peace and harmony, is the fundamental characteristic of God's universe. A proof-text frequently cited in defense of ecclesiastical as much as civil dispensations was the Vulgate rendering of Rom. 13:1, "For there is no power except from God, and whatever powers come from God are ordered."[32] Initiating a long succession of similar treatments by the controversialists (which will be discussed in more detail in chapter 5), Rhadinus demonstrated that the "most beautiful order" of higher and lower, of authority and obedience, of difference and inequality, was authorized by both divine and natural law.[33] Yet the proponents of reform seemed to the controversialists almost constitutionally unable to accept authority. "The Lutherans," Petrus Sylvius stated, "can no more stomach it than they can eat fire."[34] Sylvius wrote a pamphlet (unfortunately never published) in which he argued that any Lutheran who held any public office whatsoever contradicted himself, for Lutheranism and authority were incompatible.[35] The reformers'—and especially Luther's—apparent aversion to authority of any stripe would remain the Catholic controversialists' most self-evident proof of heresy in these first years of the Reformation.

In addition to demonstrating the implications for the emperor's power of Luther's assault on the status of his liege lord the pope, and the implications for secular authority as a whole of Luther's confusion of status and function, the controversialists also drew out the implicit anti-authoritarianism of his other doctrines. In Murner's view the very discussion of disputed doctrines in front of the laity would cause revolution. For instance, he argued, to debate publicly whether the pope alone had the right to convoke a council "would cause a revolt [*bundschu*] and a sudden, furious, and villainous uprising as much against the instigator himself as against others. And through libelous

---

32. "Non est potestas nisi a Deo; quae autem sunt a Deo, ordinatae sunt." *Ordinatus* was invariably used by the controversialists to mean "ordered" or "arranged," rather than "ordained." This was also the sense in which the text was employed in Boniface VIII's bull *Unam sanctam*, in which the superiority of the spiritual "sword" to the temporal was asserted thus: "But [these powers] cannot be ordered unless one sword is above the other" (*CICan* 1:1245). For the history of the interpretation of this text, see G. Scharffenorth, "Römer 13. in der Geschichte des politischen Denkens" (Ph.D. diss., Heidelberg, 1962).

33. Rhadinus, *Oratio*, Hi; Murner, *Tütscher nation*, Dii^v.

34. Sylvius, *Deutzscher nation*, Cii^v.

35. Ibid., Bii.

pamphlets and all manner of public insults, authority [*oberkeit*] will come to be held in low esteem."[36]

For Emser, one of Luther's most serious crimes was to suggest in *To the Christian Nobility* that vows of pilgrimage or religion could be broken for conscience's sake.[37] In Emser's view society was based on the keeping of promises, particularly oaths of obedience to higher authorities: "Dear Germans, Luther says that we should be free in perpetuity from all human law. That rhymes with 'Bundschuh'!"[38] In fact, the controversialists continued to draw out the anti-authoritarian implications of each of Luther's doctrines almost as they were formulated. In his own address "to the Christian authorities of the German nation" in 1525, Sylvius detailed the nature of the threat to secular authority posed by Luther's fundamentals: the doctrine of justification by faith alone would lead men and women to live like pigs and wild wolves, "bereft of all Christian discipline and order"; the Scripture principle would elevate the Gospel above present-day government, both spiritual and temporal; and Luther's contempt for traditional church order, bad enough in itself, was yet more threatening to secular constitutions, which were, of course, less clearly authorized by Scripture alone.[39]

It was one thing to accuse Luther of posing an implicit threat to political authority. It was quite another to prove it, particularly because, for the moment at least, he held out to the emperor and the princes the possibility of extending that authority by summoning a general council of the church. But it was precisely at this point, the controversialists argued, that his presumptuousness was most blatant: the council convoked by the emperor and noblemen of Germany had taken place a hundred years before, when the doctrines Luther now attempted to revive had been condemned outright; to demand its supersession was an insult as much to the intelligence of the reigning aristocracy as to the blessed memory of their ancestors.

The Council of Constance was something of an embarrassment to the papalist theologians who opposed Luther. As the council that had condemned and executed Huss, it was a weighty proof that Luther's teachings and his known Hussite sympathies were incompat-

---

36. Murner, *Tütscher nation*, Fi^v.
37. *WA* 6:437–43.
38. Emser, *Vorlegung*, Miii^v; see also Hiv^v, Ji, Lii, Liii, Miii, Miv.
39. Sylvius, *Deutzscher Nation*, Ai^v–ii^v.

ible with the faith of the church. At the same time, a council that had been summoned primarily to judge rival claims to the papacy could scarcely be described as a papal—and therefore a true—council. Luther's appeal in *To the Christian Nobility* for a council convoked by the laity within imperial territories resolved this dilemma overnight, for whatever else Constance may or may not have been, it was certainly that. Johannes Eck immediately seized the opportunity thus presented. His *Defense of the Sacred Council* had three goals: to demonstrate Luther's inconsistency concerning lay-convoked councils; to refute his suggestion that Huss and Hieronymus of Prague had been burned to death at Constance in violation of their safe conducts; and to prove *To the Christian Nobility* deviant in every particular from traditional *bürgerlich* and *fürstlich* virtues, leaving the reader in no doubt of the dire consequences for public order of such a pamphlet. Under a series of headings, Eck showed that Luther was opposed to peace, humility, truth, obedience;[40] the moral use of force, moderation, justice;[41] patience, constancy, mercy.[42] Within the space of just thirteen pages, Eck clearly did not intend to establish an exhaustive case against Luther. All his paragraphs began with some such disclaimer as "Ich lass stehen" or "Ich geschweich über," and one is left with the distinct impression that the author was more interested in making serious allegations of anarchy before the country's ruling classes than in substantiating them.

Catholic Attitudes to Nationality

By reasserting the validity of the Council of Constance and emphasizing the thoroughgoing anti-authoritarianism of Luther's doctrines, the controversialists attempted to counter one aspect of *To the Christian Nobility*, its appeal to the competence of the lay nobility. But the treatise contained another equally important appeal, to German nationalist and anti-Italian sentiment. How did the controversialists cope with the accusation that loyalty to the Roman Church necessarily implied disloyalty to Germany?

The Italian apologists were, of course, in a peculiarly difficult position, and their responses differed markedly. Bishop Marlianus's *Oratio* indicated that Italian snobbery, which had built up such

40. Eck, *Entschüldigung*, Aii–iv^v.
41. Ibid., Aiv^v–Bi.
42. Ibid., Bif.

resentment in fifteenth- and sixteenth-century Germany, was far from dead. In a heavily ironic passage, he dismissed the claim that German humanism equaled Italian mastery of letters, seeing it instead as a destructive force that now threatened the religion of Rome.[43] More moderate positions were represented by Catharinus and the Cremonian author. Catharinus argued that the issue of German-Italian rivalry was simply a device introduced by Luther to win over the unsophisticated. National differences, he continued, were irrelevant to Christianity: "We are divided by mountains, not by the faith which can move them."[44] The Cremonian praised the majesty of the German nation with no hint of irony but denied that the better sort had any intention of following Luther "into Bohemia."[45] Even outright German jingoism found a voice in Rhadinus, the Piacenzan nobleman of German descent, who excoriated Luther at some length as an unworthy son of a nation ever famed for its piety and glory.[46]

If Italian apologists were in a difficult position in justifying the ways of the Curia to German nationalists, German apologists of the Roman Church were surely in an impossible position. How could they convincingly dispel the inevitable suspicions of their treachery? The defense they adopted was to challenge Luther's own credentials as a German patriot, which they did in two ways. The more ambitious option was taken by Cochlaeus. In two addresses to the German nation published in 1524–25, *A Pious Exhortation* and the *Paraclesis*, he argued that any true German would naturally support the empire, by which God had guaranteed the fatherland dominion over all the world. This same empire was the result of a special relationship between Germany and Rome. Luther's revolt threatened that relationship. To call the pope Antichrist, argued Cochlaeus, was to invalidate the reigns of all anointed emperors from Charles the Great to Charles V. It was to un-church all German princes and their subjects, to deny their authority to draft and enforce laws or to exact taxes. No true German could call Huss blessed, or deny Germany the glory of its empire, or dismiss the translation of the empire as a snare of Antichrist. Like the traitor he was, Luther reserved his praise for those nations that, unlike his

---

43. Marlianus, *Oratio*, Aii.
44. Catharinus, *Apologia*, 33.
45. Cremoniensis, *Revocatio*, Eiv^v.
46. Rhadinus, *Oratio*, Aiv, Bi^v.

own, had thrown off obedience to Rome, even those who were Germany's traditional enemies. "Who cannot but suspect these calumniators (when they display so degenerate and evil a nature) of being not true Germans but rather Saxo-Bohemians and treacherous enemies of their country? For they deny that their own country is worthy of the Roman empire even as they assert the worth of others."[47] A German nationalist worth the name would, Cochlaeus believed, of necessity be an imperialist, and an upholder of the Holy Roman Empire was by definition a champion of the holy Roman Church.[48]

Cochlaeus's complex challenge to Luther's right of appeal to German national feeling was unsuitable for propaganda purposes and was not explicitly adopted by other controversialists. They preferred the simpler tactic of showing that the reformer who was so concerned to exclude foreign elements from German Christianity had borrowed his own doctrines from the arch-foreigner Jan Huss. Luther's sympathy with the Bohemian cause had been public knowledge since Leipzig. In *To the Christian Nobility*, he had continued his advocacy by raising a question over the legality of executing Huss, who had been granted safe conduct to Constance, and by urging the recognition of the Hussites' right to receive communion in both kinds.[49] Such a step confirmed his opponents' suspicions. In Eck's view Luther's questioning of the manner of Huss's execution was an attempt to cast doubt on all Constance's decisions and so to preserve Luther's adopted heresy from condemnation.[50] According to Murner, Luther was exploiting the valid grievances of the German nation as a pretext for substituting Wycliffite and Hussite heterodoxy for the Catholic faith.[51] Emser, whose debut on the stage of controversy had been in an open letter designed to dispel suspicion that Luther had defended Huss at Leip-

---

47. Cochlaeus, *Paraclesis*, Gi; cf. Cvif., Dii^v. Cochlaeus tried to remind his readers of Luther's treacherous "beatitudes" from his preface to Prierias's *Epitoma responsionis* of 1520: "Blessed are the Greeks, blessed are the Bohemians, blessed are all who have cut themselves off from Rome" (*WA* 6:329). Cf. Cochlaeus, *Christliche vermanung*, Aiii, Fi, Liii^v; idem, *Paraclesis*, Gviii^v.

48. "There are many who gnash their teeth when they hear the words 'holy Roman Church,' but to whom the title 'Holy Roman Empire' is most pleasing. Is that not downright prejudice?" (Johannes Cochlaeus, *Von der Donation des Keysers Constantini* [1537], Ciii^v).

49. *WA* 6:454–57, LW 44:195–200.

50. Eck, *Entschüldigung*, Biii.

51. See W. Kawerau, *Thomas Murner und die deutsche Reformation*, 31.

zig, now wrote to expose the "Bohemian flame of schism" that *To the Christian Nobility* had rekindled.[52] Even the Italian controversialists, who might reasonably be expected to have been less concerned with the Czech question, based their fears for the future upon it.[53]

To understand the potency of the accusation of "Bohemianism," we must remember that it was more than just a technical term used by theologians. Rather, it triggered a series of associations and reverberations within the German national consciousness, of treachery as much as heresy, of social disorder and border clashes as much as schism. Above all, "Bohemia" was the very quintessence of what was foreign to Germany. The map of Germany drawn by Erhard Etzlaub in 1512 illustrates the point—Bohemia is depicted as an area *within* Germany but ringed about with formidable peaks and forests. It was no distant threat; rather it evoked that mixture of hatred, fear, and fascination reserved for the enemy within. This feeling was expressed by Cochlaeus, in a geography textbook published in the same year:

> The Bohemians are surrounded on all sides by German peoples, but they themselves do not speak German. . . . The region itself is defended by the might of noblemen, innumerable fortresses, and even the very forest, so that it is impossible to root out this treacherous progeny of heretics who—in addition to their other thoroughly abominable and execrable practices—even frequent public baths, where they defile themselves in promiscuity.[54]

The charge of "disseminating the Bohemian virus" was made against Luther within a few months of the publication of the Ninety-five Theses,[55] and it was repeated thereafter in almost every tract written against him. (In chapter 6, the implications of comparing Luther with past heretics in general will be examined in more detail.) The specific charge of "Bohemianism," especially from Luther's fellow countrymen, had undertones of foreignness and social eversion that the "Christian nobility of the German nation" could not fail to hear. Emser and Cochlaeus in particular, who were among the most prolific of all the controversialists, consistently equated the revolutionary aims of Karsthans and the Bundschuh with Bohemianism. "When your

52. Emser, *An den Stier*, Aiii.
53. See, e.g., Modestus, *Oratio*, Biii.
54. Johannes Cochlaeus, *Brevis Germanie descriptio*, ed. K. Langosch, 110, 112. (The Langosch edition also contains a reprint of the Etzlaub map.)
55. Eck, *Obelisci* 17 (*WA* 1:302).

Karsthans-ish Bundschuh gets the upper hand, civilization will have to give way to the politics of wild beasts. Then there will be no law, no justice, and no order: just snatching, tearing, and killing. It has already happened in Bohemia, thanks to this Hussite teaching."[56]

Cochlaeus was aware of the jingoism the charge could arouse. The Taborites, he wrote, had been Germany's most vicious enemies in seven hundred years, who had put parts of the fatherland to fire and the sword and slaughtered indiscriminately without regard for age, sex, or class. "Therefore I now declare in public what hitherto I have mentioned only privately; that if any German says that Johann Huss was not a heretic, and was thus wrongly condemned and burned at Constance, he is to be rightly and justly considered an enemy and a traitor to our country."[57]

Bohemianism was the earliest and most enduring accusation made by the Catholic controversialists against Luther and his followers. It had the virtues of simplicity and of carrying with it a range of associations so wide as to affect many sections of society and so negative as to poison their minds against the reformers almost without the need of proof. The most celebrated and dramatic example is the case of Duke Georg of Saxony at the Leipzig disputation of 1519, who was instantly converted from a sympathizer to a sworn enemy on hearing Luther give Huss qualified support. Duke Georg (whose grandfather, the Utraquist King Georg Podiebrad, had died excommunicate) had more reason than most for fearing Bohemianism, but his violent reaction must have indicated to the controversialists the strength of feeling such an accusation could evoke.[58] It was therefore among the most powerful weapons in their propaganda armory.

Spiritual and Temporal Authority

In *To the Christian Nobility*, Luther had identified his own cause with German nationalism and the extension of princely jurisdiction in ecclesiastical affairs. In response, the Romanist pamphleteers turned the tables by representing Luther as a danger to the German nation

---

56. Cochlaeus, *Uff CLIIII Artikeln*, Ei, Aii, Bii, oiiiv; idem, *Adversus cucullatum minotaurum*, 18, 44; idem, *Auff den xiii Artikel*, Bi^v; Emser, *Vorlegung*, Ci^v, Miii^v.

57. Cochlaeus, *Paraclesis*, Dii^v.

58. An eyewitness, Sebastian Fröschel, has left us a graphic description of the duke's reaction: "Then Duke Georg said in a loud voice, out loud, so that he could be heard throughout the hall, 'He is obsessed,' and shook his head, and thrust his hands in his pockets. I heard and saw the whole thing" (Walch 15:1430).

and to the rule of its nobility, their defense laying considerably greater emphasis on establishing the latter point. It might surprise us that the Catholic controversialists, clerics almost to a man, should have spilled so much ink in defense of secular authority. It might have been more understandable for them to have interpreted *To the Christian Nobility* as a theological justification for secular encroachment upon spiritual affairs and consequently to have written in support of the princes of the church.[59] From this point of view, their championing of the princes of the world against Luther suggests opportunism on their part. Such a view is unjustified. Although there certainly was some special pleading, such an emphasis was entirely consistent with their attitude to authority in general. Contrary perhaps to our expectations, the controversialists did not classify men and women primarily by their ecclesiastical status, by whether they were clerical or lay, but by whether or not they exercised authority.

The Romanists' view of order as God's will for the universe meant that they believed in the continuity of all types of authority and all types of obedience.[60] The homogeneity of authority meant, for instance, that the existence of monarchy as the oldest and purest form of secular rule was considered a sound argument for papal monarchy.[61] The homogeneity of obedience meant that there was an intimate connection between theological heresy and political insurrection. Such a connection appeared to be confirmed by history. The Peasants' Revolt followed swiftly on the heels of Wycliffe's teaching, and the Bohemian heresy ushered in the bloody Hussite wars.[62] Even earlier examples of the equation between heterodoxy and revolution could be found, for instance among the Donatists.[63] Schism and civil war were simply two sides of the same coin, two manifestations of an essentially spiritual disorder, namely, a lack of love.[64] Needless to say, when the Peasants'

59. Dungersheim, e.g., interpreted *To the Christian Nobility* this way (*Multiloquus,* 16), but it was very much a minority tactic.
60. In addition to the examples cited above, note the later pamphlets prompted by the Peasants' War, such as Dungersheim's *Multiloquus:* "Luther strives to overturn, destroy, and utterly annihilate, in the name of the gospel, the peace and love of the gospel, every kind of order, and the most beautiful appearance [*facies*] of the whole Church" (p. 10). See also Emser, *Stillmess,* Aiii, Aiv^v.
61. E.g. Modestus, *Oratio,* Aiiii^v; Sylvius, *Deutzscher Nation,* Aiv.
62. Cochlaeus, *Christliche vermanung,* Eii^v–iv.
63. Ibid., Giv^v.
64. "Sedition is a crime against love" (Dungersheim, *Multiloquus,* 7); "Nothing can be more harmful to society than sedition, especially heretical sedition" (p. 26). Behind this interpretation may lie Aquinas's classification of the sin against charity into

War broke out in 1524, the controversialists considered themselves entirely vindicated. Emser and Dungersheim reviewed Luther's publications from the time of the indulgence controversy to the present, picking out supposedly inflammatory statements and showing what little wonder it was that the rabble had finally risen against lord and priest alike.[65] They were joined by Sylvius and Fundling, who accused Luther of two-facedness in first urging rebellion and then betraying the very peasants he had roused.[66]

The Romanists' belief in the fundamental unity of authority allowed them to tolerate a considerable overlap of the spiritual and worldly spheres of interest. We find repeatedly, in the lists of theological authorities cited by the controversialists against Luther, the names of kings and emperors.[67] Emperor Constantine's initiative in summoning and presiding at Nicaea (the first council of the post-apostolic era) and Emperor Sigmund's at Constance (the "German council") were held up as examples for modern Christian rulers much more by the Romanists than by the reformers, notwithstanding Luther's appeal in *To the Christian Nobility*. Certainly there was nothing unusual or innovative in Luther's call for a council convoked by the higher laity, despite Lateran V's very recent declaration that a general council could be summoned by no one but the pope. And of course the right remained with respect to local councils. When in 1518 Duke Georg of Saxony requested the Leipzig theology faculty to arrange a debate between Luther and Eck to "discover the truth," they replied without any discernible embarrassment (though with some tactical maneuvering) that a debate would increase confusion whereas the duke, through his right of summoning a synod of local bishops, abbots, and university representatives, held the power of settling the Luther affair once and for all.[68] Moreover, it is remarkable that no hint of unease was expressed publicly when Georg and Henry VIII turned

---

the sin by thought (*discordia*), by word (*contentio*), and by deed (*seditio*). See *Summa theologiae*, 2a, 2ae, qu. 39.

65. Emser, *Stillmess*; and Dungersheim, *Multiloquus*.

66. Sylvius, *Deutzscher Nation*; and Fundling, *Zwayer zungen*.

67. Dietenberger, *Von menschen leren*, Ei; Cochlaeus, *Adversus cucullatum minotaurum*, 17; idem, *Auff den xiii Artikel*, Biiff.; Blich, *Verderbe*, Ci^v; Campester, *Heptacolon*, Eiii^v. When Cochlaeus came to write his literary biography of Luther in 1547, it is significant that he chose to conclude it with the text of the Edict of Worms and not the papal bull of excommunication (*Commentaria*, 327–39).

68. See the letter from the Leipzig faculty to Duke Georg, 26 December 1518 (Gess 1, no. 63).

their hands to writing theological works against Luther. Instead, their fellow controversialists applauded the fact that princes nowadays defended the faith as much by the pen as by the sword.[69]

The *Realpolitik* of the Romanists' Pamphlets

The enormous contemporary popularity of Luther's *To the Christian Nobility* and the significance with which historians have since invested it have completely eclipsed the pamphlets printed against it by Roman loyalists in both Germany and Italy. Even modern Roman Catholic scholars have refused this literature the attention they have given to more properly "theological" works. This neglect is unfortunate, for in these pamphlets the controversialists demonstrated a high degree of skill in attempting to counteract Luther's appeal to anti-curialism and German nationalism, and in doing so revealed much about their beliefs and methods.

Luther had invited the German princes to summon a council once he realized, partly as a result of the divine right debate, that the papacy could not itself be expected to initiate reform. In the course of that debate, the Catholic controversialists had drawn upon the writings of earlier theorists of papal monarchy such as Juan de Torquemada and Augustine of Ancona to argue the pope's superiority to a council. When Luther combined his conciliarist call with an appeal to temporal authority, therefore, they might reasonably have been expected to assert the pope's superiority to emperor and princes as well. This superiority had been established as a belief "necessary to salvation" by Boniface VIII's bull *Unam sanctam* in 1302, which had conflated the Gospel accounts of Jesus's arrest to argue that Peter possessed two swords, representing the spiritual and temporal powers. Furthermore, the bull stated, the spiritual sword is above the temporal sword even as spiritual things are higher than temporal things, so that, as the Apostle says, "the spiritual man judges all things but is himself judged by no one."[70] Although the bull itself bore little relation to the actual political situation obtaining between the papacy and the crowned heads of Christendom, its theoretical basis might still have retained

---

69. See, e.g., Johannes Dietenberger, preface to *De votis monasticis*, ai[v].
70. *Unam sanctam* was issued on 18 November 1302 in the course of Boniface's struggle with King Philip IV of France over clerical taxation rights. For the full text, see *CICan* 2:1245f.; for an abbreviated version, see *DS*, 870–75.

some force two centuries later. This basis had been worked out by Giles of Rome, the general of the Augustinian order and drafter of the bull. In 1301, he had published a much fuller apology for papal supremacy entitled *Ecclesiastical Power*. Here Giles had formulated his belief in a universal monarchy in which the temporal estate is subordinate to the spiritual (even as the body is subject to the soul) and in which both are subordinate to the pope.[71]

Of the controversialists, we indeed find that the Italian writers Marlianus and Modestus, with Prierias before them, adopt *Unam sanctam*'s subordination theory, enabling them to argue cogently that because the emperor held his power from the pope, an attack on the pope was also an attack on the emperor. The majority of controversialists (including all the German writers), however, eschewed this theory for one not nearly so well-founded as a dogma of the church. This was the theory that the spiritual and temporal estates existed side by side as equal—or at least parallel—powers, so that with the pope paramount in one sphere and the king in the other, there was no immediate question of competition. Using such a model, the controversialists were able to argue that an attack on the pope was an attack on the emperor, not because one was the liege of another but because both powers were equally established by God and blessed with his *ordinatio*, or "ordering." This was the theory held for a time by Aquinas, and even by such royal apologists as John of Paris, another thirteenth-century Dominican; it was the theory that *Unam sanctam* itself had refuted in its insistence that there was just one divine ordinance and not two;[72] and it is arguable that it contributed to the development of Luther's doctrine of the "two kingdoms."

Bearing in mind their tactics in the divine right and eucharistic controversies, it is most surprising to find the Romanists deliberately ignoring a bull that declared papal supremacy an article of faith. There are a number of possible explanations. The first and most obvious is that an appeal to the German nobility on the grounds of their inferiority to the pope would not have been too compelling. Or perhaps the explanation is a more mundane one. The theoretical basis of *Unam*

---

71. See B. Tierney, *The Crisis of Church and State 1050–1300* (Englewood Cliffs, N.J.: Prentice-Hall, 1964), 198–99.

72. *Unam sanctam* (*DS*, 874). For earlier champions of the "parallel" theory, see A. Gewirth, *Marsilius of Padua: The Defender of Peace*, vol. 1, *Marsilius of Padua and Medieval Political Philosophy* (New York: Columbia University Press, 1952), 9.

sanctam had been set out by its author more than two hundred years earlier, in a treatise that had not been reprinted or resurrected in controversy in the intervening years. By contrast, in the divine right controversy the Romanists were able to quarry useful arguments out of treatises barely forty years old. Their apparent neglect of arguments for the dominance of the spiritual sword might simply be due to the absence of suitable "off-the-peg" treatments. This suggestion is not really borne out. It is true that Torquemada's trenchant refutation of conciliarism, the *Summa de ecclesia*, had been reprinted at Cologne in 1480 and possibly even more recently, and that this presumably explains Catharinus's and Rhadinus's acquaintance with it. However, such champions of the papacy's temporal claims as Augustine of Ancona were also being published at the same time, and *Unam sanctam* itself had been resurrected for use against the reigning French king, Francis I, as recently as Lateran V.[73]

The more likely explanation is therefore that German Catholics in the sixteenth century had adopted a theological *Realpolitik*, with the result that the majority of controversialists were quite happy to assert papal absolutist claims with respect to councils because conciliarism was by then a spent force, but were not prepared to defend the absolutism of *Unam sanctam* because it was clear that the argument for royal supremacy had succeeded. Be this as it may, their use of the "parallel" theory of spiritual and temporal power was certainly a propaganda victory. On the one hand, it cut the ground from beneath Luther's contention that the Roman Church had elevated the spiritual estate above the temporal; on the other hand, used in conjunction with their belief that all forms of authority were connected, it was still an effective way of interpreting an attack on one sword as an attack on both.

No less remarkable were the tactics adopted by the controversialists in trying to establish for German Catholics the better claim to patriotism. Cochlaeus's attempt to identify the true patriot with the holy Roman imperialist cannot be considered a success, for it was certainly not taken up by his colleagues. Moreover, it represented a complete about-face on the author's part. In 1512, while still a schoolmaster in Nuremberg, Cochlaeus had the distinction of writing the

---

73. Augustine of Ancona's *Summa de potestate ecclesiastica* was published at Augsburg in 1474, at Rome in 1479, and at Venice in 1487. See M.J. Wilks, *The Problem of Sovereignty in the Later Middle Ages: The Papal Monarchy with Augustinus Triumphus and the Publicists* (Cambridge: Cambridge University Press, 1963).

first historical geography of Germany, the *Brief Description of Germany*.[74] In addition to being an educational publication, it also had a polemical purpose. It described the progress of Germany's civilization after its conversion to Christianity as an *incrementum*, an advance in degree but not in kind.[75] This was a pointed criticism of Aeneas Sylvius Piccolomini (the Italian humanist later to become Pope Pius II), who in a tract published in 1457 had lavished praise upon Germany's post-conversion achievements in order to emphasize the debt it owed to Rome as the source of its good fortune. The flattering prose of this prince of humanists had the immediate effect of promoting the nationalist cause in Germany among moderates such as Conrad Celtis and Heinrich Bebel. But the more radical, anti-Italian nationalists such as Jakob Wimpheling and Franciscus Irenicus began to bridle at such a patronizing attitude.[76] Three years before Wimpheling's famous belated riposte to Sylvius, Cochlaeus took up the challenge on his fatherland's behalf by portraying its pre-Christian history as worthy of praise in its own right. So in 1512, Cochlaeus had in his *Brief Description* aligned himself with the most radical nationalists of his day, and had gone further than them in attempting to indoctrinate the German youth with patriotic history. But by the time he returned to this subject in 1523, he had gone over to the Sylvian view: Germany, he argued, owed everything to Rome and (here he went beyond Sylvius) would realize its glorious destiny only if it remained loyal to Rome.[77] Cochlaeus had already been ostracized by his nationalist humanist colleagues when he resolved to take priest's orders in Rome in 1518. The change of heart represented by the *Paraclesis* and *A Pious Exhortation* over against his earlier *Brief Description* would have served only to make him more obnoxious to German nationalists. (Indeed, it

74. For a more detailed examination of the relation of this early work to Cochlaeus's later appeals to the German nation, see my article, "'Teutschlandt uber alle welt': Nationalism and Catholicism in Early Reformation Germany," *ARG* 82 (1991).

75. Cochlaeus, *Descriptio*, chap. 3, par. 1, which he titled "The Advance of Germans under the Christian Faith" (p. 62).

76. For extracts from Aeneas Sylvius and Wimpheling, see G. R. Strauss, *Manifestations of Discontent in Germany on the Eve of the Reformation* (Bloomington: Indiana University Press, 1972), 40–48.

77. The dramatic alteration of Cochlaeus's opinions is exemplified by his differing accounts of the famous defeat of Varus's legions by Arminius. In the *Descriptio*, Arminius's achievement was magnified as a victory over Augustus's "finest legions" (*Descriptio*, chap. 1, par. 6); but in the *Paraclesis* it was played down, the legions now being described as "far from home, quarrelling among themselves and under a vacillating leader" (Eiif.).

is ironic that the Italian author Rhadinus, who lauded the religion of
pagan Germany in an attempt to criticize the irreligion that currently
prevailed, proved himself a more credible German nationalist than the
later Cochlaeus!)[78]

The case of Cochlaeus shows that the controversialists were not
on safe ground in appealing to patriotism. To have done so would
inevitably have implied the fragmentation of the essentially supra-
national Roman Church. Cochlaeus's ingenious solution of using the
Holy Roman Empire as a focus for loyalty to both Germany and Rome
misfired, because the idea of the empire was no longer taken seriously.
It says much for the good sense of the controversialists in general that
they refused to follow Cochlaeus's lead. They were more likely to
meet with success by pointing out the foreignness of Luther's own
doctrines. And it was in their accusation of Bohemianism that the
controversialists found not only an effective and accessible indictment
of the reformer, but also one that encapsulated their belief in Luther's
twofold threat: to the Christian nobility and to the German nation.

78. See, e.g., Rhadinus, *Oratio*, Aiv.

PART THREE

THE AUTHORITY OF
THE CHURCH,
1520–1525

5

THE CHURCH IN
CAPTIVITY

When Erasmus diagnosed Luther's case as incurable,[1] he was expressing a view shared by friends and foes alike that Luther's *Prelude on the
Babylonian Captivity of the Church* represented a new and irrevocable
step away from Rome. The number of Catholic defenses of the sacraments in general and of the mass in particular that followed it was
second only to that produced in defense of the papacy. Luther had
certainly touched a raw nerve with his treatise, and an examination of
the controversialists' responses is a good way of determining which
nerve that was.

The sacramental system of the Roman Church was the meeting
place of the covenant between humankind and God. Here human
obligations were faithfully discharged; here the graces of justification,
satisfaction, and sanctification were distributed in return. The fulcrum
of this system was the priest. The indulgences controversy showed
how essential the Romanist writers considered the priest's role in sacramental confession. The threat posed by Luther's *Babylonian Captivity*
was in their opinion the further diminution of priestly power and
distinctiveness, for in denying the sacrificial nature of the mass, Luther
was denying the de jure foundation of the priesthood itself. Luther's
earlier writings had, they believed, challenged the authority of the

---

1. Erasmus to Ludwig Ber, 14 May 1521, in P. S. Allen and H. M. Allen, eds., *Opus
epistolarum Desiderii Erasmi Roterodami*, 12 vols. (Oxford: Clarendon Press, 1906–58) 4:494:
"et ecce incendium Decretalium, Captivitas Babylonica, Assertiones illae nimium fortes
reddiderunt malum, ut videtur, immedicabile." For the background to *The Babylonian
Captivity of the Church* and the controversialists' reaction to it, see esp. Iserloh, *Kampf um
die Messe*; idem, *Die Eucharistie in der Darstellung des Johannes Eck*; idem, "Der Wert der
Messe in den Diskussionen der Theologen vom Mittelalter bis zum 16. Jahrhundert";
H. Sasse, *This Is My Body: Luther's Contention for the Real Presence in the Sacrament of
the Altar* (Minneapolis: Augsburg Pub. House, 1959); F. Clark, *Eucharistic Sacrifice and the
Reformation*; H. B. Meyer, *Luther und die Messe*; L. Grane, "Luthers Kritik an Thomas von
Aquin in De captivitate Babylonica," *ZKG* 80 (1969), 1–13; U. Stock, *Die Bedeutung der
Sakramente in Luthers Sermonen von 1519*, Studies in the History of Christian Thought 27
(Leiden: E. J. Brill, 1982). For general background, see A. Franz, *Die Messe im deutschen
Mittelalter* (Freiburg, 1902; repr. Darmstadt: Wissenschaftliches Buchgesellschaft, 1963).

pope, the authority of the magisterial consensus, and the social order. *The Babylonian Captivity* went further and challenged the spiritual authority of the priest over his flock.

Luther's Sacramental Theology, 1517–1520

The Babylonian Captivity was not the first occasion on which Luther's sacramental theology had brought him into conflict with his opponents. As early as 1517 his questioning of indulgences had entailed a discussion of the right use and understanding of the sacrament of penance,[2] and in 1518 the imminent prospect of his own excommunication had concentrated his mind wonderfully on the significance of the mass.[3] Furthermore, Luther's interview at Augsburg showed how his emphasis on faith related to his current assessment of the worth of sacraments both *ex opere operando* and *ex opere operato*.

In a series of four sermons printed between October 1519 and July 1520—two on the mass and one each on baptism and penance— Luther gathered the fruits of his most recent reflections on the sacraments for the edification of a general audience.[4] Here he taught that a sacrament consists of three parts: the visible sign, the grace thus signified, and faith, which connects the two and enables the believer to receive sacramental grace. The sign of baptism, for instance, is immersion; its significance is the drowning of one's sinful nature and the raising of the believer into new life. The faith involved here is not the conviction that one is no longer sinful, but that God in his mercy no longer counts sin against one. In these sermons Luther closely related baptism and penance, on the grounds that God's promise of forgiveness refers to the future as much as the past and is not nullified by post-baptismal sin: "It is as if the priest, in absolution, were saying 'God himself has now forgiven you your sin, as he promised you long ago in baptism. And he has commanded me, through the power of the keys, to assure you of this forgiveness. Now you are returning to that

2. Luther, Ninety-five Theses, theses 1–3 (*WA* 1:233, *LW* 31:25).

3. Luther, *Sermo de virtute excommunicatione*, August 1518 (*WA* 1:638–43).

4. Luther, *Eyn Sermon von dem newen Testament, das ist von der heyligen Messe* (*WA* 6:353–78) = *A Treatise on the New Testament, That Is, the Holy Mass* (*LW* 35:[77], 79–111); *Eyn Sermon von dem Sacrament der Pusz* (*WA* 2:714–23) = *A Sermon on the Sacrament of Penance* (*LW* 35:[3], 9–22); *Eyn Sermon von dem heyligen hochwirdigen Sacrament der Tauffe* (*WA* 2:727–37) = *A Sermon on the Holy and Praiseworthy Sacrament of Baptism* (*LW* 35:[23], 29–43); and *Eyn Sermon von dem Hochwirdigen Sacrament, des heyligen waren leychnams Christi. Und von den Bruderschaften* (*WA* 2:742–58) = *The Blessed Sacrament of the Holy True Body of Christ, and of the Brotherhoods* (*LW* 35:[54], 49–73).

which baptism is and which baptism does. Believe, and it is yours. Doubt, and it is lost.' "[5] Since for Luther the sacrament's center of gravity lay within God's promise and not outside it (in the recipient's merit, for example, or in the priest's virtue), he could attribute the power of absolution not only to the priest but to any Christian.[6]

On penance, therefore, Luther's position was substantially the same in October 1519 as it had been eighteen months earlier, except that now he stressed its connection with baptism. His views on baptism, except insofar as they touched on penance, were unobjectionable—to judge from the silence of the Romanist opposition. It was on the subject of the mass that his thoughts were moving in a radical direction. In his first sermon on the mass, *The Blessed Sacrament*, he dealt with the nature of eucharistic fellowship. By partaking of the natural body and blood of Christ in the elements of bread and wine, he argued, the believer was made one with the mystical body of Christ, the communion of saints. The comparatively little polemic this sermon contained was directed almost entirely against the brotherhoods or sodalities, which made the sacrament of the altar their bond of association, yet excluded others from sharing in their spiritual and material benefits. For similar reasons Luther criticized the clergy, who in keeping communion wine from the laity were likewise expressing only a partial fellowship. His second sermon on the mass, *The New Testament or Holy Mass*, published July 1520, was much more pointed. In it, Luther claimed that modern ritual had completely obscured the true meaning of the sacrament, making it a good work (*sacrificium*) we do for God rather than God's gift (*beneficium*) to us. Here for the first time Luther set himself against the view dominant in medieval eucharistic theology, which saw the mass as a "representation" of Christ's sacrifice on Calvary, performed by the priest on the altar.[7]

By conflating the argument of these two sermons, we have a reasonably full picture of Luther's theology of the mass on the eve of writing *The Babylonian Captivity*, and we can see how rich and multifaceted this theology was. The most important part of the mass, he argued, were Christ's words of institution contained in the so-called

---

5. *WA* 2:733.32–36, *LW* 35:38.
6. *WA* 2:722.33, *LW* 35:12f.
7. A particularly influential statement of this view can be found in Aquinas: "The celebration of this sacrament . . . is a representative image of Christ's passion, which is the the true immolation" (*Summa theologiae* 3, qu. 83, art. 1).

silent canon. But far from being whispered out of a mistaken reverence, they should be loudly proclaimed to all the congregation. As a dying man indicates his bequest and nominates heirs through his last will and testament, so in his "blood of the new testament" Christ has bequeathed remission of sins, won by his sacrifice on the cross, and has named as his heirs whosoever would partake. Thus the words of institution are "the entire gospel in a short summary,"[8] and are accompanied by the sensible signs of bread and wine that the promise might be apprehended by all the believer's senses. There is indeed a sacrifice in the mass, but it is not we who offer up Christ. Rather, it is Christ who offers us up in his eternal sacrifice to the Father. Our contribution is entirely dependent on that: to offer through our praise and thanksgiving a sacrifice of all that we are, and to offer through almsgiving all that we have. By virtue of this restricted role, "all Christian men are priests, all women priestesses, be they young or old, master or servant, mistress or maid, learned or unlearned."[9]

By communion, Luther writes, we receive into our bodies the very flesh and blood of Christ, and we are strengthened by his strength. But since this is also the body and blood of the Crucified, we are bound up with his death. Communion therefore has two aspects: in communion with Christ, the weight of our sins is assumed by him, and we are in turn covered by his righteousness; in communion with our fellow saints in the body of Christ, we share all the benefits of mutual love and support and, thus strengthened, remember our fellowship of martyrdom and turn to share in the misfortunes of our brothers and sisters.[10]

Such was the shape of Luther's sacramental theology as outlined in sermons printed between October 1519 and July 1520 for the Christian edification of his readers and hearers. But with the appearance of his *Babylonian Captivity* three months later, it was clear that the plowshares had been beaten into a sword. Intending to taunt his literary opponents by inventing fresh "heresies" while they were still occupied with the ramifications of earlier works, he proceeded to sharpen up his treatment of the sacraments and to add new ideas.[11] For the first time he made public a conviction he had previously confided

8. *WA* 6:374.4–5, *LW* 35:106.
9. *WA* 6:370.25–27, *LW* 35:101.
10. *WA* 2:745.19–746.15, *LW* 35:14f.
11. *WA* 6:501.7–9, *LW* 36:17.

only to Georg Spalatin, that there were only two sacraments and not seven. A true sacrament, he argued, must have a divinely instituted sign and have associated with it a promise of grace: "We can have no relationship with God except by the word of him promising and the faith of man receiving."[12] "We seek sacraments that have been divinely instituted, for there must be above all else a word of divine promise by which faith may be exercised."[13]

Baptism and the Eucharist alone remained as true sacraments, although this is not to say that the other rites were to be valued less when properly used. Luther did, however, take the opportunity of subjecting their abuse to the severest censure. The apostolic practice of the laying on of hands, for instance, was laudable but had become restricted to confirmation and to ordination, the basis of "that detestable tyranny of the clergy over the laity." Penance, too, furthered clerical tyranny over consciences, and the many legal restrictions placed on matrimony were, he believed, merely a means of making money by selling dispensations. Far more serious were the abuses and misconceptions that had accrued to the two proper sacraments. The importance of baptismal vows, which should have been regarded as the most momentous one could take, had become so obscured that the comparatively trivial monastic vows of poverty, chastity, and obedience were now thought to secure a greater share of sanctity. Baptism, however, had been relatively unscathed in comparison with the Eucharist, the significance of which had been totally obliterated by the sacrifice of the mass and, to a lesser extent, by the reservation of the chalice. At this point Luther unveiled a new critique. Transubstantiation—the thirteenth-century dogma of the annihilation of the substances of the consecrated bread and wine and their replacement by the substances of Christ's body and blood—he called a monstrous doctrine that had more to do with Aristotelian physics than with the Christian faith. Why can it not be, he asked, that the substances of the bread and wine remain, and that they share the same time and space as the holy body and blood in a wholly mysterious way?[14]

12. Luther to Spalatin, 18 September 1519 (*WA Br* 1:595.23f.).
13. *WA* 6:550.9–10, *LW* 36:17.
14. Lateran IV, *constitutio* 1, *De fide catholica* (*DS* 802). The term was first used in official circles by Innocent III in his letter *Cum Marthae circa* to Archbishop John of Lyons, 29 November 1202 (*DS* 782), and was theoretically developed by Aquinas in *Summa theologiae* 3, qu. 75–77 (Alba and Rome: Editiones Paulinae, pp. 2260–84).

Before concluding our assessment of Luther's sacramental theology, insofar as he had developed it in opposition to the Roman Church, we should consider another of his pamphlets, *Opinion on the Abolition of the Private Mass*, published with a translation exactly a year after *The Babylonian Captivity* first appeared.[15] The treatise was addressed to the ecclesiastical authorities of Wittenberg and demanded both the abolition of what he called the private mass (a mass offered, without the sacrament of communion, for the souls of the deceased) and forbearance with traditionalists who could not immediately adapt to the new order. It continued *The Babylonian Captivity*'s critique of the mass sacrifice, but for the first time explicitly associated with that critique a rejection of the sacrificial nature of the priesthood. With this development, the evolution of Luther's sacramental theology was complete—at least until the deviant theologies of his fellow reformers attracted his attention—and we can now turn to consider the response it evoked from the Catholic controversialists.

The Romanist Reaction and Critique

Up to 1525, nine Catholic titles against Luther were published on the mass, five on penance, three on sacraments in general, and a further fourteen in answer to *The Babylonian Captivity*. The sacramental debate with Luther thus represented the largest single controversy of the Catholic literary campaign.

Battle commenced in earnest with the bishop of Meissen's injunction against the publication and distribution of Luther's *The Blessed Sacrament* within his diocese, and with a formal complaint against the reformer from the bishop of Merseberg. The latter had engaged Alveld's services in the controversy over papal primacy, and it may well have been at his instigation that Alveld wrote his *Tractate Concerning Communion in Both Kinds* in July 1520,[16] which Luther refuted in the prologue to *The Babylonian Captivity*. Alveld also took the opportunity provided by the revision of a previous tract to attack Luther's *New Testament or Holy Mass*.[17] He was presently joined in this attack by another Franciscan, Thomas Murner, whose chief complaint

15. See Luther, *Vom Misbrauch der Messen* (*WA* 8:482–563) (Ger. trans. of *De abroganda missa privata* [*WA* 8:411–76]) = *The Misuse of the Mass* (*LW* 36:[129], 133–230).
16. Published in Leipzig by W. Stöckel, July 1520.
17. Augustinus von Alveld, *Ein Sermon darinnen sich Bruder Augustinus.*

was that Luther had publicly discussed matters that were best not heard by the common people, in particular the question of universal priesthood.[18]

The New Testament or Holy Mass also occasioned two pieces by a new writer, Johannes Dobneck of Nuremberg. A German humanist who took the sobriquet Cochlaeus, he had been in broad agreement with Luther as late as the summer of 1519. But *To the Christian Nobility* seemed to him to undermine the foundations of the church—particularly the priesthood—and *The Babylonian Captivity* confirmed his worst fears. His two refutations of Luther's earlier sermon, composed in retrospect, therefore concentrated on the revolutionary social implications of the reformer's sacramental theology, whose doctrine of baptism would make the common people think themselves free of sin and whose eucharistic theology would have them dispense with the duty of obedience.[19]

The first barrage of Catholic pamphlets helped Luther locate further areas for attack in *The Babylonian Captivity*. The second barrage, opened by Henry VIII's *Defense of the Seven Sacraments*,[20] was even more intense. The king's book prompted supplementary works from John Fisher, Thomas More, Edward Powell (all later to give their lives for the papal supremacy), and Queen Catherine's chaplain Alfonso de Villa Sancta. Even Murner and Eck sprang to the English king's defense. But *The Babylonian Captivity* also generated a controversy independent of Henry's involvement, which was reheated by the reformer's *Abolition of the Private Mass*, his 1523 order of communion for Wittenberg, and *The Abomination of the Silent Mass* of 1525. It involved the prolific veterans Emser, Cochlaeus, Alveld, and Murner, as well as the newcomers Schatzgeyer and Dietenberger, and the less productive Johannes Eckhart and Matthias Kretz. Of course, defenses of traditional sacramental theology continued to be published after 1525, but with a diminishing frequency and a certain staleness of repetition. Even the particularly thorough treatments of the sacrifice of the

18. Murner, *Ein christliche und briederliche ermanung.*
19. Cochlaeus, *Uff CLIIII Artikeln,* Oiii[v]–Pii[v].
20. For a summary of opinions on the authorship of the *Assertio septem sacramentorum,* see E. Doernberg, *Henry VIII and Luther: An Account of Their Personal Relations,* 21–23. A critical edition of the *Assertio* is currently being prepared by P. Fraenkel for the Corpus Catholicorum series.

mass by Johannes Mensing and Eck that appeared in 1526 drew heavily upon the books of their predecessors who had been working in this field for the previous five years.

Concerning Sacraments other than the Mass

By far the greater part of the Catholic controversialists' replies to *The Babylonian Captivity* was concerned with the novel elements it contained, in particular Luther's theologies of the Eucharist and ordination. But in the same way as much of the argument of the treatise had been adumbrated in Luther's earlier works, so the controversialists perfunctorily repeated many of the same objections they had already made in the context of the indulgence controversy.

This was the case, for example, with regard to Luther's redefinition of a sacrament and his theologies of baptism and penance. Luther had taken the traditional definition of a sacrament—Augustine's belief that it was a visible sign of an invisible grace—and altered it so that it was now a dominically instituted visible sign with a faith-evoking promise attached. He would not have considered this a substantial alteration. After all, the African was himself of the view that it was faith in the sacrament and not the sacrament itself that conferred grace.[21] But for the Catholic apologists it was a new departure. In the twelfth century, Hugh of St.-Victor had argued that the distinguishing characteristic of Christian sacraments over against the ceremonies of the Old Testament was that they actually conveyed the grace they signified.[22] With the later scholastics, the idea gained ground that this grace was infallibly given, provided that the recipient put no obstacle in the way.[23] The Romanists' aim was therefore to defend the objective nature of sacramental grace, insofar as it was produced *ex opere operato*, and simultaneously to insist on the necessity of worthy reception. Faith unformed by works of charity was insufficient disposition for

---

21. Augustine, *Quaestionum in Heptateuchem* 3, cap. 84 (*MPL* 34:712); idem, *Sermo* 112, cap. 5 (*MPL* 38:645).

22. Hugh of St.-Victor, *De sacramentis Christianae fidei* 2, pars 6, qu. 3 (*MPL* 176:448). The notion was adopted by Peter Lombard, *Sententiarum libri quattuor* 4, dist. 1 (*MPL* 192:839–41).

23. See, e.g., Duns Scotus, *Super libris sententiarum* 3, dist. 19 (Duns Scotus, *Fratris Ioannis Duns Scoti in quatuor Libros Sententiarum* (Venice: J. Baptista, 1597), 4 vols. in one, 3:73–76.

grace—according to Fisher, Cochlaeus, and Henry[24]—and God could not be expected to fritter away gifts promiscuously on unworthy recipients lest, in Henry's words, they "fell into the hands of demons."[25]

It is obvious that the controversialists meant something quite different from Luther in their use of the words "faith" and "grace," and it is not surprising that they experienced some difficulty with his new definition of a sacrament. This difficulty is particularly clear from their attitude to his theologies of baptism and penance. Against the traditional Western view, represented by Augustine and Tertullian among others,[26] that baptismal grace is irrevocably lost with the first sin committed after baptism and that the sacrament of penance is thereafter the sinner's sole recourse, Luther had maintained that the grace of baptism is never lost; indeed, the validity of the sacrament of penance derives entirely from the promise of forgiveness received once for all at baptism, which God would never withdraw from any true penitent.[27] Henry protested the unreasonableness of such a presumption. A merciful God would naturally wish to forgive any contrite sinner. But a just God could not be expected to restore anyone to baptismal grace proper who had willfully rejected it. The penitent could be admitted only to the grace of sacramental absolution, and only after due satisfaction had been made for the injury done to divine majesty by the sin.[28]

The exchange between Luther and Henry on the sacraments of baptism and penance helps to illustrate the conditions of thought that prevented the Romanists from accepting, or at least from understanding, Luther's sacramental theology. Their first and most significant presupposition was that the sacrifice Christ made on the cross did not atone for all sins. It applied, they believed, only to sins committed before baptism, which (in the era of infant baptism) effectively meant

24. "Theologians speak of two types of faith, one naked and unformed, which endures not, and one clothed with virtuous and good works, and formed by love for God" (Cochlaeus, *Uff CLIIII Artikeln*, Mi; see also, Liv[v], Niii[v]).

25. Henry, *Assertio*, Ki[v].

26. Tertullian, *De paenitentia*, cap. 4,2 (*MPL* 1:1343-60); Augustine, *Contra epistolas Pelagianorum* 4, 10.27, 11.31 (*MPL* 44:629–32, 634–36); Jerome, *Epistola* 84.6 (*MPL* 22:748), 130.9 (*MPL* 22:1115); Pope Benedict XII, *Cum dudum*, August 1341 (*DS*, 1012).

27. *WA* 6:529.24, *LW* 36:61.

28. Henry, *Assertio*, Ki[v], Nii[v], Niii.

original sin. The guilt of post-baptismal sin had to be remitted by contrition duly recognized as such in the confessional and by the performance of a penance duly imposed by the priest.[29] This is not to say that the cross was thought to have no validity for the forgiveness of post-baptismal sins, but that it could be applied only in conjunction with the sinner's own penitential works. It is this doctrine to which Cochlaeus referred when he wrote in *Against 154 Articles* that the sacrifice of the cross does not atone for all the sins of everyone.[30] This brings us to their second presupposition. Medieval theologians developed the idea that Christ's sacrifice had generated an infinite amount of merit, only some of which was required for the remission of the past sins of the baptized. The excess, it was believed, was stored away in a treasury of merits. Access to this treasury could be obtained only by the exercise of the power of the keys, which was the prerogative of the vicar of Peter and, at his dispensation, of subordinate clergy.[31] The controversialists' second presupposition, therefore, was that the benefits of Christ's Passion must be applied exclusively through the mediation of priests.[32] As is clear from this view of a store of grace, they were further predisposed to think of grace as some supernatural substance that could be variously applied or withheld, added to or subtracted from. Henry could speak of grace "falling into the hands of demons," as if it were a contingent reality that, once dispensed, continued to have an existence of its own. To such a quantitative and materialist understanding, Luther's conception of grace as God's saving will was utterly foreign.

These three presuppositions explain the difficulty the controversialists experienced with Luther's sacramental theology. If grace is understood as God's predestinating will to save, expressed in promises contained in the Bible and repeated through preaching and in the sacraments—above all in the Word "Your sins are forgiven"—then

---

29. John Fisher, *Assertionum Regis Angliae de fide Catholica adversus Lutheri Babylonicam Captivitatem defensio*, in idem, *Opera omnia*, 181; cf. 219; Cochlaeus, *Uff CLIIII Artikeln*, Niv[v].

30. "Our sins will indeed be forgiven us by the merit of the passion and the blood of Christ our Lord and Savior—but not all of them" (Cochlaeus, *Uff CLIIII Artikeln*, Mi[v]). See also idem, *De gratia sacramentorum liber unus Ioan. Cochlaei adversus assertionem Marti. Lutheri*, Aiv.

31. See, e.g., Clement VI, *Unigenitus*, 27 January 1343 (*DS*, 1025–27).

32. Murner, *Ermanung*, 58–59. Hieronymus Emser, *Quadruplica auff Luters Jungst gethane antwurt / sein reformation belangend*, Biii[v], Ciiif.; Fisher, *Adversus Babylonicam captivitatem*, 200, 223.

faith must be understood as that which comes from hearing a promise and from passively but gratefully receiving a free gift. If, on the other hand, grace is a life-giving substance dispensed conditionally, then faith must be such that it can give something in return, that is, it must be faith formed by acts of love for God.

In their response to the doctrine of justification by faith alone, the Romanists actually had little difficulty in understanding Luther's redefinitions of faith and grace, and even in acknowledging the validity of his case. Fisher, for example, accepted Luther's redefinition of grace as a promise as entirely orthodox, inasmuch as it was a tenet of later medieval covenant theology that God gives us no grace not already preordained.[33] What they found difficult, both with Luther's justification theory and with his sacramental theology, was his apparent disregard for the consequences of teaching the common people that grace could be received unconditionally, without the need of good works. Cochlaeus was particularly insistent on this point. Luther's doctrine of baptism, he feared, would make the rabble think they were free from sin, while his eucharistic theology would declare them free of the duty of obedience.[34] Both Fisher and Henry deplored Luther's doctrine that faith was a divine gift and not a human virtue. This they did, not for any theological or philosophical reasons, but because they feared that the common people would seize on the new teaching as a pretext for immorality. Fisher wrote:

> It is certainly by the very worst sort of trickery that Luther has won popular support. He teaches that faith alone suffices and that no satisfaction is required for any crime, no matter how serious. With a baleful impudence he claims that not only the guilt but also the penance of a sin is remitted simply by absolution, on condition that such absolution is firmly believed. Be one never so orthodox in other respects, who would not be easily seduced and led on to a bitter end by the prospect of sinning with impunity and of the freedom to commit all kinds of vice?[35]

Henry agreed:

> Your sole intention is to deceive men, either by the false security of having obtained faith, or by despair of obtaining it, and to

33. Fisher, *Adversus Babylonicam captivitatem*, 256.
34. Cochlaeus, *Uff CLIIII Artikeln*, oiii^v and passim.
35. Fisher, *Adversus Babylonicam captivitatem*, 232.

plunge them headlong into that licentious way of life which you strive to introduce under the pretext of evangelic liberty.[36]

The reaction of Cochlaeus, Fisher, and Henry does not suggest that Luther's concept of faith was misunderstood. It suggests rather that the controversialists thought its possibility for abuse far outweighed any claim it might have had to serious theological consideration. As Henry wrote in the *Defense*, "I do not object to the fact that Luther attributes so much to faith, so long as he does not use it to defend evil lives or to destroy the sacrament it is meant to support."[37] Precisely the same sentiments would be expressed with regard to Luther's doctrine of justification, as will be seen in chapter 6. But it was in connection with his sacramental theology that the pastoral argument had a special relevance. It was believed that the sacrament of penance in particular played a vital role in the detection, punishment, and deterrence of crime, and that to abandon it in its current form, as Luther demanded, would have had incalculable consequences for society.[38]

Luther's attack in *The Babylonian Captivity* on sacraments other than the mass, and the Romanist response to it, merely recalled issues already debated in the indulgence controversy: the insufficiency of the cross for the remission of post-baptismal sins; the necessity of worthy receipt of grace; the need for priestly mediation in the dispensing of grace; and the dangerous consequences of stressing the sufficiency of faith. The point of departure was Luther's treatment of the threefold "captivity" of the mass in *The Babylonian Captivity.* The mass was central to the daily life of the medieval church; therefore, the controversialists' assessment both of its importance and of the threat they considered Luther's writings to represent to it is of considerable interest.

36. Henry VIII, *Henrici VIII Regis Angliae, ad Martini Lutheri Epistolam Responsio,* in Fisher, *Opera omnia,* 92.

37. Henry, *Assertio,* Kiii^v.

38. "Had you taken away from the Hebrew synagogue the judgment and discretion of its priests, you would have been left with nothing but a den of thieves. Take away from the Catholic Church the sacrament of confession, which in this respect replaces the judgment and discretion of the old law, and you will see unimaginably terrible things. The children of Belial will seek to throw off the bridle and the reins and to lose themselves in carnal pleasure and in the abyss of lust" (Augustinus von Alveld, *Sermo de confessione sacramentali an confessio prorsus homini mortali ad verae beatitudinis vitam sit necessa, An ne,* Ci^v). See also Henry, *Assertio,* Kiv^v, Miif.

Concerning the Sacrament
of the Mass

The first captivity of the mass, according to Luther's analysis, was the practice of allowing the laity to receive only the bread and not the wine in communion. It was difficult for the Romanists to defend the practice as an authentic part of the church's official teaching. The reservation of the chalice had not been recognized until the Council of Constance's decrees against Huss, just over a hundred years earlier; even Constance did not enjoin it but merely declared it noninjurious to salvation. The situation was complicated by the fact that eighteen years later, in 1433, the Council of Basel ratified the so-called *Compactata* of Prague by which the Hussites were ceded the chalice. Of course, the Romanists could argue that Basel was not a true ecumenical council because it had not been summoned by a pope. But neither had Constance. Not even the condemnation of Luther's view of the matter in *Exsurge Domine* resolved the issue to universal satisfaction, for throughout the Reformation period Catholic regions petitioned Rome for concession of the cup for fear of something worse. The Tridentine fathers were unable to agree on the matter and left such ad hoc concessions to the discretion of the pope.[39]

Such a dearth of dogmatic guidance on the question of the cup ruled out a bare appeal to conciliar authority, and most of the Catholic apologists were obliged to strengthen their case in other ways. Henry and Sichem represented a fideist position. The king did not know why the clergy withheld the chalice from him, but he respected their integrity and knew they would not act against his interests in matters of ultimate salvation.[40] Similarly, Sichem confessed that the original reason was now lost in the mists of time. Nevertheless, the practice did not concern salvation and brought about no other great harm—so, he asked, why change a long-established custom simply for the sake of change?[41] Fisher represents almost the other extreme. His aim was to fight Luther with his own scriptural and patristic weapons, and he was careful not to rely too heavily on fifteenth-century decrees. He

39. Leo X, *Exsurge Domine*, art. 16, 15 July 1520 (*DS*, 1466); Trent, *sessio* 22, 17 September 1562 (*DS*, 1760).
40. Henry, *Assertio*, Ciii^v–iv.
41. Sichem, *Brevis elucidatio*, Hii^v.

therefore cited a number of supplementary reasons, among which were
the many practical dangers that had occurred to the fathers:

> For there was the danger in administration that the blood might
> be spilt, as indeed often happened, particularly when a large
> crowd was communicating. Again, there was a danger involved
> in conservation, that the species of wine might turn to vinegar,
> since parish priests always kept some in readiness for the sick.
> There was also a danger in taking it to the dying, either on foot or
> on horseback. There was a danger from those who partook, espe-
> cially from those many who feel sick when they taste wine. There
> was the danger of lack of wine, as it is in short supply in many
> parts of Christendom. (The danger was that those who could not
> partake of the species of the wine might believe that they were not
> partaking of the whole Christ.) Finally, there was just this danger
> of infidelity, that the entire Christ might have been believed to
> exist only in both species, had he never been shown to all Chris-
> tians except under both species. So you see how many and how
> great were the dangers feared of old, which have now been
> avoided by this custom.[42]

Cochlaeus, like Alveld, relied equally on conciliar authority and
common sense, and was as insistent as Fisher on the dangers of dese-
crating the blood of Christ: "You have clearly never been a country
parson, Luther, or you would know how clumsy bumpkins can be."[43]
This was an odd point for Cochlaeus to have made: he had never been
a country parson, and even if he had, he could not have spoken
authoritatively on the matter. Neither he nor Fisher nor any other
Catholic priest of the time could have had any firsthand knowledge of
the difficulties of administering the cup to lay people. It is interesting
to note that one of the Catholic dioceses that later petitioned Rome to
authorize the lay chalice in order to prevent wholesale Protestantiza-
tion was Meissen, and that the man who put its case forward was
none other than Cochlaeus himself.[44] One is left with the impression
that the Romanist appeal to reason and practical difficulties was an
attempt to compensate for the lack of official guidance rather than the
result of any deep conviction of the impropriety of the lay chalice.

The dogmatic status of transubstantiation, the target of Luther's
second attack, was much clearer. The annihilation of the substances of

42. Fisher, *Adversus Babylonicam captivitatem*, 132.
43. Cochlaeus, *Uff CLIIII Artikeln*, lii.
44. Bäumer, *Johannes Cochlaeus (1479–1552)*, 46–50, 97.

bread and wine at consecration had not been formally defined until the Council of Florence in 1430. But the word itself had appeared in a canonical document as early as 1202, and thereafter in the conciliar documents of Lateran IV (1215), Lyons (1274), Constance (1415), and Florence again in 1442. The concept had received its most thorough treatment at the hands of Aquinas, and it was his attempt to explain in terms of Aristotelian physics what Luther believed could be grasped only by faith that so angered the reformer. It cannot be necessary to salvation, he argued, to believe that the bread and wine are not as truly present after consecration as are the body and the blood.[45] Given the wealth of dogmatic statements concerning transubstantiation, the controversialists were much more confident of their case than they had been with regard to the reservation of the chalice. *Cum Marthae* and Lateran IV, they rightly argued, made it heresy to disbelieve the doctrine, and Luther had neither right nor reason to speak against it.[46] The fact that the word had been invented only in the past three hundred years made it no less the faith of the church. Henry, Sichem, and Powell maintained that the concept of transubstantiation, if not the technical term, had been taught as early as St. Ambrose's time, and that the aim of the medieval theologians in borrowing Aristotelian distinctions was simply to show that in this matter the Christian faith was intellectually defensible.[47]

The controversialists could safely have rested their case for transubstantiation entirely on arguments from authority. But Luther's reliance on arguments from reason obliged them to follow suit, in case their hand appeared weaker than his. His chief argument for the bread's continued existence after consecration had been the grammatical sense of the words of institution: "This is my body" (Mark 14:22 and parallels) must mean "This bread is my body." Fisher, Powell, and More followed Henry's argument that the Scriptures often give trans-

---

45. Luther, *Babylonian Captivity* (WA 6:508–12, LW 36:28–35).
46. Henry, *Assertio*, Fii^v; Fisher, *Adversus Babylonicam captivitatem*, 164, 175–76; Cochlaeus, *Uff CLIIII Artikeln*, Miii.
47. "For the Church does not believe this simply because theologians have disputed the matter so, but because the Church has always believed it from the beginning, and has decreed it as a matter of faith lest anyone should doubt it. For this reason, the theologians have exercised their ingenuity by deploying additional arguments from philosophy, so that they can prove by any means at their disposal that there is nothing absurd in such a belief, namely that the conversion of the bread into a new substance necessarily abolishes the former substance, and does not allow it to remain" (Henry, *Assertio*, Eiii^v). Cf. Sichem, *Brevis elucidatio*, Giii^v; and Powell, *Propugnaculum*, 45f.

formed entities the names of their previous forms. The sentence "Aaron's rod swallowed the rods of the magicians" (Exod. 7:12) refers to the rods when serpents; similarly, Christ's words at the wedding feast at Cana, "Draw some out" (John 2:8), appear from the context to refer to water but in fact refer to the water now become wine. "This is my body" must therefore mean "This flesh is my body."[48]

But Scripture did not provide the controversialists with linguistic evidence alone. Powell saw a type of transubstantiation in Jacob's deception of his blind father. When Isaac reached out to bless his firstborn, he indeed smelled and touched the "accidents" associated with Esau; but the substance he blessed was Jacob in disguise.[49] Despite such exotic exercises, the Romanists knew that transubstantiation was a dogma and ultimately needed no supplementary proof, and that by opposing the faith of the church Luther could succeed only in condemning himself.[50] The sole exception was the Franciscan provincial Schatzgeyer, who studiously avoided using the word "transubstantiation" and regarded the mode of Christ's presence as a question of theology, not of physics.[51]

The Sacrifice of the Mass

In *The Babylonian Captivity*, Luther's attacks on the reservation of the chalice and on transubstantiation had merely been preliminaries to his main assault. Both were "captivities" of the church, but they were not spiritually harmful to it. He was chiefly concerned with the opinion that the mass was a good work done by men and women to please God, an opinion promoted by the doctrine of the sacrifice of the mass.

48. Henry, *Assertio*, Div[v], Eii; Fisher, *Adversus Babylonicam captivitatem*, 160; Powell, *Propugnaculum*, 45[v]–50; Thomas More, *Eruditissimi viri Guilielmi Rossei opus elegans* (CWM 5:451–69).

49. Powell, *Propugnaculum*, 47.

50. "It is enough for us to follow what the fathers, as excellent in their learning as in the holiness of their lives, have bequeathed to us. Should a heretic wish not to believe them, let him give good reason why they are not to be believed. Otherwise, he is not to be heard" (Fisher, *Adversus Babylonicam captivitatem*, 175–76).

51. Schatzgeyer, *Tractatus de missa*, Av[v]. Note the similarity between Schatzgeyer's position in 1522 and Luther's. O. Müller (*Rechtfertigungslehre nominalistischer Reformationsgegner: Bartholomäus Arnoldi von Usingen OESA und Kaspar Schatzgeyer OFM über Erbsünde, erste Rechtfertigung und Taufe*) suggested that Schatzgeyer was a "nominalist" in the tradition of Scotus and Gregory of Rimini, and to this extent shared Luther's intellectual background. Müller's suggestion was criticized by V. Heynck ("Zur Rechtfertigungslehre des Kontroverstheologen Kaspar Schatzgeyer OFM"), who attributed these apparent affinities to Schatzgeyer's eclecticism and argued that, as a biblical humanist, he was no more indebted to the *via moderna* than to any other tradition.

This, in his view, was the Babylonian captivity of the church that spelled death.

The sacrificial nature of the mass was a far more important aspect of the Eucharist in medieval thought than was its sacramental nature. It had achieved this prominence long before the thirteenth century, and Aquinas's treatment of it was noteworthy only because it was a particularly thorough one. Yet the sacrifice of the mass had never been defined by the church.[52] The Catholic apologists were therefore put in a difficult position. With Luther, they believed that this was the most crucial of the three eucharistic doctrines he had criticized. But in contrast with transubstantiation and even with communion in one kind, there was no official guidance to which they could appeal. In light of the absence of such guidance, it will be instructive to see how the controversialists established the importance of the mass sacrifice and interpreted the nature of the threat Luther posed to it. Particularly interesting are the ways in which they explained the purpose of the mass's sacrifice and perceived the relationship, first of the sacrifice of the altar to the sacrifice on Calvary, and second, of the clerical priesthood to the priesthood of Christ and his church.

The most common description of the mass was as a memorial of Christ's death offered to the Father to remind him of his past mercy and secure that mercy in the present.[53] Its purpose was primarily intercessory. The sacrifice of Christ was again offered up to the Father in accordance with the command "Do this as a memorial to me." The propitiation once found pleasing to God would be found so again as often as it was offered, securing divine favor for those who offered it and for the intentions named in the canon of the mass: souls in purgatory, the physical well-being of the living, and worldly enterprises. Since it was performed in obedience to the Lord's command it was, according to Cochlaeus and Henry, a good and meritorious work. It was indeed an objectively good work, regardless of the personal virtue of the celebrant.[54] Against Luther's exclusive understanding of the mass as a benefit to be gratefully received, the controversialists

52. The term *sacrificium altaris / missae / eucharistiae* found its way into official documents, but was never properly defined. The pre-Tridentine occurrences are Innocent III, *Eius exemplo*, 1208 (*DS*, 794); Lateran IV *constitutio* 1, 1215 (*DS*, 802); Honorius III, *Perniciosus valde*, 1220 (*DS*, 822) and Innocent IV, *Sub catholicae professione*, 1254 (*DS*, 834).

53. Alveld, *Ein Sermon darinnen sich Bruder Augustinus* (Lemmens, 44).

54. Cochlaeus, *Uff CLIIII Artikeln*, Xi, Xivf.; Henry, *Assertio*, Giii^v, iv^v.

insisted that the mass was something we do for God. Powell believed it to be a work three times over, as an act of thanksgiving, as a transforming of the elements, and as a spiritual eating.[55] For Fisher, it was a good work insofar as it was a proclamation of the Lord's death till he returns.[56] Cochlaeus protested that no rite involving so much activity and so many different bodily postures and movements could be mistaken for some passive receipt of free gifts. We are not helpless beasts waiting to be fed, or hibernating animals waiting to be woken by the sun. Rather, "We celebrate the mass as a good work. In it we pray to the Lord God, not for ourselves only but for the living and the dead, as well generally as individually. We hope thereby to please and serve God, to earn for ourselves grace, virtue, mercy, and the like, to praise God, to strengthen our souls with spiritual food, and to improve our lives by meditating upon Christ and by other good works."[57]

A surprising omission from Cochlaeus's otherwise comprehensive balance of accounts is any mention of the forgiveness of sins. This was typical of the controversialists, who believed the sacrifice of the mass could directly remit only the sins of souls in purgatory. Fisher and Cochlaeus expressly stated that, for the forgiveness of the sins of the living, the effect of the sacrifice of the mass had to be mediated through sacramental penance,[58] by which in practice the mass was always preceded. The immediate benefits for those who heard mass were brought about not by the sacrifice but by the sacrament, the communion itself. Through the sacrament, their love was rekindled by the supreme example of Christ's self-sacrifice (Schatzgeyer);[59] as the body of Christ they grew in unity with their head and with their fellow members (Fisher)[60] and improved their lives by meditation on

---

55. Powell, *Propugnaculum*, 52[v].
56. Fisher, *Adversus Babylonicam captivitatem*, 197.
57. Cochlaeus, *Uff CLIIII Artikeln*, Jii[v], Xiv, Niv–Oi.
58. On Alveld, see n. 53 above. Cf. Cochlaeus, *Uff CLIIII Artikeln*, Miv[v], Oi; Fisher, *Adversus Babylonicam captivitatem*, 147, 180, 219. The Council of Trent was eventually to reject Fisher's and Cochlaeus's position (*sessio* 22, 17 September 1562). A mediating position between the Tridentine formulation and that of the two earlier theologians might be represented by Catharinus. In a famous passage dating from the middle of the century he argued that because there can be no remission of sins without sacrifice and because the post-baptismal sinner is deprived of the immediate grace of the cross sacrifice, the remission one obtains in the sacrament of penance must be mediated through the representation of Calvary in the sacrifice of the mass. See the helpful summary in Clark, *Eucharistic Sacrifice*, 498–500, for detail on this point.
59. Caspar Schatzgeyer, *Von dem hayligsten Opffer der Mess*, Mii.
60. Fisher, *Adversus Babylonicam captivitatem*, 147, 180, 219.

Christ's Passion (Cochlaeus).[61] The controversialists did not shrink from a near-superstitious regard for the Eucharist. Cochlaeus believed that hearing the mass ensured good health, good luck, and general protection,[62] while Emser appealed to "the common man's testimony" that attending mass in the morning guaranteed a happy issue to all one's affairs that day.[63]

The later medieval explanation of the relationship of the sacrifice of the mass to Christ's sacrifice on the cross had been greatly furthered by Aquinas's description of the former as an *imago repraesentativa*, a memorial that makes the original event present again in the same way as a portrait re-presents the subject: in the mass, Christ was not resacrificed, but neither was his Passion simply "remembered" in any weak sense. The same sacrifice was offered daily anew.[64] There is no doubt that many of the controversialists were indebted to this definition, as they were to Lombard's collation of statements from Augustine, Prosper, and Chrysostom.[65] Murner, Emser, and Alveld could subscribe to Cochlaeus's belief that "Although Christ was sacrificed only once mortally and visibly on the cross, he is offered daily in the mass immortally and invisibly through this memorial of and meditation on his passion and death, and is now a spiritual sacrifice that is made without slaughter."[66]

However, it would be a mistake to press all the controversialists into the same mold. While Eck followed Aquinas in his use of the phrase *imago repraesentativa*, he had no obvious qualms about describing the mass as a repetition (*reiteratio*) and a fresh sacrifice (*nova oblatio*).[67] Fisher and Schatzgeyer, characteristically careful in their scholarship, also manifested a certain independence of mind. In contrast with their colleagues, who interpreted Christ's words of institution ("Do this in remembrance of me") as "Remind my Father of

61. Cochlaeus, *Uff CLIIII Artikeln*, Tiiᵛ.
62. Ibid., lii.
63. Emser, *Auf Luthers Grevel wider die Stillmess Antwort* (CC 28:148f). Cochlaeus's and Emser's beliefs about the magical effects of the Eucharist may be an example of the convergence of popular and elite Catholicism. For a recent survey of popular beliefs concerning the properties of the mass and Eucharist, see R. W. Scribner, "Ritual and Popular Religion in Catholic Germany at the Time of the Reformation," *Journal of Ecclesiastical History* 35 (1984), 65f.
64. Cf. Aquinas, *Summa theologiae* 3, qu. 83, art. 1.
65. Peter Lombard, *Sententiarum libri quatuor* 4, dist. 12, cap. 7 (MPL 192:866).
66. Cochlaeus, *Uff CLIIII Artikeln*, Ziif.
67. Johannes Eck, *De sacrificio missae* (1526), 59–60, 169.

my sacrifice,"[68] they saw that the mass brought the memory of Christ's death before the participants, not before God.[69] To this extent, Fisher's and Schatzgeyer's eucharistic theologies would have proved acceptable to Luther, had not the reformer long since ceased to read his opponents' writings altogether. An independent position was also taken by Henry. His fellow controversialists made a clear distinction and separation between Christ's Passion and the Last Supper, based on their conviction that the first was commemorated in the sacrifice of the altar and the second in the communion.[70] The king, however, believed that both events of the Lord's life were jointly represented in the mass, which thus became one moment, *unum sacramentum.* "For on the cross Jesus consummated what he had begun at the supper: this commemoration is accordingly a commemoration as much of the consecration at the supper as of the oblation on the cross; and it is celebrated and represented by the one sacrament of the mass, although it is the death which is more truly represented than the supper."[71]

The existence of a general consensus on the doctrine of the eucharistic sacrifice did not preclude significant deviations from it. Nonetheless, there can be no doubt that Aquinas's teaching on the sacrifice, although not yet raised to the status of a dogma, exercised an all but normative influence on subsequent treatments: the sacrifice offered daily in the mass was identical with that of Christ on the cross, except that it was now offered in an unbloody manner. But although this formulation was designed to protect the priority of Calvary as the validation of the daily masses,[72] the relationship between the two sac-

---

68. Alveld, *Ein Sermon darinnen sich Bruder Augustinus* (Lemmens, 44).

69. "There are however not two paschas or two sacrifices, but one pascha and one sacrifice, inasmuch as one is representative of the other. For in both the same true lamb is Christ Jesus. In the same way as he was once immolated by dying on the cross, so now he is surely immolated each day, when the memorial of Christ's death is renewed before us [*apud nos mortis Christi memoria quotidie renovetur*]" (Fisher, *Adversus Babylonicam captivitatem*, 197–98). Clark translates the final clause as "when we daily renew the memorial of his death" and loses the sense of Fisher's argument (*Eucharistic Sacrifice*, 528). For Schatzgeyer, the sacrifice of the cross was not a contingent historical event but a continuous reality ever-present before God's eyes, made present before us through the sacrifice of the mass; the sacrifices are identical but exist in different modes, one *realiter,* the other *mysterialiter.* See Schatzgeyer, *Ein gietliche und freuntliche anntwort und unterricht* (Munich, 1526), Fi; and idem, *Von dem opfer,* Giii, iv).

70. See, e.g., Fisher, *Adversus Babylonicam captivitatem,* 181.

71. Henry, *Assertio,* Giii; see also Hii[v].

72. Fisher, *Adversus Babylonicam captivitatem,* 223; idem, *Sacri sacerdotii defensio,* 1270; Murner, *Ermanung,* 6, 62; Johannes Mensing, *Von dem opffer Christi,* Bii[v], Ciif.

rifices was complicated by the belief that the Passion itself was largely ineffective unless its benefits were mediated through the mass.[73] The remarkable position had been reached whereby the two sacrifices had become necessary conditions of each other. The demands of orthodoxy were satisfied inasmuch as the mass sacrifice was denied an independent value, but equally the sacrifice of Christ was to all intents denied a value independent of the mass. The sacrifice of the mass, therefore, was not an additional sacrifice but a necessary addition to the original sacrifice.

Closely related to any treatment of the relationship of the two sacrifices is the question of the agency by which the sacrifice of the mass was offered. The notion that Christ had been both priest and victim on the cross was familiar enough from the Epistle to the Hebrews, and Lateran IV had applied this twofold office to the mode of his participation in the sacrament of the altar. But if Christ were understood as the priest officiating at the mass, how was the role of the human priest to be explained? Furthermore, the First Epistle of St. Peter attributed the royal priesthood to the church as a whole and not to a caste within it. In what sense, then, could the priest be said to offer Christ in the Eucharist? The controversialists by and large accepted in principle the point that priesthood pertained primarily to Christ and to his church and only secondarily to the special priesthood. Schatzgeyer, Cochlaeus, and Henry followed Lateran IV in according Christ the chief priestly role in the Eucharist.[74] (Emser entertained no such notion, presumably because of his high evaluation of the human priesthood.) Eck, Emser, Cochlaeus, and Schatzgeyer were agreed that the priest offered Christ *in persona ecclesiae*, on behalf of all Christians living and dead.[75]

This last point suggests that the controversialists in general were much less antagonistic to Luther's doctrine of the priesthood of all believers than might have been supposed. Their objection, as with some of Luther's other teachings, was prompted largely by the pos-

73. Powell, *Propugnaculum*, 120; Henry, *Assertio*, Ri; Fisher, *Adversus Babylonicam captivitatem*, 200, 223.
74. Schatzgeyer, *Von dem opfer*, Ki; Cochlaeus, *Uff CLIIII Artikeln*, Eif.; Henry, *Assertio*, Hiv.
75. Eck, *De sacrificio missae*, 174–75; Emser, *Assertio*, Di; Cochlaeus, *Uff CLIIII Artikeln*, Eiii[v]; Caspar Schatzgeyer, *Replica contra periculosa scripta*, 88[v]; idem, *Von dem opfer*, Div[v].

sibility that the rabble might misunderstand it out of ignorance or malice. Bäumer quite correctly states that Cochlaeus, Fisher, Bartholomeus Usingen, Eck, Arnoldi von Chiemsee, Johannes Gropper, and Jodocus Clichtoveus all accepted the universal priesthood, provided that it did not detract from the special priesthood.[76] To Bäumer's list we must add the names of Emser, Murner, and Alveld. (In fact, of all the Catholic controversialists, only the little-known Wolfgang Wulffer wrote against the priesthood of all believers. His strangely Wycliffite contribution to the debate was to interpret the "royal priesthood" as a reference to a small number of Christians entirely without sin, known only to God.)[77] Nonetheless, the controversialists accepted the universal priesthood as a notion entirely secondary to the special priesthood, which alone could be described as the real priesthood of the church,[78] because a "royal priesthood" did not mean that all Christians were literal priests any more than it meant they were all literal kings.[79] The priesthood of all believers was thus considered by the Catholic apologists as no more than a metaphor suggested by the presence in the church of a special priesthood. Their understanding of it had little in common with Luther's.[80]

This brief survey shows that the attempts of the Catholic controversialists to establish a theology of the eucharistic sacrifice in the absence of conciliar definitions were greatly influenced by Aquinas's treatment. But it also shows that there were nevertheless many more differences between their teachings than would have been the case had official dogmatic guidance existed. It suggests that both F. Clark and Iserloh are correct in their conflicting evaluations of the Romanists' theologies of the mass. The consensus Clark has identified applies largely to those aspects of the sacrifice of the mass that Aquinas had described, especially in its relationship to (its "re-presentation" of) Calvary. On the other hand, the numerous divergences observed by Iserloh largely concern issues on which Aquinas had been less clear,

---

76. Bäumer, *Cochlaeus*, 94.
77. See Wolfgang Wulffer, *Wider den ketzrischen widerspruch*.
78. Emser, *Vorlegung*, Civ^v.
79. Emser, *Vorlegung*, Ciii; Sichem, *Brevis elucidatio*, Li.
80. For a more detailed discussion of the issues raised here, see D.V.N. Bagchi, "'Eyn mercklich underscheyd': Catholic Reactions to Luther's Doctrine of the Priesthood of All Believers, 1520–25."

for example the question of the identity of the priesthood that offers the sacrifice.[81]

Sacrifice and Priesthood

The controversialists were agreed that the primary purpose of the repeated sacrifice of the mass was intercessory: the church reminded the Father of his past mercy in order to secure his favor. There was, however, another justification of the sacrifice upon which they were no less insistent, namely, that it underpinned the priesthood. Without the sacrifice of the mass, Cochlaeus reasoned, there could be no priesthood.[82] The argument was reversible; Fisher, Sichem, and Eck maintained that while the priesthood stood, so did the sacrifice of the mass.[83] In this they were following the orthodoxy of the day, which defined priesthood as that which performed sacrifice and sacrifice as that which priests did. Even before the Council of Florence, priests were ordained with the words "Receive the power to offer sacrifice in the Church for the living and the dead" and received a chalice and paten containing the eucharistic elements as symbols of office.[84] An exegetical commonplace of the time was to see the Last Supper as a service of ordination in which Christ made his apostles priests so that they could offer the sacrifice of which he spoke. This commonplace was annexed by Trent into its decree on ordination, a decree that began with the words "Sacrifice and priesthood are so joined in God's ordinance that in every dispensation both have existed together."[85]

The Romanists clearly considered that the gravest threat posed by Luther's denial of the eucharistic sacrifice was to the continued existence of the priesthood. The reformer was quite conscious of developing the two attacks in tandem, and it is no coincidence that his doctrine of the universal priesthood finds its clearest expression in his

---

81. Iserloh, *Kampf um die Messe*, esp. 58; Clark, *Eucharistic Sacrifice*, 92.

82. "There would be no priests in the Christian faith if we had no sacrifice, because the primary function of the priest is to sacrifice" (Cochlaeus, *Uff CLIIII Artikeln*, fi).

83. "Moreover, the office of the priest is the office of offering sacrifice to God. . . . For a priesthood is in vain where there is no sacrifice to be offered" (Sichem, *Brevis elucidatio*, Iii^v). Cf. Fisher, *Sacri sacerdotii defensio*, 1298. Cf. also Eck, *Enchiridion*, 199, where the priestly office is cited as the primary justification of the mass sacrifice.

84. *Exsultate Deo*, 22 November 1439 (*DS*, 1326).

85. Trent, *sessio* 22, canon 2, 17 September 1562 (*DS*, 1752); *sessio* 23, cap. 1, 15 July 1563 (*DS*, 1764).

polemical works on the mass.[86] Equally, Catholic treatises on the sacraments abound in defenses of the priesthood and of its difference from and superiority to the lay estate. First, they argued, there had always been and must always be a mediator who represents humankind before God and God before humankind. The priest is such a mediator, which is sometimes described as an angel, or even a god.[87] The priest differs from lay people as much as the sun differs from the earth, or an architect from a building, or a farmer from his field (so Fisher, invoking 1 Cor. 3:9).[88] Not all Christians can be priests, or else there would be no laity to which they could minister.[89] Second, they defined the nature of this distinction. It was in Emser's words a real distinction (*mercklich underscheyd*), not only of function but also of status: "The office follows from the status, not the status from the office."[90] Only priests may officiate at the mass and offer up the sacrifice pleasing to God;[91] only priests may make God out of bread and wine; only priests may mediate the benefits of Christ's sacrifice to others.[92] (In this sense, Powell and Henry asserted, ordination was the highest sacrament of all, for all other sacraments depended upon it.)[93] On several occasions, Cochlaeus insisted that the priestly office is so mysterious that no lay person should so much as hear the canon of the mass, for pearls are not to be cast before swine.[94]

Surprisingly, the controversialists did not defend the reservation of the chalice on the basis of this "real distinction" between clergy and laity. Their silence may be due to the fact that Luther himself seems never to have attacked the practice on these grounds; or it may be that they were careful to observe the fact that reservation was a matter of order, not of doctrine, and that to associate it with the subordination of the laity would have been unwarranted. However, the controver-

86. See esp. *De abroganda missa privata* (WA 8:411–76) and its translation, *Vom Misbrauch der Messen* (WA 8:482–563).

87. Emser, *Vorlegung*, Di[v]. See also Powell, *Propugnaculum*, 145[v].

88. Fisher, *Adversus Babylonicam captivitatem*, 200; idem, *Sacri sacerdotii defensio*, 1247f., 1258.

89. Fisher, *Sacri sacerdotii defensio*, 1259.

90. Emser, *Vorlegung*, Ciii.

91. Cochlaeus, *Uff CLIIII Artikeln*, Gii, hi[v].

92. Fisher, *Sacri sacerdotii defensio*, 200, 223; Cochlaeus, *Uff CLIIII Artikeln*, fii[v].

93. "If the priesthood falls, all other sacraments fall with it" (Powell, *Propugnaculum*, 120). Cf. Henry, who makes the same point rather differently: "Luther's denial that ordination is a sacrament is as it were the fount of all his errors with regard to the sacraments. Staunch that, and the other streams must dry up" (*Assertio*, Ri).

94. Cochlaeus, *Uff CLIIII Artikel*n, Gii, Oiii, Qiv.

sialists had not previously been overscrupulous in respecting the boundaries between faith and order, and it would have been particularly odd for them to be so now. The explanation may lie in the fact that it was not only lay people who were denied the chalice, but also noncelebrating priests. Therefore, the practice of reservation could not strictly be used to establish a difference between the clerical and lay estates, despite the fact that to most ordinary people it must have seemed to have done precisely that.

Concerning the Sacrament of Ordination

By basing their defense of the mass on the prior necessity of a priesthood, the controversialists appear to have begged the question of ordination. For them the priesthood was an institution that needed no justification because it was part of the divine order of the universe. This impression is strengthened by the fact that their defense of the sacramentality of ordination was conducted primarily on the basis, not of New Testament texts, but of the witness of Dionysius the Pseudo-Areopagite.

Despite doubts raised by Laurentius Valla and Erasmus that Dionysius's Neoplatonism set him much later in date, the controversialists who cited Dionysius accepted the tradition that he was the Athenian disciple of St. Paul and accorded him quasi-apostolic status as "first and foremost" of all authorities after Scripture.[95] For them, therefore, his books on the ecclesiastical and heavenly hierarchies constituted firsthand evidence from the very infancy of the church of a comprehensive sacramental system, including a threefold ministerial order.[96] His *Ecclesiastical Hierarchy* testified to the early emergence of

---

95. See, e.g., Johannes Eck, *Commentaria de mystica theologica D. Dionysii Areopagitae*, Avi^v. Clichtoveus, Cochlaeus, Kretz, Marcello, Fisher, Wimpina, Dietenberger, Campester, Rhadinus, and Fabri also explicitly accepted the Pseudo-Areopagite's authenticity.

96. For references to Pseudo-Dionysius's authority on the sacraments and other rites, see Fisher, *Adversus Babylonicam captivitatem*, 181, 192; Cochlaeus, *De gratia sacramentorum* 1:Li, Liii^v; Matthias Kretz, *Ain Sermon inhaltend etlich spruch der schrifft von dem fegfewr*, Ai^v; Jodocus Clichtoveus, *Antilutherus tres libros complectens* 1:10, 53^v; idem, *De veneratione sanctorum*, Gi^v; Johannes Fabri, *Malleus in haeresim Lutheranam*, 272–76. For Dionysus's testimony to the sacramentality of ordination, see Fisher, *Sacri sacerdotii defensio*, 1239; Emser, *Vorlegung*, Civ^v, Div, Kiii^v; Clichtoveus, *Antilutherus* 2:63^v; Marcello, *De authoritate*, 39^v–40; Johannes Dietenberger, *Contra temerarium Martini Luteri de votis monasticis iudicium* I:Nv^{v}ff.

certain rites, while the *Celestial Hierarchy* helped to explain their theological significance.

These writings deeply influenced the controversialists, as we can
see, for example, from the third book of Powell's *Propugnaculum*. In
the longest section, a defense of the sacramentality of ordination, there
is an extended meditation on the necessity to the church of a divine
order of authority and obedience, in which ministerial orders (*ordo*)
and order (*ordinatio*) are interchangeable ideas—"omnia, quae a deo
sunt, ordinata sunt" (Rom. 13:1, Vulg.)[97] Such an order, Powell argued,
reflects the ranking of the planets, metals, and animal kingdom; as
Dionysius showed, it reflects the very order of heaven, of the ranks of
angels, and especially of the Holy Trinity, which is itself both ordered
and the source of all order. The heavenly and ecclesiastical hierarchies
each consist of a triad of triads, in which each element acts upon the
one below it and is acted upon by the one above it, in purgation,
illumination, and perfection.

> But each hierarchy also contains its own order, rapt in sweetest
> contemplation of the Trinity. And this supreme and inerrant
> Trinity, the fount and origin of all order, disposes its own family
> and household of angels in a beautiful and decorous order, to
> which Christ wishes to conform the Catholic church which he has
> redeemed with his own precious blood. He has therefore consti-
> tuted it in a threefold hierarchy of higher, lower, and middle: that
> is, of prelates, clergy, and people. The prelates, as supreme, purge
> their inferiors by correcting faults, illuminate them by teaching
> the true faith, and perfect them by the example of decent living.
> The clergy is established as the middle order between prelates and
> people, so that it first receives purgation, illumination, and perfec-
> tion from the prelacy, and afterwards diffuses it to the people. The
> people are the lowest in this subcelestial hierarchy, so that while
> they receive the hierarchical actions of prelates and clergy, they
> cannot themselves act upon one another or upon any below them,
> nor return it to those above.[98]

Another example is provided by Powell's compatriot, Fisher, who
also appealed to natural history in defense of the priesthood, although
without mentioning Dionysius by name. The heavens are rightly
located above the earth, he argued, because the earth depends upon

97. Powell, *Propugnaculum* 3:154ᵛ.
98. Ibid., 3:155ᵛ.

their heat, light, and rain for its sustenance. The church is, as it were, a "spiritual universe" in which the clergy are the heavens and the people the earth. "The heavens are telling the glory of God," sings the Psalmist. Like the heavens, says Fisher, the clergy "shine forth in their lives, make warm with the ardor of charity, moisten with their wholesome counsels, quicken with promises, thunder with threats and flash forth miracles; so that in the same psalm David can properly say of them 'their voice has gone forth throughout all the world' [Ps. 19:4]."[99] Fisher goes on to invite us to consider the human body. Its nobler functions, such as the finely discriminating senses of taste, smell, and hearing, are located in the uppermost part of the body, while the cruder functions are situated in correspondingly lower and more ignoble regions.[100]

The arguments of the two Englishmen were adumbrated by two Italians. Both Marcello and Rhadinus defended the three orders of ministry on the basis of the Pseudo-Areopagite. On the authority of Dionysius, "who learned from St. Paul the deepest mysteries of the Godhead," we know, said Rhadinus, that the divine grace of illumination must flow down from the higher echelons of the hierarchy to the lower.[101] The classic proof-texts followed: the tabernacle of Moses (Exodus 25–26), the temple of Solomon (1 Kgs. 7); the hierarchy of sun, moon, and stars (Song of Sol. 6).[102]

Clichtoveus (who took Luther's low regard for his country's patron saint as a mortal insult to France) used a similar argument, expressly citing the Pseudo-Areopagite: the entire universe is subject to a most beautiful order, with the highest heaven above all, then the lower heavens—the spheres and celestial bodies—then the earth itself, and finally the lower regions. Noah's ark, Moses' tabernacle, Solomon's temple, and the Jewish synagogue—types of the Christian church—were all marvelously ordered into higher and lower parts or offices.[103] Another Frenchman, Lambert Campester, also explicitly followed Pseudo-Dionysius in interpreting Moses' tabernacle and Solomon's temple as figures of the ecclesiastical hierarchy.[104]

99. Fisher, *Sacri sacerdotii defensio*, 1248.
100. Ibid.
101. Rhadinus, *Oratio*, Hi; Marcello, *De authoritate*, 39ᵛ–40.
102. See n. 101.
103. Clichtoveus, *Antilutherus*, 2:57–58.
104. Campester, *Heptacolon*, Giii; cf. Aivᵛ. Cf. Rhadinus, *Oratio*, Hi.

Closely related to these Dionysian, Neoplatonist emphases were other themes that recur throughout the Catholic literature of controversy. The idea of the body of Christ (1 Corinthians 12; Ephesians 4) was important to the controversialists, not because it signified the church's unity, but because it denoted difference and inequality within it: "It is clear that in the Church there is distinction of dignity, degree, and order, just as in the human body there is distinction of members and function."[105] Similarly, the controversialists referred to the figure of the church as the bride of Christ (Ephesians 5). What they found particularly attractive about this imagery was the implication of order and inequality. When the Psalms spoke of "the queen all beautiful within, adorned with vestments of gold and clothed in varied hues," or when Solomon sang of his "beautiful and ornate" bride, it was the manifold distinctions of rank within the church, the beauty of order, that was meant. "What now becomes of the Church's beauty and ornament," asked Rhadinus of Luther's supposed confusion of distinctions within church and society, "which consists in the very variety of her orders?"[106] A third proof-text frequently appealed to in connection with the church hierarchy was one we have already encountered: "Let everyone be subject to the higher powers. For there is no power except from God; and the things which are from God are *ordinata*."[107] It is

105. Campester, *Heptacolon*, Giii^v. See also Johannes Cochlaeus, *Ein Spiegel der Ewangelischen freyheit*, Cii; Murner, *Tütscher nation*, Dii^v; Emser, *Quadruplica*, Ci; Fisher, *Sacri sacerdotii defensio*, 1248; Marcello, *De authoritate*, 7^v; Clichtoveus, *Antilutherus* 2:60f.; Powell, *Propugnaculum*, 155; Rhadinus, *Oratio*, Hi, Hiv^{v}f.; Jakob Latomus, *De Ecclesia & humanae legis obligatione*, 95^v.

106. Rhadinus, *Oratio*, Hi. See also Clichtoveus: "That is to confound the beautiful order of the Church by which it is decently arranged" (*Antilutherus* 2:55^v, 57, 59f.). See also Powell, *Propugnaculum*, 136: "The Church's order is her glory, without which there can be no glory in heaven and, on earth, no beauty"; ibid., 154^v: "But where, pray, will this wrong-headed madness of yours end, this belief that all without exception are equal by right? Where else than the confounding of the beautiful appearance of the entire universe, whose only ornament is orderly arrangement?" See also Dungersheim, *Multiloquus*, 10: "Luther strives to overturn, destroy, and utterly annihilate every kind of order, and the most beautiful appearance of the whole Church." See also Paris University, *Determinatio theologice*, Aii: "The appearance of the Church is and ever shall be full of grace and most splendidly decorated, like a queen standing at the right hand of her husband, in vesture of gold and clothed with a variety of laws, ceremonies, sacraments, and all manner of things beneficial for this life and the next." See also Alveld, *Sermo de confessione*, Ci^v: "God desired that the Jews be holy. How much more did he wish to make his Church beautiful with various orders, terrible as an army drawn up for battle [*ut castrorum acies ordinata*; Song of Solomon 6:4]?" Similar formulae can be found in Adrian VI's letter to Frederick the Wise, 542, 542^v.

107. See, e.g., Powell, *Propugnaculum*, 155; Campester, *Heptacolon*, Hiv. See also Chapter 4 for the sense of *ordinatus* as "in order" as much as "ordained."

worth noting that all three texts were taken from writings attributed to St. Paul. In a sense, this is unremarkable, because the Pauline corpus includes so much of the doctrinal and ethical content of the Christian Scriptures. But the controversialists' repeated appeals to St. Paul on the theme of the church's hierarchical organization may signify more than that. They not only regarded Pseudo-Dionysius as Paul's disciple but also, like Rhadinus, believed that he had been privy to "the deepest secrets of the Godhead" revealed to the Apostle during his rapture into the third heaven (2 Cor. 12:3f.). Given this belief, it is hardly surprising that Paul's epistles were read, as it were, through Dionysius's spectacles, and that the hierarchical structure of the church and of the heaven to whose glory it conformed was seen as the key to all Paul's thought.

In their defense of the sacramentality of orders against Luther, therefore, the controversialists were thrown back onto a fundamental of their theology. Without any idea that he might be begging a question, Sichem could warn Luther: "Take away the sacrament of ordination and you take away order itself."[108] *Ordo* was the very basis of God's universe, as testified by Dionysius, apostle of Paul the apostle of Christ Jesus. It was a fact that required no explanation. To question it would have been to question the world and the God who made it.

Defending Priestly Power

After the question of the papacy, *The Babylonian Captivity* occasioned the largest number of controversial works by Catholics in the early 1520s because it was regarded as another significant attack on the church's authority. However, this identification was not made simply on the grounds of Luther's doctrine of faith in relation to the sacraments, which his Catholic opponents believed would lead to widespread immorality and anarchy. They regarded his threat as much more fundamental. In their defense of the sacramental system as a whole against Luther, the predominant concern of the Catholic controversialists was, as in their defense of secular authority, with preserving power—in this case, the power of the priest over the daily lives of lay people. If asked what they considered to be the source of sacramental grace, the controversialists would not have thought it enough to answer, as Luther did, "the sacrifice of Christ." They would not

108. Sichem, *Brevis elucidatio*, Kiv.

even have considered it sufficient to answer "the sacrifice of the mass." Rather, the source of all the other sacraments was, in their opinion, the sacrament of ordination, even as the source of all Luther's errors was his denial of the sacrament of ordination.[109] The benefits of Christ's sacrifice could not be conveyed through the mass, nor the benefits of the mass through the other sacraments, without an ordained priesthood.

Their conception of the church and the universe owed much to the hierarchical Neoplatonism of Pseudo-Dionysius, which enjoyed a revival during the late fifteenth and early sixteenth century. The sacraments were regarded as part of that hierarchy, indeed, the means by which the higher levels operated upon the lower levels. As the divine energies moved ever down and away from the Godhead, so could there be a flow of grace if and only if there were inequality. It was thus in the "real distinction" between priest and people that the source—or at least the necessary means—of all spiritual power in the church lay.

109. Powell, *Propugnaculum*, 120; Henry, *Assertio*, Ri; Fisher, *Adversus Babylonicam captivitatem*, 200, 223.

6

THE CREATION OF A
NEW CHURCH

From the time of Cajetan's warning at Augsburg that Luther desired to "build a new church," there was the threat that the reformer's teachings would create a schism by leading large numbers of people from Roman obedience. By 1522 that threat had been realized, and the controversies of the period 1522–25 both reflected and established a thoroughgoing difference between the two camps based on their opposing conceptions of God and of the church.

The Babylonian Captivity of 1520 was the last of Luther's works to attract specific replies in large numbers. Nevertheless, the annual yield of Romanist titles against him continued to increase until 1526, because the Catholic response now began to spread itself over a growing list of smaller controversies: monastic vows; clerical celibacy; the cult of the saints; faith, works, and free will; the authority of Scripture; the nature of the church; the moral consequences of the Reformation. This corpus was not, however, a ragbag of unrelated works. In addition to being connected by the overall motif of the two churches, the topics themselves dovetailed into one another. The inter-relatedness of all the disputed doctrines—the fact that one could not treat one without regard to other doctrines and practices—promoted the publication of such theological compendia as Eck's *Handbook of Commonplaces*, which represent a change in the literary genres used by the controversialists and provide a convenient finishing point for this study.

Monastic Vows and Christian Liberty

Although Catholic controversialists wrote against Luther's *Judgment on Monastic Vows* and its preparatory *Theses Concerning Vows*,[1] they did so only after religious began deserting their communities. As a result,

---

1. Luther, *Themata de votis: iudicium M. Lutheri de votis, scriptum ad episcopos et diaconos Wittenbergensis ecclesiae* (WA 8:323–35); idem, *De votis monasticis M. Lutheri iudicium* (WA 8:573–669) = *The Judgment of Martin Luther on Monastic Vows* (LW 44:[245], 251–400).

their refutations of Luther's works were directed not primarily at the reformer but at apostates and those considering apostasy. This accelerated the process whereby the Catholic literary effort moved from manufacturing polemic against its opponents to producing propaganda for home consumption.

Luther's intention in writing *Monastic Vows* had been purely pastoral. He knew from his experience as a prior in his order that there were many who tortured their own consciences, believing that vows could earn God's favor, yet perturbed either because they were incapable of observing them or because they were too scrupulous. Luther decisively cut the knot by declaring that monastic vows are unchristian and that it is therefore no sin to break them. Poverty, chastity, and obedience, he argued, may be observed as a matter of private preference, but may not be vowed or imposed. Monastic poverty is hypocritical: monks lack for nothing, yet they demand alms while widows, orphans, beggars, and ordinary people go without. Monastic obedience to deliberately chosen "superiors" is also worthless in comparison with a Christian's duty to be a servant of all. And chastity, being a gift from God, cannot be the subject of a vow. Monks, he concluded, injure God insofar as they deny justification to be by Christ alone, and they injure men and women insofar as they forswear responsibility to their parents and neighbors and so transgress the law of love. The "one in a thousand" who takes vows piously could well continue under those vows. But for the majority, it would be no sin to abandon them.

The task of the Catholic controversialists in opposing Luther, therefore, was to prevent religious from taking his advice and leaving their monasteries, and in this task more or less the same arguments were repeated by different authors. Their first objective was Luther's attempt to contrast monastic vows with Christian liberty, which Luther defined as "a freedom which liberates the conscience from works—not that no works are done but that no faith is put in them."[2] They objected that liberty is in no way infringed by vows because no one is forced to take them. But once a solemn vow has been made one is bound to perform it, because one's freedom has been voluntarily renounced: "Pay what you owe" (Eccles. 5:4); "Make your vows to the Lord God

2. *WA* 8:606.30–32, *LW* 44:298.

and perform them" (Ps. 76:11; Isa. 19:21).[3] Besides, Christian freedom means freedom from sin, not freedom from virtue.[4] Furthermore, if solemn oaths can be broken, the very ties and obligations that hold society together will be dissolved.[5] Under no circumstances, therefore, could monastic apostasy be countenanced.

Nonetheless, there were positive as well as prescriptive reasons for remaining under vows. It was true, as Luther himself insisted, that there was only one version of Christianity and not two, the regular and the secular. Be this as it may, monasticism was nearer the lifestyle recommended in the Gospels: the three vows of poverty ("If you would be perfect, sell all you have and follow me"), chastity ("some make themselves eunuchs for the Kingdom"), and obedience ("he was obedient even unto death on a cross") could all be justified from Jesus' teaching and example. Furthermore, the monk's renunciation of the world represented the perfect sacrifice required by God, and in the common brotherhood of prayer and meditation and in separation from the cares of the world, the religious comes as near as one can in this life to angelic bliss.[6] The observance of such counsels was nothing less than "a short-cut to heaven."[7] Another positive reason for the continuance of religious communities was that, contrary to Luther's assertion that they were opposed to love of neighbor, they contributed to society by their learning and by their good works among the sick, the needy, and all sorts and conditions. It was no shame to give up doing a limited amount of good in one place (providing for one's parents, for example) so that one could do a far greater amount of good elsewhere. In any case, discretion is always the better part of charity.[8]

---

3. Bartholomeus Usingen, *Sermo de matrimonio sacerdotum et monachorum*, 157, 158. Cf. Bachmann, *Czuerrettung*, Fiv[v]: "No-one is obliged to take vows, but one is beholden [*schuligk*] to whatever one does vow." See also Dietenberger, *De votis monasticis* 1:Iiii[v], Giv[v]f.; 2:Liv[v]: "Everyone is free to take vows or not. But, under the new law as much as under the old, a voluntary [*ex pectore*] promise to God must needs be fulfilled." Similar formulations can be found in Clichtoveus, *Antilutherus* 1:38[v]–39[v]; 2:32[v]; 3:175[v]–176; Eck, *Enchiridion*, 210–11.

4. Cochlaeus, *Freyheit*, Ci, Cii[v]; Eck, *Enchiridion*, 155–56; Clichtoveus, *Antilutherus* 1:43[v].

5. Emser, *Vorlegung*, Kiv; Cochlaeus, *Freyheit*, passim, esp. Bi[v].

6. Bachmann, *Czuerrettung*, Liv[v]–Miii; Dietenberger, *De votis monasticis* 1:Hiv[v]–vi[v], Mii, Niv; 2:Cvi–vii, Eviii, Fi; idem, *Ein nutzliche rede frag und antwort von dreyen personen*, Ciii[v]–iv.

7. Schatzgeyer, *Vonn christlichen satzungen*, Civ[v].

8. Dietenberger, *De votis monasticis* 1:Oiv, Pii; Blich, *Verderbe*, Ci[v]; Clichtoveus, *Antilutherus* 3:157.

Having put forward general reasons for not breaking vows, the controversialists could proceed to defend in more detail the three monastic vows. They paid little attention to the vow of poverty, possibly because the wealth of the orders was too great to argue away. Dietenberger, whose defenses of monasticism were quantitatively the most impressive, could argue only that much good was done with this wealth, while Simon Blich simply accused Luther of trying to stir up envy on the part of the common people and of encouraging them to sack monasteries and slaughter "the servants of God."[9] By far the most controverted vow was that of celibacy, Luther's chief concern as the area most likely to produce a conflict of conscience. His reasoning was weak at this point, and his opponents did not spare him. It was inconsistent of him, they said, to divide people according to whether they possessed the gift of chastity. As with every other virtue, we need God's grace to live chastely. If we pray in faith, we will receive this grace. To do otherwise is to make provision for the flesh.[10] These *pistologoi*, punned Usingen, delight in attributing everything to faith and call us by contrast *papistae*: but by their faithlessness in this matter they prove themselves to be *priapistae*.[11]

From the point of view of all the Catholic writers, monastic celibacy was commended by the fact that both Jesus and Paul considered it a higher way of life. Clerical celibacy was even more important. Sexual purity was required of the Old Testament priests (as explained in the incident of the shewbread in 1 Samuel 21, for example) and of such pagan officiates as the vestal virgins, who celebrated the divine mysteries. How much more essential was this for Christian priests, who daily confected God upon the altar![12] Dietenberger at least was well aware of the reformers' picture of the ideal Christian man: one who earns his modest living by honest toil, who is not supported in idleness by the great wealth of a monastery; one who lives chastely with his wife and with her raises a family "as the book of Genesis says we should," not whoring about or committing acts "which we are not

9. Blich, *Verderbe*, Bi.
10. Bachmann, *Czuerrettung*, Miv^v–Nii; Blich, *Verderbe*, Bi^v, Biv; Dietenberger, *De votis monasticis* 1:Miv; 2:Dii^v, Oii^v–Qvi^v.
11. Usingen, *De matrimonio*, 152.
12. Dietenberger, *De votis monasticis* 1:Nvii^v; Powell, *Propugnaculum*, 137^v, 138; Usingen, *De matrimonio*, 159.

allowed to mention."[13] Dietenberger countered this with what he trusted was the revolting thought of a priest who had slept with a woman all night offering mass in the morning.[14] In order to strengthen their case, the controversialists often blurred the distinction between a priest (who by virtue of the sacrament of ordination could never cease to be a priest) and a religious (who could in principle be released from his or her vows). This enabled Blich to thunder against the marriage of ex-religious as incest and adultery, worthier of divine displeasure than the traffic of the sons of God with the daughters of men.[15]

The vow of obedience, dismissed by Luther as a piece of worthless hypocrisy in the context of monasticism, was also stoutly defended. The theme that runs through Paulus Bachmann's entire *Encouragement of a Vacillating Religious* is the virtue of obedience to higher authority. (His first chapter is titled "That in These Dangerous Times It Is Important to Cleave to Righteousness and Obedience.") He was able to find obedience or its opposite in everything from the canonical hours to the monk-calf of Freiburg.[16] Obedience, he argued, was paramount in all cases, even when the authority concerned was evil or its ordinances unjust. All sins are rooted in self-will. Vows and strict obedience to them are essential because they remove our actions from the realm of self-will and bind us instead to the will of another. Our behavior then becomes selfless and therefore meritorious: "a vow, which is a surrender of the will, ennobles every good work." Therefore, Bachmann believed, the vow of obedience was the highest of all.[17] Dietenberger preferred to confer that distinction on celibacy, but could still speak in glowing terms of "the most beautiful order of

13. Dietenberger, *Rede*, Ciii–Di^v. "Unmentionable acts" was a customary medieval way of denoting male homosexuality.

14. Ibid., Ci.

15. Blich, *Verderbe*, Aiii, Bii, Eii; Dietenberger, *De votis monasticis* 2:Pv–Qii^v. See also Henry VIII, *Ad Lutheri epistolam*, 86, referring to the wedding of Luther and Katharine von Bora as "a most incestuous marriage."

16. This creature (so called because it was reported to have a bald patch on its head resembling a tonsure and a flap of skin on its back resembling a cowl) was a deformed calf born near Freiburg in Saxony at the end of 1522. It became a favorite subject of popular pamphlets and was variously interpreted as an omen against Luther and an omen against Catholic monks. For a recent treatment, see R. W. Scribner, *For the Sake of Simple Folk: Popular Propaganda for the German Reformation* (Cambridge: Cambridge University Press, 1981), 127–33.

17. Bachmann, *Czuerrettung*, Bi^v, Ciif., Div^v–Ei, Eiii, Fif., Fii^v, Hi^v, Ki.

superiority and inferiority."[18] Like Henry VIII, Bachmann could argue that, while it was not always clear why the church had ordained certain practices (fasting, for instance), it was nevertheless necessary for salvation to obey them for the sake of the church's authority: neither food nor anything else in God's creation is forbidden because it is evil in its own nature, but the church of Christ has forbidden it that our obedience might be exercised.[19] Similarly, Cochlaeus again stressed the importance of a system of authority and obedience in his own attack on *Monastic Vows*. According to Cochlaeus, the body of Christ is not some undifferentiated jumble of organs but, as St. Paul taught, a structure in which each member has its appointed place and function. In such a body, which implies levels of superiority and inferiority, obedience is the cardinal virtue and whosoever sets himself against any authority, which is ordained of God, will merit eternal damnation.[20]

We began this survey of the Catholic defense of monasticism with the general remark that it was directed mainly at monks and nuns who were considering apostasy. Typical is the attitude of Bachmann, abbot of the Cistercians at Altzelle. His encouragement of an unnamed vacillating religious was based on the premise that Luther's arguments against monastic vows were no more than a routine temptation sent to test a monk's faithfulness and that they could be averted by the usual methods of avoiding those occasions for sin with which the religious life is beset.[21] We shall see later in this chapter how this attitude helped to depersonalize Luther and to deny the force of his criticisms by interpreting them as delusions prompted by the devil.

The Invocation and Veneration
of the Saints

Luther's attitude toward the cult of the saints bore a close resemblance to his critique of monasticism. Both, in his view, transgressed Christ's summary of the Law, to love the Lord God and one's neighbor as oneself. As the religious were guilty of blasphemy for magnifying human achievement at God's expense, so saint worship detracted from the worship of God. As monasticism conflicted with the demands of

---

18. Dietenberger, *De votis monasticis* 2:Fiii.
19. Dietenberger, *Rede,* Biii^v; idem, *Widerlegung des Lutherischen buechlins / da er schreibt von menschen leren zu meiden &c.,* Bii^v–iv.
20. Cochlaeus, *Freyheit,* Ci^v–ii; cf. Bi^v.
21. Bachmann, *Czuerrettung,* Nii^v.

neighborly love, so "the living saints"—the poor and the sick—suffered while money was wasted on the dead saints. The Virgin Mary, rightly honored by us as the Mother of God, is a model of humility. She would be appalled, protested Luther, to be worshiped as a pagan goddess, "the queen of mercy," by those who should know better. The pious are encouraged to visit shrines containing fragments of the true cross. Even if they were genuine—and there are enough pieces of the true cross in Germany to build a house—the one true cross is the cross that Christ himself bade us to bear, and we need travel no further than our own hearts to find and honor it.[22]

Luther's sermons of 1522 show that he was attempting to recall to its spiritual basis a practice that had become externalized. But in 1524 an event took place that exhibited a more sinister side to the cult of the saints. The canonization process of Benno, a twelfth-century bishop of Meissen, which had been promoted by Duke Georg of Saxony and assisted by Emser's biography of the bishop, reached a successful and apparently innocuous conclusion with the promulgation of Adrian VI's bull *Excelsus Dominus* (May 1523) and the solemn translation of the new saint's bones to a place of honor in the Cathedral of Meissen the following June. But in Luther's view (and not without justification) the entire affair was intended as Romanist propaganda. A pope who from the outset had attempted to recall Saxony to its once proverbial loyalty to the Apostolic See had now canonized a Saxon bishop, not for any exceptional sanctity or erudition or miracle-working but simply for upholding papal interests during the investiture contest. So blatant a political appointment to the glorious company of saints was to be exacerbated by a triumphant festival of Romanism just across the border from Wittenberg. For Luther this showed the cult of the saints in its true colors—as a political weapon of the papacy.[23]

Nonetheless, Luther was, in the main, moderate in his critique of the cult of the saints and of images, and indeed wrote as much against

22. Luther publicized these views on the saints in *Sermon von der Geburt Mariae*, given on 8 September 1522 and reprinted eleven times before 1524, excluding editions of collected sermons; and *Sermon von der Heiltumen*, given on 14 September 1522 and reprinted five times before 1524, excluding editions of collected sermons.

23. See Luther, *Widder den newen Abgott und alten Teuffel der zu Meyssen soll erhaben werden*.

the destroyers of images as against their devotees.[24] Partly because they could make capital out of lumping Luther with the iconoclasts, but mainly because they genuinely held him responsible for the more extreme actions, the Catholic controversialists now began to include in their works refutations of positions other than Luther's.[25] This tendency grew to such an extent that after 1522 it becomes increasingly difficult to speak of a Catholic response to Luther, and nearly impossible to do so for any date after 1525. The following survey attempts to take this diversity into account, but concentrates on those arguments directed specifically against Luther.

The Sorbonne theologian Clichtoveus declared his intention of steering a middle path between the Scylla and Charybdis associated with saint worship. There were those who attributed too much to the saints, believing, for instance, that we may never approach God except through heavenly intermediaries, or that our worship is offered ultimately to them and not to God.[26] There were others, from Vigilantius to the present day, who would deny any veneration whatsoever and who were blind to the fact that it was God's good pleasure that we ought to approach whenever possible through members of the heavenly court[27]—in particular, that we should beseech the Blessed Virgin Mary "through whom we have access to his Son."[28] This rambling work (which Clichtoveus with exasperating modesty entitled an *opusculum*) achieved little more than an unintentional demonstration of the impossibility of justifying the cult of the saints directly from Scripture. One proof-text he used for the practice of burning candles in honor of the saints was the parable of the wise and foolish virgins. Another, for the intercessory function of Mary, was Bathsheba's approach to King Solomon on Adonijah's behalf—scarcely a recommendation, one might think, in view of the fact that the king promptly had his brother killed for making this petition.[29] The foremost French editor of the fathers and early schoolmen had rather more success in adducing evidence from the four doctors, John Damascenus, Bernard,

---

24. See the Invocavit sermons of 1522 (*WA* 10.3:1–64), *Eight Sermons at Wittenberg, 1522* (*LW* 51:[69], 70–100).
25. See, e.g., Johannes Femelius, *Eyn kurtz Sermon sso die heyligen Gottes belangenn.*
26. Jodocus Clichtoveus, *De veneratione sanctorum libri duo*, Civ^v, Hiii^v, Iii^v, Mi.
27. Ibid., Aiii^v, Di, Eiii, Gi, Iiv.
28. Ibid., Aii, Gi, Gi^v–ii^v.
29. Ibid., Hii, Niv.

and the Victorines.[30] He was safest in his appeal to the binding force of "the customs of the people of God": the sheer number of observances, practices, and prayers, both universal and local, connected with the saints confirms the rightness of the cult.[31] It may be, however, that Clichtoveus was attempting no more than a *dégustation* of the sort of defenses of saint worship that had or could be made. Certainly he refers the reader at various points to other, dare one say, more adequate works on the subject by Thomas Netter, Gabriel Biel, and Johannes Eck.[32]

Much more successful in his use of Scripture was the Franciscan provincial Schatzgeyer, who based his arguments on the "manifold unities" implicit in the doctrine of Christ. The first is the unity of the divine and human natures, the *communicatio idiomatum*, by which Christ the man can receive our prayer and praise.[33] The second is that of Christ with his mother, from which it follows that Mary is the mediator of our salvation and the mother of Christ's fellow heirs.[34] The third is the unity of Christ with his bride, the church. This is the the body of Christ in which all the members must care for each other, those in heaven for those on earth, and those on earth for those in purgatory.[35] Having established this basis, Schatzgeyer proceeded to explain that the saints hear our prayers by virtue of their complete unity with the Godhead[36] and that we should implore their help in all those matters touching our salvation and our temporal welfare where we would otherwise pray to God directly.[37] As will become clear later in this chapter, while Schatzgeyer was firmly opposed to the Scripture principle, he was equally firmly convinced that the Lutherans could and should be defeated with their own weapons. His work on the saints was typically full of references to biblical passages employed not as proof-texts but in order to construct a "biblical theology."[38] He

30. Ibid., esp. Ci^v–ii.
31. Ibid., Biii^v–Ci.
32. Ibid., Ei^v, Iii, Mi^v, Riv.
33. Caspar Schatzgeyer, *Von der lieben heiligen Eerung unnd Anrueffung*, Aii^v, iii^v.
34. Ibid., Aiv–Bii^v.
35. Ibid., Biii–iv^v.
36. Ibid., Cii–Di.
37. Ibid., Di^v–Eiii.
38. See, e.g., Schatzgeyer, *Von der heiligen*, Aii^v, where the verse "The Word became flesh and dwelt among us" (John 1:14) is used to demonstrate the unity of the divine and human natures in Christ, the principle on which Schatzgeyer justifies the cult of the saints.

also differed from Clichtoveus in having a systematizing principle that ran through this treatise as through his other work, relating all his assertions to the three theological virtues of faith, hope, and love.

In his verse dialogue between a "worldling" and a "spiritual brother," Dietenberger was able to make many of the same points as the other authors much more concisely. For instance, a chapter's worth of Clichtoveus is in Dietenberger reduced to three couplets:

> Be sure that you don't get me wrong:
> Supreme praise is for God alone
> (Called in Latin "latria").
> But saints are praised with "dulia";
> In just the same way as you would
> Laud in this life the great and good.[39]

A chapter of Schatzgeyer is reduced to two couplets:

> Since they now are counted blest
> So their power has increased,
> To help by many prayers on their part
> One who prays to them in his heart.[40]

Like Schatzgeyer, Dietenberger preferred to support the cult of the saints by scriptural reference, but unlike the Franciscan the passages he cited were mere proof-texts. However, this was enough to convince the worldling of his error, even to the point of eventually conceding that only priests have the power to interpret Scripture.

Against Luther's contention that saint worship detracted from divine worship, the controversialists were unanimous. Any honor done to the saints is, they argued, done ultimately to God as the first cause of their great merits, and prayers to them are also meant ultimately for God.[41] The position of Christ as "the one mediator between man and God" (1 Tim. 2:5), however, was the occasion of some divergence. Clichtoveus maintained that the force of *unus* in this instance did not exclude auxiliary mediation.[42] Schatzgeyer, on the other hand,

---

39. Johannes Dietenberger, *Cristliche underweisung / wie man gotes heiligen in dem hymmel anrüffen*, Giii[v].

40. Ibid., Gii.

41. Schatzgeyer, *Von der heiligen*, Bi[v], Fi[v]–Fi[v]ff, Fiv, Gii, Giii, Hif., Jiv, Ki; Femelius, *Eyn kurtz Sermon*, Ci; Dietenberger, *Underweisung*, Eiv, Ki[v]; Clichtoveus, *De veneratione sanctorum*, Giv[v], Hiii[v].

42. This argument is similar to one he used to gloss 1 Tim. 1:17—"soli Deo honor et gloria." See Clichtoveus, *De veneratione sanctorum*, Niii[v].

preferred to interpret Christ's mediation as pertaining only to salvation and not to intercession.[43] Against Luther's contention that it conflicted with love of neighbor, the controversialists were equally unanimous. New Testament exhortations to mutual love and support were most perfectly fulfilled when the members of the body of Christ prayed for one another. If holy Christians prayed for others in this life, how much more will they do so when they are taken up into heaven, when their charity will be made perfect and their compassion for their former fellow sufferers in the vale of tears increased?[44] Luther's objection, of course, concerned the neglect of practical charity in favor of vast expenditure on the cult. This met with a standard Romanist *reductio ad horrendum* from Alveld, Emser, and Schatzgeyer: such was the argument of Judas Iscariot, who covered his own treachery with just such talk of giving to the poor.[45] Dietenberger took a different tack when he counseled that God rewards equally both the one who honors the saints and the one who gives alms. His concern was for the meritoriousness of the deed rather than for its practical consequences.[46]

Luther's fundamental objection to the cult of the saints was that it had multiplied the objects of Christian worship and charity beyond necessity. All Christian teachers were agreed that the sanctity of the saints lay in their perfect transparency of God, that everywhere they pointed from themselves to him. And yet the cult encouraged the pious to regard the saints as self-sufficient objects of worship. How did the controversialists, therefore, defend the cult? An author such as Blich could base his objection on purely pragmatic grounds. If the cult of the saints were abolished, he protested, how many goldsmiths, silversmiths, jewelers, painters, and other craftsmen would be out of jobs, or worse, be obliged to prostitute their art on profane subjects?[47] Blich's colleagues adopted a more traditional defense of the invoca-

43. Schatzgeyer, *Von der heiligen*, Jiii.
44. Schatzgeyer, *Von der heiligen*, Hiii^v, Jiv^v; Dietenberger, *Underweisung*, Gii; Eck, *Enchiridion*, 180–81.
45. Augustinus von Alveld, *Wyder den Wittenbergischen abgot Martin Luther*, 45–46; Hieronymus Emser, *Antwort auff das lesterliche buch wider Bischoff Benno zu Meissen*, cited in H. Smolinsky, *Augustin von Alveldt und Hieronymus Emser: Eine Untersuchung zur Kontroverstheologie der frühen Reformationszeit im Herzogtum Sachsen*, 293; Schatzgeyer, *Von der heiligen*, Kiv. Schatzgeyer protested that gambling, for example, took even more money each day from charitable uses and was in itself a less worthy object of expenditure than saint worship. Alveld taunted the "new Judas" with wishing to spend the money thus saved on prostitutes.
46. Dietenberger, *Underweisung*, Kii.
47. Blich, *Verderbe*, Cii^v, Eiii^v.

tion of the saints. Because of human sin and unworthiness, none may approach God directly in prayer; that is why Christians pray through the Son. But there are many times when a Christian will feel unworthy even to approach Christ (who will after all be the merciless Judge on the Last Day, who will reward every man and woman according to strict justice). On such occasions, it is helpful to approach the Son through his special friends in heaven—particularly, of course, his mother. As Christ's mother the Blessed Virgin is also the mother of every member of Christ's body. What could be more natural, Schatzgeyer asked, than for children to run to their mother when they are in trouble?[48] Once again employing his talent for biblical malapropism, Clichtoveus established the same case by reference to the wise woman of Tekoa (2 Sam. 14:1-20), whom he took as a figure of Mary's mediating role. "But what does this story mean for us? It means that when we offend against the divine majesty by our sins, we may resort to that wise woman, the mother of infinite wisdom, the Blessed Virgin Mary, imploring her to placate God that we might approach him in prayer through her."[49]

Dietenberger accorded the saints an altogether more positive role. Instead of simply placating God, they actually had the power of bringing the Christian into the body of Christ.

> But that we might have membership
> Of this great kindly fellowship,
> By prayer and by the sacrament
> To acquire it are we meant;
> Lest it might be that our Saviour
> Does not know us for a member.

God requires evidence of suitability for membership of the body of Christ, states Dietenberger, and what better recommendation can there be than that of a valued member of long standing?[50] In effect, therefore, Dietenberger brought the cult of the saints into the realm of things necessary to salvation. By this reasoning, there was no room for an agnosticism toward the cult such as Luther held: either one observed it or one risked exclusion from the fellowship of heaven. Indeed, the

48. Schatzgeyer, *Von der heiligen*, Bi.
49. Clichtoveus, *De veneratione sanctorum*, Fiv^v.
50. Dietenberger, *Underweisung*, Hii–iii^v.

effect of the controversy as a whole was to polarize attitudes toward the veneration of the saints, so that Luther's moderate critique was portrayed by his opponents as extreme, and a de facto cult was elevated to the status of an article of faith.

Faith, Grace, and Free Will

One of the more surprising aspects of the Catholic response is that the controversy concerning justification by faith alone constituted such a small part of the literature that it must be ranked with the treatment of such topics as monastic vows and the cult of the saints. The fact that justification was sometimes treated in works primarily devoted to other subjects alters the picture only slightly.

What was the reason for this apparent neglect of what we regard as the most significant doctrine of the Reformation period? One possibility is that such neglect was a function of the "reaction principle" that dominated so much of the controversialists' work: the doctrine did not figure largely in their writings because it did not figure largely in Luther's. While this suggestion is not so absurd as it might first appear (after all, Luther was more likely to expound justification by faith in his homiletic works, and these were less likely to draw his opponents' fire than his disputatory writings), it cannot be seriously maintained. Did they then ignore it simply because they did not understand it? It is clear that they did understand what he meant by "faith" and "justification"—only the popularizers reduced the debate to the formula "faith versus works," which was then, as now, misleading theological shorthand. They fully appreciated that the debate set trust in God over against trust in works. A more likely alternative is that the controversialists deliberately chose to ignore the doctrine. Notwithstanding the reaction principle, the controversialists were ultimately responsible for selecting the subjects on which they wrote, and their choice might have been dictated by factors such as the relative unimportance they accorded the doctrine in comparison with their high estimation of the papacy or the mass.

I think that the answer is to be found somewhere between these possibilities. To serve the purposes of controversy, Luther's opponents had either to cite his more offensive statements without comment or else to draw out the offensive consequences of his innocuous statements. Many of Luther's statements on justification itself were considered too orthodox to be publicly refuted, and these the controversialists passed over. Far more important to them was the task of alerting their readers to the social consequences of the doctrine.

In accordance with historic Christian sources, the controversialists accepted that there was a sense in which justification comes about by faith alone. It applies, for instance, in the case of children below the age of discretion who cannot perform morally good works.[51] Moreover, in the hierarchy of the so-called "causes of justification," faith is prior to works, which perform a solely confirmatory function. This view was clearly stated in a number of places by Dietenberger and Clichtoveus,[52] and a related point was made by Schatzgeyer in a work dedicated to exploring the relationship between faith and works: "A man who is born again in Christ by the Holy Spirit and baptism, and who is old enough to distinguish between good and evil, must have in addition to faith good works, in order to receive Christian perfection in this life and, in the life to come, eternal blessedness. I do not speak of justification, which happens through faith, which such a person will already have received."[53] For the controversialists, faith was a primary cause of justification whether one meant by it *fides*, intellectual assent to the truths of Christianity, or *fiducia*, trust in God's promise that we are saved by God alone. Dietenberger went so far as to concede that we are indeed justified by the merits of Christ alone, in the sense that they are the first and special cause of our justification, but that they must be followed by our works.[54]

51. Dietenberger, *De votis monasticis* 2:Hvii; idem, *Der leye*, Bi; Clichtoveus, *Antilutherus* 1:48ᵛ.

52. Dietenberger, *De votis monasticis* 2:Hviif., Lv: "Works justify in this sense, not that they are effective causes of justification, but that they prove and perfect justification. . . . [Works justify] perfectively, not effectively." Cf. Clichtoveus's statement that good works justify "in their own way . . . at the least they assist and dispose one to receive grace, and are as it were necessary instrumental causes" (*Antilutherus* 1:48ᵛ; see also 3:136ᵛ).

53. Schatzgeyer, *Vonn christlichen satzungen*, Aiiᵛ. Inasmuch as Schatzgeyer divides the process of salvation into three stages in which first faith and then works prevail, we might justly suspect him of being an early exponent of a double justification theory. See the discussion in V. Heynck, "Zur Rechtfertigungslehre des Kontroverstheologen Kaspar Schatzgeyer OFM." Heynck's conclusion that there is no evidence of any such theory in Schatzgeyer's work is not entirely convincing and suggests special pleading. Certainly the same distinction was current enough in 1526 to have been made by Hochstraten, who could write of his *Catholicae aliquot disputationes contra Lutheranos*, "The whole point of the book is this: good works do not justify, they beatify" (Pijper 3:545). The distinction appears to be based on chapter 14 of Augustine's *De fide et operibus*, which contains the statement that good works "follow the act of justification and do not precede the process of justifying" (*MPL* 40:211).

54. Dietenberger, *De votis monasticis* 2:Ivii.

The cautious and qualified approaches of Dietenberger, Clichtoveus, and Schatzgeyer suggest that Luther's *sola gratia* doctrine, viewed in the light of historic Christian sources, was by no means to be instantly dismissed. Of course, this is not to say that the doctrine was thereby any more acceptable to them, for it struck at the heart of the theory, maintained by nearly all the controversialists, that God has in some way to be compensated by us for God's grace.[55] But even their own compensation theory was complicated by Augustine's dictum, which they quoted freely, that when God rewards our good works God does no more than crown God's own gifts.[56] The controversialists therefore found themselves once again in the position of needing to refute Luther but by no means having all the theological authorities on their side.

The solution they adopted was to demonstrate the untoward pastoral effects the *sola gratia–sola fide* doctrine would have. Eck, who can hardly be described as a moderate, claimed that he fully accepted justification by faith alone. His opposition was prompted solely by the thought that the common people would misunderstand it and neglect virtuous actions.[57] In his *Diatribe* on free will, Erasmus went so far as to say of the sacrament of penance that he would uphold it even if he did not believe it, simply because it kept the people in check. (Erasmus was not alone in his attitude toward Luther's doctrine of penance. It prompted Fabri's extraordinary confession "I agree with almost everything Luther says . . . I wish that everybody would become real Lutherans.")[58] The entire *Diatribe* was an attempt to preserve the priority of grace while at the same time allowing just enough to human initiative for "simple people" to see that there was some purpose *sub specie aeternitatis* in good behavior:[59] abolish merit and the free will it presupposes and you abolish morality. This was also the motto of Erasmus's less-renowned fellow defenders of free will such as

55. We first encountered the compensation theory in the course of the indulgence controversy. That it still underlay the Catholic response was evidenced by Dietenberger's emotive reference to "robbing God of his grace" (*Von menschen leren,* Biv) and by numerous implicit appeals to a covenant theology that required the sinner to do his or her best in response to or as a precondition of God's grace. See Bachmann, *Czuerrettung,* Aiv; Dietenberger, *De votis monasticis* 2:lvii; idem, *Obe die christen mügen durch iere gute werck dz hymel reich verdienen,* 102.

56. Dietenberger, *Obe die christen,* 107; Clichtoveus, *Antilutherus* 3:144.

57. See Iserloh, *Theologen* 1:70.

58. Fabri to Vadian, summer 1520. See Iserloh, *Theologen* 1:90.

59. See, e.g., Erasmus, *Diatribe,* Av[v], Evii[v].

Dietenberger, Bachmann, and Blich.[60] Even the controversialist who elicited from Luther his most scholarly exposition of justification by faith alone, Jacobus Latomus, argued only that this doctrine was heretical "in the sense which Luther uses and expounds," that is, with apparent prejudice to morality.[61] Their defense of good works was primarily pragmatic. But they also put forward other reasons for commending them: good works provide a moral certitude that one is in a state of grace;[62] they edify one's neighbors;[63] and they mortify the flesh.[64] For Bachmann, they ensured such worldly benefits as protection from enemies and a long life.[65] For Schatzgeyer, it was evidence of Christian immaturity to bring forth leaves and flowers of faith but not the fruit of works.[66] None of these supplementary reasons, however, could prove or were intended to prove the necessity of good works for salvation.

It is tempting, in light of the controversialists' vehement rejection of *sola gratia–sola fide* in spite of the equivocation of the theological tradition on this question, to suggest that they were helping create a division between themselves and Luther where there was no such great gulf in fact. Such a conclusion would support the general theory of this chapter that the period 1522–25 saw the polarization of the two churches, and is itself supported by ecumenically minded historians and theologians such as Lortz,[67] who held that the controversialists devoted so little attention to *sola fides* only because it was self-evident, and that the Reformation was therefore based on a misunderstanding. I think that we are entitled to assert this only to a very limited extent. In this case, if not in others, the gulf between the two sides was uncrossable from the outset. The theology against which Luther set himself from the time of the *Disputation against Scholastic Theology* was that God must be recompensed by humankind for grace. This compensation theory was so deep-seated that even when the controver-

---

60. Dietenberger, *Obe die christen*, 100; idem, *Rede*, Bii[v]; Blich, *Verderbe*, Fiii[v]; Bachmann, *Czuerrettung*, Ai[v]. Cf. Eck, *Enchiridion*, 317.

61. Latomus, *De ecclesia*, 87[v]. Cf. idem, *Contra articulos quosdam Martini Lutheri a Theologis Lovan. damnatos* ("*Ratio*"), 25.

62. Bachmann, *Czuerrettung*, Hiv[v]; Dietenberger, *De votis monasticis* 1:Eiii[v].

63. Bachmann, *Czuerrettung*, Hiv[v]; Schatzgeyer, *Vonn christlichen satzungen*, Ai[v].

64. Ibid. Two similar lists of the benefits and the necessity of good works occur in Caspar Schatzgeyer, *Scrutinium*, 61–62, 140–59.

65. Bachmann, *Czuerrettung*, Hiv–v.

66. Schatzgeyer, *Vonn christlichen satzungen*, Aiii[v].

67. Lortz, *Reformation in Germany* 2:200–201.

sialists were aware that there was little justification for it in the traditional sources, they tried to defend it on other grounds (the pastoral argument, for instance). Lortz is right to say that the controversialists accepted *sola fides* as the historic faith of the church—they could hardly do otherwise—but he is wrong to conclude that they therefore believed it in any deep sense. Their thoroughgoing compensationism made this impossible.

Scripture and Consensus

It is a truism that, while *sola gratia* was the material cause of the Reformation, *sola scriptura* was its formal cause. As with the controversy over faith, works, and free will, the Scripture principle did not draw as much direct Catholic fire in the first years of the Reformation as one might expect. In contrast, it played a more significant part in the controversy overall because it had such a bearing on the counterstrategy adopted by individual Catholics, who had to decide whether to fight Luther on the ground he had chosen and base their case on Scripture alone or to demonstrate the insufficiency of Scripture by appealing to other authorities as well.

Luther's characteristic position was that no doctrine not found in Scripture can be enjoined as generally necessary for salvation. This view was universally condemned by Catholics,[68] principally on two grounds that were themselves drawn from Scripture. First, Christ said much to his apostles that is not recorded in Scripture (John 21:25).[69] This apostolic tradition was reputed to include such practices as praying toward the east and observing Sunday as the Christian sabbath, and such doctrines as the generation of the Son from the Father. Second, Christ told his apostles that they could not yet bear the whole truth and promised them the Holy Spirit, which would lead them into all truth (John 16:12-13).[70] This was taken as a guarantee of the trustworthiness of established custom, *consuetudo ecclesiae*.[71]

---

68. Dietenberger, *Von menschen leren*, Aii; idem, *De votis monasticis* 2:Av[v]; idem, *Underweisung*, Eiii[v], Ki; Schatzgeyer, *Von der heiligen*, Eiii[v]–iv[v]; idem, *Vonn christlichen satzungen*, Bi[v]; Clichtoveus, *Antilutherus* 1:9; 3:117; Cochlaeus, *Wideford*, passim; Powell, *Propugnaculum*, 41; Fabri, *Malleus*, 306.

69. Cochlaeus, *Wideford*, Aiii[v]; Henry, *Assertio*, Hiii, Niv, Oi.

70. Schatzgeyer, *Von der heiligen*, passim; idem, *Vonn christlichen satzungen*, Fiii; Powell, *Propugnaculum*, 42; Henry, *Assertio*, Eiv, Uiv; Fisher, *Confutatio*, 280.

71. Latomus, *De ecclesia*, 96f.; Clichtoveus, *Antilutherus* 1:23, 26f., 34; Cochlaeus, *Wideford*, Aiv[v]–Bi.

The controversialists laid great store by the positive evaluation of precedent contained in the preamble to Gratian's decrees, and even took it to extremes not countenanced in canon law. Augustine's dictum that the customs of the people of God have the force of law came readily to their lips once again. Since the Holy Spirit and the Holy Scriptures themselves belonged to the church, correct interpretation of the Scriptures could be found only within the church.[72] For Erasmus, Campester, Fisher, and Cochlaeus, the "church's" interpretation meant in effect the classic expositions of the early fathers.[73] Consequently, heretics and schismatics, being outside the church, were held legally and actually incapable of interpreting Scripture according to the Spirit. They were deprived, as Fisher pointed out, of the right to interpret Scripture (*ius tractandi scripturas*), and could therefore understand it only in a literal sense. Conversely, the literal interpretation of Scripture itself produced many heresies.[74] Scripture was therefore to be considered the property of the church. Being part of a consensus of authorities, it was neither separate from nor above the church.[75] Latomus even went so far as to assert that, in certain cases, Scripture should be considered as of less weight than other authorities.[76] The church decided which books should constitute the canon; therefore the church had jurisdiction over Scripture and not vice versa. As Augustine put it, "I would not have believed the Gospel had the authority of the Catholic church not prompted me."[77]

To understand the intention and the task of the Romanists in this

72. Latomus, *De ecclesia*, 95ᵛ; Fisher, *Confutatio*, 287.

73. Erasmus, *Diatribe*, Aviiiᵛ; Fisher, *Confutatio*, 280, 288, 291; Campester, *Heptacolon*, Hiv. Cochlaeus's views were expressed on this occasion by his republishing of the condemnation of Wycliffe by the fourteenth-century London Carmelite William Wideford in *Ob nichts anzünemen sey*, of which see esp. Biii.

74. Latomus, *De ecclesia*, 92ᵛ–93, 95; Dietenberger, *Von menschen leren*, Civᵛ; idem, *Der leye*, Biᵛ; Clichtoveus, *De veneratione sanctorum*, Oi; Cochlaeus, *Wideford*, Biif.; Fisher, *Confutatio*, 278, 286; Henry, *Assertio*, Oiiiᵛ, Riiif.

75. Fisher, *Confutatio*, 290, 291, 296, 299; Henry, *Assertio*, Oiiiᵛ. Cf. Alveld's letter to his patroness Margarethe of Anhalt, 11 February 1527, in which he advised her not to take to heart the Lutheran claim that they had Scripture on their side. Catholics had the whole church on their side, he wrote, which is stronger than Scripture just as the body is stronger than an individual member (Lemmens, *Aus ungedruckten Franziskanerbriefen des XVI. Jahrhunderts*, 40).

76. "Although the authority of Scripture is not diminished, in this case the consensus of the whole world has the force of a commandment" (Latomus, *De ecclesia*, 91; cf. 96).

77. MPL 42:176. Quoted by Alveld, *Abgot*, 41; Fisher, *Confutatio*, 285; Henry, *Assertio*, Nivᵛ, Rii.

controversy, it is important to dismiss any simplistic formulation that sees them combating the Bible's authority with that of the church, or the Scripture principle with a tradition principle.[78] I believe we should speak rather of a Catholic consensus principle. The *consensus ecclesiae* was wider than the church, in the sense of its teaching office, in that it included the teaching of the fathers; it was also wider than tradition, in the sense of apostolic tradition, because it included both precedent and positive law established outside it. Most significantly, it included the Holy Scriptures. These were considered part of the holy church, in no sense separate from or contrary to it, and open to interpretation only by the Holy Spirit, which resided exclusively within the church. Luther's great mistake, in the Romanist view, was to take the Bible in isolation, to claim that it was its own interpreter. In reality, they believed, that would leave one with the literal interpretation alone, with the letter that kills. The true, spiritual interpretation existed solely within the community of the Spirit, the church, and could be divined only from the consensus of the church. The Scriptures were, as we might say, a blank check: they could be written on by Catholics or by heretics, but had no value they were not assigned. This was Erasmus's view, who stated quite clearly that the controversy between Luther and his opponents had never been about the importance of Scripture, but about its meaning.[79] Such a conviction also lay behind Fisher's advice that it is more profitable to study the fathers than Scripture.[80]

Luther's belief in the internal clarity of Scripture was therefore a mistake, but also a threat. It threatened the *consensus ecclesiae* itself, because it presupposed a distinction between God's word and humankind's: God's teaching, he maintained, was to be found primarily (though by no means exclusively) in Scripture, while ecclesiastical constitutions and customs, together with the teachings of individual theologians, were often (but not always) the doctrines of human beings. Although such a distinction was alien to Romanist thinking, it was sometimes adopted by them in the course of controversy. These

78. G. H. Tavard (*Holy Writ or Holy Church? The Crisis of the Protestant Reformation*) dispelled the mistaken contrast between the Bible and the church thirty years ago. The misconception of a so-called Catholic tradition principle has yet to be exorcized.

79. "But the controversy in this case is not about Scripture, because both sides embrace and honour the same Scripture. The battle is about the sense of Scripture" (Erasmus, *Diatribe*, Aviii^v).

80. Fisher, *Confutatio*, 281.

"defenses of the doctrines of men"[81] became predictable arguments for obedience to higher authority, familiar from earlier stages of the controversy. In order to press Luther on this point, the Romanists abandoned, at least for the sake of argument, their belief in the indivisibility of the Spirit-led consensus. But this was an aberration. On the whole, the consensus was too valuable a weapon for the Romanists to neglect altogether because it allowed any belief or practice to be justified simply on the grounds that it was believed or practiced.

Such a tendency is apparent from their interpretation of custom. The early canons of Gratian, especially *Ecclesiasticarum, In his rebus,* and *Catholica,* are clear that Scripture, apostolic tradition, and local and universal customs (provided that they contravene neither positive law nor the law of reason) have equal force.[82] Apostolic tradition was, of course, a fixed body of instructions, the contents of which were well known from references to it made by the fathers. What local and universal customs embraced was, however, not so evident. Clearly they were less ancient than the apostolic traditions, but how ancient did a custom have to be for it to be traditional? The fact that many of the beliefs and practices the Romanists defended as traditional or customary were of recent date caused them little embarrassment. This must not surprise us, for their appeal was ultimately not to antiquity, nor to catholicity, but to the fact that the doctrine or discipline at issue belonged to that church to which Christ had promised the Spirit of truth. The process of being led into all truth was one that nullified all considerations of antiquity and universality, "for the Spirit blows not only where it will, but also when it will."[83]

The greatest impact of the debate over Scripture on the controversy as a whole was on the way in which the Catholic controversialists wrote their books. In light of Luther's reliance on Scripture, were his opponents to refute him on other grounds or to carry the fight to him? Three different strategies were adopted. For those such

---

81. "Whosoever transgresses sins directly and immediately against human law, but indirectly against divine law" (Latomus, *De ecclesia,* 102). See also Campester, *Heptacolon,* Aiv[v], Giiif.; Clichtoveus, *Antilutherus* 1:23–26; 2:55[v]–61[v]; Dietenberger, *Von menschen leren,* Biv. Schatzgeyer's *Vonn christlichen satzungen* represents a transition from the consensus argument toward one that accepted the existence of "human laws" within the church. For the coexistence of both approaches, see ibid., Div[v]–Ei.

82. See, e.g., Dist. XI, canon *Ecclesiasticarum (CICan* 1:24), canon *In his rebus (CICan* 1:25), and canon *Catholica (CICan* 1:25).

83. Henry, *Assertio,* Eiv.

as Dietenberger who agreed with Luther that Scripture was the most important of all ecclesiastical authorities, it was necessary that Scripture be clearly shown to provide no support for the reformer's positions. A few authors, believing that the use of Scripture in disputes was at best indecisive and at worse dangerous, chose to avoid it so far as they could and to prove Luther's impiety on other, usually scholastic, grounds. A middle position was taken by the scholastic humanists who, like the scholastics, utterly rejected any attempt to drive a wedge between the Bible and the schoolmen, yet in spite of this—or rather because of it—based their defenses squarely on scriptural evidence. Undoubtedly the finest exponent of this method was Schatzgeyer, whose polemical works, with their thoroughgoing biblical theology, have led to the mistaken belief that he was a biblical humanist.[84] While never so skillfully employed as by Schatzgeyer, this third method became the one most usually adopted by his colleagues: Catholic biblicists were obliged to appeal sooner or later to extrabiblical authorities, while scholastics were under an equal and opposite obligation to appeal to Scripture because their masters so frequently did. The necessity of consensus made itself felt once more.

A notable feature of the Romanists' reaction to Luther's use of Scripture was the way in which they reversed their customary process of argument. With individual points of doctrine, their usual method was to examine Luther's pronouncements and to conclude from these that he was a heretic. But in this case they proceeded from the prior assumption of his heresy and concluded that he was therefore unable to interpret Scripture properly.[85] This was an important step, because it made the Romanist argument that Luther was a heretic completely circular, an argument as convincing to those who accepted its various premises as it was unconvincing to those who did not. It has already been argued that this phase of the Catholic literary effort between 1522 and 1525 was characterized by polarization between two camps, two churches. It is therefore appropriate that the argument for Luther's heresy should also have become closed during this period. If the conversion of Luther or his followers had ever been uppermost in the controversialists' minds, the possibility of rational engagement

84. According to P. L. Nyhus ("Caspar Schatzgeyer and Conrad Pellican: The Triumph of Dissension in the Early Sixteenth Century," 194–95), even Schatzgeyer's contemporaries were led to believe in his biblical humanism.
85. See nn. 72, 73 above.

between the two camps had now vanished. Rational argument presupposed one's opponent's own reasonableness. But heretics, by per-
severing in error, were believed to be beyond reclamation.[86] The only
appropriate course of action was to confront them with the authority
of the Catholic church and oblige them either to submit or else to
condemn themselves out of their own mouths.[87] By disallowing
Luther's appeal to Scripture during this period the Roman controversialists proved once more that their intention was to silence criticism,
not to encourage public debate.

The Moral Fruits of
Luther's Teaching

A vital plank in the Roman controversialists' platform was that the
public dissemination of Lutheran ideas would result in widespread
immorality. The proclamation by a senior churchman and academic of
difficult doctrines easily misinterpreted would, they believed, be taken
by the simple and the unscrupulous as a license for acts of criminality.
The controversialists had already used the pastoral argument as a fatal
objection even to those of Luther's teachings they believed theologically impeccable, such as justification by faith alone, his views on
penance, and the universal priesthood. The Peasants' War was to stand
as a bloody fulfillment of their warnings, and well-publicized cases of
immorality in towns such as Wittenberg that had supposedly under-
gone "reformation" were to disgust not only Luther himself, but
several of his followers who would consequently defect to Rome.
(Nevertheless, it should be noted that, until 1525, the Roman controversialists' conviction of having seen bad fruit borne by the tree they
had always claimed to be bad was based almost entirely on examples
of monastic apostasy and monastic and clerical marriage, which was
not yet the sort of "immorality" to falsify Lutheranism from the Lutherans' own point of view. At this stage the best evidence the controver-

---

86. "The heretic adheres obstinately to falsehood, the bad Catholic does not. For
this reason, the one case is incurable, the other curable" (Latomus, *De ecclesia*, 92ᵛ). See
also Eck, *Enchiridion*, 281: "They are incorrigible, obstinate, and are not teachable of
God, but rely on their own sense and thus obstruct the Holy Spirit."

87. Latomus, *De ecclesia*, 92ᵛ. The reference, presumably to Augustine's letter to
Jerome (*MPL* 33:277) was made by so early an opponent of Luther as Tetzel (*Vorlegung*,
in Löscher 1:484), but then seems to have fallen from the Roman controversialists'
repertoire. Its reappearance at this polarizing stage of the pamphlet war is significant.

sialists could cite was gossip, innuendo, and damning by association.)[88] It was important, therefore, for the Romanists to demonstrate the moral failure of the Reformation, which they normally did by means of asides in their works of controversial theology. But five authors— Cochlaeus, Dietenberger, Blich, Slegel, and one anonymous writer— produced books specially devoted to this theme, and these were stylistically the most popularizing of all the Catholic works produced in the first eight years of the Reformation.

It is tempting to compare Blich's *Shame and Desolation of the Nation and Its People* with an opposition party's election literature. After four years of religious and economic decline, and the erosion of law and order during that time, the author declared, no one would want to admit to being Martinists. The Lutherans, he pointed out, made much of brotherly love, which they believed had been neglected by the medieval church. But how caring was it, he asked, to put out of work woodcut makers, painters, goldsmiths, jewelers, and illuminators who depended on ecclesiastical decoration for their livelihood?[89] Purple passages abound:

> Moreover, churches, cloisters and foundations which our ancestors built (and without doubt it was our ancestors who made such buildings wealthy and who maintained them in their wealth) have fallen into such poverty and necessity that they can scarcely be

88. Luther did not lack skeletons in his own cupboard, and his fellow monks at Erfurt (who considered themselves betrayed when he took Staupitz's side in the question of the reform of the German Augustinians) seem to have been only too glad to furnish interested parties with stories of his litigious and even demonic behavior. Cochlaeus (*Paraclesis*, Cii^Vf.) reports Luther's litigiousness and betrayal of the seven conventual monasteries. For the story of Staupitz's reform and the part Luther played on both sides, see, e.g., H. Boehmer, *Martin Luther: Road to Reformation* (New York: Meridian Books, 1957), 77–81. Bachmann is, I believe, the first to record the famous incident in which Luther is said to have fallen writhing from his stall while the story of Jesus's healing of the young demoniac was being read, crying "It does not mean me" (*Czuerrettung*, Ciii^V). This colorful narrative was eventually included in Cochlaeus's influential *Commentaria Iohannis Cochlaei, de actis et scriptis Martini Lutheri*, fol. 2^V, by virtue of which it became an indispensable element of the Luther myth, lasting even into the 1960s: see John Osborne's play *Luther*, at the end of act 1, scene 1. Titillating as such reports were, they did not indicate the scale of the Lutheran virus. Cochlaeus (*Christliche vermanung*, Fii) accordingly obliged with scandal about the married women of Wittenberg and hinted that the Elector Frederick's complaisance with the immorality (that is, the matrimony) of his clergy was entirely consistent with the prince's own irregular matrimonial arrangements. He also related suitably gory accounts of past massacres of good German Catholics at the hands of heretics, to suggest the shape of things to come (Giv^V–Hi).

89. Blich, *Verderbe*, Ci, Cii–iii.

kept up. So much for the love of neighbour, which these men preach, as far as the houses and servants of God are concerned![90]

In short, a runaway monk has turned everything upside down. . . . Pious virgin nuns have become whores, devout monks wicked carnal unchaste men, and good Christians evil heretical dogs. . . . The people's deep devotion has been destroyed; instead of good works there are works of base carnality; for freedom of the Spirit, the freedom of the flesh; . . . for love of God, hatred of neighbour; for moderation, eating and drinking and feasting.[91]

It is not too far-fetched to regard Blich's antitheses as the Romanist equivalent of the Lutheran propaganda technique identified by S. E. Ozment, in which anxieties were first created by reference to current ecclesiastical malpractice, then the resolution of those anxieties offered in the form of the new teachings.[92] Blich's technique is the reverse of this. Those who had cried so incessantly for moral reform now had to admit that the present state of society was worse for the changes and not better.

If *Shame and Desolation* should be compared with criticism of a government's record, the anonymous *Game of Skittles* is more like a satirical dramatic sketch, in which different public figures step forward and reveal in asides their true hopes and fears. The followers of Luther are playing skittles, but the skittles they try to strike are the poor, simple lay folk; the bowl they use is Holy Scripture; and the mark at which they aim is faith. Luther, the "mother of them all," tells us his concern is just to scatter the skittles, regardless of the consequences.[93] The clerical "disciples of propaganda" follow him for expected rewards, a wife perhaps, or an increased stipend.[94] Observing this spectacle are the followers of the "right old way of the Gospel," the pope, the emperor, a bishop, and assorted priests, who each in turn express their doubts and fears. By far the longest complaint is put into the mouths of the so-called rank-and-file priests, and this may indicate the author's own station in life. It troubles them, they say, to see these young men make sport of the right old way and of ordinary folk. Their sole intention is to knock everybody down, especially the

90. Blich, *Verderbe*, Ci.
91. Blich, *Verderbe*, Eii^v.
92. S. E. Ozment, *The Reformation in the Cities: The Appeal of Protestantism to Sixteenth-Century Germany and Switzerland*, 116–20. Cf. Dickens, *German Nation*, 132.
93. *Kögel spil gebracttiziert ausz dem yeczigen zwytracht des glaubens* (1522), Aii.
94. Ibid., Aiii^v.

pope and the emperor, and they encourage the religious to abandon works of piety. They claim to have rediscovered the gospel, but in fact have just unearthed Hussitism.

> They say that under the men of old
> Scripture-truth got covered in mould.
> The true bowl which in chains was bound
> They boast that they themselves have found.
> They're under the Hussites' magic spell—
> I can't believe that's the true Gospel.[95]

Finally, the mayor of Upper Esslingen gives his own point of view. He does not claim to understand the Lutherans' game. All he knows is that, while the game is on, peasants can laugh and disobey the commandments, and a fool's cudgel will answer a bishop's authority.[96]

Despite an ending that dissipates its partisan force, the *Game of Skittles* is a sparkling piece of popular propaganda. With its versified speeches and its setting in a bowling alley, one could imagine that it was intended as a play in the *Fastnachtspiel* tradition, or was at least inspired by this form. Certainly the title-page woodcut of the major protagonists facing each other across the alley that divides the picture in two is a striking visual image, although it is doubtful whether its unfamiliar scene and signification would have been accessible to anyone who could not read its verbose legend.[97]

It is something of a shock, after the lighthearted *Game of Skittles*, to read Matthias Slegel's *What Good Has Come of the False Lutheran Cats?* a short, violent piece crammed full of sarcasm, abuse, popular prejudice, and superstition—altogether something we would more readily expect from a Thomas Müntzer than from a Catholic contro-

---

95. Ibid., Biii.
96. Ibid., Biii[v].
97. My impression is that the *Kegelspil* grew at the hands of two or more authors. The first (who was probably a humanist, to judge from his sympathetic evaluation of Erasmus and Melanchthon) wrote the bulk of the pamphlet, up to and including the speech of the mayor of Upper Esslingen, which is consistently pro-Roman (Aii–Biii[v]). The final two paragraphs (on the separate sheet Biv in the two editions I have seen), namely, the "Conclusio" and "Lenhart zů der Eych," give the piece a quite different flavor: both sides are in it for what they can get, and the old and the new sound much the same if your belly is empty. The average syllabic length of these twenty-four lines is also shorter than that of the preceding lines. Between these two stages the woodcut and the title-cum-legend were added. These continue the partisan theme of the greater part of the pamphlet, but contain references to themes not elaborated elsewhere in the work (e.g., the three holy teachers, the four evangelists, and the twelve apostles).

versialist. Only four pages long, it is eminently qualified to be considered a classic *Flugschrift*: it relates Lichtenberger's fifteenth-century prophecy of a black monk to Luther;[98] it plays up the violent, anti-authoritarian tendencies of the opposition (*bundtschuh, plutzapffen*)[99] and its mendacity.[100] Humanism is a chief target, damningly associated with insurrection and Jewry,[101] but once again the emphasis is on the damage done to piety. "They propose to introduce a 'German mass,' for which little enthusiasm will be found. They also propose that the holy sacrament be received daily by young and old alike. But such daily use will bring with it annoyance and reluctance, and the mass will be as much revered by Mr. and Mrs. Bloggs as an ordinary meal."[102] This is a comparatively restrained passage. In its final lines the pamphlet reaches a peak of bombast: "Hell, Devil, Hell take them all! Slaughter the cats! Slaughter the Lutheran cats! Slaughter the heretics!"[103]

The pamphlet with which Cochlaeus, using the pen-name "D.J.K.," exposed the bad fruit of Lutheranism was also popularist, though it never reached Slegel's pitch of hysteria. Once again, the emphasis was on distinguishing between the two churches, between Lutheran and true evangelical freedom.[104] His *Mirror of Evangelical Freedom* developed an inventive color-coding of Luther's heresies: black were the lies he spread about the immorality of the spirituals, while remaining silent about the far worse crimes of worldlings; green stood for the lying, envious, mendacious, faithless, and topsy-turvy doctrine of faith alone without works; blue was for the harsh doctrine that we are brute beasts with no free will before God.[105] True evangelic

---

98. On Lichtenberger's *Prognosticatio* of 1488, see Dickens, *German Nation*, 14–15. For a more detailed treatment and for the use of Lichtenberger by other controversialists, see D. Kurze, *Johannes Lichtenberger: Eine Studie zur Geschichte der Prophetie und Astrologie*, 58ff.

99. Matthias Slegel, *Wass nützung enntspring von den falschen Lutherischen Catzen*, Aii, Aiiif.

100. "False cats" (an idiomatic expression meaning "hypocrites"), passim; "false ambassadors," Aiii; "false evangelists," Aii, Aii^v, Aiii^v; "Antichrist," Aii, Aii^v.

101. Slegel, *Wass nützung*, Aiii, Aiii^v.

102. Ibid., Aii^v.

103. Ibid., Aiii^v.

104. "I have resolved to show with God's help what the difference is between true Christian freedom and Lutheran freedom, and how one may distinguish them and follow the holy Gospel of Christ and the teaching of the holy apostles" (Cochlaeus, *Freyheit*, Aiii).

105. Ibid., Bii^v–iii, Civ.

liberty, on the other hand, is to be found by selfless incorporation into the body of Christ, the Catholic church, and by voluntary subjection and obedience to its nobler members.[106]

The theme of these pamphlets—the immorality of self-appointed reformers of other people's morals—was excellently suited to the rumbustious treatment it received. But in fact these four pamphlets were very close in style and purpose to the pamphlets written in support of the Reformation, and the comparison with election literature indicates their deliberate appeal to public opinion. The authors of these four pamphlets, therefore, shared the intentions of the Reformation publicists. But it is significant that such popular pamphlets constituted only a tiny part of Catholic publishing. Two authors, Blich and Slegel, are known only from the two pamphlets here described—in other words, they did not make a significant literary contribution to the Catholic cause. Again, few unequivocal conclusions can be based on the anonymous *Game of Skittles* because of its ambiguity. The remaining author, Cochlaeus, elected to adopt a nom de plume which perhaps suggests his recognition that this particular pamphlet differed in some way from the rest of his output. What is undeniable about these pamphlets is that their lurid depictions of the moral and doctrinal depravity of the reformers fit well with the policy of the mid-1520s, which had abandoned controversy (and the possibility of dialogue, however limited, which that entailed) for outright condemnation.

Catholic Compendia, 1521–1525

Alongside the vast numbers of pamphlets devoted to single themes, such as formed the bulk of the works discussed so far in this chapter, there emerged a class of writings that dealt with several subjects at once. While a number of factors contributed to its development, one of the most important was the proliferation of the minor controversies described in this chapter, because such controversies demonstrated that the Luther affair involved much more than a secession over one or two issues. In a way that the minor pamphlets with their limited scope could not, these compendia bore eloquent witness to the existence of two churches because as they developed they became little less than *summae* of the Roman faith.

The compendia fall into three categories. Some are not much

106. Ibid., Ci–iii.

more than collections of unrelated treatises that happened to be published in the same volume. An example is Latomus's *The Church* (1525), a collection of short disputations on secret confession, on the types of individuals opposed to the church, and on the church itself. No attempt was made by the author or publisher to establish a line of thought between the disputations, and they were presumably published together only because separately none would have constituted a decent-sized book. A better attempt at giving his work coherence was made by Clichtoveus. The three books of his *Antilutherus* (1524)—on the church's power to pass and enforce laws, on orders and the mass, and on monastic vows—are linked by a conviction that these are the three pillars on which the "ecclesiastical commonwealth" (*respublica ecclesiastica*) stood, and that the Lutherans had set about systematically to subvert the Christian state in these three areas.[107]

A second category consists of replies that owed their comprehensiveness to the wide-ranging nature of the works they were meant to refute. These were Latomus's so-called *Rationale* (1521), Sichem's *Confutation* (1521), and Fisher's rather larger work of the same name (1523). The *Rationale* was written in support of the Louvain theologians' condemnation of some of Luther's pre-1520 statements. It therefore ranged over a number of issues including free will, sacramental confession, the nature of sin, purgatory, and indulgences, but there was no coherence or systematization to it. Fisher's work was equally derivative, being a refutation of Luther's defense of the articles condemned in *Exsurge Domine*. Some coherence was lent the Englishman's work by his addition of ten introductory "truths" that establish the basis on which the refutation is to be conducted. But even this section was prompted by Luther's introduction to his *Defense of All the Articles*, in which the Scripture principle was set out.

The third category comprises those works that owe their comprehensive nature neither to accident nor to derivation. Catharinus's two books of 1520 and 1521, Schatzgeyer's *Investigation of Holy Scripture* (1522), Fabri's *Hammer of Lutheran Heresy* (1524), and Eck's *Handbook of Commonplaces* (1525) were genuinely original works.[108] Typically

107. See, e.g., Clichtoveus, *Antilutherus* 2:55ᵛ.
108. The traditional view that the form of Eck's *Enchiridion* was not original but inspired by Philipp Melanchthon's *Loci communes* has been questioned. In the introduction to his critical edition, P. Fraenkel argued that "We have to do not so much with a reply to Melanchthon's *Loci communes* as with a pamphlet, made possible by the Catho-

they drew on a number of Luther's books at once. This meant that instead of slavishly following his argument point by point in the way that Emser, for instance, refuted the reformer's individual works, they were able to take a longer view, to select and compare, to decide their own priorities, and generally to free themselves from any pattern dictated by their opponent. In Schatzgeyer's case this was the result of a deliberate policy, and he was able to plan his discussion on the basis of what seemed to him a descending order of magnitude: grace and free will, faith and works, whether good works are sinful, the origins of true repentance, and so forth. In Catharinus's case, it was the result of a happy chance. Controversialists in Germany and the Low Countries (and consequently in France and England) were able to buy Luther's works as they were published. But the Alps were a formidable barrier to the free movement of so burdensome a commodity as books. It was not until Johannes Froben published a "collected works" of Luther in Basel in 1519 that Italians outside the Curia were able to read him. When they answered him, therefore, they answered a number of books at once. Catharinus's *Apology* could address itself to a particular work (e.g., to Luther's *Thirteenth Proposition* in Book Two of the *Apology*), to a group of works on the same subject (books three and four on the indulgences controversy), or to the entire corpus, from which general trends could be revealed and retractions and contradictions exposed (Book One, *Eleven Tricks Played by Luther on the German People*, and Book Five, *A Clear Mirror of Martinian Theology*).

The differences between the categories of compendia make worthwhile generalization difficult. One characteristic that emerges strongly, however, is their tendency in the direction of authoritarianism. The purpose of many Catholic writers was, as we have seen in earlier chapters, simply to reinforce official condemnations. If they supplied rationales to support these condemnations, it was not meant to lessen their authority. With regard to Lutherans, they stressed the impossibility of dialogue. Writing in his *Dispensation from Disputing*

---

lic controversialists, which arranged the materials necessary for developing an answer to Reformation teachings, using a 'modern' literary form preferred by their opponents" (*Johann Eck: Enchiridion locorum communium adversus Lutherum et alios hostes ecclesiae (1525–1543)*, CC 34 (Münster-Westfalen: Aschendorff, 1979), 15*). Fraenkel's work is now supplemented by N. H. Minnich's investigation into the immediate circumstances of the *Enchiridion*'s production, "On the origins of Eck's *Enchiridion*," in E. Iserloh, ed., *Johannes Eck (1486–1543) im Streit der Jahrhunderte*, 37–73.

in 1521, Catharinus had been an early and isolated exponent of the futility of literary debate with Luther. By 1525, such pessimism had become the generally accepted position of the compendiarists. Even Eck, who was still to participate in disputations with the Swiss reformers and in the religious colloquies, revealed in his *Handbook* an absolute disbelief in the value of debating with heretics. "There can be no doubt that Luther and the Lutherans are condemned heretics and are to be treated as such. For they recall the heresies, frequently condemned in the past, of Arius, Manichaeus, Jovinian, Aerius, Vigilantius, Eutyches, Felix, the Albigensians, the Waldensians, John Wycliffe, John Huss, and other heretics with whom there can be no disputing."[109]

With regard to their own laity, the authors of compendia stated unequivocally that this was the Catholic faith, which except a man believe faithfully he cannot be saved. Eck is once again a helpful witness. His German-language version of the *Handbook* was written "for many laity of high and low estate . . . that the simple layperson, and others who have not been instructed in Latin, might have something wherewith to fight and defend themselves against the errors and heresies of the new sects."[110] But popular propaganda did not mean that the controversialists imputed theological ability or understanding to the laity. The divisions of Eck's *Handbook* were *loci* (grounds of proof), not the traditional *quaestiones* (questions) or *dubia* (disputed points). They were not where theological enquiry started, but where it finished.[111]

The development toward ever greater degrees of entrenchment reached its culmination in 1530 in the so-called Confutation of the Augsburg Confession, the official theological basis of imperial opposition to the Lutheran princes. The way to the Confutation was paved with the theological compendia, which were not only written in many cases by the theologians—such as Eck, Fabri, Wimpina, Cochlaeus—who were to become the emperor's advisers, but which also marshaled the arguments and authorities to be drawn upon at Augsburg. As well as being historically their most significant achievement, the Confutation—imitative in style, reactive in content, and directed at

109. Eck, *Enchiridion*, 280.
110. See E. Iserloh, ed., *Johannes Eck Enchiridion*, vi.
111. This aspect of Eck's method in the *Enchiridion* was elucidated by Fraenkel in the introduction to his critical edition (*Johann Eck: Enchiridion* 18*f.).

those with religious and political power—was a paradigm of the controversialists' policy of the preceding decade.

Heresy and Schism

Common to the Catholic genres of 1522 to 1525—both the pamphlets of the minor controversies and the compendia—was the growing appreciation that Luther's threat consisted not in aberrant views on one or two aspects of the medieval church but in the development of a total alternative system of belief and practice, in other words, the creation of a new church. Increasingly after 1522, and exclusively after 1525, Catholic controversial literature both reflected and furthered this polarization, as published exchanges between theologians gave way to treatises for home consumption. In the process, Luther was depersonalized and dehumanized. His doctrines became devilish poisons, not positions to be engaged with rationally. His followers became depraved dregs of society, driven on by the basest of motives. In almost all the pamphlets and books of the Romanists, of course, Luther's threat to the church was summarized in the charge of heresy. This charge occurs so frequently in the literature that it is easy to take it for granted. But by identifying more precisely the implications that this charge had in the minds of those who leveled it, it is possible to explain the process seen at work in this and in preceding chapters.

In the sixteenth century, heresy was always "obstinate heresy" or "heretical depravity." In other words, a distinction was drawn between simple error, a genuine mistake, and persistence in it after being shown one's error. The test of heresy, therefore, was obedience to one's superiors in the faith. An error perpetrated by a loyal Catholic was not considered heresy; but a schismatic, orthodox in all doctrine save the question of communion with Rome, was already a heretic on the grounds of having transgressed the principal article of belief in one, holy, catholic, and apostolic church.[112] The loyal Catholic had not sinned, at least not so seriously, because he or she had remained within the bond of peace, living charitably with fellow members of the body of Christ. It was this love that covered a multitude of sins.[113] But the body of Christ was not thought of as an indifferent collection of organs.

---

112. Latomus, *Ratio*, 1ᵛ; idem, *De ecclesia*, 85, 86ᵛ.
113. Latomus, *Ratio*, 2. The notion of schism as a symptom of a lack of love was developed by Aquinas, who distinguished between sin against charity in thought (*discordia*), in word (*contentio*), and in deed (*seditio*). See *Summa theologiae* 2a, 2ae, qu. 39.

One of the most important associations the image had for the controversialists was that of the deliberate ordering of its members into a complex of inferiority and superiority, obedience and authority.[114] To live charitably within this body was, therefore, to be subject to its order. Therefore, heresy (and schism, the sting of heresy) was primarily thought of as sin against God's order, an equation encountered on almost every page of the Catholic literature.

From such a point of view one can see how the controversialists could readily explain the conjunction of Wycliffe's and Huss's religious revolts with social revolution, and how they could predict the Peasants' War of 1525. As symptoms of a lack of charity, heresy and schism were not simply errors—they were spiritual disorders. On many occasions Luther or his followers were described as suffering some physical or mental illness.[115] This explains the strong conviction on the part of the controversialists that all schisms and heresies were essentially manifestations of the same, recurring disease in the body of Christ. The same symptoms were always present: reliance on the literal meaning of Scripture, the uncharitable rejection of authority, the appeal to the common people, the resort to violence. The disease recurred because it was a trial sent by the devil, but the true church could rest assured that the gates of hell—even the thirteen general persecutions, the twenty-one schisms, and the three hundred heretics that from time to time had beset it—could never prevail.[116]

Such a dismissive attitude to heresy was most convenient. As a madman and an unthinking agent of the devil, the heretic could not profitably be answered rationally. He could be confronted with the brute assertion of the church's authority, that his disobedience

114. Cochlaeus, *Freyheit*, Cii; Emser, *Quadruplica*, Ci; Fisher, *Sacri sacerdotii defensio*, 1248; Marcello, *De authoritate*, 7ᵛ; Clichtoveus, *Antilutherus* 2:57, 60f.; Powell, *Propugnaculum*, 155; Rhadinus, *Oratio*, Hi, Hivᵛf.; Latomus, *De ecclesia*, 95ᵛ. Campester wrote: "It is clear that in the Church there is distinction and dignity of degree and order. For in a natural body there is distinction of members and functions" (*Heptacolon*, Giiiᵛ).

115. Clichtoveus, *Antilutherus* 2:113ᵛff.; Latomus, *De ecclesia*, 92ᵛ; Powell, *Propugnaculum*, 35ᵛ; Eck, *Enchiridion*, 286, 313, 317, 415; Fisher, *Confutatio*, 300, 313; Modestus, *Oratio*, Biᵛ. Alveld gave two of his early pamphlets the names of medical remedies, while many of the Wimpina-Tetzel theses—the first response to the Ninety-five Theses— conclude with the formula "insanit," "he is mad." Campester (*Heptacolon*, Eiiᵛ) explained the fact that Luther had ignored both the *rationes* of the controversialists and the *auctoritas* of condemnations by universities, emperors, and popes by the fact that the very mind and conscience of the unbeliever is corrupt (Titus 1:15).

116. Alveld, *Abgot*, 29. Cf. Eck's descriptions of heresy as a many-headed Hydra and as self-perpetuating (*Enchiridion*, 405, 415).

might be made clear. An alternative strategy—consciously adopted by Catharinus, for example—was to "answer the fool according to his folly, lest he think himself wise,"[117] which in effect meant paying Luther back tenfold in abuse, invective, and sarcasm. In either case, a controversialist would not have to engage seriously with Luther's criticisms. Even the staunchest *Neinsager* conceded that there was some truth in his arguments. But truth in the mouth of a heretic was a delusion of the devil and a snare for the unwary.

It was not simply on account of a belief in the organic or pathological unity of all heresies that Luther was so closely associated with the heretics of the past. There was a more practical reason as well. Many reform-minded Catholics believed that Luther's condemnation had been improper, either because he had not been given a fair hearing, or else because he had not been condemned by a general council.[118] But if it could be proved that his teachings had already been legally condemned as the teachings of past heretics, such reservations could safely be dismissed:

> There is not one single heresy of Luther that is new and which did not exist before. His heresies are those of the Waldensians, the Poor Men of Lyons, the Wycliffites and Hussites, and of even older sects such as the Jovinians and the like, which have already been condemned by councils. So there is no necessity for fresh decisions, because the old ones suffice. As Gelasius says in the canons *Achatius* and *Maiores*: "Achatius was not an inventor of new errors but an imitator."[119]

For both forensic and pathological reasons, "catalogues of heretics" such as Bernard Luxemburg's and Wimpina's were produced, and numerous other references were made to Luther's heretical pedigree. "Wycliffe, Huss, Luther: grandfather, father, grandson."[120] Ironi-

117. Catharinus, *Apologia* (Lauchert, 33). See also Powell, *Propugnaculum*, 3ᵛ. The quotation is from Prov. 26:5.
118. Latomus, *De ecclesia*, 88ᵛ.
119. Latomus, *De ecclesia*, 88ᵛ–89. The reference is to *Decretum Gratiani*, pars II, causa XXIV, qu. 1 (*CICan* 1:966). Cf. Alveld, *Abgot*, 36; Johannes Eck, *Epistola ad divum Caesarem Carolum*, Aii.
120. Clichtoveus, *Antilutherus* 1:5ᵛ. See also Alveld, *Abgot*, 32, 34–36, 37; idem, *Sermo de confessione*, Dii; Blich, *Verderbe*, Aii, Fi; Cochlaeus, *Freyheit*, passim; Clichtoveus, *De veneratione sanctorum*, Aii, Di; idem, *Antilutherus* 1:2; Dietenberger, *Underweisung*, Fiᵛ; Eck, *Ermanung*, Aiᵛ, Aiif.; idem, *Enchiridion*, 24, 75, 280, 289, 313, 324; Sichem, *Confutatio*, 234–35; idem, *Brevis elucidatio*, Aivᵛ, Iivᵛ; Powell, *Propugnaculum*, 6, 35ᵛ, 159 (concerning Wycliffe in particular), 7, 13ᵛ, 24, 27ᵛ, 35, 40, 46ᵛ, 49, 146ᵛ, 150, 181ff.

cally, here we have the origins of the concept of Reformation fore-runners—particularly the Wycliffe-Huss-Luther family tree—which Protestants later adopted as a means of justifying their beliefs on the rather "Catholic" basis of tradition and long usage. But Luther's heresy could be traced further back than Wycliffe, further back even than Jovinian. According to Alveld, the Sadducees of Jesus's time held to a "Lutheran" Scripture principle, accepting only the Pentateuch.[121] Korah, Dathan, and Abiron, who rebelled against Moses, maintained the priesthood of all believers.[122] The first member of the church of which Luther was merely the most recent adherent was Cain, for this was the church called by David the congregation of the wicked (Ps. 21:17, Vulg.) and by John the synagogue of Satan (Rev. 2:9), which had its beginnings in the fall of Lucifer.[123] In the same way as Luther was "not an innovator but a renewer of old heresies,"[124] neither could he be the creator of a new church—only the modern representative of an extremely old one.

121. Alveld, *Abgot,* 33.
122. Alveld, *Abgot,* 32. For the frequent comparison of Luther with Korah and his companions (Gen. 9:20-27), see also Cochlaeus, *Auff den xiii. Artikel,* Civ[v], Di[v]; *Uff CLIIII Artikeln,* Ei; Dietenberger, *Underweisung,* Ji; idem, *Rede,* Di[v]; Clichtoveus, *Antilutherus* 3:152[v]; Fisher, *Adversus Babylonicam captivitatem,* 123; Campester, *Heptacolon,* Fiv, Gi[v], Hiii[v]; Powell, *Propugnaculum,* 139[v], 146[v]; Eck, *De primatu Petri* 1:1; idem, *Enchiridion,* 1; Emser, *Assertio,* 697; idem, *Auff Luthers grewel,* Div[v]; Rhadinus, *Oratio,* Ii[v]; Leib, *Endschafft und frucht,* Aii; Murner, *Ermanung,* Eiv.
123. Alveld, *Abgot,* 31; idem, *Super apostolica sede,* Iii; Petrus Sylvius, *Ein sunderlich nutzlicher Tractat von der eynigen warhafftigen: gemeyne Apostolischer heyligen Christlichen Kirche,* Ai[v]; Eck, *Ermanung,* Biv.
124. Alveld, *Abgot,* 36.

PART FOUR

"HANDS OF PRINTERS,
TONGUES OF DOCTORS"

7

THE BATTLE OF
THE BOOKS

Instructive as a close reading of Luther's earliest opponents is, it does not answer—at least not directly—all the questions that might be asked of their writing. Why, for instance, did the volume of their literature compare so unfavorably with that of Luther and his colleagues, assuming that there were at least as many Romanists as evangelicals capable of putting pen to paper? And how closely was the Catholic literary campaign coordinated with the Roman Church's overall strategy against Luther? To answer these questions, we must take a step or two back from the cut-and-thrust of debate and attempt to set the controversialists' enterprise in a wider context. Their relationship to the spiritual and temporal arms of the ecclesiastical establishment will be explored in chapter 8. The immediate concern is with attempting to understand the character of the Catholic literary response. What sort of people became controversialists and why? What genres and styles of writing were open to them? Which did they choose? What were their aims in writing? How did they understand the role of their controversial theology? This investigation of relatively uncharted areas begins by taking bearings from the well-documented phenomenon of pro-Reformation pamphlets.

Printing for the Reformation

The study of printing as an element contributing to the rapid spread and acceptance of Lutheran ideas is at least 150 years old. Recently, however, the pace of this study has accelerated and we are now in a much better—though still not ideal—position to give an account of the importance of the new technology for the Reformation, and of the Reformation for printing. Although they are inexact, the statistics show a phenomenal increase in printed matter. Total book production in Germany quadrupled between 1518 and 1520 and doubled again by 1524. The number of German-language titles rose from a yearly average of 40 at the beginning of the sixteenth century to 498 in 1523, of which 418 related to the Reformation, the vast majority in its favor.[1]

These figures are impressive, but it is appropriate at this point to enter two caveats. First, the Reformation was primarily a theological, not a technological, event. Lutheran ideas spread rapidly because they spoke of God's free gift of love through Jesus Christ; social, economic, and political factors helped to condition, and were in turn changed by, the religious message and its response; but these factors remained secondary.[2] If the invention of printing was a cause of the Reformation, it was so only by general, indirect, and subtle cultural transformations of the sort suggested by E.L. Eisenstein.[3] Second, the contemporary literacy rate should also be borne in mind when considering Reformation publishing statistics. Recent estimates suggest that only between 5 percent and 10 percent of the population of Germany could read. Although the percentage was higher in towns than in the countryside (no doubt contributing to the urban character of the German Reformation), the generally low figure must disqualify printing as even the chief secondary factor in the spread of Lutheran ideas. The black art was in fact only one of several media pressed into the service of reform. Other visual phenomena, such as demonstrations and riots, and oral forms, such as disputations, everyday conversations, and official announcements, also played their part in conveying Reformation propaganda.[4] But, as can be demonstrated from the evidence of numerous cities, it was through preaching that the masses appropriated the new doctrines.

Such caveats guard one against assigning to the book a role it never had. But equally one should not underestimate its importance for the Reformation. Not a few opinion-formers were actually converted by reading pamphlets, and the literary bombardment that lasted from 1519 to 1524 cleared intellectual ground for the Reformation message and consolidated it thereafter. A close association of printing's advent with Protestantism's spread is not, after all, only a modern interpretation: Luther himself hailed the technology as "God's

---

1. R. Engelsing, *Analphabetentum und Lektüre: Zur Sozialgeschichte des Lesens in Deutschland zwischen feudaler und industrieller Gesellschaft* (Stuttgart: Klett-Cotta, 1973), cited in Wohlfeil, *Einführung*, 126.

2. Dickens, *German Nation*, 103.

3. E. L. Eisenstein, *The Printing Press as an Agent of Change: Communications and Cultural Transformations in Early Modern Europe* 1:367–78.

4. R. W. Scribner, "Reformation, Carnival and the World Turned Upside Down."

highest and extremest act of grace whereby the Gospel's work is furthered."[5] The ways in which the champions of the Reformation
exploited this act of grace provides reference points for a study of
their opponents' use of printing.

The most important and certainly the most enduring propaganda
for the German Reformation was provided by vernacular Bibles, hym-
nals, prayer books, and catechisms. But the years 1518–25 saw the rise
of a phenomenon no less remarkable in its way—the *Flugschrift* (flying
pamphlet), "a self-contained, occasional, and unbound publication
consisting of more than one page, addressed to the general public
with the aim of agitation (i.e., the influencing of events) and/or propaganda (i.e., the influencing of beliefs)."[6] It was a development of the
single broadsheet that emerged in the previous century, consisting of a
report of some natural, historical or contemporary event illustrated in
its upper half by a colored woodcut. The pamphlet differed from this
ancestor of the modern newspaper in that the illustration tended to
become little more than a title-page decoration while the text was
expanded into a small book. The means of producing pamphlets in
large numbers was also readily available to the champions of reform,
because the humanist movement to which so many of them belonged
had established a network of printers, distributors, retailers—and even
a readership—in towns the length and breadth of Europe. In Germany,
the humanist network was as much geared to translating as to editing
Greek and Latin literature.[7] In addition to popularizing the classics,
the humanist presses were also producing political and religious critiques, although such efforts had little in common except the vague
attribution of social and economic ills to the clergy and Roman Curia.

Reformation propaganda therefore had at its disposal an appropriate literary form and the means of its production. It also had a
corps of willing and able propagandists. Their vernacular style was
simple, direct, unashamedly for the common people, and, as P. Bockmann showed, written from the common person's point of view.[8]
Admittedly, few such writers were genuinely lay or proletarian, and it

5. Dickens, *German Nation*, 109.
6. H.-J. Köhler, "Fragestellungen und Methoden zur Interpretation frühneuzeitlicher Flugschriften," 2.
7. See R. Hirsch, "Printing and the Spread of Humanism in Germany: The Example of Albrecht von Eyb," 31.
8. P. Bockmann, "Der gemeine Mann in den Flugschriften der Reformationszeit."

is difficult to entertain the attractive notion that *Flugschriften* really do reflect the common person's verdict on contemporary events when we read self-styled "illiterate peasants" quoting fathers and schoolmen![9] However, few were of high social standing. The majority of Reformation pamphleteers would seem to have come from the rising middle orders, with learning enough to articulate complex ideas yet at this stage still sharing the outlook and interests of the lower classes.[10]

What did these pamphlets actually say? They seem to have set out first to create or to rekindle certain anxieties within the reader and then to present the new doctrines as a resolution of those anxieties. The endlessly repeated ceremonies of the church that gave no answer to the conscience, the priest's control over all aspects of life, and the greed of the Roman Curia were all portrayed as an intolerable burden invented and perpetuated by human teaching, by the writers of oppression. This burden was then lifted by a corresponding stress on inward religion, confidence of salvation in Christ, the primacy of God's teaching expressed in Scripture, and the priesthood of all believers.[11] The contrast was painted in the starkest possible colors: no redeeming feature was attributed to the old system and no defect allowed to the new. The aim of the pamphleteer was not to create an informed climate for discussion, but to change opinions and to incite action.[12]

The most striking aspect of these Reformation *Flugschriften* is that they were designed to reach as low as possible down the social strata. The message and the language in which it was expressed were kept simple, and the pamphleteer started from the hopes and fears of the common man and woman, or at least tried to. Steps were taken to obviate the low literacy rate by using woodcut illustrations as teaching aids,[13] and the contents of pamphlets were evidently read out aloud on occasion by a literate member of a community for the benefit of his or her unlettered colleagues.[14] Although there was some profi-

9. See, e.g., the case of Diepold Peringer, cited in Ozment, *Reformation in the Cities*, 66.

10. See R. W. Scribner, "Practice and Principle in the German Towns: Preachers and People," Tables 3 and 4, for evidence that the "vast majority" of Reformation preachers were working class elite, but with an extraordinarily high standard of education.

11. Dickens, *German Nation*, 132; and Ozment, *Reformation in the Cities*, 116–20.

12. Wohlfeil, *Einführung*, 125.

13. For a detailed study of many of these illustrations and the part they played in propaganda, see R. W. Scribner, *For the Sake of Simple Folk: Popular Propaganda for the German Reformation*.

14. Rupp, "Battle of the Books," 45.

teering by unscrupulous dealers,[15] retail prices were kept low by the brevity and technical simplicity of most of these books and by the size of their production runs.[16]

Striking as this phenomenon was, it begs a question. The attempt to mobilize public opinion at all levels of society is a tactic more appropriate to the era of universal suffrage than to the early sixteenth century. The humanist presses went some way toward popularizing social critiques, but it was the Reformation that first provided writings for the people. Why was this? The most important single factor was Luther himself. He was responsible for 94 percent of all pamphlets expounding Reformation theology (excluding controversial literature) published between 1518 and 1520. He was responsible, too, for giving this theological publication its vernacular stamp at a time when more than two-thirds of traditional theology was published in Latin.[17] And yet Luther seems to have discovered the popularizing potential of printing quite by accident, to judge from his surprise at the rapidity with which unauthorized translations of the Ninety-five Theses spread through Europe.[18] The theses—curt, allusive, and provocative headings for a university disputation—had not been designed for public consumption, and Luther feared he might be misunderstood. The solution he adopted in this case—publishing the *Explanations of the Ninety-five Theses* and the *Sermon on Indulgence and Grace*—serves almost as a paradigm for the rest of his writing career. In extended Latin treatises he could present his ideas and dispel misconceptions about them in a scholarly manner; he had room to elaborate with technical references and to embellish with literary allusions. In his German pamphlets, on the other hand, he could write clearly and concisely and use a more homely style. Of course, this is not to say that he practiced theological reserve; exactly the same matters were discussed, but in two different ways.[19] While printing was still modeled on oral forms of communication, these two ways were, I believe, literary versions of the academic disputation and the vernacular sermon. Luther rapidly eschewed the first for the second, and after 1519

15. Dickens, *German Nation,* 113.
16. A recent study suggests that most (62.1 percent) pamphlets printed during the first half of the sixteenth century were of sixteen pages or less. See R. G. Cole, "The Reformation Pamphlet and Communication Processes," Table 3.
17. See R. A. Crofts, "Books, Reform and the Reformation," Table 4.
18. See Luther's letter to Christoph Scheurl, 5 March 1518 (*WA Br* 1:152.1–24).
19. M. Gravier, *Luther et l'opinion publique,* 33.

his Latin works never again outnumbered the German. In his opinion, God's purposes demanded at that time not large tomes but little sermons.[20]

From this brief survey of recent literature on printing and the Reformation, it can be seen that the real questions have not been, and perhaps cannot be, answered. How many people read or otherwise experienced these pamphlets? To what social groups did they belong? Were they the social groups targeted by these works? What effects did these pamphlets have upon those who read them? Were they the desired effects? But the results so far collected are not entirely unhelpful and at least provide some background against which to examine the far less documented phenomenon of anti-Reformation printing.

Printing against the Reformation

To compare the Romanists' effort with that of the Reformation writers, let us look first at the authors themselves. Fifty-seven Catholic controversialists were active between 1518 and 1525. Of these, twenty-one belonged to a religious order. This percentage (37 percent) is very close to the level of monastic participation in pamphleteering on the Catholic side throughout Europe for the entire period from 1518 to the end of the century—39 percent. Moreover, such a profile is not significantly different from that of the first generation of Reformation pamphleteers. While biographical information for many of the evangelical authors is hard to come by, comparable evidence suggests that approximately one-third were ex-religious.[21] Of the Catholic religious, the Dominican order was best represented with twelve authors, the Franciscans a poor second with five. The Franciscans, however, were more than twice as prolific and actually produced more titles than the Dominicans. At the other extreme, the two Augustinians wrote only one book apiece. It is interesting to note that this is precisely the reverse order of monastic participation in evangelical pamphleteering, if we take the comparable evidence as a guide.[22]

20. Luther's Dedication to Duke John of Saxony in *Von den guten Werckenn* (*WA* 6:203.11–14, *LW* 44:22).
21. Scribner has collected biographical data on 176 Protestant preachers active in Germany up to about 1550. He found that 32.4 percent of those for whom there was appropriate information had backgrounds in religion. See Scribner, "Practice and Principle," Table 1.
22. Of the ex-religious identified by Scribner, eighteen were Augustinians, thirteen Franciscans, and only four were Dominican. See Scribner, "Practice and Principle," Table 1.

In other respects, the differences between the two sides are starker. While several women are to be found in the ranks of the Reformation controversialists, none contributed to the Catholic cause in print at this stage.[23] And although both sides were able to attract lay writers, those who supported the Reformation "represented the full spectrum of sixteenth-century urban society"[24] from the proletariat to the patriciate, while lay participation in defense of the Roman Church up to 1525 was limited to the social and intellectual elite—King Henry of England, Duke Georg of Saxony, Erasmus, Sir Thomas More.

Nineteen of the authors who wrote against Luther in the period before 1526 had received an exclusively scholastic training, compared with twelve humanists. In addition there were five authors—Cellarius, Clichtoveus, Cochlaeus, Eck, and Fabri—who fall into the hybrid category of scholastic humanism. The average tally for each controversialist works out at three books apiece, and as groups both the scholastics (average 2.9) and humanists (2.75) fit unremarkably into this pattern. But these averages of prolificity are misleading. The majority (thirty of the fifty-seven controversialists) wrote only once, so the bulk of the Catholic effort was the responsibility of a handful of stalwarts: 10 percent of the authors produced 44 percent of the writings. When we consider that the four most prolific writers (Cochlaeus, with fourteen works during this period; Eck, Alveld, and Emser with thirteen each) represent scholasticism, humanism, and scholastic humanism, it becomes clear that no tradition had a particular aversion to, or a particu-

---

23. Perhaps the most famous female evangelical writers were Argula von Grumbach and Katharine Zell (see R. H. Bainton, *Women of the Reformation [Germany and Italy]* [Minneapolis: Augsburg Pub. House, 1971], chaps. 3 and 5). When Grumbach published a reasoned defense of the reformer Seehofer against the members of the Ingolstadt theology faculty who had condemned him, and challenged them to a disputation, she received no answer except the present of a distaff from Johannes Eck (see G. Strauss, "The Religious Policies of Dukes Wilhelm and Ludwig of Bavaria in the First Decade of the Protestant Era," 359). A pamphlet appeared under the name of Caritas Pirckheimer, abbess of the Poor Clares at Nuremberg, in support of Emser (*Eyn missyve odder Sendbrieff so die Ebtissche von Nürnberg an . . . bock Emser geschriben* [Wittenberg, 1523]), but this was simply a pirated version of a private letter, heavily glossed with innuendo by an anonymous Lutheran at Wittenberg. The first female Catholic controversialist was the Dutch schoolteacher Anna Bijns, whose anti-Reformation poems were published in 1528. Bijns's example was later followed by Elizabeth Gottgabs, abbess of the convent at Oberwesel, and by the Rem sisters of Augsburg. See M. Wiesner, "Women's Response to the Reformation," in R. Po-chia Hsia, ed., *The German People and the Reformation* (Ithaca and London: Cornell University Press, 1988), 148–71, esp. 158f.

24. M. U. Chrisman, "Lay Response to the Protestant Reformation in Germany, 1520–1528," 51.

lar predilection for, publicity. What these figures do show is that the Catholic literary response was actually more poorly supported than appears at first sight: those who came to Rome's literary defense tended to write just once or twice, and perhaps only a dozen or so Catholics can be regarded as committed propagandists.

How did they set about writing? Their primary requirement would have been for a suitable literary form through which to fulfill their two principal aims: the negative, defensive one of countering Luther's arguments, and the positive, aggressive one of setting forth their own. A number of options were available to a Catholic writer who wished to refute Luther in print. One was to adapt the academic disputation to the demands of literary controversy. There were precedents for this. In 1500, the Tübingen professor Konrad Summenhart published the transcript of the case he had put in a disputation on tithing, because he believed that academic activities had a practical application in such circumstances.[25] The Cologne theologian Peter of Ravenna had also made public a debate within his university. His motive had been more directly polemical—to appeal over the heads of the university authorities to educated lay opinion.[26] The disputation-type publication was used in the controversy between the orders of St. Francis and St. Dominic over the doctrine of the immaculate conception,[27] and of course it was the form Luther had used in replying to scholarly criticisms of his Ninety-five Theses. It was a literary genre that readily appealed to academics, for whom the disputation—as a regular feature in the curriculum, as a quodlibetal exercise, or as a requirement for the award of higher degrees—was a routine means of both teaching and research.

An alternative, but no less scholarly, genre was that of the polemical pamphlet, used in pamphlet wars in the early years of the six-

25. See H. Oberman, *Werden und Wertung der Reformation: Von Wegestreit zum Glaubenskampf*, Spätscholastik und Reformation II (Tubingen: J.C.B. Mohr, 1977), 145ff; abridged Eng. trans. *Masters of the Reformation* (Cambridge: Cambridge University Press, 1981). The text of Summenhart's *Tractatulus de decimis* is partially reprinted in Oberman's book (pp. 381–411). That it was largely a transcript is suggested by the title, which describes the *Tractatulus* as "solemniter anno domini 1497 per eundem [sc. Summenhart] disputatus" (p. 381, ll.11–12). Oberman reminds us that the same belief in the practical value of academic debate was held by the man who in a dispute at Bologna in 1515 argued on the Fuggers' behalf for an interest rate of 5 percent—Johannes Eck (p. 161).

26. See Nauert, "The Clash of Humanists and Scholastics," 6, 8ff.

27. Ibid., 6.

teenth century among writers influenced by humanism. (These wars are often characterized as clashes between humanists and scholastics, but in view of the sympathies and backgrounds of most of the so-called "scholastic" participants, it seems more accurate to regard them as debates between different wings of humanism.)[28] Notable among these was the storm Wimpina created with his *Apologeticus in sacrae theologiae defensionem* in 1500, in which he argued that philosophical theology was the highest of all human sciences and that poetry was the lowest.[29] The cause célèbre of the next decade was the Reuchlin affair, but less sensational controversies bubbled away quietly as well.[30] This type of publication was in Latin and, given its subject matter, directed at an educated readership. It had a family resemblance to an academic disputation that even extended to its style, for these pamphleteers would use irony, ridicule, the *reductio*, and the *argumentum ad hominem*, just as in the schools.

The decision to use the disputation, whether in print or viva voce, proceeded from the assumption that one's opponent was mistaken but still Catholic.[31] Once the Romanists had become convinced of Luther's heterodoxy, however, the additional possibility presented itself of using the literary form reserved for the refutation of heresy. The sixteenth century saw a number of republications of patristic writings. From these it would have become clear that the anti-heretical treatise was a characteristic form used by the fathers. The form had not remained dormant during the Middle Ages, even though systematic heresies became rarer. The last great example of the genre was Thomas Netter of Saffron Walden's five-volume *summa* against Wycliffe, in which it seemed that every possible argument and authority was brought to bear on every supposedly unorthodox statement made by Wycliffe. Netter was reprinted in Paris in 1521, given a new

28. See J. H. Overfield, *Humanism and Scholasticism*, 174, 300.

29. Konrad Wimpina, *Apologeticus in Sacretheologie defensionem, adversus eos qui nixi sunt eidem fontem Caput et patronam Poesim instituere: ac per hoc nec sacram theosim: iure religionis nostre monarchum et architectonicam habituum scientialium agnoscere revererique* (Leipzig, 1500). For details of the ensuing pamphlet war, see Overfield, *Humanism and Scholasticism*, 174–77.

30. See Nauert, "The Clash of Humanists and Scholastics," 6.

31. See, e.g., Luther's protestation in his *Asterisci* concerning the Ninety-five Theses: "Therefore I have asserted nothing, but have disputed and sought to be Catholic, since only obstinate error in the faith makes one a heretic" (*WA* 1:302.22–4). Although in theory one could not dispute with a heretic, the disputation form was still used against Luther into the 1530s.

lease on life, no doubt, by the appearance of the German Wycliffe.[32] Thanks to this Paris edition, Netter's arguments were able to find their way into the works of Eck, Emser, and, in the course of time, into the Catholic theologians' refutation of the Augsburg Confession.[33] It was with the Paris edition in mind that the man most probably responsible for it, the Sorbonne theologian Clichtoveus, wrote his own magnum opus against heresy, the three-volume *Antilutherus* (1524). Clichtoveus was probably not alone in taking Netter as his model. In the third edition of his *Handbook* (Cologne, 1529), Eck changed its subtitle from *adversus Ludderanos* to *adversus Martinum Lutherum et asseclas eius*. The alteration was necessary to reflect the widening scope of the manual; but it also echoed the title of the Netter reprint, *In Witcleffistas et eorum asseclas*. In itself, this alteration signifies little. But in view of Eck's special regard for and use of the Englishman's writings,[34] one can reasonably suppose it to indicate a claim to Netter's mantle: if Luther was the new Wycliffe, Eck was the new Waldensis.

Closely related to the genre of the treatise against a specific heresy or group of heresies was the treatise on the nature of heresy in general. Drawing upon such works as the classical studies of heresy by Johannes von Freiburg and Thomas of Brabant, Wimpina and Bernard of Luxembourg produced *catalogi haereticorum*, in which the new heterodoxies were shown to be merely the most recent manifestations of a single, organic heresy that from time to time assailed the church.[35] Both the *summa* and the *catalogus* presupposed, on the

32. Thomas Netter, *Doctrinalis antiquitatum ecclesiae Jesu Christi liber quintus, ac tomus secundus de sacramentis editus in Witcleffistas et eorum asseclas* (Paris, 1521). Netter also collated the documentation relating to Wycliffe's posthumous trial in *Fasciculi zizaniorum magistri Johannis Wyclif cum Tritico*. See the Rolls series edition by W. W. Shirley (London, 1858).

33. Eck in particular relied heavily on Netter. Some indication of this can be gauged from the remarkable fact that Netter's was the only non-contemporary name in the list of theologians active against Luther with which Eck prefaced his *Enchiridion* (p. 1f.). Fraenkel's apparatus on the *Enchiridion* reveals some 270 implicit references to Netter's *Doctrinale*, the majority relating to the chapters on prayer, church buildings, the priesthood, and the Eucharist. The following year, Eck explicitly acknowledged his indebtedness to Netter's collection of authorities on the sacrifice of the mass (*De sacrificio missae*, 189). Emser's work on the mass was by his own admission equally dependent on Netter (see *Missae assertio*, Bii). Netter's influence on the *Confutatio confessionis Augustanae* seems to have been limited to the refutation of the articles on clerical celibacy and reception in both kinds (see H. Immenkötter, *Die Confutatio der Confessio Augustana vom 3. August 1530*).

34. See n. 33.

35. See Luxembourg, *Catalogus;* and Wimpina, *Anacephaleosis*.

one hand, that the heresy of Luther and his followers had been duly defined and, on the other, that they had expressed their heresies with sufficient clarity and detail to be systematically refuted. Neither genre, therefore, could be employed by the Romanists in the earliest stages of the controversy.

A literary genre associated with humanism available to Catholic writers for refuting Luther was the dialogue. It had its origin in the philosophical dialogues of classical antiquity and survived in this form into the early Middle Ages, for instance in Anselm's *Cur Deus homo.* Thereafter, it all but disappeared,[36] although a trace of it can perhaps be detected in such major theological works as Lombard's *Libri sententiarum* and Aquinas's *Summa theologiae,* which were essentially harmonizations of the statements of earlier theologians. The dialogue reemerged during the Renaissance, first in Italy and then in Germany, where the author of *Pope Julius Locked Out of Heaven* and Hutten adapted it for satirical purposes by giving it a much more dramatic character. Its debut in the service of the Reformation was the satire *Eck Polished Off,* aimed at Luther's opponent in the Leipzig disputation.[37]

Such were the means available to the controversialists for the purpose of refuting the reformer. But there were other genres that allowed them to present a more positive case of their own without having to adopt their opponent's terms of reference. Within the devotional literature of the pre-Reformation period, printed sermons were an important element and an option open as much to Catholic as to evangelical writers. In contrast to the disputation or treatise forms, the sermon was generally short and delivered in the vernacular, which made it particularly suitable for use by popularizers. Another possibility was the open letter, nominally addressed to some friend or patron but in fact intended for a far wider audience. This was a favorite genre with humanists; but when Luther adopted it with his *Sendbriefen* to whole towns and communities, his inspiration was more probably the

---

36. See R. Hirzel, *Der Dialog,* 2 vols. (Leipzig, 1895), 2:384.
37. See T. W. Best, *Eccius Dedolatus: A Reformation Satire* (Lexington: University Press of Kentucky, 1971), for a brief survey of the question of authorship of this pamphlet. On the use of the dialogue form at this time, see W. Lenk, *Die Reformation im zeitgenössischen Dialog* (Berlin, 1968). For the view that the Reformation dialogue was entirely dramatic in form and origin and (against Hirzel and Lenk) owed nothing to the philosophical dialogue of antiquity, see B. Balzer, *Bürgerliche Reformationspropaganda: Die Flugschriften des Hans Sachs in den Jahren 1523–25,* Germanistische Abhandlungen 42 (Stuttgart, 1973), 99–104.

epistles of the New Testament and the fathers than the published correspondence of contemporary *literati*.[38] Another, more specialized, option was that based on the *Klageschrift* or *gravamen*, the plaintiff's sworn testimony. Luther had imitated this form, which had long been used as a vehicle for parliamentary complaints against the Curia, in his address *To the Christian Nobility* (1520), and it may also have informed his appeals to the knights of the Teutonic order on the subject of true chastity (1523) and to the city councilors of Germany on primary education (1524).[39]

Some literary forms used woodcut illustrations, and these might have been considered a particularly effective polemical tool. The most basic type was the broadsheet (*Flugblatt*) already mentioned, which was usually employed as a sort of newspaper.[40] It was developed into a series of cartoons with accompanying text, such as Lucas Cranach's *Passional Christi und Antichristi* and the woodcuts he did for Luther in 1523 and 1545.[41] The apocalyptic *Weissagung* genre, associated with both prophecies (for example, those of Joachim of Fiore and Johannes Lichtenberger) and astrological predictions, was often illustrated with woodcuts and could easily be adapted to polemical use.[42] Finally, of course, there was the poem or song—used to good effect by the Meistersinger Hans Sachs to convey evangelical theology—and the play,

38. See, e.g., Luther, *Epistel oder Unterricht von den Heiligen an der Kirche zu Erfurt* (1522), WA 10.2:164–68; and idem, *Ein Brief an die Christen zu Strassburg wider den Schwärmergeist* (1524), WA 15:391–97. For an example of a more deliberate imitation of Pauline epistolography, see R. Keen's study of Bugenhagen's *Epistola ad Anglos* (1525) in his *Johannes Cochlaeus: Responsio ad Johannem Bugenhagium Pomeranum* (Nieuwkoop: De Graaf, 1988), 17–22.

39. See Luther, *An die Herren Deutschen Ordens, dass sie falsche Keuscheit meiden* (*WA* 12:232–44); and idem, *An die Ratherren aller Städte deutschen Lands, dass sie christliche Schulen aufrichten und halten sollen* (*WA* 15:27–53).

40. See M. Kortepeter, "German Zeitung Literature in the Sixteenth Century."

41. See Luther, *Deuttung der zwo grewlichen Figuren Bapstesels zu Rom und Munchkalbs zu Freyberg in Meyssen funden* (1523), WA 11:362–85; and idem, *Wider dem Papst zu Rom gestifft durch dem Teuffel* (1545), WA 54:206–99.

42. For the publication of Joachite prophecy in the sixteenth century, see M. Reeves, *The Influence of Prophecy in the Later Middle Ages* (Oxford: Clarendon Press, 1969). The most recent study of Lichtenberger is D. Kurze, *Johannes Lichtenberger: Eine Studie zur Geschichte der Prophetie und Astrologie*. For astrological *Flugschriften*, see M. Steinmetz, "Johann Virdung von Hassfurt, sein Leben und seine astrologischen Flugschriften," in Köhler, *Flugschriften als Massenmedium*, 353–72; and P. Zambelli, ed., *"Astrologi hallucinati": Stars and the End of the World in Luther's Time* (Berlin and New York: Walter de Gruyter, 1986).

particularly the rumbustious *Fastnachtspiel*-type, which could be as much an aid to indoctrination as to satire.[43]

The literary forms actually adopted by Luther's Catholic opponents active between 1518 and 1525 are surprisingly varied, bearing in mind the small number of their publications compared with those of Luther and his colleagues. From Emser there is a poem and a four-part song to "celebrate" Luther's marriage;[44] from Murner a lengthy illustrated poem, *The Great Lutheran Fool*; and from an anonymous author a dramatic poem, the *Game of Skittles*. On the other hand, it should be noted that these are the only examples in the Romanist corpus of the use of such forms. Other unique attempts include an example of *Weyssagung* in Sylvius's translation of Vincent Ferrer's *Miraculous Little Work Concerning the End of the World* (though in the course of otherwise nonapocalyptic pamphlets, Emser, Cochlaeus, and Slegel interpreted the "black monk" of Lichtenberger's *Prognostication* as Luther) and an example of consolation literature in Bachmann's *Encouragement of a Vacillating Religious*, subtitled *Eyn Trostlich Rede*. In fact, 79 of the 172 Catholic works (46 percent) fall into a single category, that of scholarly treatises and disputations, trailed distantly by the open letter (12.8 percent), the sermon (7 percent), the dialogue (5.8 percent), and the oration (4.6 percent). The remaining works fall either into no recognizable category or into two or more of the other categories.

Breaking down each category by language, the treatise/disputation and letter forms are found to be heavily biased toward Latin (9.9 to 1 and 4.4 to 1, respectively), while a high proportion of the sermons and, perhaps significantly, of the unclassified publications (75 percent and 83 percent, respectively) were vernacular. Breaking down the categories by year, we find that the oration, which was essentially an Italian forensic imitation of the *Klageschrift* employed exclusively to answer Luther's *To the Christian Nobility*, disappeared completely after 1521, while the letter form declined noticeably. The treatise form, on

---

43. See Hans Sachs, "Die wittembergisch Nachtigall, die man ietz horet uberall," in *Hans Sachsens Ausgewählte Werke* (Leipzig: Insel-Verlag, 1923)1:8–24. See also Niklaus Manuel's six-act play, *Die Totenfresser*, which was performed in Bern during Lent 1523, in F. Vetter, ed., *Niklaus Manuels Spiel evangelischer Freiheit: Die Totenfresser. "Vom Papst und seiner Priesterschaft"* 1523 (Leipzig: Frauenfeld, Huber & Co., 1923).

44. See Hieronymus Emser, *Der Bock dryt frey auff disen plan*; and idem, *Epithalamium Emseri in nuptias Lutheri*, which I have been unable to trace except for nine verses reprinted in Cochlaeus, *Commentaria*, fol. 128.

the other hand, increased throughout the period, so that by 1525 it accounted for half the pamphlets and books published against Luther. Finally, in matching authors with literary genres, we see that some significant writers (Emser and Sylvius, for instance) occasionally experimented with more exotic forms such as song and apocalyptic; and while Dietenberger consistently preferred the vernacular dialogue, Eck and Cochlaeus stood by the treatise and disputation. The many controversialists who wrote only once or twice also preferred to use the scholarly styles.

In the absence of a comparable classification of pro-Reformation pamphlets, it is difficult to make much sense of these figures. From a random sample of three thousand religious and political pamphlets of all allegiances published between 1501 and 1530, H.-J. Köhler has calculated that 48 percent were in a "discursive" style.[45] This corresponds closely to my figure of 46 percent for the category "treatise/disputation." Indeed, this figure seems rather conservative when compared with the 56.5 percent "discursive" established by J. Schwitalla for the period 1520–25.[46] These three figures are not, however, strictly comparable. Apart from the fact that Köhler and Schwitalla were studying the entire pamphlet corpus of their selected periods and not Protestant pamphlets alone, the definition of "discursive language" is subjective and in any case differs from my "treatise/disputation" classification. The most important difference, however, is that the Catholic pamphlets from the years 1518 to 1525 with which we are concerned, while accounting for some three-quarters of the total Catholic polemical output of the period, is in statistical terms neither a random sample nor a universe, but a selection comprising those pamphlets written exclusively or predominantly against Luther.

It might, therefore, be a sounder procedure to compare the Catholic controversialists' output directly with that of their antagonist. M. U. Edwards, Jr., has analyzed Luther's first editions in five-year intervals using categories more strictly comparable with my own.[47] Of 192 works published between 1521 and 1525, 33 (17 percent) were open letters, 84 (44 percent) were sermons, 45 (23 percent) were trea-

45. H.-J. Köhler, "The Flugschriften and Their Importance in Religious Debate: A Quantitative Approach," 163.

46. J. Schwitalla, *Deutsche Flugschriften, 1460–1525. Textsortengeschichtliche Studien,* cited in Köhler, "Flugschriften," 163.

47. M. U. Edwards, Jr., *Luther's Last Battles,* Fig. 7, p. 14.

tises, and 2 (1 percent) were disputations or theses. Other categories—forewords, lectures, expositions of Scripture, woodcuts, glosses, and so forth—accounted for the remaining 28 works (15 percent). If we compare Edwards's figures for Luther with those for the Catholic controversialists over the same period, a number of significant differences emerge. Open letters form nearly one-fifth (17 percent) of Luther's corpus, but only 8 percent of his opponents'. While 44 percent of Luther's output consisted of published sermons, they accounted for a mere 6 percent of Catholic pamphlets. And while half (or perhaps even as much as 58 percent)[48] of the Catholic works were published in the form of treatises and disputations, only a quarter of Luther's works answer to this description. It would, however, be a mistake to build too much on a detailed comparison of Edwards's analysis with my own, not least because the samples of the two studies are perforce so different: in the years 1521–25, Luther had 192 titles published, while the Catholics between them had only 128.

The literary character of the Romanists' response can be explained in a number of ways. First, as a response their publications would naturally be of the occasional, reactive type described above—disputations, point-by-point refutations, polemical pamphlets, dialogues. There would be relatively less opportunity for the more positive modes of communication, such as sermons and letters; when these were used, it would often be in deliberate imitation of Luther's original, the better to engage and neutralize his teachings. Second, it should be borne in mind that the printed sermon was not a viable literary form for many of the more prolific controversialists. His duties in the Black Cloister and at the castle-church in Wittenberg required Luther to preach several times a week. It was inevitable not only that many of these sermons would find their way into print, but also that Luther would almost automatically think of writing in a homiletic style. In contrast, the principal Catholic controversialist, Cochlaeus, could declare at the age of sixty-two that he had never preached in his life.[49] The various chaplaincies and canonries he held had simply not required it. We may presume that the preaching experience of

48. The higher figure is obtained by combining the classifications "treatise/disputation," "dialogue," and "oration." The reason for doing this is that the latter two categories were not used by Edwards, who would certainly subsume these highly specialized styles under his general classification "treatise."

49. G. Wiedermann, "Cochlaeus as a Polemicist," 200.

Cochlaeus's predecessor in the royal chaplaincies at Dresden and Zerbst, Emser, was of a similar order. Eck did not assume parochial responsibilities until 1525, the year at which our survey ends. Indeed, of the four most prolific Romanists (who between them were responsible for one-third of all Catholic controversial publications during this period), only Alveld was a preacher and published sermons. Third, it should be remembered that the adoption of a literary style was often determined by language. The disputatory style obliged one to write in Latin and was therefore more convenient for foreigners who wished to participate in the debate: of seventy-nine such pieces published between 1518 and 1525, only eight were in a vernacular, while no less than thirty were of non-German authorship. The opposite principle applied to the traditionally vernacular printed sermons, which made them suitable only for the home market, so that all but one of the eight Catholic authors of such works in this period were German.

Finally, we come to the question of the volume of Catholic controversial publishing. In recent years there have been a number of statistical studies of the use of the press at the time of the Reformation.[50] A consistent result of such studies is the apparent quantitative disparity between pamphlets and books published in favor of the Reformation and those published against. M. U. Chrisman's study of polemical pamphlets published in Strasbourg between 1520 and 1529 shows an overall ratio of Protestant to Catholic publications of 5.5 to 1.[51] R. G. Cole's analysis of the Freytag collection of sixteenth-century pamphlets (a collection biased in favor of the major Protestant reformers) produces a ratio of 7.8 to 1.[52] R. A. Crofts based his research on the British Library's holdings of early printed books from German-speaking countries, which he believes to be a more random collection than the Freytag. His figures for the years 1521–30 produce a ratio

50. See, e.g., M. U. Chrisman, "From Polemic to Propaganda: The Development of Mass Persuasion in the Late Sixteenth Century"; R. G. Cole, "The Reformation in Print: German Pamphlets and Propaganda"; idem, "The Reformation Pamphlet"; Crofts, "Books, Reform and the Reformation"; idem, "Printing, Reform and the Catholic Reformation in Germany (1521–1545)"; Edwards, "Catholic Controversial Literature"; idem, "Statistics on Sixteenth-Century Printing"; Köhler, "Flugschriften."
51. Chrisman, "Polemic to Propaganda," 176.
52. See Cole, "Reformation Pamphlet." The 7.8:1 ratio is obtained by combining figures from Cole's Table 1 (for the category "Luther," after allowing for Luther's non-polemical works) and Table 4 (for the category "Polemics," after excluding anonymous pamphlets).

close to that of Chrisman, 5.7 to 1.[53] Edwards has analyzed Luther's total output and compared this with W. Klaiber's bibliography, supplemented where necessary by other standard biographies of individual controversialists. By excluding from the count Luther's non-polemical titles and polemical works directed against other Protestants, Edwards obtained a Luther to Catholic controversialist ratio of 1.7 to 1 for the years 1518 to 1544.[54] This would also be consistent with a Protestant to Catholic ratio of 5 or 6 to 1 over the same period.

Of course, these statistics have to be used with care, not least because the evidence we have comes largely from titles that have been collected—and therefore selected—at some stage, and it almost certainly gives no very accurate representation of the actual output of sixteenth-century presses. The cumulative evidence can cut both ways, either canceling out the biases of collectors or compounding them. But the cumulative evidence strongly suggests that there was a significant disparity.

Does this disparity reflect a lack of demand for Catholic polemic, and therefore quantify to some extent the degree of their unpopularity and thus of their failure? Or does it reflect an inadequate supply of prolific writers, indicating a reluctance among Roman loyalists to take up the pen to the extent that their Reformation counterparts did? The immediate cause of the discrepancy was, of course, lack of demand. The statistics that show the 5:1 predominance of Protestant pamphlets are drawn from the catalogues of private and public collections. By their very nature, they record only those books that found a purchaser. Generally speaking, books that remained unsold and were otherwise disposed of by printer and retailer cannot be counted. As a matter of fact, these low-budget publishing ventures seem to have depended heavily on demand. This, in turn, would mean that publishers would tend to refuse work offered by Catholics; indeed, we find controversial-

---

53. See Crofts, "Printing, Reform and the Catholic Reformation." The ratio is derived from his "Graph A: Works by Reformers" and "Graph C: Works by Catholic controversialists." From Crofts's figures for the period 1531–45, we can obtain a ratio of 3.8:1, giving an overall ratio for the period 1521–45 of 4.95:1. According to Croft, if Luther's works are excluded from the reformers' total, Catholic writers outpublished their opponents. As Edwards has pointed out, this statement rests on the questionable assumption that all Catholic works, and not just those of a polemical nature, should be included in the equation ("Statistics on Sixteenth-Century Printing," 154).

54. Edwards, "Catholic Controversial Literature," 199f.

ists such as Emser and Murner having to bear their own publication costs.[55] When a printer did produce Catholic tracts it was more likely to be a matter of conviction rather than of business sense, and he had to subsidize them by producing anti-Catholic tracts too. In addition, he (no women were involved in the printing of Catholic pamphlets at this stage, to my knowledge) ran risks from Protestant authorities because they enforced libel laws selectively and from Catholic authorities because they did not.[56] But this raises the question, Why didn't Catholic works sell?

The problem was to a large extent one of presentation. Defenses of the Roman Church were more likely to be in Latin and were often written in a heavy, "scholastic" style. They were rarely as short as their Reformation counterparts.[57] Their content was also unexciting compared with that of their rivals. The controversialists' work lacked the appeal of the new, and unlike the reformers they could not draw upon the anti-curialism that was particularly prevalent in Germany. Romanist pamphlets did not sell because they were too long and boring. But why did their authors adopt such an unattractive style? Was it perhaps because they were ignorant of the propaganda possibilities of shorter tracts? This is unlikely, because religious writers before the Reformation both exploited the vernacular tract and perceived its potential for agitation. While theological works printed before the Reformation mostly appeared in Latin, nearly three-quarters (74.5 percent) of the devotional literature published in Germany between 1510

55. Smolinsky, *Alveldt und Emser,* 44–47; Dickens, *German Nation,* 113.

56. Gravier, *Luther et l'opinion publique,* 74; K. Schottenloher, "Buchdrücker und Buchführer im Dienste der Reformation," 272.

57. Cole analyzed the Freytag collection of sixteenth-century pamphlets according to their length in pages, but did not indicate the formats of the pamphlets ("Reformation Pamphlet," Table 3). His results show that Luther's own pamphlets tended to be quite short: the majority (59.6 percent) were of sixteen pages or less, while only 3.6 percent were of fifty pages or more. His category "Polemics" (which includes the writings of both Protestant and Catholic controversialists) demonstrates much the same overall pattern: 53.4 percent of sixteen pages or less, and 4.7 percent of fifty pages or more. Cole did not isolate data for Catholic polemicists, but it is possible to adapt my figures to make them comparable with his. Because Cole specified only length, not format, I have used as a basis for comparison only the 114 Catholic works published in quarto. Of these, only 39.5 percent were of sixteen pages or less, while 21.2 percent were of fifty pages or more. Although this profile is taken from a relatively small number of pamphlets published over a relatively short period, it indicates that Romanist polemical works were longer than those of their contemporaries. One reason that Cole's "Polemics" category suggests slightly greater prolixity on the part of Luther's contemporaries compared to the reformer himself may be that it includes the output of Catholics.

and 1520 was vernacular.[58] In the same period, more than half (56 percent) of the sermons that went to press appeared in German, and it was the printed German sermon that constituted the most powerful influence upon the development of the religious pamphlet.[59] Furthermore, his study of anti-Semitic tracts has led H. A. Oberman to conclude that the potential of pamphlets for agitation was a pre-Reformation, not a Reformation, discovery.[60] It is therefore clear that the Catholic controversialists deliberately chose the literary style they used.

We should also remember that, while there was a disparity between Catholic and Protestant output, there was not a complete absence of literary activity in defense of the status quo. What is needed is an explanation that can account for both the use by some Romanists of a medium of mass communication and the reluctance of most fully to exploit its potential.

The Controversialists' Self-Understanding

Luther concluded his Ninety-five Theses with a challenge: let these conscientious questionings of the people, he demanded, be answered by reason, not crushed by authority.[61] Much of the controversialists' motivation and intention, behind the bare statistics, can be discovered by understanding how they related these two elements, reason and authority, to one another in their campaign against Luther. Although it does not appear that he was explicitly referring to Luther's challenge, Latomus used the two categories to explain his own reason for first taking up the pen. There were many intellectuals, he wrote in the preface to the *Rationale* of 1521, who were unhappy that Louvain had condemned Luther's writings out of hand with no explanation of the reason for the condemnation.[62] Such discontent could easily give rise,

---

58. See Crofts, "Books, Reform and the Reformation." The figure of 74.5 percent is obtained by aggregating the vernacular percentages of each of Crofts's literary categories in his Table 5, titled "Traditional Religious Books by Category," and excluding the explicitly theological categories of "medieval theologians" and "Catholic theology."

59. The figure given is derived from Crofts's category "Sermons (Catholic)" in Table 5 ("Books, Reform and the Reformation," 34).

60. H. A. Oberman, "Zwischen Agitation und Reformation: Die Flugschriften als 'Judenspiegel,'" 287.

61. From Luther's ninetieth thesis (*WA* 1:238.9–11; *LW* 31:33).

62. Latomus, *Ratio*, 3ᵛ.

he thought, to the suspicion that there were no grounds for such a condemnation after all, and the net result of the faculty's action would therefore be to increase interest in and sympathy with the very doctrines it had wanted committed to the flames. Clichtoveus used precisely the same argument in the general introduction to the three books of his *Antilutherus*—although what he had in mind was not the doctrinal condemnation of some university theology faculty but the papal bull *Exsurge Domine* itself. It may well be, he wrote, that there are those who outwardly acknowledge Luther's error on the authority of others, but who will secretly harbor doubts until they see it for themselves.[63]

To these examples from the writings of Latomus and Clichtoveus can be added similar statements that support the view that many controversialists understood their role as providing a rationale for the condemnations of Luther issued by authoritative bodies such as universities or even the Holy See. Writing in 1523, Campester explained that it was now futile to hope for Luther's recantation, for he had ignored so many warnings in the past.

> As regards proofs from Scripture and reason [*rationes*], it is clear that the most outstanding writers of our day have left nothing to be desired—his orthodox majesty King Henry, the most reverend Cardinal Thomas de Vio, the lord Bishop of Rochester, Joannes Antonius Modestus, Johannes Eck, Hieronymus Aleander, Hieronymus Negusantius [Emser], Ambrosius Catharinus, Johannes Cochlaeus, Jacobus Hochstraten, Jacobus Latomus, and Thomas Rhadinus. Nor has authority [*authoritas*] been lacking in the Luther affair. From the outset, his writings were rejected as impious and inept by Leipzig and Erfurt, the foremost universities of Germany. Soon the poisonous cargo was borne across the Rhine, only to be condemned by the judgment of Cologne. When this statue of Dagon was carried to Louvain, it received the just censure of heresy. This ark of Babylon with its lethal brew was then taken to Paris, the highest seat of learning and here, its leprosy revealed, was consigned to the flames it so well deserved. Moreover, the whole world bears witness to what the diets of two emperors, Maximilian and Charles, at Augsburg and Worms, and what anathematization, proscription, edict, and conflagration by the holy Apostolic See have achieved.[64]

63. Clichtoveus, *Antilutherus* 3.
64. Campester, *Heptacolon*, Eiiif.

Campester's clear distinction between the reasons provided by the controversialists and the authority provided by the universities, the pope, and even the emperor, was echoed in Bachmann's pamphlet of a year later. "You know," he reminded the reader, "that Luther's writings have been condemned by the power or authority of the pope and the emperor."[65] But there were also, he continued, many scholars who had attempted to reason with the heresiarch and his followers. Bachmann then gave a list of controversialists and disputants considerably more comprehensive than Campester's.[66]

Campester and Bachmann followed Latomus and Clichtoveus in distinguishing between *ratio* and *auctoritas*. As their statements imply, this distinction was not thought of as a separation, for both means complemented each other in the suppression of heresy. Reason needed authority. This was, not surprisingly, the Curia's view. In the letter that conferred upon Henry VIII the title "Defender of the Faith," Pope Leo claimed he was happy to accord a work of *rationes*, drawn from Scripture and the writings of the fathers, his "authorization."[67] Outside the Curia, however, it was felt that authority needed reason. Writing in 1521, the Dutch theologian Sichem suggested that official pronouncements, though definitive, ran the risk of seeming too bald, too insensitive, for a public that felt it deserved better and that consequently dismissed such edicts from above as "deaf testimonies."[68] In a series of private memoranda addressed to Popes Adrian VI and Clement VII in the year 1523, Eck ventured the same opinion rather more cautiously.

---

65. Bachmann, *Czuerrettung*, Aii.

66. Ibid., Aii^{v}f. Bachmann's list contains thirty-one names, arranged by nationality, but it is not entirely reliable—under the entry *in Welschenlanden*, for instance, Cardinal Cajetan and Thomas de Vio occur separately.

67. See the letter of Leo X to Henry VIII (prefacing the first edition of Henry's *Assertio*, but independently signed), Aii^v.

68. Sichem, *Confutatio*, 229. The point made by Clichtoveus and Sichem in the context of the judicial process against Luther has a parallel in Aquinas's attitude to disputations. In dealing with the question of whether a master, in determining a theological question being disputed in the schools, ought to rely more on reason or authority, Aquinas comes down on the side of reason. "Otherwise, if the master should determine the question by authority alone [*nudis auctoritatibus*], the member of the audience will register what has been decided, but will gain nothing in knowledge or understanding, and will go away empty-handed" (*S. Thomae Aquinatis Quaestiones Quodlibetales*, ed. R. Spiazzi, 7th ed. [Turin: Marietti, 1949], 87–88). See also F. A. Blanche, "Le vocabulaire de l'argumentation et la structure de l'article dans les ouvrages de Saint Thomas," *Revue des sciences philosophiques et théologiques* 14 (1925), 183.

It would be an unwise judge who gave an explanation [*causa*] in the course of his judgment. For although one ought never make any definition without cause, yet neither should one include this in the judgment itself, lest it provide matter for dispute. Nonetheless, it would be good to commit this task to one, or even to a number, of learned men. With the authority of Holy Scripture, of the holy fathers, and of councils, they could refute these heresies and explain why their articles had been properly, justly, and duly condemned as heretical. They should however take care to avoid sophisms and references to the more recent theologians—particularly those of religious orders—or they will only be mocked.[69]

It is interesting that Eck begins this piece of advice with a nod in the direction of what he takes to be the Curia's own position. As will be seen in chapter 8, Eck was correct in his analysis of the Curia's attitude. The idea that authoritative condemnations needed rational justification was quite foreign to Rome.

In their own minds, therefore, the job of the controversialists was to provide the *rationes* or *causae*, which lay behind the bare proscriptions, by referring the reader to the Scriptures and other writings that the church considered canonical. But while this seems to account for the Romanists' self-understanding from, let us say, the beginning of 1520 (and certainly from the middle of that year, when *Exsurge Domine* had been promulgated in northern Europe), we must ask how those Catholic writers active in the two years before that date, who enjoyed no such official backing for their activities, perceived their role. As a papal inquisitor and a preacher who prided himself on his popular appeal, Tetzel launched into a campaign against Luther designed both to guard the faithful from the Wittenberger's errors and to delate him before the Curia. The question of his own *auctoritas* was uppermost in Tetzel's mind—while Tetzel held inquisitorial office, which Luther did not, Luther had a doctorate, which Tetzel did not. Tetzel had been eligible to proceed to his doctoral disputation since 1509,[70] but it was not until the spring of 1518 that he actually did so, and it cannot be a coincidence that he delayed this step until the height of his controversy with Doctor Martinus. In this disputation, he argued among other things that the preaching of any Catholic preacher should be accepted

69. Eck, *Memoranda* (ARC 1:117).
70. Paulus, *Deutschen Dominikaner*, 2.

as Catholic truth.[71] This attempt to pass off his own teaching as the church's faith has been deplored by modern Roman Catholic scholars.[72] It is nonetheless highly significant, for it demonstrates that, before a decision arrived from Rome or from the universities, the controversialists did not employ a hard and fast distinction between *ratio* and *auctoritas*.

The same confusion was evident in the strategy adopted by Prierias. As master of the Sacred Palace, with ultimate responsibility for the censorship of theological books, he had been appointed to investigate the charge of heresy brought by the procurator-fiscal against Luther. It is remarkable, then, that as one of Luther's judges he should have gone into print with his *Dialogue* against the Ninety-five Theses. Indeed, it is quite astonishing that he should not only have published it, but even have adopted the style of a literary adversary declaring that he, the pope's champion, had "descended into the arena" to challenge Luther to "single combat" over the issue of papal power.[73] By virtue of his office, therefore, Prierias's *Dialogue* was a hybrid product, being both a controversial work and a legal document, both *ratio* and *auctoritas*.

For Eck it was absolutely vital that an authoritative condemnation of Luther be reached as quickly as possible, to which end he worked tirelessly to arrange first the Leipzig disputation and then a university verdict upon it. At first, Eck saw absolutely no purpose in literary activity against Luther: without *auctoritas* there could be no *ratio*. But as the summer of 1519 turned to autumn, with the Lutheran propaganda machine at full pitch and both Paris and Erfurt silent, Eck was obliged to change his mind. The danger in leaving the literary field open to the reformers was in his opinion that their distortions might be mistaken for the teachings of the church. Eck therefore set about answering the works of Luther and Melanchthon in a way that presented what he believed to be orthodoxy. But these answers were of an entirely provisional nature, pending the verdict of an authorita-

---

71. Tetzel, *Subscriptas positiones*, thesis 39 (Löscher 1:521).
72. See, e.g., Iserloh, *The Theses Were Not Posted*, 109, where Tetzel's theses are described as "a good example of the extent of this thoughtless identification of personal theological opinion with dogma."
73. Prierias, *Dialogus* (Löscher 2:14, 39).

tive body.[74] If such a verdict were not forthcoming (which by October 1519 seemed highly likely) or if Luther questioned the fairness of the Leipzig debate in any way, Eck's solution was to propose that another debate be held before competent judges who could give a decision on the spot.[75] This contrasts with Luther, who felt the Leipzig debate had gone badly and believed that publication offered a chance to restage the debate under conditions more favorable to his case.[76]

It is ironic that Eck, who was regarded by contemporaries and is represented in much modern literature on Luther as a bombastic, contentious figure, should actually have been a reluctant pamphlet warrior. The comparatively little remembered Alveld was by contrast an eager publicist entirely wanting in Eck's inhibitions. So far as we can tell, Alveld shared Luther's aim of reaching the widest possible readership with his concise, memorable pamphlets based exclusively on arguments from Scripture. Indeed, he even copied verbatim one of Luther's statements of intent and used it as his own in an early work.[77] It might be that Alveld considered himself sufficiently furnished with *auctoritas* for his prolific publishing campaign. He had been specially commissioned by his bishop to refute Luther's *Explanation of the Thirteenth Proposition*, and it is possible that this commission was extended to include his subsequent publications, or else that Alveld regarded it as so extended. Moreover, it seems unlikely that so stout a champion of the controversialists as Duke Georg of Saxony would not have made known his support to a Romanist author active a stone's throw from his Leipzig court. But this is conjecture. What can be said with certainty is that the Franciscan Alveld took up the mantle of vernacular writing that had fallen from the Dominican Tetzel, and that the concern with providing a rational explanation for some authoritative decision did not greatly exercise him.

74. Cf. Johannes Eck, *Disputatio et excusatio* 320.22–24: "I see that I shall have to take care that the weak-minded are not scandalized. For they are likely to agree with my disparager if they receive no explanation from me." Cf. also idem, *Expurgatio*, Aiv^v: "I had decided, Reverend Father, to hold my peace after the Leipzig disputation, awaiting the judgments of Paris and Erfurt. But I am forced to respond lest Lutheran beliefs (which in my humble opinion are of less weight and which conflict with the fathers of the Church) become more firmly entrenched." For a similar statement, see idem, *Responsio pro Emser*, Ci^v.

75. Eck, *Responsio pro Emser*, Aivf., Bivf.

76. "Because the disputation went badly, I shall re-publish the *Explanations* [of the Ninety-five Theses]" (Luther to Spalatin, 20 July 1519, *WA Br* 1:423.105).

77. See Augustinus Alveld, *Von dem elichen standt*, Eiif. For this evidence of plagiarism, I am indebted to Smolinsky, *Alveldt und Emser*, 121.

The situation can therefore be summed up as follows. Before the condemnations from Louvain and Cologne in late 1519 and *Exsurge Domine* in mid-1520, the Roman loyalists who took up the pen against Luther, though few in number, represented a wide variety of motives and different understandings of their actions. After the publication of the authoritative condemnations, the ranks of the controversialists were swelled considerably, but the reasons they gave for writing against Luther were now much more uniform—generally speaking, they saw themselves as providing rational explanations of the actions taken by "authority." Naturally, there were exceptions to this rule. Emser and Murner cannot be said to have been thoroughgoing popularists, nor to have related their publications to authoritative condemnations of Luther. Rather, their motives in writing were purely personal, and their contributions literary duels with Luther and other opponents.

Emser's rapid exchange with Luther of eight replies and counter-replies within as many months during 1521 is particularly illuminating. The concern uppermost in Emser's mind in writing these replies was to protect his honor. What mortal can be like Zeus, he asked, and laugh at his enemies as if their insults could not harm him?[78] His letter to the diocesan administrator at Prague on the Leipzig disputation had been published under the Emser family crest, a goat. When Luther made fun of "the goat without horns," therefore, he had insulted Emser's name and his person, and "the bull at Wittenberg" was repaid in kind. That Emser saw literary activity as a matter of personal honor is confirmed by a piece of doggerel he composed to accompany Bachmann's *Encouragement of a Vacillating Religious*, which describes the types of pamphlet in circulation—he made special mention of those that bore the "shame" of anonymity.[79] Some indication of the highly personal nature of Emser's replies can be gauged from his first, the *Assertion*. This contained an apologia of his life and character, and even, as independent testimony, an extract from a private letter of support he had received from an unnamed bishop.[80] The remainder of the pamphlet was taken up with a point-by-point refutation of Luther's original. The point-by-point method was one Emser favored

---

78. Emser, *Assertio*, 729.
79. In Bachmann, *Czuerrettung*, Niii^v.
80. Emser, *Assertio*, 727–29, 704.

in his exchanges with Luther. As a tactic it had the advantage of not letting one's opponents get away with anything that might help their case; it was therefore particularly well-suited to the demands of a controversy with a pronounced personal element. An extension of this tactic was to adopt the same style and language as one's opponent, so as to ensure as much as possible that one's reply reached the same readership. Therefore, when Luther wrote his *Addition* in Latin, Emser responded with the *Assertion* in the same language. When Luther pressed home his attack with the German *Answer to the Goat at Leipzig*, Emser followed suit with his vernacular *Reply to the Bull at Wittenberg*. Emser's addressing his 1521 *Refutation* to "the whole German nation" should thus be seen more as a way of scoring a point off the author of the address "to the Christian nobility of the German nation" than as indicating a program of popular propaganda. Indeed, the *Refutation*— a staunch defense of civil and ecclesiastical authority—continued the anti-popularist theme Emser had already pursued in his earlier works, namely, the rabble's invariable preference for the novel and the bad.[81]

Emser was neither a popularist nor one who wrote in support of authoritative condemnations, but a literary duelist for whom it was of paramount importance that Luther's assertions did not go unanswered.[82] Such a description also fits Murner. This may seem surprising, for his *Great Lutheran Fool* of 1522 is normally held up as a masterpiece of popularizing satire, with its inventive verses and eye-catching cartoons.[83] In fact, the pamphlet was primarily intended as literary revenge for the attacks launched on him by his Strasbourg opponents—"As they have done to me, so have I done to them." Nothing was further from Murner's mind than an appeal to popular opinion on the religious issues at stake—in earlier publications he had consistently identified Luther's chief crime as the discussion of advanced theological matters before the simple folk.[84] Following his own advice, he had been careful to keep his controversy with Luther and other reformers at a personal, rather than a doctrinal, level, and *The Great Lutheran Fool* was simply the culmination of such a policy.[85]

81. Ibid., 704–5; idem, *Vorlegung*, Riv[v].
82. Emser, *An den Stier*, Aii.
83. See esp. Gravier, *Luther et l'opinion publique*, 70–72, 206–17; Dickens, *German Nation*, 124; Scribner, *Simple Folk*, 235–39.
84. Murner, *Ermanung*, passim, esp. Hiii.
85. J. Schütte reaches a similar conclusion in his detailed study, *"Schympff red": Frühformen bürgerlicher Agitation in Thomas Murners "Grossem Lutherischem Narren" (1522)*,

It would, however, be a mistake to suppose that the popularist tradition of Tetzel and Alveld went unrepresented in the period after 1520. Alveld himself was intermittently active against Luther until his death in the early 1530s, but the cause was now taken up by Cochlaeus and Petrus Sylvius. Both believed fervently in combating the reformers in kind, using the presses to produce a great quantity of literature aimed at the common people. But both had trouble initially in getting their work published. The breakthrough for Cochlaeus came at the end of 1522, when the Strasbourg printer Johannes Grüninger printed his *Grace of the Sacraments I*, which belatedly tackled Luther's sacramental teaching of 1519–20. The floodgates were now open. Over the next three years he penned seventeen pamphlets and books—many of considerable size and most directed against Luther—and was responsible for editing and/or translating a further fourteen by other authors. In addition, he wrote much that was not published until later, or not at all. He made his intentions quite plain: to reach the common people in precisely the same way as Luther had already done.[86] His ambitious popularizing program included the translation of classic texts such as Cyprian's *De unitate ecclesiae* "as a fair warning to the common people of our nation";[87] even his Latin publications were intended not for an elite but for the still wider dissemination of his writings in foreign countries. Dietenberger's literary career was closely associated with that of Cochlaeus. Dietenberger's works were published and translated by Cochlaeus, and some of Cochlaeus's work, such as *A Pious Exhortation*, was translated by Dietenberger.[88] It can safely be assumed that Dietenberger was a supporter of his patron's popularizing policy. The third popular writer, Sylvius, shared the problem of being unable at first to find a publisher. He began writing against Luther before the Leipzig debate, but was not published until 1524. Between 1524 and 1536 Sylvius published some thirty titles, all in German, including his own republications of works by Bachmann and Cochlaeus.

---

esp. 40. Schütte argues that *Von den grossen Lutherischen Narren* differs from Murner's pre-Reformation satires in that the author himself becomes a character in the satire. This confirms my impression that Murner's motive in writing was predominantly personal.

86. See, e.g., Cochlaeus, *Auff den xiii Artikel*, Ai^v; *Uff CLIIII Artikeln*, Aiif.

87. Johannes Cochlaeus, *Tractat S. Cypriani*, Aii^v. See also Cochlaeus's edition of William Wideford's anti-Wycliffite theses, *Ob nichts anzünemen sey* (1524).

88. Due to publishing difficulties Dietenberger's translation, *Ein christliche vermanung* (Tübingen, 1524), actually came out before Cochlaeus's original (Tübingen, 1525).

Over the period from 1518 to 1525, Cochlaeus was the single most prolific Catholic controversial author. He is therefore an extremely significant figure for any study of the literature of these years. But even when we set alongside him the names of Sylvius and Dietenberger, it is clear that the vast majority of the fifty-seven Romanists active at this time did not subscribe to the vision of a Catholic popular propaganda effort matching that of the Lutherans. Most of them, as Cochlaeus himself complained in 1521, wrote one or two books and then left the field:

> Will no-one oppose Luther in writing besides Emser alone? What of Prierias? What of the Franciscan Alveld? What of Eck? What of the Cremonian? What of Murner? What of the scholars of Cologne or Louvain or Paris? Emser alone remains unbowed. The others publish one book and then, either because they are unpopular or fear becoming so, they fall silent. And what of this brilliant Ambrosius [Catharinus] of yours? What did he do? He published—then left the matter to God. True, he wrote a most scholarly treatise. But the belligerent Germans don't like it when so brave a soldier leaves the field of battle so early![89]

It is clear that, with scarcely a handful of honorable exceptions, the controversialists had a much more limited conception of the role of publishing than did their Lutheran counterparts.

The Dangers of Publishing

What can be inferred of the intentions of the Catholic controversialists? The fact that they chose to go into print at all was significant. Had they simply wanted to refute Luther, they could have tried to convince him privately, as Dungersheim attempted through personal correspondence with the reformer.[90] Or they could have circulated their views confidentially among friends, as Eck did with his annotations on the Ninety-five Theses. The fact that they published their writings shows that they wished their views made known to a wide public—the same public, we may assume (unless there are specific indications to the contrary), their opponent had reached, and for the

---

89. Cochlaeus to Aleander, 27 September 1521 (*ZKG* 18:124).
90. For Dungersheim's correspondence with Luther, see *WA Br* 1:518–22, 574–94; 2:112; and T. Freudenberger, ed., *Hieronymus Dungersheim Schriften gegen Luther: Theorismata duodecim contra Lutherum; Articuli sive Libelli triginta*, CC 39 (Münster-Westfalen: Aschendorff, 1987).

same reasons. But it is also clear that the Catholic controversialists operated under two constraints that did not apply to Luther. These constraints severely limited their literary activity and made them suspect in the eyes of fellow Catholics and—on occasion—of one another.

The first was the danger of appearing to be debating with heretics. This danger was felt very early on in the controversy—in fact, long before Luther had been formally condemned as a heretic! Alluding to Luther's demand that the laity's questions be answered rationally, Tetzel reminded the readers of his *Refutation* of Augustine's dictum that one corrected erring Christians by reason, but heretics were to be confronted with authority alone.[91] After Luther's formal condemnation, this danger was much more widely recognized. The aversion of the German nuncio Aleander to disputations—which led him to blame the entire Reformation and its continuance on "two plagues: the tongues of doctors and the hands of printers"[92]—was shared by a number of Catholic writers, including Eck and Fabri.[93] Disputing with heretics, they feared, implied the negotiability of the Catholic faith; or it suggested something equally unacceptable, that heretics were *docibiles Dei*, open to the Spirit of Truth. It was for this reason that some refused to engage in public controversy with Luther.[94] Those who did had to be careful that their efforts could not be construed as disputing with a heretic, but this was often a delicate business. As late as 1523, the Frenchman Campester could write a pamphlet directly addressed to Luther in which he clearly stated on its title page his intention of bringing this erring sheep back to the straight and narrow road. But within the space of a few pages he had reverted to the more

91. Tetzel, *Vorlegung*, 485. Cf. Augustine, *De utilitate credendi*, chap. 33 (*MPL* 42:259); and idem, *Confessiones* 6, chap. 5, sec. 8 (*MPL* 32:105).

92. Hieronymus Aleander, *Consilium*, 275. See also p. 245: "Public and prearranged disputations are to be avoided like the plague, because they make what has been our universal faith for so many centuries a matter for debate before hostile and unsuitable judges. In particular, they bring into question the papal bull [*Exsurge Domine*] and the imperial edict [of Worms]. However hard your champion might try to avoid debating such issues, he would immediately find the proceedings of the disputation published by Lutherans in a thousand books, in which they will boast that the apostolic nuncio had been defeated before sworn witnesses. We saw this happen first at Leipzig and most recently at Zurich: I need not mention other evil disputations too numerous to mention."

93. Eck, *Enchiridion*, 280–81; Fisher, *Confutatio*, 272, 279; Fabri, *Malleus*, 23. Cf. Conrad Pellican's preface to Schatzgeyer's *Scrutinium*, p. 1.

94. E.g., the theology faculty of the University of Paris. See Powell, *Propugnaculum*, 3ᵛ.

orthodox view that Luther, having steadfastly ignored all attempts to correct him by *ratio* as much as by *auctoritas*, was now beyond reclamation and, as St. Paul said of all heretics, "corrupted in his very mind and conscience" (Titus 1:15).[95] Campester was by no means alone in his confusion. Emser sailed even closer to the wind: his detailed, point-by-point refutations of Luther were indistinguishable from the process of disputing; and yet he had no doubt of Luther's identity with the great heresiarchs of the past.[96] Furthermore, it was ironic that Catharinus devoted his *Dispensation from Disputing with Martin*—two hundred pages of painstaking doctrine-by-doctrine refutation—to proving the futility of disputing with Luther!

To avoid the suspicion of attempting to dispute with heretics, several controversialists chose to state that their intended readership was not Luther and his supporters but the *gemeine volck*, meaning at times "the whole people" and at times "the common people." Their intention was, they proclaimed, to warn the people against the new doctrines and to instruct them in the true faith.[97] But this option also carried with it dangers of its own because there was, many believed, only a fine distinction between offering instruction on the contested points of the religious controversy and inviting the general public to make up their own minds. The "judgment of the people" was the Romanists' pet hate, and they frequently characterized Luther's motive in writing pamphlets as the courting of it. Even in the period after Leipzig, his opponents maintained their polemic along these lines. As late as 1525, Fisher could accuse Luther of developing the doctrine of the theological competence of the laity simply because he knew that the rank and file supported him.[98] In the same book, Fisher devoted an entire chapter to a discussion "on the judgment of the people," in which he argued that the laity had a right of assent (*ius assentiendi*) but

95. Campester, *Heptacolon*, Aii^v; Eii^v–iii.
96. Emser, *An den Stier*, Aiv^v.
97. Cochlaeus, *Tractat S. Cypriani*, Aii^v; idem, *Auff den xiii Artikel*, Ai^v; idem, *Uff CLIIII Artikeln*, Aii–ii^v, pi^v; idem, *Wideford*, Aii; Dietenberger, *Der leye*, Aiii; Emser, *Vorlegung*, Siii^v; Femelius, *Eyn Kurtz sermon*, Ai; Prierias, *Epitoma*, 329.30f. (with reference to the *Replica*); idem, *Replica*, 51 (with reference to the *Dialogus*); Tetzel, *Vorlegung*, theses 1 and 12 (the latter with reference to *Subscriptas positiones*).
98. "The clever old fox takes care that the people applaud his pestilential opinions, and therefore extols the people's judgment as the most reliable kind of oracle, and then attempts to prop it up with Scripture. But on the subject of public approval there is an apt saying of Seneca's: 'Underhand tricks always win the people's favour.'" (Fisher, *Adversus Babylonicam captivitatem*, 232).

not a right of dissent (*ius dissentiendi*) or a right of judgment (*ius iudicandi*).[99]

The controversialists themselves were often at pains to show that they desired the people's agreement and not their judgment. The case of Johannes Femelius illustrates the point. In 1522, the Erfurt authorities arranged a disputation on the cult of the saints,[100] in which Femelius was to defend the practice. He published a short sermon in order, as he put it, to bring his own case to light and to prove to his critics that it had a sound scriptural foundation. In other words, he was attempting to present the case he would eventually make in a disputation to the wider audience that might be expected to read a short, vernacular pamphlet,[101] and was therefore presumably trying to gain public support for his position before the debate began. And yet a consistent theme of the pamphlet was his ridicule of those common people who had set themselves up as judges in matters of which they knew nothing: the "doctors of Erfurt," as he sarcastically addressed them, "both young and old, male and female."[102] Femelius thus represents the tension between the practical necessity of winning public opinion over to the "old" church and the same church's minimal regard for the opinion of a public that had at most only the right to agree.

In their attempt to use reason in defense of authority, the Romanists trod a hazardous path between two pitfalls of controversial writing. The danger of seeming to conduct an illegal disputation with heretics was faced by Campester, for example, while Femelius struggled with the problem of appearing to encourage the people to exercise their judgment in theological matters. The dilemma was eventually resolved in favor of authority. This was inevitable: on the one hand, a heretic who had stubbornly rejected the authority of the church would not and could not listen to reason; on the other, while it was

---

99. Ibid., 232–54.

100. Luther himself published a pamphlet on the subject at the same time, as a contribution to the Erfurt debate, the *Epistel oder Unterricht von dem Heiligen an die Kirche zu Erfurt* of 10 July 1522 (*WA* 10.2:164–68).

101. "Stilo populari et lingua patria," as H. Hurter described it (*Nomenclator literarius theologiae Catholicae: ab exordiis theologiae scholasticae usque ad celebratum concilium Tridentinum: theologos exhibens aetate, natione, disciplinis distinctos* 2:1242).

102. See Femelius, *Eyn Kurtz sermon*, Ai; see also Biii, Aii^v: "By the blood of Christ we beseech the simple people, who are not so well-versed in Scripture, not to judge wantonly and maliciously in this great matter."

perfectly permissible for a Catholic to instruct the faithful rationally, such a writer had to remember that authority, and not reason, should have the last word.

This dilemma explains, I think, why so few Catholics were willing to use the printing press in support of their beliefs. Most could see no role for printing that did not compromise the writer in one direction or another. The majority of those who did write wrote only once or twice because a sustained publishing program ran a correspondingly greater risk of being misconstrued as either futile disputation or an illegitimate appeal to public opinion. It explains why the controversialists preferred non-popular forms of writing. Finally, it explains the lack of support, even outright distrust and opposition, with which the controversialists met from the church hierarchy.

8

ESTABLISHMENT
REACTIONS

Despite differences of background and of approach, the Catholic controversialists can be seen—indeed, many saw themselves—as constituting a coherent literary movement. What role, if any, did this movement play in the wider counter-Reformation strategy of the Roman Church? The controversialists were men of letters in more than one sense, and from their correspondence with curial officials and with spiritual and temporal magnates nearer home, it is possible to gauge the seriousness with which the Catholic authorities regarded the practitioners of controversial theology.

Catholic Opinion beyond Rome

Perhaps the most obvious advantage enjoyed by the Catholic controversialists over their opponents was the possibility of help from Rome. The Reformation propagandists were, at least at first, isolated figures. Freelancers, they championed a minority cause that, if they were priests or monks, undermined their own status. They lacked organization and coordination and could by no means count on the humanist network of printing, retailing, and distribution as uniformly on their side. In all these respects, the defenders of the "old" faith were potentially far better off. From the surviving correspondence of the German Catholic controversialists with the papal staff appear the makings of a centralized "office of propaganda." News and copies of heretical publications were sent to Rome,[1] and there preliminary sketches of refutations were referred for official scrutiny prior to publication.[2] From Rome came ideas for counter-pamphlets and moral and material support for individual controversialists.[3] Moreover, the various chains of command and communication from Rome through diocesan *curiae*,

---

1. Cochlaeus to Aleander, 11 May 1521 (*ZKG* 18:112); Aleander to Fabri, n.d. (*ZKG* 20:64).
2. Cochlaeus to Aleander, 5 May 1521 (*ZKG* 18:111).
3. Ibid., 109; Cochlaeus to Aleander, 22 May 1521 (*ZKG* 18:114); Cochlaeus to Leo, 19 June 1521 (*ZKG* 18:117).

religious provinces, and universities laid the foundations for a truly international propaganda effort, which the proponents of the Reformation could never hope to have.

By and large, however, this advantage was not pressed home. Indeed, for those controversialists who looked to Rome for support, life was cheerless. They lacked encouragement and companionship; but most of all they lacked cash, and printing was an expensive business. Generally speaking, printers would work without charge to the author only if they could be confident of selling enough copies to cover their costs and make a profit. Because a Romanist's work was unlikely to sell that well, he would frequently have to pay the costs in advance.[4] Even then, he could not be sure that the printer would make a good job of, for example, the proofreading, either because the printer or his staff were unsympathetic to the Catholic cause or because he was a bad printer and an anti-Reformation treatise was the only work he could get. These difficulties hit Catholics in Germany particularly hard. Even when, in 1536, the German Catholics found a reliable printer, they claimed that their fixed stipends became increasingly inadequate as the price of paper rose.[5] Money was needed also to engage the services of trustworthy couriers who were neither crooks nor Lutheran spies and who could safely convey letters, proofs, books, and cash.[6] The controversialists solicited this money either in the form of lump sums granted in recognition of a particular work or as ecclesiastical appointments in the gift of officials at Rome. They met with little success in the latter, normally because all significant appointments seem to have been contested in the sixteenth century as a matter of course by members of the papal household or by ecclesiastical and lay magnates nearer home. The defenders of the Roman Church thus fell foul of the very abuses of pluralism and absenteeism that its critics had been pointing out for decades. In 1525, just four years after Luther had attacked the same practices in his *To the Christian Nobility*, Eck wrote to Clement VII, "Who can tolerate this buying and selling of benefices, these 'commencements,' 'returns,' accumulations of pensions, suits at law, and a thousand other such scandals that on several

4. Cochlaeus to Aleander, 27 September 1521 (*ZKG* 18:123).
5. Cochlaeus to Alessandro Farnese, 7 October 1537 (*ZKG* 18:278).
6. Cochlaeus to Aleander, 22 May 1521 (*ZKG* 18:113); idem, to Aleander, 27 September 1521 (*ZKG* 18:121).

occasions I have brought to the attention of your Holiness and of your predecessors Leo X and Adrian VI?"[7]

To make matters worse, the controversialists complained, they lacked the time, the inclination, and the wherewithal for lengthy litigation. Even when they put up a fight, they were at a hopeless disadvantage. Eck continued his letter to Clement by protesting the unfairness of competing against a household official at the center of things in Rome. "Now all the expenses which I incurred in making my submission to the judges, in my citation, and in my action, as well as all my exertions, have been in vain thanks to this revocation. And to make me even more of a laughing-stock I, who live far away, have been cited by this courtier in the very heart of the Church."[8] It was particularly galling to a professional theologian like Eck that cathedral chapters were often staffed by noblemen who had not even taken orders and who had certainly never studied theology in their lives. As late as 1540, Eck still found it necessary to complain to Contarini: "How poorly do such men serve their churches! They rarely come into the city, rarer still to the cathedral precinct, and most rarely of all into their stalls. Even when their salaries are paid they just roll up, take the money, and are out again quicker than a dog out of the Nile."[9]

Even more serious than the threat of unsuitable Catholic canons was that of suitable Lutheran ones. Eck was scandalized that in 1525 the younger brother of the Protestant margrave Georg von Ansbach could enjoy the pope's support in pursuit of an ecclesiastical position,[10] or that, years later, highly placed ecclesiastics of his acquaintance could boast openly of their Wittenberg education and of their familiarity with Luther himself.[11] More embarrassing even than having to contest a benefice with a Lutheran was contesting one with a fellow controversialist. No examples of this have survived from the early period with which we are concerned, but in the winter of

---

7. Eck to Clement VII, 17 September 1525 (*MRL,* 539).

8. Ibid. (*MRL,* 540).

9. Eck to Contarini, 13 March 1540 (*ZKG* 19:225).

10. Eck to Clement VII, 25 July 1525 (*MRL,* 497f.). Cf. Eck to Contarini, 3 March 1540 (*ZKG* 19:241).

11. Eck to Aleander, 15 December 1536 (*ZKG* 19:225). On the phenomenon of Protestant noblemen being appointed to Catholic canonries, see P. S. Fichtner, *Protestantism and Primogeniture in Early Modern Germany* (New Haven and London: Yale University Press, 1989).

1536–37, Cochlaeus and Eck both petitioned for annuities from the vacant provostship of Würzburg cathedral.[12] The following winter Eck was beaten to a canonry at Regensburg by Johann Haner, an ex-Lutheran whose services as a controversialist had been secured by Cochlaeus.[13]

Clearly Rome did not provide the controversialists with either sufficient or sustained material help. But accident more than design seems to be the explanation in many cases, for the system of appointments necessitated a slow and complicated legal procedure that favored those who could manipulate it. We should therefore ask whether this lack of support indicated a more general coolness toward the controversialists from Rome. There can be little doubt that it did. It is pathetic that Eck—the man who at Leipzig had so publicly and so dramatically demonstrated Luther's rejection of the papacy was himself rejected by the papacy. At the height of the Peasants' War in July 1525, Eck wrote to Clement VII:

> Now I shall slip away for a short time to northern Germany and England, to see whether there is a peaceful spot where I might study; and the while to try to besiege your Holiness with my humblest prayers for your help. But why should I worry? The Apostolic See makes so free in conferring churches and dignities even upon ungrateful recipients, it will surely be generous to Eck, who has run so many dangers and undertaken so many labors for the orthodox faith and for the honor of the Apostolic See.[14]

Cochlaeus, in contrast, felt that he had been abandoned as soon as he entered the lists against Luther in 1521. Ordered to remain in Frankfurt am Main by Cardinal Aleander to facilitate his publishing, he complained that he was now deserted by his humanist friends, surrounded by Lutheran sympathizers, threatened with death by Ulrich von Hutten's anticlerical forces, and deprived of the intellectual and literary resources of a loyal university such as Cologne or Louvain.[15] We have already seen how frustrated Cochlaeus became with his controversialist colleagues who wrote one book and then left

---

12. Ibid., 224–25; Cochlaeus to Morone, 31 August 1537, and to Aleander, 7 October, 1537 (*ZKG* 18:271–74).
13. Eck to Aleander, 11 December 1537 (*ZKG* 19:223).
14. Eck to Clement VII, 25 July 1525 (*MRL*, 500).
15. See Cochlaeus to Leo X, 19 June 1521 (*ZKG* 18:118), and to Aleander, 27 September 1521 (*ZKG* 18:122–23).

the field. He was even more scathing about the lack of official action from Rome: "You clearly do not believe that our cause can be furthered by bulls, mandates, speeches to princes, force, threats, or other terror tactics. Pray tell me, then, by what other means do you intend to ensure our victory? Do tell us. Conspiracy? Bribery? Poison? Deceit? Or is there some other underhand method you have in mind?"[16]

So stung was Cochlaeus by the thought of the risks he ran for the faith while officials in Rome sat safely doing nothing that he even contemplated desertion, as he wrote to Aleander in the same letter: "If I am ignored by you any longer, I shall wash my hands of the Catholic cause and denounce all bishops and prelates before God and before men. I need only say the word and the Lutherans would welcome me with open arms. No—away with such as would take me from the Church! I can live with it and be as happy in it as the next man. But you see how little you need give me, and how much I am worth to you."[17] However hypothetically put, and allowing for exaggeration, this was a threat. Cochlaeus as Protestant reformer is an intriguing "what if" of history.

The frustration to which Eck and Cochlaeus bear a surprisingly frank witness is to be explained, I believe, by the dissonance between their view of the controversialist's role and that of their superiors in Rome. Those controversialists whose letters to Rome we still possess were generally humanists and, like the ancients they imitated, clients dependent on the generosity of patrons of the arts. (Cochlaeus referred to himself as the client of Aleander and Fabri, while Eck regarded as his patrons Aleander and Bishop Giberti—"my Maecenas," as he predictably called Giberti.)[18] This meant that they were subject to the changes of fortune of their patrons, who were primarily Vatican careerists more concerned with their own promotion and with the Curia's domestic conflicts, and who inevitably saw their clients' literary activity as theological belles-lettres rather than weapons in a mortal combat for the hearts and minds of ordinary people. In this attitude there was undoubtedly an element of Italian snobbery toward the barbarous Teutonic tongue and the barbarous Teutonic mob. But this

16. Cochlaeus to Aleander, 27 September 1521 (*ZKG* 18:120).
17. Ibid., 123.
18. Cochlaeus to Aleander, 11 June 1521 (*ZKG* 18:115); idem, to Fabri, 24 June 1539 (*ZKG* 18:293); Eck to Giberti, 29 June 1525 (*ZKG* 19:213); idem, to Aleander, September 1534 (*ZKG* 19:215).

is easily exaggerated: it was natural that these figures of considerable personal authority should think that the church's position could be improved only in a changed political climate.

The case of Aleander provides a good illustration. He took Cochlaeus under his wing during his first German nunciature (1520–21).[19] At the same time, he commissioned Cochlaeus to write a history of the Waldensians, so his own sights were set rather nearer home than Germany.[20] He did not take as much interest in Cochlaeus's subsequent anti-Lutheran works, and one suspects he would have preferred to play patron to the humanist "poet" Cochlaeus had earlier shown himself to be than to a theological polemicist. His connection with other German Catholic controversialists and his commitment to their labors were of about the same level. Aleander's priorities are perhaps most clearly seen from an undated letter he wrote to Fabri. Here he lamented the German schism, not for the danger it posed to the souls of so many, but because at the time of the disaster Germany had been a focus of the renewal of letters and Italy's sole bulwark against the Turkish hordes.[21] It would be unfair to suggest that Aleander had no religious interest in German affairs, but he certainly thought it admitted only of a political, not a literary or ideological, solution.

Aleander was a champion of *auctoritas* over *ratio*. After making the taunts about bribery, plots, and poison in his letter of September 1521, Cochlaeus addressed an appeal to Aleander and, through him, to the Curia: the Catholic cause, he wrote, has no need to stoop to such depths. "Have we on our side no intelligence? Have we no *rationes*? Have we no Scriptures? It is by these weapons alone that the German people will be most readily subdued." Cochlaeus then went on to announce his desire of engaging Luther himself, or else some other leading reformer, in a disputation.[22] In marginal comments to this letter, Aleander revealed that his own perception of the troubles was more political than theological: "The cause of the revolution in Germany is something other than the sacraments. Besides, *rationes* and disputations achieve nothing."[23] He also appreciated that the holding

19. Bäumer, *Johannes Cochlaeus (1479–1552)*, 22.
20. Cochlaeus to Aleander, 5 May 1521 (*ZKG* 18:109).
21. Aleander to Fabri, n.d. (*ZKG* 20:63–64).
22. Cochlaeus to Aleander, 27 September 1521 (*ZKG* 18:120–22).
23. Ibid., 120 n. 6.

of a disputation *after* the promulgation of the edict of Worms would be not only unnecessary but also positively detrimental to the cause.[24] "You are a man who normally sees everything," he replied to Cochlaeus the following month, "so I marvel that you do not see this. Suppose that you do join battle with the enemy on this issue. And suppose that this had the approval of Emperor and Empire alike. The Lutherans would deliberately misconstrue this as a definitive verdict, and all authority [*auctoritas*] would be undermined."[25]

Aleander recalled that Eck, the veteran of many disputations, had at Leipzig vanquished Luther and Carlstadt in a virtuoso exhibition of learning and ingenuity. Lutheran propaganda, however, depicted the result quite differently, and did so to such effect that the heretics drew greater strength from Leipzig than they had had before. Cochlaeus, he warned, should take heed: "You can therefore see why, in these circumstances, it would be wrong to permit or to conduct such an untimely disputation. Had our friend Eck followed such advice at the outset, perhaps this disaster would never have overtaken the Church."[26] If Aleander's attitude was at all typical (and we know it was shared at least by Joannes Glapion, the Emperor's confessor, whose advice on this matter Aleander had sought),[27] one can readily see why the Catholic controversialists could not expect support from their own hierarchy: they were held partly to blame for the Reformation in the first place!

Much more of Aleander's correspondence survives than that of his colleagues. This is particularly true of correspondence with the controversialists. It makes almost unanswerable an important question: How representative of other Roman officials was Aleander's low opinion of the Catholic authors? There is a sense in which this is a non-question, because Aleander's nunciature spanned the most significant years of the period up to 1525, so that, in a manner of speaking, Aleander *was* Rome as far as the controversialists were concerned. But more can be said. Circumstantial evidence suggests that Aleander's attitude was indeed typical of his colleagues and successors. Like him they were humanists and presumably shared his distaste for public

24. Ibid., 122 n. 1.
25. Aleander to Cochlaeus, October 1521 (*ZKG* 18:128).
26. Ibid., 129.
27. Glapion expressed his disapproval of Cochlaeus's "descent into the arena" with Luther or with any other Lutheran. See his letter to Aleander, 10 October 1521 (*ZKG* 18:131).

disputations, which humanists frequently dismissed as a disruptive influence. We also know that the complaints made by the controversialists against Rome in the period 1521–25 were repeated almost word-for-word even into the 1540s, from which we can deduce that their relationships with Rome had not changed significantly for the better during that time.[28] It seems, therefore, that the attitude of Roman officials toward the controversialists between the outbreak of the Reformation and the summoning of Trent was consistently negative. Hubert Jedin concludes that "their efforts were occasionally rewarded, but their ultimate aims were ignored; and no attempt was made either to engage with Lutheranism at any deep intellectual level, or to conduct a deliberate propaganda campaign in support of Catholicism, by assisting Catholic writers and printing-houses."[29]

There was a short-lived exception to this rule. Although Pope Adrian VI's reign lasted less than two years before his untimely death in September 1523, he appears to have undertaken a systematic program that bore a close resemblance to the aims of the controversialists themselves. Indeed, it seemed for a few months that the German controversialists at least were to be turned into a coherent and indispensable element of the Roman strategy against the Reformation. Adrian was a Dutchman, educated by the Brethren of the Common Life, and a scholastic theologian of some renown. As a cardinal, he provided his former colleagues at Louvain with a foreword to their condemnation of Luther.[30] Three years later, after his elevation to the pontificate, he reminded the theologians at Cologne of the condemnation they too had issued, and spurred them to yet greater diligence:

28. E.g., Eck's complaint to Pope Clement VII in 1525 that he had been forgotten by Rome was repeated for the benefit of Paul III in 1537 (*Briefmappe* 1:163–64), and of Cardinal Contarini in 1540 (*ZKG* 19:225). Jedin believed that Aleander's low opinion of the controversialists was shared by the Curia and its representatives during Clement's "unglückselig" reign, but that a change of policy occurred under Paul III, since in the briefing for the new nuncio Morone in 1535 it was suggested that proper provision be made for Eck, Fabri, Cochlaeus, Nausea, Witzel, Haner, Marstaller, and Appel (Jedin, "Bedeutung," 74–75). That Eck (to say nothing of Fabri and Cochlaeus) continued to beg for the least financial help shows that this later plan for assisting the controversialists went unheeded. Jedin therefore exaggerates the case for a policy change in 1535. There are much sounder reasons for supposing such a change of direction under Adrian VI, which Jedin, surprisingly, ignores.

29. Jedin, "Bedeutung," 74.

30. Adrian VI to the Louvain theology faculty, 4 December 1519 (*WA* 6:174–75).

From the beginning you have ever despised this most pestilential and pernicious teaching which, like a cancer, spreads further and further each day, not so much by its subtlety (for it has none) as through the negligence and lack of zeal for God's house of those whose duty it is to prevent it. We therefore urge you and yours in the Lord to strive to expose *by teaching, writing, and preaching* to the faithful whomsoever in your opinion opposes sound doctrine and conceals poison in the honey of the words of the saints, with which they are accustomed to mix their perverse doctrines. Their doctrines will thus appear to be that much crasser and less defensible.[31]

Adrian accepted the literary option as a valid means of countering religious innovation. With such an attitude—unusual for Rome— went an equally unusual resolve to take the controversialists themselves seriously. Adrian saw them as men ideally situated to give tactical advice on two fronts, the treatment of the heresy and the implementation of the "head and members" reform he so fervently desired. He invited Eck, for instance, to supply information

on the question of the desperate and infamous heresy of Martin Luther and his many followers, that we might see how this pestilential disease might best (with God's help) be stopped, and an effective remedy applied. . . . Because we are not sufficiently informed, we request and ask you in the Lord to render us in writing (should you be unable to attend us in person) the fullest possible account of your advice in this matter, and of what you consider needs be done for its successful execution, as much by us as by others.[32]

This was almost certainly a sort of circular letter sent to all the German controversialists of whom Rome had heard. The replies of Eck, Cochlaeus, and Fabri have survived.[33] All three believed that the

31. Adrian VI to the Cologne theology faculty (*Quoniam unicuique*), 1 December 1522, quoted in Cochlaeus, *Adversus cucullatum minotaurum*, 25 (emphasis mine). On this letter, see P. Kalkoff, "Kleine Beiträge zur Geschichte Hadrians VI," 53–62.

32. Adrian VI to Eck, 1 December 1522 (*Briefmappe* 1:226–28).

33. Also extant is the reform proposal of Jakob von Salza, bishop of Breslau (2 April 1524). Although not a controversialist himself, he advised among other things the publication of pamphlets in Latin and in the vernacular, sparing no expense: "They should obtain all Luther's pamphlets and refute them, with moderation and discretion, in pamphlets in Latin and also in the common tongue. To ensure that this is done properly, no expense should be spared, even though a large sum of money might have to be spent each year" (S. Ehses, "Ein Vorschlag des Bischofs von Breslau an Papst Klemens VII [1524]," 835). Bishop Jakob's advice, like Fabri's, Cochlaeus's, and some of Eck's, was either not complete or not received in Rome until after Adrian's demise.

Reformation had been fueled by a widespread and justified indignation at abuses in the church. The best solution, in their opinion, was to summon a reforming general council. They were realistic enough, however, to recognize that this was a counsel of perfection and to put forward second-best proposals. Fabri proposed that the German bishops encourage their learned clergy to pen refutations of the heresiarch and of his disciples such as Carlstadt.[34] Eck's suggestion was threefold: first, he advised, the pope should issue a "bull of reformation" in order to correct abuses; then a "bull of condemnation," which would take into account the new elements of Luther's teaching and the other heresies that had sprung up since *Exsurge Domine*; and finally, a bull that would allow the setting up of a national synod, with extensive inquisitorial and reforming powers.[35] Literary activity played only a limited role in Eck's proposal, which envisaged "three or four of the most learned" providing an explanation of the new bull of condemnation.[36] Cochlaeus, on the other hand, had printing play an important role in both wings of the twofold assault on heresy essayed in his proposal. "The way of moderation" included the reform of clerical abuses and the inculcation of Catholic piety by sermons and pamphlets on the cult of Mary and the mass, for example. He believed that much capital could be made out of the Lutheran abolition of masses for the souls of the departed, which had apparently proved deeply unpopular with the people.[37] "The way of force" involved taking to task recalcitrant princes and bishops for permitting heresy to flourish within their jurisdictions. Cochlaeus pinpointed their allowing Luther's books to be printed, and expressly requested that bishops subsidize those Catholic controversialists who had not been published.[38]

All three memoranda were extremely frank. The German bishops, for example, were condemned as "negligent" (Fabri), "neutral" (Eck),

34. Fabri to Clement VII, 9 September 1525 (*MRL* 537–38).
35. Eck, *Memoranda* (*ARC* 1:109, 116, 119–20).
36. "Once the new condemnation has been issued, three or four very learned men should explain point-by-point in books written especially for the purpose why these articles and others like them have been condemned. It should be done dispassionately so that those who at the present time are ensnared in the tradition of Martin might be able to recognize themselves and see their own deformity as if in a mirror" (*ARC* 1:143).
37. Cochlaeus, *Duae viae*, 113–15. See R. Bäumer, "Johannes Cochlaeus und die Reform der Kirche," 339.
38. Cochlaeus, *Duae viae*, 115^v–16^v. See Bäumer, "Cochlaeus und Reform," 339–40.

and "dead-drunk shepherds" (Cochlaeus). This in itself said nothing of Adrian's own open-mindedness, of course: he could have commissioned these reform proposals and ignored them as surely as his successor, Clement VII, did. Unfortunately, Adrian died before the process of consultation with the controversialists was concluded. But he would certainly have taken some of their points to heart.

In November and December 1522, Adrian addressed a series of letters to selected allies and opponents in Germany. His purpose was to ensure the enforcement of the edict of Worms. The letters are therefore noticeably concerned with the suppression of the printing, selling, and reading of evangelical pamphlets.[39] But Adrian took the remarkable step of going beyond the written word of the edict, in attempting to secure for pamphleteers on the Roman side free access to the presses. In a letter of 30 November to the city council of Bamberg he wrote:

> If what we have heard is true, the printers working in your city have (if it is to be believed) been bribed by the Lutherans, so that they most willingly publish Lutheran works but will under no circumstances publish those written against them by Catholics in defence of the truth. I must solemnly warn you that, should you fail to correct and mend this attitude of theirs, you shall not escape God's awful retribution, be you ever so Christian in all other respects.[40]

Adrian was here taking up with an alleged offender a complaint that almost certainly came to the Curia's attention from a controversialist. Cochlaeus, for example, had made this specific charge to Leo X in 1521. In the same year Aleander could tell Cochlaeus it was an accusation he had heard before.[41] There is certainly no reason to believe that the complaint was made any less frequently to the new pope. The concern Adrian demonstrated in this letter for the conditions

39. Adrian VI, *In hoc libello*, Ai^v, Aii; idem, to Bamberg, 30 November 1522 (*Op. Lat.* 2:539ff.).
40. Adrian VI to Bamberg, 30 November 1522 (*Op. Lat.* 2:540).
41. Cochlaeus to Leo X, 19 June 1521 (*ZKG* 18:117): "I have not however published anything yet because many things have held me up: the fraud and treachery of printers, the wrath of the mob, the abuse of Lutherans, and the contempt of the people. I am at a loss to know which printer I can trust, they are all so infected! Had I resources of my own I could guarantee the printing not only of my own books but also those of Emser and the Italians. But you cannot rely on these rogues to publish anything against Luther." See also Cochlaeus to Aleander, 27 September 1521 (*ZKG* 18:123): "The printers are almost all secret Lutherans. They will print nothing for us without payment, and they will do nothing reliably unless we stand over them." Aleander replied curtly, "You allege nothing new" (*ZKG* 18:123 n. 3).

under which the controversialists worked was equally apparent in the instructions he gave his legate Chieregati at the time of the first Nuremberg diet: "We understand that many virtuous and erudite men in Germany are paupers; and that certain men of outstanding talent have become cool towards this see, for it has made them provision more suited to actors and stable lads than to learned men. It is therefore our wish that you determine the identity of these men and forward their names to us, so that we can provide for them *proprio motu* as German benefices fall vacant."[42]

Adrian's relationship with the controversialists seems, however, to have gone deeper than a concern for the practical problems they faced. The letters he sent out to all quarters, encouraging the faithful and warning the suspect, so bristle with arguments and appeals typical of the Romanist authors that they should be regarded as controversial pamphlets in their own right.[43] Like Cochlaeus, he praised Germany's former greatness and piety.[44] Like Fabri, he marveled that a man who claimed, as Luther did, to have rediscovered Pauline theology should have ignored Paul's characteristic appeals to charity and peace.[45] Like nearly all the controversialists, he warned the German princes that one who had attacked ecclesiastical authority would not leave secular authority unmolested;[46] that Luther had merely renewed past heresies, not invented new ones;[47] that, like all heretics, he based his doctrines on the literal meaning of Scripture alone;[48] that the worse part of humankind (which is the majority) is always attracted to

42. Adrian VI, *In hoc libello*, Biii. It is tempting to interpret the "men of outstanding talent" who "have become cool towards this see" as a reference to Cochlaeus's threatened defection of the previous year. *Proprius motus* was the means in law by which the pope could bestow a benefice upon whomever he wished (regardless of the validity of other claims to it) on the basis of *reservatio pectoralis*, the notion that he had already secretly reserved to himself the right of appointment. See *LThK* 7:664; 8:1250f.; 10:563.

43. At the end of 1522, Adrian sent with his nuncio Chieregati a packet of letters addressed to the first diet of Nuremberg (25 November); Archduke Ferdinand (26 November); Mainz, Bamberg, Strasbourg, Speyer, and Constance (28–30 November); Archduke Ferdinand and Duke Henry of Mecklenburg (30 November); Elector Frederick (n.d.); Cologne University and Erasmus (both 1 December). On these, see Kalkoff, "Kleine Beiträge."

44. Adrian VI, *In hoc libello*, Aiii[v]; idem, to Bamberg, 539. See also Cochlaeus, *Paraclesis;* and idem, *Pia exhortatio*, passim.

45. Adrian VI to Frederick, 542[v]. Cf. Fabri, *Malleus*, 24.

46. Adrian VI, *In hoc libello*, Aii, Aiii; idem, to Bamberg, 539; idem, to Frederick, 542. For this charge on the lips of other controversialists, see chap. 4 above.

47. Adrian VI, *In hoc libello*, Ai[v]; idem, to Bamberg, 538[v]. See also chap. 6 above.

48. Adrian VI to Bamberg, 539[v]; idem, to Frederick, 542. See also chap. 6 above.

novelty;[49] that no less than the orderedness of the church, manifested in the special priesthood, was at stake;[50] and that those who opposed this order would suffer the fate of Korah, Dathan, and Abiron.[51] Nor was Adrian loath to give these letters the widest publicity. While pirated and suitably annotated editions were put out by Lutherans,[52] official printed versions in Latin and German also appeared, replete with imperial privileges.[53]

Both in his support for the controversialists and in his own published appeals to various bodies in Germany, Pope Adrian VI demonstrated his belief in the value of reason alongside authority. It is tempting to ascribe this attitude to his background, which was in academic theology rather than canon law, the more usual qualification for high ecclesiastical office. Whatever the reason, he was at odds with his colleagues at Rome not only in desiring a reform in head and members, as much of the Curia as of the parish priest, but also in appealing to the hearts and minds of those in a position to influence events in Germany. In such a climate it is hardly surprising that currency was soon given to rumors that his death was not entirely natural.

Catholic Opinion beyond Rome

Rome could have acted as a center for the coordination of the literary attack on Luther; however, partly for reasons having to do with the structure of the Curia and partly because the aims of the Catholic polemicists were generally considered suspect, it did not. Institutions nearer home had the opportunity of redressing the balance by providing the necessary encouragement and support. Although officially subordinate, the local jurisdictions of dioceses, religious provinces, and universities would have been far more effective in most cases than Roman jurisdiction. Moreover, local secular authorities could provide the physical protection the controversialists from time to time sorely missed. What evidence is there to test such a hypothesis?

49. Adrian VI to Bamberg, 539^v.
50. On Luther's threat to the beauty of orderliness, see Adrian VI to Frederick, 542, 542^v, and chaps. 4 and 5 above. On the centrality of the priesthood to the church, see Adrian VI to Frederick, 541^v, 543f.; and chap. 5 above.
51. Adrian VI, *In hoc libello*, Aiii^v; idem, to Frederick, 544. See also chap. 6 above.
52. E.g., Luther's translation of Adrian VI's letter to Bamberg, *Ein päpstlich Breve*, and the Latin versions of letters to Adrian VI and Chieregati by Wilhelm Nesen or Joachim Camerarius. See WA 11:337–38.
53. E.g., Adrian VI, *In hoc libello*, and its translation, *Was auff den Reichsstag zu Nüremberg*.

A potential source of assistance to which one might reasonably look in the first instance is diocesan curias. Unfortunately, however, the records even of dioceses in the front line of the battle with the Reformation are silent about the controversialists.[54] By itself such silence might denote no more than that we are looking in the wrong place for the evidence we require; however, when taken in conjunction with Eck's, Fabri's, and Cochlaeus's description of the German episcopate as fence-sitting, negligent, and dead-drunk, we can suspect that it is as eloquent a testimony as can be got—the controversialists simply did not figure in the bishops' religious policies. Nor did this situation alter over the years. In 1534, almost ten years after the period of this study, Cochlaeus wrote to Aleander: "The talk here is of nothing but Witzel and his new patron, a count and a layman, who does more for literary men than ten bishops, deans, or wealthy provosts."[55]

There were exceptions, of course. Abroad, the ranks of the controversialists were adorned by the presence of the bishops of Rochester and Tuy, the archbishop of Corfu, and the cardinal of St. Sixtus. This was a reflection of the fact that foreign participants in the Luther controversy were generally higher-ranking than their counterparts in Germany, where the literary fray was a relative—but by no means absolute—free-for-all. At home, Jakob von Salza, bishop of Breslau, was eager that Rome should make proper provision for the controversialists. More direct assistance was provided by Johannes von Schleinitz, bishop of Meissen, and Adolf von Anhalt, bishop of Merseburg, the diocesans of Albertine Saxony. These two cooperated closely with Duke Georg in banning Luther's publications and in sponsoring Catholic works even before the edict of Worms was published. They also gave Cochlaeus, for one, sufficient financial assistance for him to have exempted them from his blanket condemnation of the

54. For an overview of the German bishoprics at this time, see G. May, *Die deutschen Bischöfe angesichts der Glaubensspaltung des 16. Jahrhunderts*. There are also specialist studies of individual dioceses and their incumbents: A. Willburger, *Die Konstanzer Bischöfe Hugo von Landenberg: Balthasar Merklin, Johann von Lupfen (1496–1537) und die: Glaubensspaltung*; K. Schottenloher, *Tagebuchaufzeichnungen des Regensburger Weihbischofs Dr Peter Krafft*; A. Amrhein, *Reformationsgeschichtliche Mitteilungen aus dem Bistum Würzburg 1517–1573*; K. Reid, *Moritz von Hutten Fürstbischof von Eichstätt und die Glaubensspaltung*; and A. Sabisch, *Die Bischöfe von Breslau und die Reformation in Schlesien: Jakob von Salza (gest. 1539) und Balthasar von Promnitz (gest. 1562) in ihrer glaubensmässigen und kirchenpolitischen Auseinandersetzung mit den Anhängern der Reformation*.

55. Cochlaeus to Aleander, 6 May 1534 (ZKG 18:250).

prelacy.[56] However, due to the loss of diocesan records for Saxony, it is impossible to say how much the bishops' cooperation was spontaneous. One suspects that, had Johannes and Adolf not been blessed with a single-minded and interfering duke, their commitment on the controversialists' behalf would have more closely resembled that of their fellow bishops.

The balance of episcopal inaction was redressed to some extent when the controversialist Fabri was made bishop of Vienna in 1530. He was now in a position to act as spokesman for his colleagues, and in particular to present them as expert witnesses on the nature and extent of sixteenth-century heresy. He wrote to Cardinal Morone on the eve of the abortive Council of Mantua in 1536, recommending that certain invitations be issued: to Eck for his internationally acknowledged erudition; to Friedrich Nausea for his special study of the seditious nature of these heresies; to Cochlaeus for his knowledge of the history of Protestantism in general and of Luther's self-contradictions in particular; to Mensing for the treatment of "the heart of the matter," the sacrifice of the mass; to Witzel for his inside information as a former Lutheran.[57]

Fabri's letters of this time represent something of a high-water mark for the Catholic literary effort. But it is perhaps significant that the controversialist Fabri had been awarded one of the least attractive sees in the empire. In addition to the long and costly defense of Vienna against the Turks in 1529, which had seriously depleted the reserves of the diocese, the area occupied by the Turks had been devastated and depopulated, so that, according to Fabri, its income was now worth scarcely a quarter of its pre-war assessment.[58] Bishop Fabri had risen in ecclesiastical status, but had suffered a severe drop in income by comparison with his previous position. It apparently prevented him from maintaining secretaries for his own controversial work and certainly made it no easier for him to subsidize the endeavors of others.

It seems, therefore, that the Romanists received very little moral or material encouragement in their enterprise from Rome itself, and even less from their bishops. There remains the possibility that they

56. "I have no complaints, however, about our bishops and prelates. My lord the prince has two bishops in his territories who have this winter made it their business to assist me financially. Without their aid I could never have borne these heavy expenses" (ibid., 250).
57. Fabri to Morone, 17 December 1536 (*ZKG* 20:78–80).
58. Fabri to Aleander, 14 March 1532 (*ZKG* 20:70).

could have received help from secular sources. Their most illustrious princely supporter was, of course, Henry, king of England. He not only mobilized his own subjects such as More, Fisher, and Powell to write as part of a vigorous anti-Lutheran campaign waged between 1521 and 1534, but even entertained such polemicists from abroad as Murner and Eck.[59] An equally highly placed sympathizer was King James V of Scotland, although Cochlaeus found to his cost that royal generosity could be moderated by episcopal canniness: "My messenger was given forty crowns by the king. That is to say, he told me that the king had instructed a hundred crowns be handed over, but his treasurer, the bishop of Aberdeen, counted out only forty."[60]

The Catholic princes of Germany appear at first sight to have made more use of the controversialists, who took a full part in the formation of the Regensburg Union of 1524, which united the Catholic territories of south Germany, and of the northern alliance forged at Dessau the following year. The culmination of the controversialists' political activity came five years later, when they collaborated on the Confutation of the Augsburg Confession.[61] But although the two roles married neatly at Augsburg, the controversialists were required at these meetings as Catholic theologians, not controversialists as such. In fact, of all the German princes who remained loyal to Rome, only two can reasonably be described as patrons of controversial theology.

Georg, duke of Albertine Saxony, stands out as the Catholic ruler most single-mindedly committed to the use of propaganda. He pursued a deliberate policy of maintaining a team of Catholic writers by appointing them to benefices in his gift. In 1525, he installed the redoubtable Dungersheim in the Church of Our Lady at Mühlhausen; on Emser's death in 1527, he made Cochlaeus his personal chaplain; the following year, he appointed the popularist pamphleteer Sylvius

59. For Murner's trip to England and Henry's handsome gift of £100, see Doernberg, *Henry VIII and Luther*, 39. For details of Eck's visit, see Fraenkel, "John Eck's Enchiridion," 111. Cochlaeus's mission to England was badly timed, with his contacts More and Fisher already incarcerated.

60. Cochlaeus to Fabri, 28 October 1534 (*ZKG* 18:261). The only payment recorded in the bishop of Aberdeen's accounts for 1534 in connection with the visit is: "Item, to ane servand of . . . cocleus, quhilk brocht fra his maister ane buyk intitulat . . . , to his reward 1 li." See J. B. Paul, ed., *Accounts of the Lord High Treasurer of Scotland*, vol. 6, 1531–38 (Edinburgh, 1905), 236. The book in question was *Pro Scotiae Regno Apologia, adversus personatum Alexandrum Alesium Scotum, Ad serenissimum Scotorum regem* (Dresden, 1534).

61. For the controversialists' contribution to the Diet of Augsburg, see esp. Immenkötter, *Die Confutatio der Confessio Augustana*.

to a chaplaincy at Rochlitz. Moreover, he used his legislative powers to obstruct the printing of Reformation pamphlets and to encourage the publication of Catholic works. Duke Georg and King Henry could justifiably congratulate themselves and each other on their vigor in suppressing Lutheran propaganda while promoting Catholicism through the presses.[62] Like England, Albertine Saxony saw wholesale burnings and confiscations of Luther's books,[63] while its ban on the printing of evangelical pamphlets was maintained despite the economic hardship this caused. In April 1524, the Leipzig town council passed on to Duke Georg the complaint of local printers that because of the ban printers in neighboring regions were getting rich at their expense and were threatening to put them out of business.[64] This was no exaggeration. One Leipzig printer, Jakob Thanner, eventually went to prison for bankruptcy; another, Wolfgang Stöckel, had to flee ducal jurisdiction to avoid the same fate.[65] For those who violated these sanctions the penalties were harsh. In March 1521, Duke Friedrich the Younger and the Dresden town council reported to Duke Georg that, in accordance with his instructions, the printer Valentin Schumann and his assistants had been incarcerated "for some weeks" for publishing a defamatory tract against Emser, and that they had been released only after Emser himself had interceded on their behalf. In the same letter we read of another printer being jailed for publishing a pro-Lutheran pamphlet without the permission of the ordinary, in contravention of the edict of Worms.[66]

Georg's activity against Lutheran literature was complemented by more positive steps taken to promote Catholic literature. Emser's New Testament—specially commissioned to counter Luther's translation—was granted a two-year privilege by Duke Georg in recognition of the author's "diligent labors."[67] Georg was not content simply

62. The correspondence between the two princes was published by Emser in 1523 as *Serenissimi ac potentissimi regis Angliae Christianae fidei defensoris invictissimi, ad illustrissimos et clarissimos Saxoniae principes de coercenda abigendaque Lutheranae factionis et Luthero ipso Epistola. Item illustrissimi princeps Ducis Georgii ad eundem Regem rescriptio.*

63. See, e.g., Adolf, bishop of Merseburg, to Chancellor Dr. Kochel, 1 February 1521 (Gess 1:153); and Wolf von Schöberg, ducal officer in Meissen, to Duke Georg on the confiscation of four copies of Luther's New Testament in January 1523 (Gess 1:452–53).

64. Leipzig town council to Duke Georg, 7 April 1524 (Gess 1:640–41).

65. Dickens, *German Nation*, 112.

66. Duke Friedrich the Younger to Duke Georg, 4 March 1521 (Gess 1:155–58).

67. Duke Georg's foreword of 1 August 1527 to Emser's *Annotationes uber Luthers Naw Testament* (Gess 2:780).

with expecting his officers to execute his instructions, but tried to win their hearts, too. We know, for example, that he sent a copy of Emser's Testament as recommended reading to his officer at Quedlinberg.[68] Georg also used his influence as a secular prince to cajole Erasmus into throwing his considerable weight against Luther. The present crisis, he argued, summoned all, not just the professional theologians, to put their shoulders to the wheel. As good as his word, the duke himself wrote against the Reformation both in poetry and prose. Two of his polemical poems have survived. One scored Frederick the Wise for his arrogance in striking the legend *Verbum Dei manet in aeternum* (the Word of God endureth forever) on his coins in 1522. The other attacked Luther for mocking the translation of Bishop Benno's bones in 1524.[69] In addition to his numerous mandates and edicts, Georg also penned letters to Luther that were later published and, according to a common opinion, even tried his hand at writing pamphlets.[70]

Although uncharacteristic because of its very quantity, the propaganda put out by ducal Saxony in the twenty years up to Georg's death in 1539 shows what could be achieved for the Catholic literary cause under a combination of a strong and committed ruler and cooperative bishops. Becker's statement that hardly anything was published by Luther that did not evoke counter-measures from Georg is only a slight exaggeration.[71] In 1519, the duke initiated a propaganda campaign that was to have no parallel on either side of the religious divide in terms of its centralization. The campaign exploited the talents of the printers Stöckel, Martin Lotther, Martin Landsberg, Schumann, and Thanner, who operated from the twin capitals of ducal Saxony, Dresden and Leipzig. Through their publishing of original titles and reprints, they handled more than a quarter of all Catholic authors in Europe who wrote against Luther between 1518 and 1525, and almost a third of all titles.[72] These figures are particularly impressive when it is remembered that in 1525 the duke's campaign was in its infancy,

68. Duke Georg to Ulrich Gross, 31 August 1527 (Gess 2:783).
69. For the full text of these poems, see H. Becker, "Herzog Georg von Sachsen als kirchlicher und theologischer Schriftsteller," 164–67.
70. Ibid., 171, 198, 252, 263; see also Edwards, *Luther's Last Battles*, 46, 57.
71. Becker, "Georg als Schriftsteller," 162–63.
72. The authors represented by the Saxon presses included the Italians Prierias, Catharinus, Rhadinus, and Marlianus and the Englishmen Fisher and King Henry in addition to the local writers Alveld, Bachmann, Blich, Emser, Fabri, Sylvius, Tetzel, Usingen, and Wulffer. The Leipzig presses produced thirty-nine titles, the Dresden eleven.

that these figures do not include works against reformers other than Luther or anti-Lutheran works published without means of identifying their provenance, and that the most prolific writers of the period did not use the Saxon presses (Cochlaeus was still printing at Strasbourg until 1527; Eck was at Ingolstadt; and Schatzgeyer was at Munich, Tübingen, and Ulm). Moreover, Duke Georg was not content simply to produce the works of his own local authors, numerous as they were. During these years, his presses produced twenty-one reprints of pamphlets originally printed outside Saxony, of which eight were originally printed outside Germany.

In comparison with the duke of Saxony's strenuous efforts to assist the Catholic literary response, the action of other Catholic princes seems almost negligible. After Georg, the most committed and devout German monarch on the Catholic side was undoubtedly his cousin, Margarethe, princess of Anhalt. As Georg had originally been trained as a priest, so she had received a convent education and seemed destined at first to follow her sisters into the cloister. Like her cousin she also wrote devotional poetry, and like him was a notable benefactor of religious communities in her realm.[73] And it was to her own court at Dessau in 1526 that she summoned the Catholic princes of north Germany to conclude an anti-Reformation treaty. In addition, she conducted a voluminous correspondence with her chaplains and other spiritual advisers, who included the foremost Catholic controversialists of the day: Emser, Cochlaeus, Alveld, Sylvius, Bachmann, and Mensing.[74] They exchanged information about political and ecclesiastical developments in the religious crisis and drew one another's attention to noteworthy pamphlets, both orthodox and heretical.[75]

---

73. See Lemmens, *Franziskanerbriefen*, 23f., 43.

74. Much of this correspondence has been published in O. Clemen, ed., *Briefe von Hieronymus Emser, Johannes Cochlaeus, Johannes Mensing und Petrus Rauch an die Fürstin Margarete und die Fürsten Johann und Georg von Anhalt;* and Lemmens, *Franziskanerbriefen*.

75. Emser to Margarethe, 21 April and 25 December 1526 (Clemen, *Briefe*, 3), enclosing his own collected Latin works, an unnamed German work, and Erasmus's *Diatribe;* Cochlaeus to Margarethe, 28 October 1529 (Clemen, *Briefe*, 14), enclosing a copy of Emser's New Testament and a vernacular work of his own; Alveld to Margarethe, 21 April 1525 (Lemmens, *Franziskanerbriefen*, 35), replying to her request for advice on whether the mass was a sacrifice or, as Luther held, a testament; idem, to Margarethe, 18 April 1527 (Lemmens, *Franziskanerbriefen*, 36), on how to deal with defamatory pamphlets; idem, to Margarethe, 11 February 1527 (Lemmens, *Franziskanerbriefen*, 40), on the use of Scripture by heretics; idem, to Margarethe, 13 March 1529 (Lemmens, *Franziskanerbriefen*, 41f.), on the doctrine of the enslaved will; Mensing to Margarethe, 21 April 1528 (Clemen, *Briefe*, 6), acknowledging receipt of a Lutheran tract and enclosing two books purchased at the most recent Frankfurt book fair.

Margarethe even rewarded her controversialists' literary efforts with occasional cash payments.[76] But the interest she took in their work seems to have been entirely personal. She did not regard herself as leader of a propaganda campaign against the Reformation. Her concern with Luther's *The New Testament or Holy Mass*, for example, was not (as it was with Duke Georg) how best to suppress it, but whether one should indeed regard the mass as a testament rather than a sacrifice.[77] Similarly, when pamphlets libelous of the Franciscan order were brought to her attention, her reaction was not to have the printer or colporteur clapped in irons, but to enquire of the local Minorites whether the accusations of malpractice were justified.[78] Nor does it seem, notwithstanding her occasional financial contributions, that she was particularly interested in ensuring the wide dissemination of Catholic controversial work. Princess Margarethe can therefore be considered a patron of the controversialists only inasmuch as she patronized a number of priests who happened to be controversialists: her assistance and promotion of the Catholic literary effort cannot be compared with that of her cousin Georg.

None of the other Catholic princes of Germany took any interest whatever in the controversialists' work. It is true that Archduke Ferdinand regularly called upon the services of Fabri,[79] and the Bavarian dukes Wilhelm and Ludwig on those of Eck.[80] But Fabri and Eck were employed not as controversialists but as negotiators with other princes and with Rome. Only in ducal Saxony was propaganda taken seriously, and one is obliged to ask the reason for this. It seems that Duke Georg genuinely believed that ordinary lay people deserved guidance from professional theologians, and that it was his duty as a Christian prince to ensure that they received it.[81] This impulse was particularly clear during the preparations for the Leipzig debate. The duke was astonished by the efforts of the Leipzig theology faculty and of the bishop of Merseburg to call off the disputation, interpreting their actions as a dereliction of duty. He tauntingly suggested that the faculty's reluc-

---

76. For evidence of lump-sum payments, see Emser to Margarethe, 22 February 1527 (Clemen, *Briefe*, 5); and Cochlaeus to Margarethe, 28 November 1529 (Lemmens, *Franziskanerbriefen*, 15f.).
77. Alveld to Margarethe, 21 April 1525 (Lemmens, *Franziskanerbriefen*, 35).
78. Alveld to Margarethe, 18 April 1527 (Lemmens, *Franziskanerbriefen*, 36).
79. See Willburger, *Die Konstanzer Bischöfe Hugo von Landenberg*, 139.
80. See Strauss, "Religious Policies of Dukes Wilhelm and Ludwig," 360f.
81. Duke Georg to Bishop Adolf, 17 January 1519 (Gess 1:60).

tance to host the debate was due to cowardice, or to fear of being shown up by more competent theological disputants.[82] Georg felt aggrieved that although he maintained the University of Leipzig, a *universale studium* where even articles of faith might be freely debated within the confines of the faith, it would not so much as provide a venue for a dispute over a simple rhyme about a penny and a money-box, which was "not even an article of faith." Although it was he who paid the theologians' wages, they reacted to the suggestion of a debate like soldiers who take fright on hearing the first shot.[83] He would therefore ask other, more learned men to judge the disputation, men who would earn their supper by bringing the truth to light.[84]

Duke Georg's enthusiasm for bringing the truth to light never waned. Georg was genuinely convinced before the Leipzig debate that Luther had, in his questioning of indulgences, hit upon a subject that deserved further investigation; once Georg learned of Luther's leanings towards Hussitism, he knew precisely where the truth lay. Replying to Erasmus in 1525 he wrote:

> I do not deny your assertion that I too was taken with Luther's fables at first. For it seemed that the opportunity had presented itself for correcting the abuses and corruptions which had grown apace. But after he began to re-kindle the Hussite heresies, Satan stepped in and impelled him to leave almost nothing in the entire Church untouched and undefiled, beginning with the Supreme Pontiff and thence ruinously corrupting all the traditions of the fathers.[85]

Luther's patrocination of the Hussite cause was decisive in earning Duke Georg's displeasure. The duke's grandfather was the excommunicated Utraquist King Georg Podiebrad of Bohemia, and his mother, Sidonie, was deeply troubled by the thought of her father's

---

82. Cf. Georg's instructions to Dr. Dietrich von Werthern for a reply to Bishop Adolf, before 17 January 1519 (Gess 1:59): "Perhaps [their reluctance to stage the debate] stems from their faintheartedness, because they realize that they shall have to trouble their heads slightly with something they can't do while they sit drinking. Or perhaps they themselves realize that they are not clever enough to dispute solemnly with such learned men and will be confounded. Or perhaps they realize that this disputation will show that they are not up to the fight, and they don't like that. For they mislead us poor folk and lead us where they will, so they can take our money and leave us holding the empty purse."

83. Duke Georg to Bishop Adolf, 17 January 1519 (Gess 1:61).

84. Duke Georg to Dietrich von Werthern, before 17 January 1519 (Gess 1:59).

85. Duke Georg to Erasmus, 13 February 1525 (Gess 2:40).

dying outside the protection of the church. Sidonie herself retreated behind the ceremonies and works-righteousness of the Roman Church, and the correspondence between the two shows that her son inherited this piety.[86] As we saw from Georg's reaction to the legend his cousin struck on the coinage of electoral Saxony, he took exception to Lutherans' using such words as "Word of God" and "Gospel" to describe their own singular beliefs. The only gospel Duke Georg knew was that handed down through the centuries and authoritatively interpreted by the church. The fruits of the new Lutheran gospel— violence, sedition, and impiety—showed it for what it was, the heresy of Huss: "It is our hope before God that all who truly know us will agree that we have always wished to obey the Gospel and the Word of God as it has been received by the Christian Church; and that we have prohibited from our lands not the true Gospel and Word of God, but only the counterfeit doctrines, sermons, and writings of Luther and of those other evangelicals, falsely so-called."[87]

The case of ducal Saxony, atypical as it was, illustrates the weakness as well as the strength of relying upon the personal commitment of secular rulers. The controversialists worked under excellent conditions while a Duke Georg or a Margarethe lived. But these monarchs were succeeded by Protestant heirs, so that such circumstances could— and did—alter overnight.

Self-Imposed Limits and External Pressures

Many of the Catholic controversialists were highly apologetic about their decision to go into print at all. To what extent, they wondered, was it legitimate for them to attempt to give account (*rationem reddere*) of an authoritative judgment of the Holy See, corroborated by the emperor? Would it bring the judgment itself publicly into doubt? Would it imply negotiation with heretics? Would it imply the courting of popular opinion? It was a genuine difficulty that prevented Catho-

---

86. See I. Ludolphy, "Die Ursachen der Gegnerschaft zwischen Luther und Herzog Georg von Sachsen," 35. It is interesting to note that Margarethe of Anhalt was also a grandchild of Georg Podiebrad (Lemmens, *Franziskanerbriefen*, 23); it might be that this spurred her to oppose Lutheranism as it did her cousin.

87. Duke Georg's foreword to Emser's New Testament, 1 August 1527 (Gess 2:776).

lics from writing more, or even from writing at all. This was a limitation the controversialists imposed upon themselves.

But there were also external pressures that may well have limited the extent of the Catholic literary response to the Reformation. Generally speaking, propaganda played no part in the policies of the Curia or of the royal courts of Catholic Europe, which put their trust in a political and military solution to the problem of the Reformation. Pope Adrian, the academic who believed that rational explanation could win hearts and minds, and Duke Georg, the Christian prince whose duty was to win and preserve the souls of his people, were exceptions. Their examples serve only to show what their colleagues might have achieved had they been similarly inclined. People such as Aleander, who were well-informed of the controversialists' activities, saw the controversialists as a liability that could actually exacerbate an already difficult situation. The less-knowledgeable majority—in the cities and in provincial councils of the empire, for instance—viewed all religious publishing with the blanket suspicion engendered by the edict of Worms. Catholic authorities, in other words, were not able so much as to regard controversial writing for the church as an honorable profession; much less were they prepared to provide central funding and set up Catholic presses and networks of distribution, as the authors themselves would have preferred.

9

MESSAGE, MEDIUM, AND MOTIVE

This book began with a question: Given the conventional theory that Protestantism and printing were natural allies at the time of the Reformation, what is to be made of the Catholic use of the press in the same period? Is it possible to develop a general theory of the relationship between print and Catholicism? This book was intended as a contribution to answering such a question, by taking as an example the work of Luther's first Catholic opponents. The theological evidence that emerges from this literature was presented in chapters 1 to 6, and the literary and historical evidence in chapters 7 and 8. It remains for this chapter to make explicit the connections between them. It will be seen not only that the character of the Catholic literature was determined to a large extent by the theological presuppositions of the authors, but also that the style and content of their arguments were themselves largely the result of the particular literary form adopted.

The Theological Contribution

It is a sound procedure to attempt to relate the controversialists' theology and their literary style. They wrote and published works of controversy, not spiritual journals or systematic *summae*, and this undoubtedly affected the way in which their theology was presented. Nonetheless, certain aspects of their theological achievement can be assessed independently of literary considerations. Three aspects in particular have emerged as a result of the methods adopted in this book. Because of their importance for a full appreciation of the controversialist effort, I propose to summarize them before going on to examine the relationship of medium and message.

Results of the Chronological Approach

The approach taken to this study of the controversialists' work has been largely chronological, because this was the best way of identifying any development their response underwent over the course of time. It has shed considerable light on the question of their literary

development, and the evidence for this will be reviewed later in the
chapter. It is more difficult to find evidence of changes, refinements, or
deteriorations with respect to their theology or argumentation. As controversial writers, of course, they were obliged to follow the lead of
their opponent—Cochlaeus and Fisher complained that it was always
Luther who called the tune[1]—and so to a great extent their changing
concerns reflected Luther's own theological development.

This is not to say that the controversialists' arguments did not
develop. For instance, the charge of "Bohemianism" contained in Eck's
Obelisci led eventually to the controversialists' finding Luther's fore-
runners in the heretics of the Middle Ages and antiquity, until they
had traced his spiritual genealogy back to Cain himself. This argument developed into the important contrast between two churches,
the *ecclesia Dei* and the *ecclesia malignantium*. On the other hand, Tetzel's
complaint that a reliance on Scripture "would lead everyone to believe
what he likes" was never improved upon.

Nonetheless, it is revealing that all the major arguments employed against Luther in these years were in essence leveled against
him in the first few months of the indulgence controversy: biblicism,
antinomianism, anarchism, and Bohemianism. This is surprising, for
Luther's questioning of indulgences was extremely mild in comparison with the violence of his later attacks on aspects of the church's life.
It suggests that the early controversialists very quickly perceived the
implications of Luther's basic approach; in the same way as his
approach never altered, neither did their criticism of it. But there was
also a subtle sense in which Luther grew into the accusations laid
against him. At first they seemed to bear almost no relation to the
positions they were meant to refute. But as Luther's critique of the
church developed, these allegations appeared less and less wide of the
mark. (A reason for this will be suggested later in this chapter.)

Results of the Comparative Approach

Another intention of this book was to compare and contrast the arguments used by the controversialists against Luther. The most dramatic
differences centered on the question of the pope. At one extreme was

---

1. Cited in Iserloh, *Kampf um die Messe*, 31; and Lortz, "Wert und Grenzen," 18,
respectively.

the papal absolutism of Prierias and Marcello—both Italians; at the other was the more or less muted conciliarism of the Franciscans Murner, Alveld, and Schatzgeyer. The other controversialists represented the gamut of intermediate positions, with Dominicans tending toward the first extreme, Franciscans toward the second. The dangers of reading too much into these differences was signaled in chapter 2—after all, the controversialists were united in their implacable opposition to Luther. But this variety of opinions is interesting nonetheless, not least because it qualifies Jedin's assertion that conciliar theory was dead by the beginning of the sixteenth century:[2] the attitude of the Franciscan controversialists shows that signs of life could still be found. Other doctrinal differences between the controversialists tended not to be so marked. For instance, there seems by this date to have been no theologian trained exclusively in the *via moderna* who opposed Luther (with the sole exception of Usingen, his teacher in the Erfurt arts faculty).

In addition to the similarities and differences between the Roman loyalists on individual points of doctrine, the comparison has revealed an overall pattern, namely, that they were more likely to agree when there were doctrinal definitions to work from and less likely when there were none. Thus the champions of indulgences put forward different defenses of the practice, and with regard to the mass the reservation of the chalice, transubstantiation, and certain aspects of the theology of the sacrifice were treated very differently. On the question of papal jurisdictional supremacy, however, there was no dissent even from the conciliarists and the semi-conciliarists.

The question of similarity and dissimilarity between the controversialists' presentations brings us within the purview of the influential theory of *Unklarheit*. This theory was developed by the Roman Catholic historian Joseph Lortz as part of his general characterization of the period immediately prior to the Reformation as a time of disintegration, in which religious devotion became formal and externalized and relationships at all levels of the church, society, and commerce suffered from widespread alienation. The particular cause of theological confusion was nominalism, which, he believed, had fostered an arid skepticism and an obsession with peripheral issues. Lortz sug-

2. Jedin, *History of the Council of Trent* 1:30.

gested that this confusion both made the Reformation possible and hindered an authentically "catholic" response to it.[3] Of course, a number of methodological objections have been leveled against the theory since it was formulated.[4]

The question arises whether this study of the controversialists supports the theory of *Unklarheit*. The conclusion that the controversialists concurred in some respects and disagreed in others seems to support the theory as formulated by Lortz, who conceded that "in the midst of far-advanced theological vagueness, there were quite clear signs of a unified Catholic foundation, very much along the lines of what Trent was to lay down as definitive."[5] But I do not believe that the matter is as straightforward as that. The immediate cause of the variety of opinions was the absence of doctrinal definitions, not *Wegestreit*. And if it can be argued that, particularly in the early phases of the controversy, Luther had deliberately sought out for his own academic safety areas in which dogma was incompletely defined, it is possible that this variety was less significant for contemporary theology in general than Lortz believed. Moreover, it is questionable to what extent this variety was indeed a confusion or simply an example of diversity

3. "The emergence of the Reformation was entirely dependent upon the widespread vagueness of the age; vagueness, indeed, in the mind of the Church" (Lortz, *Reformation in Germany* 1:233); "Das Nebeneinander verschiedenster theologischer Schulen, Strömungen und Gruppen, von vielleicht gutem, aber schwachem Wollen bis zu leeren Phrasen, von kurialistischem Superlativismus bis zu radikalem Evangelismus, erzeugte eine uns beinahe unvorstellbare *theologische Unklarheit* über das, was katholisch sei. Es herrschte eine wahre 'confusio opinionum', die ausdrücklich auch auf dem Konzil von Trient beklagt wurde." (Lortz and Iserloh, *Reformationsgeschichte,* 19).

4. The main problem with the theory lies in its use of terms. It depends on the supposition of a standard of "clarity" that owes more to the later development of the Roman Catholic Church than to anything that actually existed in the high Middle Ages. "Nominalism" itself is such a vague term, with different meanings ascribed to it by different scholars, that it seems unfair to blame anything upon it at all. (See esp. the survey in W. J. Courtenay, "Nominalism and Late Medieval Thought: A Bibliographical Essay," *Theological Studies* 33 [1972], 716-34.) Moreover, the idea of "disintegration" is a value judgment put forward by those who wished to explain how the Age of Faith could possibly have spawned the Reformation. It could have happened, they believed, only if there had been an intervening stage that was itself an illegitimate development of medieval theology. From another point of view, it is equally possible to see the Reformation as a natural development, a coming to fruition, of the previous tradition. See esp. H. A. Oberman's Spätscholastik und Reformation series: *The Harvest of Medieval Theology: Gabriel Biel and Late Medieval Nominalism* (Cambridge, Mass.: Harvard University Press, 1963) and *Masters of the Reformation*. A similar task has been undertaken by S. E. Ozment, esp. in *The Age of Reform 1250–1550: An Intellectual and Religious History of Late Medieval and Reformation Europe* (New Haven and London: Yale University Press, 1980).

5. Lortz, *Reformation in Germany* 2:198.

of theological opinion. It would be illuminating to compare the variety of opinions that existed on the eve of the Reformation with other periods of church history for which the theory of *Unklarheit* has not been adduced. For instance, the period following the Council of Trent was presumably one of absolute doctrinal clarity for the Roman Catholic Church. But this did not preclude significant theological diversity, as the significant controversies associated with the names of Baius, Bañez, and Jansen show.

Results of the Thematic Approach

The theme that has repeatedly emerged throughout the course of this investigation is that the Catholic controversialists consistently identified Luther's chief threat as the overthrowing of order. By order (*ordinatio; ordenung*) was meant the divinely ordained system of superiority and inferiority, higher and lower, authority and obedience, which permeated the entire universe. If one part was questioned, they believed, the system itself was called into question. This accusation lay behind the controversialists' responses at every stage of the debate. Thus Luther's critique of indulgences was related to the supreme authority of the pope, while his critique of the *ius divinum* was related to the monarchical rule of God on the one hand, and to secular sovereignty on the other. His rejection of the authority of scholastic authors, his appeal to the educated layperson to decide his case, and his denial of any external criterion by which to judge Scripture were all regarded as conducive to doctrinal anarchy. His critique of the mass and other sacraments was related to a denial of the sacramentality of orders, where God's *ordinatio* was most clearly apparent. This concern with authority and order was a common feature of the controversialists' response to Luther even when, on specific issues, they differed over the detail of his error.

   At this point it would be wise to sound a note of caution, for such an interpretation of Luther's Catholic opposition raises a number of questions. To what extent were matters of authority and order raised merely as a rhetorical device? Did this concern dominate their writings to the exclusion of others? Was it an issue of equal importance to all controversialists? Clearly, there is a case for arguing that the polemics of these theologians are misunderstood if regarded as entries in private spiritual journals. They were intended to be read, and moreover to achieve certain objectives. There can be no doubt that the controversialists used the claim that Luther posed a special threat to authority as an *argumentum ad hominem* in the indulgences and the divine right disputes and in the response to *To the Christian Nobility*.

Against this it can be argued that the controversialists' concern with order is far too deep-seated to be simply a device. Not only does it appear on practically every page of their work, but it even appears when it is not particularly relevant to the matter in hand. For instance, in Cochlaeus's *Mirror of Evangelical Freedom*, the author is discussing the incorporation of Christians into the true body of Christ when he suddenly interpolates a passage on the question of authority that concludes: "As St. Paul says, every power and authority is instituted by God, and it is the duty of all to be obedient subjects. Whosoever withstands authority withstands God's order. And whosoever withstands God's order will be rewarded with eternal damnation."[6] An even more dramatic non sequitur occurs in Cochlaeus's *Against 154 Articles*. Replying to Luther's argument that the manifold laws of the Jewish dispensation succeeded only in creating sects and parties, Cochlaeus contends that the law of Moses was meant for unity, not for diversity, and that the divisions within Judaism arise from sin.[7] But he then changes tack and devotes two pages to a defense of diversity and variety: "for if we were all the same, there would be no order amongst us."[8]

An interesting point about the second of Cochlaeus's digressions is that it is a classic exposition of "the most beautiful order," with all the quotations from Paul's epistles and the Song of Solomon with which we are familiar from the other Catholic writers.[9] The verbal similarities between the controversialists on this theme are so close that one immediately suspects plagiarism on a grand scale (involving, incidentally, at least one pope!), but they can in fact be traced back to the common influence of Dionysius the Pseudo-Areopagite. There is some highly suggestive evidence connecting Dionysius with some of the Catholic writers from a date before their public engagement with

---

6. Johannes Cochlaeus, *Ein Spiegel der Ewangelischen freyheit*, Cii.
7. Idem, *Uff CLIIII Artikeln*, Ei.
8. Ibid., Ei[v].
9. See, e.g., Campester, *Heptacolon*, Giii[v]; Cochlaeus, *Spiegel*, Cii; Murner, *Tütscher nation*, Dii[v]; Emser, *Quadruplica*, Ci; Fisher, *Sacri sacerdotii defensio*, 1248; Marcello, *De authoritate* 7[v]; Clichtoveus, *Antilutherus* 2:60f.; Powell, *Propugnaculum*, 155; Rhadinus, *Oratio*, Hi, Hiv[v]f.; Latomus, *De ecclesia*, 95[v].

Luther. For instance, when Cardinal Cajetan delivered the opening sermon of the second session of Lateran V in 1512, he used the occasion to expound the Pseudo-Areopagite's view of the consonance of the earthly church with the heavenly hierarchies.[10] In 1517, when he first came to hear of the Ninety-five Theses, Eck had just completed work on a commentary on Dionysius's *Mystical Theology*.[11] This commentary was remarkable for the way in which it interpreted Dionysius's negative theology in terms of the hierarchism of the same author's *Ecclesiastical Hierarchy* and *Celestial Hierarchy*. Two years earlier, Clichtoveus had published a commentary on the same book.[12] This leads me to believe that the concern with order was not something trumped up by the controversialists overnight with the sole intention of making Luther odious, but something that, through their concern with Dionysian hierarchism, had exercised them for some time.

This suggestion is not new. In 1978, Fraenkel put forward the thesis that the writings of Pseudo-Dionysius might have been a normative influence upon the controversialists' response to Luther.[13] On the basis of Eck's commentary on the *Mystical Theology*, Fraenkel suggested that behind much of the controversialists' thought lay the idea of the *Wertskala*, the ladder of being. This belief, he argued, allowed the controversialists to use a fortiori arguments, justifying Christian practices by reference both to lower forms of animal life and to the higher forms of the celestial hierarchy.[14] It also allowed them to believe that ecclesiastical and theological authorities should be respected simply because they had been respected in the past.[15] Fraenkel's position was challenged five years later in H. Smolinsky's study of Alveld and Emser.[16] Smolinsky accused Fraenkel of making unwarranted generalizations about the controversialists as a whole on the basis of very slim evidence. He argued that it was difficult to prove that the authors used Dionysius, and even more difficult to prove "influence." Even if

---

10. See Hendrix, *Luther and the Papacy*, 57f.
11. Johannes Eck, *D. Dionysii Areopagitae De mystica Theologia lib. I Graece.* See G. Epiney-Burgard, "Jean Eck et le commentaire de la 'Théologie mystique' du Pseudo-Denys."
12. See Klaiber, ed., *Katholische Kontroverstheologen*, no. 699.
13. P. Fraenkel, "An der Grenze vor Luthers Einfluss."
14. Ibid., 24f.
15. Ibid., 26f.
16. Smolinsky, *Alveldt und Emser*, 418f.

it could be shown that a Neoplatonist view of the universe was one of the models used by the controversialists, it would not mean that other models were not of equal or greater significance for them: unity and peace were more important than order to Alveld, Emser, and Duke Georg, for example. Moreover, the controversialists should not be regarded as a homogeneous group. Even if Dionysius was important to some of them, the same would not necessarily apply to all.[17]

These are weighty methodological objections to Fraenkel's thesis, although Fraenkel himself suggested that the influence of Neoplatonism was just one of several factors that may have limited Luther's appeal. It is true that the only evidence adduced by Fraenkel was Eck's commentary of 1519.[18] Nevertheless, the present study bears out this impression in spite of Smolinsky's objections. In the discussion of the ordination controversy at the end of chapter 5, I documented the extent of the controversialists' use of Pseudo-Dionysius. Some (Kretz, Fabri, Henry, Emser, and Dietenberger) cited his *Ecclesiastical Hierarchy* simply as an early witness to the establishment of the sacraments and other rites. But others (Fisher, Powell, Rhadinus, Marcello, Campester, and Clichtoveus) were more interested in the way in which Dionysius expounded the sacrament of orders as an expression of the hierarchical ordering of the universe. Pope Adrian, the Sorbonne theologians, Murner, Latomus, and Dungersheim, while not citing the Pseudo-Areopagite by name, nevertheless defended the "most beautiful order" of the church and the universe along Dionysian lines.

In light of these findings, Smolinsky's objections—that there was at best only a minority and unrepresentative interest in Dionysius and Neoplatonist cosmology and that other models were probably equally important—seem less sustainable. Fourteen of the most prolific writers, or a quarter of all Catholic controversialists active between 1518 and 1525, refer directly to Pseudo-Dionysius. These fourteen are fully representative of different nationalities (seven German, three English, two French, and two Italian), intellectual background (six scholastics,

---

17. Ibid., 419.
18. Fraenkel restated this claim in a conference paper given in 1982: "Le schema, l'image et la cible: Luther vu par ses adversaires romains," 346.

three humanists, and three scholastic humanists), and ecclesiastical status (nine secular clergy, four religious, and one layperson).[19]

While Smolinsky was, of course, correct in his identification of peace and unity as the concerns uppermost in the minds of the controversialists with whom he was dealing, he was wrong to attempt to dissociate these concerns from the question of order. St. Paul's numerous exhortations to charity were consistently seen by the controversialists in the context of his view of order: "Be subject to the governing authorities"; "Let all things be done decently and in due order."[20] They were baffled that Luther should have chosen Paul, of all sacred writers, to justify schismatic and seditious teaching. I suggested in chapter 5 that they might have been disposed to thinking of order as the key to all Paul's thought precisely because they believed Dionysius was a disciple privy to his secret teaching.[21]

The present study therefore supports Fraenkel's suggestion that the hierarchically ordered cosmos of the Pseudo-Areopagite was a central feature of the controversialists' response to Luther. But its very importance is problematic: How is one to account for its pervasive influence, which, as we have seen, does not appear to have been restricted to any particular tradition? The Catholic theologians seem to have been exposed to Dionysian influences from two quarters. As a supposed witness to the early emergence of the sacraments, he was assured of a place in the standard medieval texts such as Hugh of St.-Victor's *De sacramentis* and Aquinas's *Summa theologiae*. But in the later Middle Ages there was also something of a Dionysian revival, which manifested itself in Dante's poetry in the fourteenth century, and in the theology of Nicholas of Cusa and Marsiglio Ficino in the fifteenth. Indeed, the rediscovery of Dionysius during the Renaissance explains why Neoplatonist tendencies are to be found among the humanist controversialists as well as among their scholastic colleagues.

19. No Franciscan controversialists are included in this list. Given that their participation in the struggle against Luther was relatively minor in any case, it is difficult to say whether their absence here is significant. Certainly, it explains why Smolinsky gained the impression that Dionysius was not important for the controversialists, for one of his two subjects was the Franciscan Alveld. But it should be remembered that the Franciscans, particularly Alveld and Schatzgeyer, differed from their fellow controversialists in appealing to no other authority than Scripture. Given this factor, it is perhaps not surprising that Smolinsky found no specific references to Pseudo-Dionysius in Alveld.

20. Fabri, *Malleus*, 24; Catharinus, *Apologia*, 36.

21. See, e.g., Rhadinus, *Oratio*, Hi.

Given the widespread influence of Dionysian Neoplatonism at the time of the Reformation, it is all the more remarkable that Luther himself should have been completely immune to it. Of course, Luther knew of Dionysius and of the revival of interest in him, and indeed was obliged on occasion to justify his low opinion of the Pseudo-Areopagite's writings.[22] Much more work needs to be done on the significance of the Dionysian revival of the sixteenth century and of Luther's criticism of it—I have merely indicated something of the extent of the problem. Particular attention would have to be paid to delineating the picture of St. Paul refracted in the Dionysian tradition, because it is clear that the "existential" Paul of Luther was quite at odds with the hierarchical and cosmological Paul of the controversialists.

The Message's Effect on Medium

While the scores of pamphlets and books published by Luther's Catholic opponents up to 1525 represent a diversity of backgrounds, motives, and approaches, a common theme runs through them all—that Luther posed a threat to the God-given authority and order of the church and of the universe. His perceived anti-authoritarianism shaped the Catholic response from the outbreak of the indulgence controversy. His demand that the hierarchy account to the laity for apparent weaknesses in the theory and practice of indulgences was seen as a dangerous development, likely to lessen the people's obedience to their spiritual superiors. His emphasis on the Christian's

22. Luther's famous rejection of negative theology in the *Operationes in Psalmos* was in fact more a reflection of his disgust for the spiritual dilettantes who took it up as the latest fashion: "I say this by way of warning, because everywhere, in Italy and Germany, there are circulating commentaries on Dionysius' *Mystical Theology* which are no more than bags of hot-air and opportunities to show off. They believe they are mystical theologians if they read, understand, and teach it—or rather, if they are seen to understand and teach it. It is not by understanding, reading, and speculating that one becomes a theologian, but by living, or rather by dying and being damned" (G. Hammer and M. Biersack, eds., *D. Martin Luthers Operationes in Psalmos 1519–21*, Archiv zur Weimarer Ausgabe 2,2 [Cologne and Vienna: Böhlau, 1981], 296.5–11). His rejection of Dionysius's hierarchism in *The Babylonian Captivity of the Church* was more direct: "If one were to read and judge without prejudice, is not everything in it his own fancy and very much like a dream? But in his *Theology*, which is rightly called mystical, of which certain very ignorant theologians make so much, he is downright dangerous, for he is more of a Platonist than a Christian. So if I had my way, no believing soul would give the least attention to these books. So far indeed from learning Christ in them, you will lose even what you already know of him. I speak from experience" (*WA* 6:562.7–12, *LW* 36:109).

assurance of forgiveness, based on God's promises, was considered detrimental to the church's sacramental system, on which its power over the laity was built. His rejection of scholastic theology would, they believed, just as surely undermine the intellectual foundations of much of the church's life and belief. Because these errors were compounded by being publicly broadcast, Luther's earliest literary opponents, who were also competent legal prosecutors, accused him of heresy in order to secure his silence. It is significant that the charge made against him by a number of different bodies was not one of doctrinal irregularity on this or that point of indulgence theory, but nothing less than *lèse papauté*. Within a matter of months, Luther's threat to authority in the church was made as pointed as it could be.

The controversialists' determination to defend authority did not slacken in the ensuing debates. Their defense of the divine institution of the papacy was based on the equivalence of *factum* and *ius*—that what is is what should be—and on such deductive arguments as the propriety of monarchy as the best system of government.[23] In the wake of the Leipzig disputation of 1519, Luther's rejection of scholastic theology and his courting of educated lay opinion were regarded as attacks on the authority of the church's *magisterium*. And the following year, his appeal to the German nation was countered by the argument that his anti-authoritarianism made him as much an enemy of the social order as of the ecclesiastical hierarchy. Luther's assault on the sacramental system in general and on the mass sacrifice in particular was interpreted by the Catholic controversialists as an attempt to lessen the authority of the priesthood by destroying the foundations on which it was based and on which its separation from the laity depended. The extension of his criticism in the early 1520s to so many more areas of the church's life than simply indulgences and the papacy signified, in Romanist opinion, the creation of an entirely different but parallel church.

The mid-1520s therefore mark the logical end of the controversialists' effort. With the creation of two churches the battlelines had been drawn up and, from their point of view, no man's land was uninhabited: "there is no middle ground between the Catholic Church

---

23. See, e.g., Eck, *De primatu Petri* 2, chap. 27; Marcello, *De authoritate* 1, sec. 1, chap. 5.

and schismatical heresy."[24] Moreover, they believed that by 1525 there were no new aspects of the Roman Church that Luther could attack. As a result, the controversialists' own role (at least with regard to Luther) became redefined as the consolidation of positions already reached. Most importantly of all, the year 1525 marked the height of the Peasants' War. With it came the apparent vindication of the Romanist strategy of interpreting all Luther's doctrines as threats to authority. It is significant that Protestant publication, which had risen almost exponentially between 1518 and 1524 and showed no signs of decline, dropped markedly in 1525 and never recovered. The aims of popular propaganda and agitation became almost as suspect among the reformers and their civil leaders as they had always been among the Catholics.

The controversialists' overriding concern with authority imposed three constraints upon their publishing activity. The first constraint was the fear of criticizing authority itself. The role most frequently claimed for themselves by the controversialists was providing intellectual support for the authoritative condemnations of Luther. These included not only the papal bull *Exsurge Domine* and its confirmation by the secular arm, the edict of Worms, but also the pronouncements of the Universities of Cologne, Louvain, and Paris. They were, of course, bare condemnations that simply listed Luther's offending articles without showing what teachings of the church they infracted or in what respects. The controversialists saw their role as a supplementary one: to provide *rationes* or *causae* by citing the relevant teachings and applying them to Luther's case. But in thus supporting *auctoritas* they had to be careful not to compromise it, for the premise of their activity was that these authoritative condemnations were in some degree inadequate.

The second constraint, closely related to the first, was the fear that their writings might be construed as an attempt to dispute with a heretic. The controversialists were fully aware of the tradition that heretics were not to be reasoned with but simply confronted with the choice of either submitting to the church's authority or rejecting it and therefore, as it were, condemning themselves. But in supplying

24. Latomus, *De ecclesia*, 89ᵛ.

auctoritas with *rationes,* the controversialists could be seen as bringing these matters into dispute. The resulting tension was expressed by Eck when, in 1523, he urged that the pope issue a new bull of condemnation to take account of Protestant heretics other than Luther. He noted with approval the convention that legal judgments never contained reasoned opinions in case they invited argument and so lessened the authority of the court. But was there not a greater risk to the Curia's authority, he wondered, if such reasons were again to be omitted from such a bull, as they had been from *Exsurge Domine*?[25]

Unlike the first two limitations on the controversialists—which applied only from 1519, when authoritative condemnations began to be issued—the third constraint operated on them from the beginning. The controversialists frequently criticized Luther for discussing in public undecided theological matters, on which not even professional theologians had reached agreement, so that every Tom, Dick, or Harry and every little old woman gossiped about them on street corners.[26] This they regarded as a serious attack on the authority of the church's *magisterium.* But of course, precisely the same criticisms applied to them when they chose a mass medium in which to debate these matters with Luther. It was for this reason that the controversialists tried to limit the potential readership of their theological works by writing them in Latin and adopting an academic style. It also explains why Murner could publish a deliberately popular work such as *The Great Lutheran Fool* only by concentrating on personalities rather than on theological doctrines.

As a result of these tensions, the Catholic response to Luther divided itself into two stages. In the first stage, publications were aimed primarily at refuting Luther and addressed him in the second person; in the second stage, the general public became the primary addressee, and the reformer himself was referred to in the third person. Jedin suggested that the transition between these phases took place in 1525, the year Eck published his *Handbook,*[27] but there are sound reasons for pushing this date back to 1522. This was the first full year in which Luther could be regarded unambiguously as a here-

---

25. Eck, *Memoranda (ARC* 1:117).
26. See esp. Murner, *Ermanung,* passim; Schatzgeyer, *Scrutinium,* 4f.
27. Jedin, "Bedeutung," 78–80.

tic. The authority of *Exsurge Domine* (1520) was at first widely questioned, and even afterwards was considered inadequate;[28] it was therefore left to the edict of Worms (1521) to put his error beyond doubt. Once declared a heretic, Luther could not be disputed with, and the Catholic publicists were obliged to turn their attention elsewhere. In the same year, the fragmentation of the Catholic response into numerous minor controversies and the simultaneous emergence of anti-Lutheran compendia bore witness to the drawing up of lines of demarcation between the two churches. It was now safe for the controversialists to address the general public without fear of such a course of action being understood as an invitation to them to judge the religious question for themselves. Indeed, the stage was set for Catholics to develop a positive attitude to publishing, which would fully manifest itself after the Council of Trent.

The Medium's Effect on Message

The theological presuppositions of the controversialists, particularly their concern with authority, largely determined the shape their literary activity took between 1518 and 1525. Half of their publications took the form of academic treatises precisely because they wished to limit their potential audience when discussing the theological issues at stake. The same tension between the need to refute Luther publicly and the dangers public refutation entailed explains why the majority of the fifty-seven Catholic controversialists wrote only one book each. Moreover, it could be suggested—although it would be an argument from silence—that other Catholics might even have been deterred from writing for the same reasons. In the second part of this chapter I want to show that the reverse was also true: that the literary style the controversialists preferred—the printed "disputation" style—had an effect on their argumentation.

---

28. For the refusal of the Wettin and Leipzig authorities to publish the bull on these grounds, see Boehmer, *Luther,* 355f. To Boehmer's list should be added the prestigious University of Vienna, which in a formal *protestatio* to Pope Leo outlined its legal objections to the bull. See *Protestatio universitatis Viennensis,* 10 December 1520 (*MRL,* 11–15). These refusals are interesting because they came from sources unsympathetic to Luther himself: the objections were purely technical. Eck was of the opinion that *Exsurge Domine* became obsolete as soon as it was published, because it did not, for example, deal with the revolutionary treatises of 1520. See Eck, *Memoranda* (*ARC* 1:116).

Controversy as Disputation

It is impossible to read far into the Catholic controversial literature without gaining the impression that at many points in the controversy the Romanists were fundamentally failing to engage with Luther's arguments. Typically, at least in the early stages, Luther would question a doctrine at its weakest point, the gray area where the church had made no binding definitions. The controversialists would, however, ignore the gray area and attack Luther instead from assured positions that had been the subject of dogmatic decrees. When, for example, Luther argued that the papacy existed by the permission but not the precept of God, the controversialists based their case on the recent decree of Lateran V, which had confirmed papal superiority over councils. The usual explanation given for this failure to engage is that the controversialists simply did not understand the level on which Luther was conducting his theological investigations. There is, however, an alternative explanation.

The academic disputation for which Luther composed the Ninety-five Theses never took place at Wittenberg as planned. Instead, it became a disputation in print, with Luther taking the role of "respondent" in the unpublished "Asterisks" and the published *Explanations* against his "opponents" Eck and Wimpina.[29] Luther continued to put forward many of his radical views in thesis form even after the indulgence controversy (thus maintaining the posture of a respondent) and, as we have seen, the literary genre most commonly adopted by the controversialists was the disputation style. Having taken the form of the academic disputation, it was inevitable that the controversy between Luther and the controversialists would also follow its procedures. The disputation was a game with strict rules, in which the cogency or validity of an argument was not enough in itself to achieve victory. To win a disputation, it was necessary to force one's opponent into a position in which he either contradicted some part of divine or natural law or contradicted his own earlier positions.[30] If one regards

29. The possibility that the disputation might have to be conducted on paper had occurred to Luther when he routinely requested at the head of the theses "that those who cannot be present to debate orally with us will do so in writing" (*WA* 1:233.1–5, *LW* 31:25).
30. For details concerning the conduct of theological disputations, see, e.g., G. Kaufmann, *Die Geschichte der deutschen Universitäten*, 2 vols. (Stuttgart: J. G. Cottas-

the controversial work of Luther and his opponents as part of a disputation in print that lasted many years, many of the otherwise odd features of the controversy become intelligible.

The necessity of proving that Luther had transgressed divine law explains why the controversialists tried to steer him onto the rocks of dogmatic definitions. It also explains why they tended to agree between themselves when they had such definitions from which to work. The rules of debate meant that they could not simply contradict Luther or throw across his path indiscriminately any and every objection that came to hand. This limitation is confirmed by their use of what I have called their "pastoral argument." One of the most surprising results of this investigation is that in a number of important respects the controversialists put up no substantive objection to Luther's teachings. We saw that his views on justification by faith alone, on the relationship between faith and the sacraments, and on the priesthood of all believers were criticized not for infracting some part of the church's teaching, but for the way in which they were expressed or for the effect they might have on the common people. Of course, this was still a serious charge, inasmuch as even official condemnations of heretics listed not only their erroneous articles, but also those that were true but were expressed in a provocative manner—for example, those deemed "scandalous, temerarious, seditious, or offensive to pious ears." This was how the Council of Constance had condemned Huss[31] and how Luther himself was condemned in *Exsurge Domine*.[32] The same formula of censure was used against Luther by at least one controversialist.[33] But it is nonetheless surprising that these relatively weak charges were the strongest objection the controversialists could bring to bear on what we regard as two of Luther's most characteristic doctrines, justification and the universal priesthood. Since it is quite clear that they were not oblivious to the implications

---

chen, 1888–96) 2:369–400; F. Paulsen, *Die deutschen Universitäten und das Universitätsstudium* (Berlin: A. Asher, 1902); M. Grabmann, *Die Geschichte der scholastischen Methode nach den gedruckten und ungedruckten Quellen bearbeitet*, 2 vols. (Freiburg im Breisgau: Herder, 1909–11; reprinted, Basel and Stuttgart: B. Schwabe, 1961); H. Hermenlink, "Luther als Disputator," in *WA* 39.2:xxxiii–xxxvii; and E. Wolf, "Zur wissenschaftsgeschichtlichen Bedeutung der Disputationen an der Wittenberger Universität im 16. Jahrhundert," in E. Wolf, ed., *Peregrinatio II: Studien zur reformatorischen Theologie, zum Kirchenrecht und Sozialethik* (Münster, 1965), 38–51.

31. Constance, *sessio* VIII, 4 May 1415 (*COD* 414.26–32; 415.12–15).
32. *DS*, 1492.
33. Tetzel, *Subscriptas positiones* (Löscher 1:517).

of these doctrines for faith and order, their decision to argue in this limited way can only have been deliberate. We can attribute this to the constraints of the disputation: Luther had not manifestly contradicted revealed truth in these doctrines; therefore, they could not be considered fatal weaknesses in his overall argument.

The necessity of proving that Luther had transgressed natural law explains the attractiveness to his opponents of the argument from order. Luther's rejection of a supreme head of the church was simply absurd, they argued, because every society on earth has had a king. They regularly cited Aristotle's *Politics,* in which monarchy was justified on similar grounds.[34] Luther's confounding of the ministerial orders and of the priestly and lay estates was equally absurd, because the very fabric of the universe was shot through with variety and inequality. Here appeals to Pseudo-Dionysius came into their own, for his arguments from natural philosophy were considered no less than an exposition of St. Paul's thought and therefore tantamount to the revealed truth of divine law.

An extension of the objection from natural law—that is, that one's opponent's argument was demonstrably absurd—was the objection of self-contradiction. The laws of logic did not allow a disputant to contradict himself in the course of a debate.[35] This explains, I think, the almost obsessive concern of such writers as Catharinus, Henry VIII, Cochlaeus, and Fabri painstakingly to document Luther's "self-contradictions." Their seeming inability to grasp the fact that Luther's thought might have developed over the years and, worse, their naive comparison of sentences abstracted from different books written with different emphases strike the modern reader as puerile.[36] But if we regard the controversy with Luther as a disputation—a written disputation of immense length and of international dimensions!—then this obsession becomes more understandable. In a disputation, self-contradiction was simply not permitted. It proved that Luther's positions were absurd. When he continued to make contradictory

34. Marcello, *De authoritate,* 7ᵛ. Cf. Prierias, *Errata* 1:2, iii, pp. iv–v; Eck, *De primatu Petri* 2:27; Murner, *Von dem babstentum,* Aiiᵛ; Modestus, *Oratio,* Aiiiᵛ; Powell, *Propugnaculum,* 8ff.

35. For the rules governing the *disceptatio* in logic, some of which applied to theological disputations, see G. R. Evans, "Wycliffe the Academic: The Old and the New," *Churchman* 98 (1984), 315.

36. See, e.g., Wiedermann's astonishment at this style of argument in "Cochlaeus as a Polemicist," 200.

statements long after being shown his inconsistency, there was good reason to suspect the influence upon him of the Father of Lies.

The Effect on Luther

The disputation model seems to account adequately for the nature of the Catholic literary response to Luther in general terms. Certainly, it explains many features of it that are otherwise unintelligible and have prevented modern scholarship from regarding these authors with much seriousness. But I believe that the value of the disputation model is not thereby exhausted. It helps us to see that the response to Luther did not take place in a vacuum. The Romanist writers responded to Luther, and he responded to them. The disputation was most emphatically not a means of convicting one's opponent of heresy. Divine and natural law merely marked out the limits within which the disputation could be conducted.[37] It therefore seems likely that the controversialists often deliberately confronted Luther with dogmatic definitions in order to set before him a sort of rhetorical dilemma in which he had either to return to the fold or take a yet more radical step. I believe that on several significant occasions this had the less desirable effect, so that the controversialists succeeded only in pushing Luther ever further from their vision of the truth.

It was certainly Luther's own view that he was pushed rather than that he fell. In a fragment of autobiography from the preface to the 1546 edition of his German works he claimed that he was "deeply indebted" to his papists.[38] What he meant by this can best be seen from a confession he made at the beginning of his career as a reformer: "Believe it or not, there is no-one, in my opinion, to whom I am more indebted or for whom I should more ardently pray than Johann Tetzel, the author of this tragedy (may he rest in peace) and you, Emser, and

---

37. There seems indeed to have been some flexibility, so that if an erroneous position was inadvertently reached in the course of the disputation, the usual questions of legality could be suspended. This seems to have been Luther's own understanding of his position in the months after the publication of the Ninety-five Theses, when he repeatedly protested his immunity as a disputant: e.g., "I myself have asserted nothing, but have disputed and sought to be Catholic. Only obstinate error in the faith makes one a heretic" (*Asterisci, WA* 1:302.22–24). He repeated this claim in connection with the Leipzig disputation: "My twelfth proposition was forced out of me by Eck, but although the pope will have his supporters in the forthcoming debate, I do not think it will be dangerous for me, unless they forget the freedom of the disputation" (to Spalatin, 24 February 1519, *WA Br* 1:351.39–352.1).

38. *WA* 50:660.5–16.

Eck, and all my adversaries, so much do I think they have furthered me."[39] It was also the explanation he gave the Emperor Charles: "First, you should know that I came out into the public eye against my will. Whatever I have written, I have written after being provoked by the violence and conspiracy of others. I desired nothing more earnestly than that I should stay in my own corner."[40] More telling than these public protestations are the confidences he exchanged with his close friend, the court-chaplain Spalatin: "I have always been dragged into this affair and it is not right to withdraw now so long as Eck keeps shouting. I have to entrust this affair to God and let myself be led, yielding the ship to wind and wave."[41]

Luther's view of his revolt was undoubtedly, therefore, one of a gradual and forced development. But we might well suspect its proximity to the truth, because it was a most convenient way of blaming almost everyone for the Reformation but himself. It was also a convenient way of resolving first the Catholic charge of inconsistency and, later, Protestant confusion over the rather conservative tenor of his early works. Luther does use the theory of gradual coercion expressly in this context (the preface to the first volume of the Latin edition of his complete works), but that does not mean it was an interpretation specially devised for the occasion. I believe rather that Luther's view was not only sincerely held, but that it has also been borne out by the events reviewed in this book.

The papacy had not been in Luther's sights when he criticized indulgences, and although "papal indulgences" could not be considered entirely without reference to the pope, his criticism was shared by contemporaries whose absolute loyalty to the Holy See was beyond reproach. The connection between an attack on indulgences and an attack on the pope seems therefore to have been made largely by Luther's opponents, Tetzel and Prierias, on the grounds that, while not all that was currently practiced or preached with regard to indulgences could be directly justified from existing definitions, it did all fall under the unwritten code of the church's rule of faith, which was itself under the patronage of the pope.

---

39. *WA* 2:667.15–19. Cf. *LW* 39:150 (*WA* 7:627.9f): "I was driven into this game against my will" (*Against the Hyperchristian Book of Goat Emser*).
40. *WA Br* 2:176.32–37.
41. *WA Br* 2:41–42.

This was how Luther himself understood the Romanist response. In May 1518 he wrote in his dedication to Staupitz of the *Explanations*: "So when these most agreeable people, schooled in the most blatant trickery, could not refute what I actually had said, they invented the story that, with my theses, I had injured the power of the Supreme Pontiff."[42] Twenty years later, he reflected for the benefit of his students: "Soon Sylvester [Prierias] came along with this syllogism: 'Whosoever has doubts about one word or deed of the Roman Church is a heretic; Luther has doubts about the word of the Roman Church and its method of action; therefore etc.' Then things really got started!"[43]

The implication for Luther was that papal power could be used as an effective and indiscriminate check to any call for reform, no matter how legitimate.[44] He considered this to be a clear abuse of papal authority by sycophants who exaggerated it not out of respect for the papacy but in order to serve their own ends, "who desire to build Babylon among us in the name of the Roman Church."[45] Luther was therefore obliged by this controversialist ploy to turn his attention from the immediate question of indulgences to that of papal authority. In March 1521 he conceded that while it had never been his intention to destroy the papacy—reform, as he explained, always implies continuance, not destruction—"it is true that in previous books, impelled by their driving and hunting, I have been forced to write that the pope does not derive from God's order."[46] At first, he believed that papal authority would be less open to abuse of this kind (which ultimately sought to claim God's authorization for anything done in the pope's name) if it were understood as a human rather than a divine institution, and this was the purpose of his *Explanation of the Thirteenth Proposition*. However, the Romanists steered the subject of debate from *ius divinum*, which was questionable, to papal magisterial superiority to a council, which had been recently determined at Lateran V and therefore was not. In the process, their charge of *lèse papauté* became the more concrete one of violating a dogmatic decree, and Luther was obliged to abandon all hope of reform from within the clerical estate. His alternative, set out in the manifesto *To the Christian Nobility*, was to

---

42. *WA* 1:526.30–32.
43. *WA Tr* 3:564.18–21.
44. *WA* 2:675.30–34.
45. *WA* 2:22.23–24.
46. *WA* 7:645.11f., *LW* 39:172.

demand a reformation at the hands of the higher laity. I believe that even this work was originally prompted by the Catholic controversialists.

The dominant Catholic response to *To the Christian Nobility* was to accuse Luther of fomenting sedition. However suited to the ears of an oversensitive aristocracy the charge may have been, it was not one fabricated for the purpose of refuting this pamphlet. The fear that Luther's writings could fire an anticlerical revolution had been present from the outbreak of the indulgence controversy and was a stock reply to the reformer's demand for the abolition of those practices and doctrines that could not adequately be explained to the laity. Eck declared the Ninety-five Theses liable to cause "tumult" and "sedition," because of which clerics could "no longer be defended from the insults, let alone the swords, of the prattling laity."[47] In the following year, Emser lamented Luther's impatience for reform and warned that such public and irate utterances would rouse princes' cohorts and the rabble to open rebellion against the pope.[48]

Given the persistence of this counter-argument and its serious misrepresentation of Luther's own position, it is surprising that he never attempted to refute it. On the contrary, he appears at times almost to have accepted the Romanist analysis, albeit with grim resolve. In a letter to Spalatin of February 1520 he reminded himself as much as his friend that "the Gospel cannot be preached without tumult, scandal, and sedition. The Word of God is a sword, it is war and scandal and perdition and poison."[49] His use of the word "sedition," in light of the Catholic conviction that his teaching would produce it, suggests that Luther was prepared even for that eventuality.

It was in opening Luther's mind to the possibility of popular unrest, I believe, that his opponents gave him the idea of a reformation conducted by the laity. We have seen how the doctrine of papal supremacy was invoked by Luther's earliest opponents in order to remove the possibility of reform, by using the syllogism that all church practice (however dubious) derives from the head of the church; to attack an "abuse" is therefore to attack the pope himself. In order to break this syllogism at some point, Luther argued against the divine

47. Eck, *Obelisci* 29 (*WA* 1:312–13). Cf. also *Obelisci* 26 (*WA* 1:313.1–2).
48. Hieronymus Emser, *A venatione Luteriana aegocerotis assertio*, esp. at Löscher 3:717, 722–23, 725–26.
49. Luther to Spalatin, 16 February 1520 (*WA Br* 2:43–4).

right, but not even this succeeded in instituting a reform from within the ecclesiastical hierarchy. The only solution, therefore, was to initiate a reform from without. The Catholic fear of insurrection indicated to Luther the vast reservoir of lay power, and it was through this power that he now saw a way of bringing about that reformation of the church he felt so necessary if God's teaching were to prevail over men's.

In the middle of June 1520, some months after his letter to Spalatin and more than a year after he had finally abandoned hope of a reform backed by the Curia, Luther was annotating Prierias's *Epitome*. One of the comments made in the afterword has been held against him ever since.

> Since the Romanists realize that they can never prevent a council, they have invented the pope's superiority to a council, that without his authority none may be assembled, continued, promised, or brought about, and that the pope himself is the infallible rule of truth, the authoritative interpreter of Scripture. It seems to me that, if they continue to rage in this way, no remedy will remain except for emperor, kings, and princes, armed with weapons of war, to attack this earthly pestilence and settle the matter not with words but with steel.[50]

For our purposes, the striking thing about this annotation is not the violence of its language but the threat of direct action to bring about a general council. A month later, Luther suggested to Spalatin that the Elector Frederick use a similar threat in response to Cardinal Riario's latest approach:

> Perhaps the Prince should add this too: Lutheran doctrine is now so widespread and deep-rooted in Germany and beyond that the Romans must defeat it with reason and Scripture. From censure and violence nothing can be expected but that Germany should become Bohemia twice over. As the Romans well know, Germans have fierce temperaments, and unless they are taken captive by Scripture and by reason, it would not be safe to anger them even with many popes, especially now, when the study of literature and languages reigns in Germany, and when the laity has begun to think for itself. It is therefore proper for a Christian prince to warn and prevent them, lest they are perhaps tempted to resort

50. *WA* 6:347.10–13, 17–20.

to any force at all (without first rendering account of themselves rationally) and thus incite against themselves an uncontrollable riot. I do believe that these untaught and timid Romanists will be badly shaken.[51]

This is the negative, reactive side to Luther's thought in the summer of 1520. *To the Christian Nobility* represented the positive side, for here the same theme of the laity's ability to bring about reform is repeated in a key more suited to Luther's own voice: reformation must be by peaceful means, for the fight is with diabolical powers, and it must be conducted by the natural leaders in society, to whom such a responsibility has been entrusted by God.

It would, of course, be wrong to attribute the famous reform manifesto exclusively to the inspiration of Luther's adversaries, for the ideas it expressed had been implicit in his ecclesiology for several years, and the possible impact on him of letters of support from the knights Sickingen and Schaumberg ought not to be ignored. But there is enough evidence, I think, to suggest the inadvertent effect of his opponents' writings as at least a contributory factor.

The December following the publication of *To the Christian Nobility*, Luther committed the papal bull of excommunication to the flames in revenge for the burning of his own books. Along with the bull he also incinerated three large folios of canon law, a penitential manual, and about twelve smaller volumes of the writings of Emser and Eck. In fact, it appears that the burning of the bull was an afterthought, and that Luther's initial intention was limited to the destruction of canon law and the other "papal books."[52] Certainly his justification of the bonfire in *Why the Books of the Pope and His Disciples Were Burned* was concerned not with the bull, but with what he saw as the canon-law basis of papal absolutism used as an effective bulwark against reform: "Therefore the canon law is rightly to be destroyed and rejected as a poisonous thing. For from it follows, as it actually has happened, and is evident to everyone, that one can check no evil and demand no good."[53] Luther had originally been alerted to the abuse of papal authority for this purpose by Tetzel, Prierias, and Cajetan, and his deeper study of canon law was prompted by his clash with Eck at

---

51. Postscript to Luther's letter to Spalatin, 10 July 1520 (*WA Br* 2:138.40–49).
52. For this view, see Boehmer, *Luther,* 369.
53. *WA* 7:169.13-16, *LW* 31:388.

Leipzig. That Luther consigned representative works of the Romanists to the same flames in which the canons and decretals were consumed was therefore highly appropriate.

Apart from a general awareness that he was being driven by his opponents, Luther had not hitherto specified the ways in which he felt he was being driven, which is the reason I have attempted the present reconstruction. But by October 1520 this had changed. In the preface to *The Babylonian Captivity* he related how the controversialists had forced him to become "more learned." Originally, he had criticized indulgences, but thought that they should continue in existence despite their abuse. But now, "aided by Prierias and his brothers," he had become convinced that indulgences were Roman impostures designed to rob God of the faith due to God and people of their money. After this, Eck, Emser, and others taught him that his early attempt to preserve the legality of papacy by denying only its divine institution had been mistaken: "I am not completely unteachable in these matters, and now I know that the papacy is the kingdom of Babylon and the empire of Nimrod the mighty hunter." Most recently, he claimed, they had attempted to educate him concerning communion in both kinds and other great issues, and Luther presents *The Babylonian Captivity* as the result of his latest studies under the controversialists' direction.

We see immediately that this work differs considerably from Luther's previous productions. It was designed to provoke his opponents: "Since I see they have an abundance of time and paper, I shall give them plenty to write about. For I shall run ahead of them, and while the glorious conquerors are triumphing over one of my heresies (as it seems to them) I shall in the meantime be inventing a new one."[54] In other words, he knew the work was extreme and expected a storm of protest. All this is not to say that Luther wrote anything in *The Babylonian Captivity* he did not mean, but simply that it was not sufficiently worked out for teaching purposes. A primary aim was to annoy the Romanists.

I think there can be little doubt that Luther was pushed by the controversialists into increasingly radical solutions to the problem of a church that had so successfully fortified itself against reform. But equally, I think that by the time of *The Babylonian Captivity* the relationship between the two parties had altered. He was now not only aware

54. *WA* 6:501.6-9, *LW* 36:17.

of their tutelage, but on the basis of this awareness he could deliberately exploit it. There was no longer a simple relationship in which the Romanists (wittingly or not) set dilemmas to which Luther reacted. It had become a complex, interactive relationship in which, on the basis of what they already knew of their opponents, each probed what they believed were the others' weak or sensitive spots, and on the basis of this new information continued their probing.

This relationship can be seen at work in the process which led Luther to write *The Misuse of the Mass* (1521). His first discussion of the reservation of the chalice and the sacrifice of the mass occurred in homiletic pamphlets. It clearly touched a nerve, particularly with Alveld and Murner. Luther therefore sharpened his treatments of them and added a polemical discourse on the other sacraments for good measure in an avowedly provocative book, which was itself meant as a prelude to some even more revolutionary treatise. The Catholic reaction to *The Babylonian Captivity* was, as Luther had predicted, considerable and oriented toward a defense of the sacrificial priesthood. Now that their presuppositions had become clear, Luther could in *The Misuse of the Mass* launch an attack on the relationship between the sacrifice of the mass and the priesthood that struck at the very foundations of the spiritual power of the Roman Church.

We may conclude that it was not Luther's intention in writing the Ninety-five Theses ultimately to deny the papacy. But by the time he came to write about the sacraments in *The Babylonian Captivity*, he knew what response to expect and had already written *The Misuse of the Mass* in his head. For their part, the controversialists engaged in precisely the same process of exploration. They could be spectacularly successful—for instance, in the self-fulfilling prediction that their opponent would reject the papacy. They could occasionally be unsuccessful—for instance, in their belief that he intended to extinguish eucharistic devotion. If Luther was more often right about what motivated the Romanists than they were about what motivated him, that is scarcely surprising: he had been a Romanist, and a devout one at that, while they had never been "Lutherans."

The Limits of Publicity

In this chapter I have attempted to draw together the results, literary and theological, that have emerged from the study as whole. On the literary side, it has been shown that Catholic publications against

Luther in the period 1518 to 1525 cannot justly be compared with the contemporary published work of Luther or his colleagues. In most cases, this is not because the Catholic writers lacked the necessary awareness or ability to be successful publicists, but because under the circumstances they could perceive a role for only limited publicity: one in which Luther's error could be plainly demonstrated, but one which could not be construed as submitting the matter before the bar of public opinion. On the theological side, it has been shown that the restrictions the controversialists imposed on their literary activity (in particular, the adoption of the disputation form) also affected their argumentation, and I believe that this accounts for many of the features of their writing that have proved so inaccessible—and therefore unattractive—to modern scholarship.

THE PREOCCUPATION
WITH AUTHORITY

The early Catholic literary response to Luther can best be characterized by its preoccupation with authority. The words *auctoritas, authori-
tas,* and *oberkeyt,* with their synonyms and antitheses, appear many
times in the controversialists' writings, and the notion informs almost
every page. It was authority, above all, that Luther seemed to attack,
even when his teachings were doctrinally unobjectionable. It was
authority that the controversialists set out to defend with their pens
and, as importantly, with the printing press. The irony of the Catholic
use of the press in these early years is that while authority was its
inspiration, authority—and the fear of offending it by use of the
press—was also the cause of its most serious shortcomings.

The controversialists identified Luther's threat to authority at
each stage of the controversy. The Ninety-five Theses and their eluci-
dations were revolutionary documents: by their fawning attitude to
the common people, by their rejection of the schoolmen, and by their
denial of the church's continuing right to legislate in spiritual matters,
Luther had signaled his anarchic intentions from the outset. His attack
on authority in the church was pressed home by his questioning the
limits of papal power before and during the Leipzig debate in 1519.
The debate and its aftermath demonstrated the radicalism of a theological method that elevated Scripture above other doctrinal authorities and that ominously boasted of its accessibility to the common
people.

The address *To the Christian Nobility* was an unambiguous assault
on the authority of the church; but precisely because of their anti-
authoritarian tendencies, Luther's teachings were as much a threat to
the social as to the ecclesiastical order. As the earlier writings had
challenged authority in the church, so the writings of 1520 and beyond
challenged the authority of the church: *The Babylonian Captivity*
attacked the sacramental system as a whole and in particular the
priesthood, the source of all other sacraments; the numerous minor

controversies of 1522 to 1525 revealed that Luther's aim was not the revision of one or two points of doctrine, but the creation of a new church—a diabolical inversion of the true church of God.

The controversialists had diagnosed the danger posed by Luther as a threat to authority. But a pamphlet war, open to all comers, in which the validity of the doctrines of the church (many of them still undefined) and the question of Luther's deviation from them could be debated in public—was that not equally subversive of the church's authority? Most of Luther's opponents of 1518 had a degree of authority themselves: Tetzel as papal inquisitor, Prierias and Cajetan as papal theologians. But after the bulls of excommunication of 1520 and the imperial edict of 1521, the controversialists became sensitive to this question. They typically regarded themselves as providing reasoned explanations of the authoritative decisions. This was a risky tactic, because such explanations might imply that the decisions themselves were deficient or open to discussion. By using the printing press, the most indiscriminate means of broadcasting ideas, there was the further risk of seeming to submit the Luther question to public opinion. The alternative was to imitate the style of some of the great controversies between humanists and scholastics earlier in the century and conduct a published dialogue or disputation with Luther. The general public would then be a silent audience, not the object of an explicit appeal. But again, was this not tantamount, in the climate after 1521, to the illegal practice of disputing with a heretic?

The danger that using the press might undermine the very authority they sought to uphold was brought home to the controversialists by the reaction of the Catholic establishment itself, which ranged from ill-disguised irritation to open hostility. When Aleander blamed the Reformation on Eck, or bewailed the "two plagues" that beset the church, "the hands of printers and the tongues of doctors," he was voicing the general attitude held at Rome. Had Pope Adrian survived, things might well have been different, and the controversialists might today be remembered as an important element of an early Catholic reform and indeed of an early counter-Reformation. But he did not survive. If Adrian was the exception to prove the rule so far as Rome was concerned, Georg of Saxony stood out among local Catholic leaders. His ecclesiastical and secular fellows, together with conservative city authorities, seem to have regarded all religious publishing with a blanket suspicion, and they suppressed Catholic and Protestant literature with equal vigor.

The fear of compromising authority and the action or inaction of their own authorities made the use of the press by Catholics for the purposes of controversy an enterprise fraught with danger. This explains, I think, the otherwise odd fact that the majority of Catholic polemicists wrote only once against Luther, as well as the reluctance of others to write at all, even though, in these early years, he ushered in a new heresy (to use his words) with almost every publication. It also explains why those who did write tended to use academic literary forms, and why some of the most popularizing works, such as Murner's celebrated *Great Lutheran Fool*, concentrated on personalities rather than on theology. There were exceptions, of course. Alveld and Petrus Sylvius could, for instance, write about theological matters in the vernacular and in a popular style, expressly imitating Luther's own tactics, in apparent ignorance of the constraints I have mentioned. But such writers were a small minority: the majority chose academic styles and Latin for discussing the disputed issues.

The decision to use such styles imposed on the author further constraints, because each style had its own rhetorical conventions. The disputation style in particular used a grammar of argument quite bewildering to any reader unfamiliar with it: the wearisome sentence-by-sentence method of refutation, the "reaction principle," the painstaking exposure of contradictions, the elaborate cataloguing of similarities with past heresies. Such conventions did nothing to increase the accessibility of Catholic controversial literature to contemporary readers (any more than they have helped its case in the courts of modern scholarship). But to suppose that all the Catholic controversialists considered accessibility an unalloyed virtue would be a mistake.

The picture I have drawn is, of course, incomplete. The Catholic use of printing before 1525 was subject to pressures that disappeared soon afterward. Polemicists were open to the charge of disputing with heretics or of appealing to the judgment of the people. The substitution of propaganda for polemic (to borrow Chrisman's terminology) largely resolved this problem, because Catholic writers, editors, and printers could work relatively unfettered by authority—and the fear of offending it—while they concentrated on producing devotional aids and theological *summae*, especially in the period after Trent. Until the sort of study attempted here is extended to include these later developments, a complete understanding of the relationship between print and Catholicism in the sixteenth century will continue to elude us.

PRIMARY
BIBLIOGRAPHY

Page and signature numbers refer to the extent of the text itself, excluding end papers, title pages, and errata. Where possible, references are given to printed editions and to the microform reproductions of early sixteenth-century pamphlets held in West German libraries, published as *Flugschriften des frühen 16. Jahrhunderts*, ed. H.-J. Köhler et al. (Zug and Leiden: Inter-Documentation, 1978–87), here cited as *Flug*.

Adrian VI. *In hoc libello pontificii oratoris continetur legatio, in conventu Norember-gensi, Anno M.D.xxij. inchoato sequenti vero finito exposita &c. Cum gratia et privilegio imperiali.* Nuremberg: Friedrich Peypus, 1523. 4°, Ai^v–Piv.

———. *Was auff den Reichsstag zu Nüremberg / von wegen Bebstlicher heiligkeit / an Keyserlicher Maiestat Stathalter und Stende / Lutherischer sachen halben gelangt / un darauff geantwort worde ist / Auch etliche andere mer nutzliche ding / wie die volgende kurtz vorred und register anzeigt. Cum gratia et privilegio Imperiali.* Nuremberg: Friedrich Peypus, 1523. 4°, Aii–Kiv^v.

———. Letter to Frederick, elector of Saxony. 1523. In *Op. Lat.*, 541–44^v.

Aleander, Hieronymus. *Consilium super re Lutherana.* 1523. In J. J. Döllinger, *Beiträge zur Politischen, Kirchlichen- und Cultur-geschichte der sechs letzten Jahrhunderte* 3:243–67. Vienna: G. J. Manz, 1882.

Altenstaig, Johannes. *Ain nutzlich unnd in hailiger geschrifft gegründte under-richt, was ein Christen mensch thun oder lassen sol, dz er salig und nit verdambt werd.* Augsburg, 1523. 4°, ai–yiv.

Alveld, Augustinus von. *Super apostolica sede, an videlicet divino sit iure nec ne, anque pontifex qui Papa dici caeptus est, iure divino in ea ipsa praesideat, non parum laudanda ex sacro Bibliorum canone declaratur.* Leipzig: M. Lotter, 1520. 4°, Ai^v–Kiii [*Flug.* 947].

———. *Eyn gar fruchtbar und nutzbarlich buchleyn von dem Babstlichen stul: und von sant Peter: und von den / warhafftigen scheflein Christi sein / die Christus unser herr Petro befolen hat in sein hute und regirung.* N.p., 1520. 4°, Ai^v–Diii [*Flug.* 5].

———. *Malagma optimum contra infirmitatem horribilem duorum virorum, fratris Ioannis Loniceri theologistae, Et fratris Martini Lutheri ordinis eremitani de vicariatu, ut sanetur Ad percuciendam Vituperij citharam.* N.p., [?1520]. 4°, Ai^v–Fiv [*Flug.* 325].

———. *Ein Sermon darinnen sich Bruder Augustinus von Alveldt . . . des so in Bruder Martinus Luther . . . under vil schmelichen namen gelestert / und geschent / beclaget / und wie Augustinus forder wyder Martinum (tzu erkennen wie gesunt sein lere sey) tzu schreyben wiln hat. Auch mith eynem tzu satz / etlichs dinges sso vom Bruder Martinum Luther newlich von der messe geschriben ist.* N.p., [?1520]. 4°, Ai^v-Ciii^v [*Flug.* 761].

————. *Tractatus de communione Sub utraque Specie quantum ad laicos: An ex sacris litteris elici possit, Christum hanc, vel praecepisse; vel praecipere debuisse, Et quod in re hac sentendium pie sane, catholice sit, iuxta veritatem evangelicam.* N.p., [?July 1520]. 4°, Ai^v-Giv^v [*Flug.* 949].

————. *Pia collatio F. Augustini Alveldiani ad R.P. Doctorem Martinum Luderum super Biblia nova Alveldensis.* N.p., [?August 1520]. 4°, Ai^v-Biv [*Flug.* 3820].

————. *Von dem elichen standt widder bruder Martin Luther Doctor tzu Wittenberg.* Leipzig, [?1520/21]. 4°, Ai^v-Eiii^v [*Flug.* 915].

————. *Wyder den Wittenbergischen Abgot Martin Luther.* Leipzig: V. Schumann, 1524. In K. Büschgens, ed. CC 11 (1926).

————. *Oracio Theologica, quam Magdeburgis Ad Clerum habuit, De Ecclesia bipartita, Et Martini Luderi omniumque Luderanorum Ruinoso ac stultissimo fundamento.* Leipzig: V. Schumann, 1528. 8°, Ai^v-Eiii^v [*Flug.* 3814].

————. *Assertio Alveldiana in Canticum Salve Regina misericordie, Contra Impios deipare Virginis Marie detractatores deo odibiles nuper restituta. Et emendata.* Leipzig: V. Schumann, 1530. 4°, Ai^v-Eiv [*Flug.* 1950].

————. *Sermo de confessione sacramentali an confessio prorsus homini mortali ad verae beatitudinis vitam sit necessa, An ne.* N.p., n.d. 4°, Ai^v-Dii [*Flug.* 262].

————. *Ein Sermon von der Sacramentlichen beycht / Ob dieselbig / dem sterblichen menschen / tzu der seligkeit gentzlich von notten / ader nicht not.* N.p., n.d. 4°, Ai^v-Eii [*Flug.* 2186].

Bachmann, Paulus Amnicola Kemnicianus. *Czuerrettung den schwachen Ordenspersonen / so ytzr yn dysen ferlichen / Bosen Gotlossen zeytten / schwerlich betrubt / und angefochten werden durch falsche vorfurliche lere ad schrifft / eyn Trostlich Rede.* Dresden: [?H. Emser], 1524. 4°, Aii–Niii^v.

Blich, Simon. *Verderbe und Schade der Lande und Leuthen am gut leybe / ehre und der selen seligkeit auss Lutherischen mund seines anhangs / lehre zugewant / durch Simonen Apt zu Begawe mit einhelliger seiner Bruder vorwilligung hirinnem Christlich angetzeigt und aussgedruckt.* Leipzig: W. Stöckel, 1524. 4°, Ai^v–Fiv^v [*Flug.* 2503].

Cajetan, Cardinal Thomas de Vio, O.P. *De divina institutione Pontificatus Romani Pontificis super totam ecclesiam a Christo in Petro.* Rome: Silber, 22 March 1521; Cologne: P. Quentell, 4 June 1521. In F. Lauchert, ed., CC 10 (1925).

————. *Opuscula omnia.* 3 vols. Lyons, 1562.

Campester, Lambertus. *L. Campestri theologi Heptacolon in Summam scripturae sacrilegae Martini Lutheri in Apologia eius contentam.* Paris: S. Colinaeus, 1523. 4°, Ai–Hiv^v.

Catharinus, Ambrosius, O.P. *Apologia pro veritate Catholicae et Apostolicae fidei ac doctrinae. Adversus Impia ac valde pestifera Martini Lutheri Dogmata.* Florence: Junta, 20 December 1520; Vienna, 27 April 1521. In J. Schweizer and A. Franzen, eds., CC 27 (1956).

————. *Excusatio disputationis contra Martinum ad universas ecclesias.* Florence: Junta, 30 April 1521. 4°, 1–105.

————. *Contra Martinum Lutherum super his verbis: Tu es Petrus &c. Et tibi dabo claves regni celorum &c. Mathei xvi. Dialogus non minus disertus quam elegans ac festive.* Dresden: [?H. Emser], 1524. 4°, Aii^v–Di [*Flug.* 2236].

Cellarius, Johannes. *Ad Volphangum Fabricium Capitonem, Theologiae Doctorem et Concionatorem Basiliensem, Joannis Cellarii Gnostopolitani, Lipsiae Hebraicae linguae Professoris, de vera et constanti serie Theologica Disputationis Lipsiacae, Epistola.* Leipzig, 31 July 1519. In Löscher 3:225–32.

————. *Nullus Lipsiensis respondet Nemini Wittenbergensi.* Leipzig: W. Monacensis, 1519. In Löscher 3:799–803.

————. *Iudicium de Martino Luthero.* N.p., 1519. 4°, Aii–Aiv [*Flug.* 1846].

Chieregati, Franciscus. *Die verdeutscht Oration und Werbung, so päpstlich Heiligkeit durch ihnen Legaten hat tun lassen.* N.p., n.d. 4°, Aii–Bi^v [*Flug.* 2550].

————. *Des Bepstlichen redners potschafft Francisci Cheregati erwelten Bischoff zu Aprutin / fürsten von Teram / zu Nurmberg in der teütschen fursten rhat.* N.p., 1522. 4°, Ai^v–Aiv^v [*Flug.* 3626].

Clichtoveus, Jodocus. *Antilutherus tres libros complectens.* Paris: S. Colinaeus, 13 October 1524. Small folio, 2–181.

————. *De veneratione sanctorum libri duo (Primus, honorandos esse ab ecclesia ostendit. Secundus, rationes esse, qui contendunt non esse venerandos, nec orandos a nobis sanctos, dissoluit).* Cologne: P. Quentel, April 1525. 4°, Ai^v– riv [*Flug.* 594].

Cochlaeus [Johannes Dobneck]. *Brevis Germaniae descriptio tum a rebus gestis moribusque populorum, tum a locorum situ.* In K. Langosch, ed., *Johannes Cochlaeus: Brevis Germanie descriptio (1512), mit der Deutschlandkarte des Erhard Etzlaub von 1512.* Ausgewählte Quellen zur deutschen Geschichte der Neuzeit 1. Darmstadt: Wissenschaftliche Buchgesellschaft, 1960.

————. *De gratia sacramentorum liber unus Ioan. Cochlaei adversus assertionem Marti. Lutheri.* Strasbourg: J. Grüninger, 5 December 1522. 4°, Ai^v–Tiv^v [*Flug.* 2378].

————. *Adversus cucullatum minotaurum Wittenbergensem. De sacramentorum gratia iterum.* Cologne: [?G. Hittorp], July 1523. 4°. In J. Schweizer, ed., CC 3 (1920).

————. *Glos und Comment Doc. Johannes Dobneck Cochlaeus von Wendelstein / uff CLIIII Artikeln gezogen uss einem Sermon Doc. Mar. Luterss von der heiligen mess und nüem Testament.* Strasbourg: J. Grüninger, 20 September 1523. 4°, Ai–piv [*Flug.* 263].

————. *Glos und Comment auff den xiii. Artikel von rechtem Mess halten widr Luterische zwispaltung. Johanes Dobneck Cochlaeus von Wendelstein.* Strasbourg: J. Grüninger, [?October] 1523. 4°, Ai–Div^v [*Flug.* 636].

————. *Duae viae agendi ad tollendam in religione dissidium Lutheranum.* December 1523. In idem, *Miscellanea,* Ingolstadt: A. Weissenhorn, 1545, 113^v–116^v.

————. *Ad semper victricem Germaniam, Iohannis Cochlei paraclesis; ut pristinae constantiae fidei & virtutis memor, insolentissima Lutheranorum factione ab dictata in errores se abduci non patratur.* Cologne: H. Alopecius, 1524. 8°, Ai–Iviiᵛ [*Flug.* 1816].

———. *Ein Christliche vermanung der heyligen stat Rom an das Teütschlandt yr Tochter im Christlichen glauben. Durch Johannem Cochleum. Verteütscht durch Doctor Johannem Dietenberger.* [?Tübingen: U. Morhart, 1524.] 4°, Ai–Liv [*Flug.* 634].

——— [D.J.K.]. *Ein Spiegel der Ewangelischen freyheit / wie die Christus warhafft-iklich gelert / und Martin Luther yetz, in unseren zeyten die Selbigenn unnütz-lich für geben hat.* Strasbourg: J. Grüninger, 23 August 1524. 4°, Aii–Diiiᵛ [*Flug.* 1799].

———. *Pia exhortatio Romae ad Germaniam, suam in fide Christi filiam, per Johannem Cochleum.* Tübingen: [?Morhart], February 1525. 8°, Ai–Givᵛ [*Flug.* 1805].

———. *De Petro et Roma adversus Velenum Lutheranum, libri quatuor, Johannis Cochlaei, artium et sacrae Theologiae professoris egregrii atque ecclesiae divae virginis Frankfordien. Decani.* Cologne: P. Quentel, February 1525. 4°, Bi–Qiv [*Flug.* 1788].

———. *Adversus latrocinantes et raptorias Cohortes Rusticorum. Mar. Lutherus. Responsio Cochlaei Vuendelstini,* Aiᵛ–Ciiiᵛ; *Cathalogus tumultuum & praelio-rum in superiore Germania nuper gestorum,* Civ–Eiiᵛ; *CXXXII articuli excerpti ex seditioso et impio libro Martini Lutheri contra ecclesiasticos. Responsio brevis Iohannis Cochlaei ad singulos,* Eiii–Hiᵛ. Cologne, September 1525. 4° [*Flug.* 639].

———. *Articuli CCCCC Martini Lutheri. Ex sermonibus eius sex et triginta, quibus singulatim responsum est a Johanne Cochlaeo Wendelstino, partim scripturis, partim contrariis Lutheri ipsius dictis.* Cologne: P. Quentel, September 1525. 4°, Aiᵛ–Siiᵛ [*Flug.* 1531].

———. *Confutatio XCI articulorum e tribus Martini Lutheri Teuthonicis sermoni-bus excerptorum, Authore Johanne Cochlaeo.* Cologne: P. Quentel, 1525. 4°, Aii–Eiiᵛ [*Flug.* 2189].

———. *Commentaria Iohannis Cochlaei, de actis et scriptis Martini Lutheri Saxonis, Chronographice, Ex ordine ab Anno Domini M.D.XVII. usque ad Annum M.D.XLVI. Inclusive, fideliter conscripta.* Mainz: F. Behem, 1549. Reprint. Farnborough: Gregg Press, 1968. 6°, aii–civᵛ + 1–339.

———, ed. *Ein heilsamer Tractat S. Cypriani von einfaltigkeit der Prelaten und einigkeyt der Kirchen wider die Ketzerey und zertrennung.* Strasbourg: J. Grüninger, Friday after All Saints' Day, 1524. 4°, Aii–Eii [*Flug.* 1855].

———, ed. *Ob nichts anzünemen sey / dann was klar in der heyligen geschrifft ist auss getruckt. Wilhelmus Widefordus contra Johannem Wicleff.* N.p., 1524. 4°, Aiᵛ–Diiiᵛ [*Flug.* 1854].

Cologne University. *Condemnatio facultatis theologiae Coloniensis adversus doctri-nam F. Martini Lutherii.* In *WA* 6:178–80.

Dietenberger, Johannes, O.P. *Obe die christen mügen durch iere gute werck dz hymel reich verdienen.* Strasbourg: J. Grüninger, 27 October 1523. 4°, Aii–Eii [*Flug.* 2757].

————. *Antwurt, das Junckfrawen die klöster und klosterliche glübd nümmer götlich verlassen mogen.* Strasbourg: J. Grüninger, 31 October 1523. 4°, Ai^v–Div [*Flug.* 1564].

————. *Widerlegung des Lutherischen buchlins / da er schreibt von menschen leren zu meiden &c.* [?Strasbourg]: J. Grüninger, 10 November 1524. 4°, Aii–Eii [*Flug.* 2596].

————. *Der leye. Obe der gelaub allein selig macht.* Strasbourg: J. Grüninger, St. Peter and Paul's Eve, 1524. 4°, Aii–Eii [*Flug.* 2756].

————. *Cristliche underweisung / wie man gotes heiligen in dem hymmel anrüffen / und das heilthum auff erden Eeren soll.* N.p., 1524. 4°, Diii^v–Kii [*Flug.* 2588].

————. *Iohan. Dytenbergii theologi, contra temerarium Martini Luteri de votis monasticis iudicium: Liber primus: quo singulatim illius rationibus, quas omnes ex ordine passim autor praetexit, ex sacris literis luculentissime respondet: de multis obiter disserens, videlicet Castitate, Paupertate, Obedientia, Libertate evangelica, Iustitia fidei & operum, Fide & legibus, alijsque id genus plurimus: omnes Martini strophas & sententiam, acute, eleganter, & vere dilvendo.* 8°, Ai^v–Qiv. *Liber secundus.* 8°, Ai^v–Tviii. Cologne: E. Cervicornus, 13 August 1524.

———— [Sebastian Felbaum]. *Ein nutzliche rede frag und antwort von dreyen personen sich uben im lutrischen sachen / Gezogen uss ewangelischer / apostolischer leer / durch sebastian felbaum von Breten.* N.p., 1524. 4°, Aii–Di^v [*Flug.* 2588].

————. *Wider das unchristlich buch Mart. Luth. von dem missbrauch der Mess.* N.p., 1524. 4°, Ai^v–Hiv [*Flug.* 270].

————. *Grund unnd ursach auss der heiligen schrifft / wie unbillich und unredlich / das heylig lobsangk Marie Salve regina / verspolt und abgestesst.* 1524. 4°, Ai^v–Hiv^v [*Flug.* 2016].

————. *Das ander buch wider Martin Luther von der heimlichen orenbeycht.* Tübingen, 1525. 4°, ai^v–tiii^v [*Flug.* 2581].

Dungersheim, Hieronymus von. *Multiloquus de concitata seditione ex dictis Lutheri p. d. Hie. q. supp. in futurorum cautelam, recollectus.* N.p., 1525. 4°, Aii–Div [*Flug.* 1859].

Eck, Johannes von. *Adnotationes (Obelisci).* 1518. In *WA* 1:281–314.

————. *Defensio contra amarulentas And. Bodenstein invectiones.* 1518. In J. Greving, ed., *CC* 1 (1919).

————. *Contra novam doctrinam scheda disputatoria. In studio Lipsiensi disputiat Eckius propositiones infra notatas contra D. Bodenstein Carlestadium Archdiaconum et doctorem Wittenbergensi.* 29 December 1518. In Löscher 3:210–11.

————. *Disputatio et excusatio D. J. E. adversus criminationes F. Martini Lutheri ordinis eremitarum.* 1519. In *WA Br* 1:320–22.

————. *Articuli per fratres minores de observantiae propositi Reverendissimo domino Episcopo Brandenburgen. contra Lutheranos.* 1519. In Löscher 3:115–21.

————. *D. Dionysii Areopagitae De mystica Theologia lib. I Graece. Joan. Sarraceno, Ambrosio Camaldul., Marsilio Ficino Interpret. Cum vercellen. extractione. Joan. Eckius Commentarios adiecit pro Theologia negativa Ingolstadii.* Augsburg: J. Miller, 25 May 1519.

———. Letter to Hochstraten, 24 July 1519. In Löscher 3:222–24 [*Flug.* 497].

———. *Excusatio Eckii ad ea, quae falso sibi Phil. Melanchton Grammaticus Wittenb. super Theologica Disputatione Lipsica adscripsit.* 1519. In Löscher 3:591–96.

———. *Expurgatio Joan. Eckii Theologi. Ingoldstadien. adversus criminationes F. Martini Luther Vuittenbergen. ordinis heremitarum.* N.p., 2 September 1519. 4°, Aiv–Eiv.

———. *Joannis Eckii pro Hieronymo Emser contra malesanem Luteri venationem responsio.* N.p., 28 October 1519. 4°, Aiv–Cii.

———. *Des heiligen concilii tzu Costentz, der heylgen Christenheit und hochlöblichen keyssers Sigmunds und auch des teutzschen adels entschüldigung, das in bruder Martin Luder mit unwarheit auffgelegt, sie haben Johannem Huss und Hieronymum von Prag wider babstlich, christlich, keyserlich geleidt und eydt vorbrandt.* Leipzig: M. Landsberg, 3 October 1520. 4°, Ai–Biiiv. In K. Meissen and F. Zoepfl, eds., CC 14 (1929), 1–18.

———. *Epistola ad divum Caesarem Carolum V. Imp. Ro. Maximum & Hisponiarum regem Catholicum de Luderi causa.* N.p., 18 February 1521. 4°, Aii–Ci [*Flug.* 3682].

———. *De primatu Petri adversus Lutherum libri tres.* Paris: P. Vidovaeus, September 1521. Folio, 1–78, 1–46, 1–69v.

———. *Determinatio theologice facultatis Parisiensis super Doctrina Lutheriana hactenus per eam visa. Hie werdent ciiij. artickel der Lutherischen leer verdampt, durch die loblich universitet von Paryss darumb Martin Luther die disputation zu Leiptzig verlorn hat. Ein teutsche ermanung zu ennd dar zu gesetzt.* N.p., n.d. 4°, Aiv–Ei.

———. *Enchiridion locorum communium adversus Lutherum et alios hostes ecclesiae.* 1525. In P. Fraenkel, ed., CC 34 (1979).

———. *Ad invictissimum Poloniae regem Sigismundum, de sacrificio missae contra Lutheranos, libri tres* (1526). In E. Iserloh, V. Pfnür, and P. Fabisch, eds., *Johannes Eck: De sacrificio missae libri tres (1526).* CC 36 (1982).

Eckhart, Johannes. *Ain Dialogus das opfer der heyligen Mess betreffent.* 1521. 4°, aiv–eivv [*Flug.* 1861].

Emser, Hieronymus. *De disputatione Lipsicensi, quantum ad Boemos obiter deflexa est.* 13 August 1519. In F. X. Thurnhofer, ed., CC 4 (1921), 29–40.

———. *A venatione Luteriana Aegocerotis Assertio.* 1519. In Löscher 3:694–731.

———. *Wider das unchristliche Buch Martini Luthers Augustiners an den Teutschen Adel ausgangen Vorlegung Hieronymi Emser an gemeyne Hochlöbliche Teutsche Nation.* Leipzig: M. Herbipolensis, 20 January 1521. 4°, Aiv–Siii.

———. *Bedingung auf Luters orsten widerspruch.* Dresden: [?H. Emser], 13 November 1521. 4°, Aii–Div [*Flug.* 2871].

———. *An den Stier zu Wuiettenberg.* N.p., 1521. 4°, Ai–iv.

———. *Auff des Stiers zu Wiettenberg wiettende replica.* 1521. In F. X. Thurnhofer, ed., CC 28 (1959).

———. *Quadruplica auff Luters Jungst gethane antwurt / sein reformation belangend.* Leipzig: [?H. Emser], 1521. 4°, Aiv–Hiv [*Flug.* 321].

————. *Schutz und Handthabung der Sibenn Sacrament wider Martinum Luther von dem aller unuberwintlichisten Konig zu Engelandt und Franckreych und hern in Hibernia, hern Heinrichen dem achten dis nhamens aufzgangenn.* N.p., 1522. 4°, Ai^v–Riv [*Flug.* 1568].

————. *Ausz was grund und ursach Luthers dolmatschung, uber das nawe testament, dem gemeinen man billich vorbotten worden sey.* Leipzig: W. Stöckel, 26 September 1523.

————. *Wider den falsch genannten Ecclesiasten Martin Luther.* Leipzig: M. Herbipolensis, 1523. 4°, Ai^v–Riv [*Flug.* 665].

————. *Antwort auff das lesterliche buch wider Bischoff Benno zu Meissen und erhebung der heyligen iungst ausgegangen.* Leipzig, 1524. 4°, Ai^v–Eiv [*Flug.* 997].

————. *Missae christianorum contra Luteranam missandi formulam assertio.* Dresden: [?H. Emser], 1524. In T. Freudenberger, ed., CC 28 (1959).

————. *Auff Luthers grewel wider die heiligen Stillmess. Antwort. Item wie / wo / und mit wolchen worten Luther yhn seyn buchern tzur auffrur ermandt / geschriben und getriben hat.* N.p., 1525. 8°, Ai^v–Fiv^v [*Flug.* 667].

————. *Der Bock dryt frey auff disen plan.* N.p., 1525. 4°, Ai^v–iii.

————. *Das New Testament / so durch L. Emser saligen verteutscht.* Leipzig: V. Schumann, 1528. 8°, 48 + Ai–Yiv + 7.

Erasmus, Desiderius. *De libero arbitrio Diatribe sive collatio.* N.p., [?1524]. 8°, aii–fviii [*Flug.* 2000].

Fabri, Johannes Heigerlin. *Johannes Fabri Constantiensis in spiritualibus vicarii opus adversus nova quaedam et a christiana religione prorsus aliena dogmata Martini Lutheri.* Rome: M. Silber, 1522. Reprinted as *Malleus in haeresim Lutheranam.* Cologne: J. Soter & P. Quentel, 1524. In A. Naegele and F. Meyer, eds., CC 23/24 (1941/52).

Femelius, Johannes. *Eyn Kurtz sermon sso die heyligen Gottes belangenn / An alle doctores tzu Erffurdt / sie seynt jung ad alt / man ad frawe.* [?Erfurt: H. Knappe, 1521.] 4°, Ai–Dii [*Flug.* 1868].

Fisher, John. *The sermon of Iohan the bysshop of Rochester made agayn the pernicyous doctryn of Martin Luuther within the octaves of the ascensyon by the assignement of the moost reuerend father in god the lord Thomas Cardinall of Yorke & Legate ex latere from our holy father the pope.* [?London]: W. de Worde, 1521. In J.E.B. Mynor, ed., *The English Works of John Fisher* 1:311–45. Early English Text Society, Extra Series 27. London, 1876.

————. *Assertionis Lutheranae confutatio.* 1523. In idem, *Opera omnia*, 272–745. Würzburg: G. Fleischmann, 1597. Reprinted Farnborough, 1967.

————. *Roffensis Episcopi loca quaedam quibus predictam auctoritatem cum duabus alijs Matthei scz. xviij. & Ioannis xx. eiusdem monetae sed non eiusdem valoris comparat. & discrimen earum evidenti scripturarum testimonio declarat.* [?Dresden: H. Emser], 1524. 4°, Di^v–Diii^v.

————. *Sacri sacerdotii defensio contra Lutherum.* 1525. In idem, *Opera omnia*, 1232–98. Würzburg: G. Fleischmann, 1597. Also in H. Klein-Schmeink, ed., CC 9 (1925).

————. *Assertionum Regis Angliae de fide Catholica adversus Lutheri Babylonicam Captivitatem defensio.* 1525. In idem, *Opera omnia,* 101–271. Würzburg: G. Fleischmann, 1597.

————. *Was die Christelischen Alten von der beycht haben gehalten. Getzogen aus dem Erwirdigen und Hochgelerten Herrn Joan. Bischoff zu Roffen yn Engelland.* Dresden: [?H. Emser], 1525. 4°, Aii–Diii^v [*Flug.* 3844].

Freiburger, Johannes. *Ein bruderlich ermanung zu den die sich nennen Ewangelisch / wie der Christenlich Glauben sein anfang hab von dem haupt Christo / und durch des Ewangeli. Und was ein Ewangelische leer billich genent und erkent werd / und was kein Ewangelische leer sey.* Landshut, Feast of the Ascension 1523. 4°, Aii–Biv^v [*Flug.* 3827].

Fundling, Johannes. *Anzaigung zwayer falschen zungen des Luthers wie er mit der ainen die paurn verfüret / mit dem andern sy verdammet hat / durch Admiratum den Wunderer, genant Johann Fundling.* Landshut: J. Weissenburger, 1526. 4°, Aii–Hiii^v.

Gebweiler, Hieronymus, ed., *Contenta in hoc libello. Ysidorus de sectis et nominibus haereticorum. Divi augustini Libellus aureus de fide et operibus. S. Hieronymi liber de perpetua gloriosae Virginis Mariae virginitate. Epistola eiusdem contra vigilantium de venerandis sanctorum reliquis.* Strasbourg: J. Grüninger, 12 March 1523. 4°, Aii–Mii.

————, ed., *Compendiola Boemice seu Hussitane haereseos ortus & eiusdem damnatorum Articulorum descriptio Lectu non iniucunda nuper a theophilo tectono congesta.* Strasbourg: J. Grüninger, 16 February 1524. 4°, Aii–Biv [*Flug.* 2472].

Hangestus, Hieronymus. *De libero arbitrio in Lutherum.* Paris: J. Petit, 1525. 4°, aii–riv.

Hauer, Georg. *Drey christlich predig vom Salve regina / dem Evangeli unnd heyligen schrift gemess.* Ingolstadt, 1523. 4°, Aii–Giv [*Flug.* 2586].

Henry VIII. *Assertio septem sacramentorum adversus Marti. Lutherum, aedita ab invictissimo Angliae et Franciae rege et dom. Hyberniae Henrico eius nominis octavo.* Rome, 1521. 4°, viii + Ai–Xi^v + xi.

————. *Henrici VIII Regis Angliae, ad Martini Lutheri Epistolam Responsio.* 1526. In John Fisher, *Opera omnia,* 81–100. Würzburg: G. Fleischmann, 1597.

Hochstraten, Jakob. *Destructio Cabale seu Cabalistice perfidie.* 1519. Dedication to Leo X in *WA* 2:384–85.

Illyricus, Thomas, O.F.M. *Libellus de potestate summi pontificis editus a Fratre Thoma Illyrico, minorita verbi dei precone famatissimo & apostolico: qui intitulatur Clipeus status papalis.* Turin: J. Angelus, 23 January 1523. 8°, Aii–Hvii.

Isolanis, Isidorus de. *Disputata catholica.* Pavia, 1522. 4°, Ai^v–Fii.

J. N. [pseudo.]. *Von der rechten Erhebung Bennonis ein sendbrief.* 1524. Reprinted in Clemens, ed., *Flugschriften ans den ersten Jahren der Reformation,* 4 vols. Nieuwkoop: de Graaf, 1967.

Kȯgel spil gebracttiziert ausz dem yeczigenzwytracht des glaubens zů eym tail ain geselletz, Alle so dann Martino Luther annhangent. Zům tail die dann dem Rechtten alten weeg des Euangeliums nach jrem vermügnn nach volgent, mit sampt andren so hye dysem spil zů lugen hyerinn vergriffen genentt werdent. Die Kugel ist die hailig Geschrifft. Das zyl ist der glaub. Der platz des Jamertal, Kegel seind die armen schlechten einfeltigen leyen, Die abentheyer ist das ewig leben, die dreyer seind die hailigen lerer der Paulus, iiij. Euangeli und die xij. poten. Jm Jar. M.D.XXII. [?Augsburg: M. Ramminger], 1522. 4°, 8 unpaginated pages [*Flug.* 2548].

Kretz, Matthias. *Ain Sermon inhaltend etlich sprůch der schrifft von dem fegfewr durch D. Matthiam Kretz zů Augspurg zů unser frawen im Thům gepredigt.* N.p., 1524. 4°, Ai^v–Aiv^v [*Flug.* 2872].

———. *Ain Sermon von der Peicht / ob sie Gott gebotten hab / Durch D. Matthiam Kretz zů Augspurg / zů unser frawen in Thům gepredigt.* N.p., 1524. 4°, Ai^v–Bii^v.

———. *Von der mess, und wer der recht priester sey / der Mess habe / auch zum tail ob sie ain opffer sey.* Augsburg, August 1524. 4°, Aii–Bi.

Latomus, Jakob. *Contra articulos quosdam Martini Lutheri a Theologis Lovan. damnatos ("Ratio").* January 1521. Reprinted in idem, *Opera omnia*, 1–53^v. Louvain: B. Gravius, 1579.

———. *Ad Lutherum responsio.* 1521. In idem, *Opera omnia*, 54–59. Louvain: B. Gravius, 1579.

———. *De primatu romani pontificis adversus Lutherum.* 1525. In idem, *Opera omnia*, 59^v–86. Louvain: B. Gravius, 1579.

———. *De confessione secreta. Eiusdem de quaestionum generibus quibus Ecclesia certat intus et foris. Eiusdem de Ecclesia & humanae legis obligatione.* 1525. In idem, *Opera omnia*, 86–105. Louvain: B. Gravius, 1579.

Leib, Kilian. *Von der endschafft und frucht der auffruer und empörungen des gepouels unnd gemainen volcks wider die oberkeit.* N.p., Feast of St. Ulrich 1525. 4°, Aii–Bi^v [*Flug.* 3767].

Lombard, Peter. *Von dem hochwürdigen Sakrament unter beider Gestalt.* N.p., n.d. 4°, 2 unpaginated pages [*Flug.* 2553].

Louvain University. *Facultatis Theologiae Lovaniensis doctrinalis condemnatio doctrinae Martini Lutheri.* December 1519. In *WA* 6:175–78.

Luther, Martin. *Disputatio pro declaratione virtutis indulgentiarum.* 1517. In *WA* 1:233–38.; Translated as Ninety-five Theses. In *LW* 31:[19], 25–33.

———. *Ein Sermon von den Ablass und Gnade.* March 1518. In *WA* 1:243–46.

———. *Resolutiones disputationum de indulgentiarum virtute.* 1518. In *WA* 1:529–628. Translated as *Explanations of the Ninety-five Theses.* In *LW* 31:[77], 83–252.

———. *Asterisci Lutheri adversus Obeliscos Eckii.* 1518. In *WA* 1:281–314.

———. *Eyn Freyheyt des Sermons Bebstlichen Ablas und gnad belangend Doct. Martini Luther wider die vorlegung, szo tzur schmach seyn und desselben sermons ertichtet.* 1518. In *WA* 1:383–93.

———. *Ad dialogum Silvestri Prieratis de potestate papae responsio.* 1518. In *WA* 2:647–86.

———. *Appellatio a Caietano ad Papam.* 1518. In *WA* 2:28–33.

———. *Disputatio et excusatio F. Martini Luther adversus criminationes D. Johannis Eccii.* 7 February 1519. In *WA* 2:158–61.

————. *Scheda adversus J. Hochstratum.* 1519. In *WA* 2:386–87.

————. *Resolutio Lutheriana super propositione sua decima tertia de potestate papae.* 1519. In *WA* 2:181–240.

————. *Ad Aegocerotem Emserianum M. Lutheri Additio.* 1519. In Löscher 3:668–93.

————. *Contra malignum Johannis Eccii iudicium super aliquot articulis a fratribus quibusdam ei suppositis Martini Lutheri defensio.* 1519. In *WA* 2:625–54.

————. *Ad Iohannem Eccium Martini Lutheri epistola super Expurgatione Ecciana.* 1519. In *WA* 2:700–708.

————. *Eyn Sermon von dem Hochwirdigen Sacrament, des heyligen waren leychnams Christi. Und von den Bruderschaften.* 1519 In *WA* 2:742–58. Translated as *The Blessed Sacrament of the Holy True Body of Christ, and of the Brotherhoods.* In *LW* 35:[54], 49–73.

————. *Verklärung D. Martin Luthers etlicher Artikel in seinem Sermon von dem heiligen Sakrament.* 1520. In *WA* 6:78–83.

————. *Ad schedulam inhibitionis sub nomine episcopi Misnensis editam super sermone de sacramento eucharistiae M. Lutheri Augustiniani responsio.* 1520. In *WA* 6:144–53.

————. *Responsio Lutheriana ad condemnationem doctrinalem per magistros nostros Lovaniensis et Coloniensis factum.* 1520. In *WA* 6:181–95.

————. *Von dem Papstthum zu Rom wider den hochberühmten Romanisten zu Leipzig.* 1520. In *WA* 6:285–324. Translated as *The Papacy at Rome.* In *LW* 39:[49], 55–104.

————. *Eyn Sermon von dem newen Testament, das ist von der heyligen Messe.* 1520. In *WA* 6:353–78. Translated as *A Treatise on the New Testament, That Is, the Holy Mass.* In *LW* 35:[77], 79–111.

————. *Der allerdurchleuchtigsten, Grossmechtigsten Keyserlichen Maiestet, und Christlichen Adel deutscher Nation, etlicher stuck Christliches stands besserung belangend.* 1520. In *WA* 6:404–69. Translated as *To the Christian Nobility of the German Nation Concerning the Reform of the Christian Estate.* In *LW* 44:[115], 123–217.

————. *De captivitate Babylonica ecclesiae praeludium.* 1520. In *WA* 6:484–573. Translated as *The Babylonian Captivity of the Church.* In *LW* 36:[3], 11–126.

————. *Von den neuen Eckischen Bullen und Lügen.* 1520. In *WA* 6:576–94.

————. *Wider die Bulle des Endchrists.* 1520. In *WA* 6:614–29.

————. *Warum des Papstes und seiner Jünger Bücher von D. M. Luther vorbrannt sind.* 1520. In *WA* 7:161–86. Translated as *Why the Books of the Pope and His Disciples Were Burned by Dr Martin Luther.* In *LW* 31:[279], 383–95.

————. *An dem Bock zu Leyptzck.* 1521. In *WA* 7:262–65. Translated as *To the Goat in Leipzig.* In *LW* 39:[105], 111–15.

————. *Auff des bocks zu Leypczick Antwort.* 1521. In *WA* 7:271–83. Translated as *Concerning the Answer of the Goat in Leipzig.* In *LW* 39:[118], 121–35.

————. *Auff das uberchristlich, ubirgeystlich und ubirkunstlich buch Bocks Emszers zu Leypczick Antwortt D. M. L. Darynn auch Murnars seynsz geselln gedacht wirt.* 1521. In *WA* 7:621–88. Translated as *Answer to the Hyperchristian, Hyperspiritual, and Hyperlearned Book by Goat Emser in Leipzig—Including*

Some Thoughts Regarding His Companion, The Fool Murner. In *LW* 39:[136], 143–224.

———. *Ad librum eximii nostri Ambrosii Catherini defensoris Silv. Prieratis acerrimi responsio M. Lutheri.* 1521. In *WA* 7:705–78.

———. *Rationis Latomianae pro Incendiariis Louaniensis Scholae Sophistis redditae. Lutheriana Confutatio.* 1521. In *WA* 8:43–128. Translated as *Against Latomus. Luther's Refutation of Latomus' Argument on Behalf of the Incendiary Sophists of the University of Louvain.* In *LW* 32:[133], 137–260.

———. *Ein Urteil der Theologen zu Paris über die Lehre D. M. Luthers. Ein Gegenurteil D. Luthers.* 1521. In *WA* 8:291–93.

———. *Eyn widderspruch D. Luthersz seynis yrthumsz erczwungen durch den aller hochgelertisten priester gottis Herrn Hieronymum Emser, Vicarien tzu Meissen.* 1521. In *WA* 8:247–54. Translated as *Dr Luther's Retraction of the Error Forced on Him by the Most Highly Learned Priest of God, Sir Jerome Emser, Vicar of Meissen.* In *LW* 39:227–34.

———. *Vom Misbrauch der Messen.* 1521. In *WA* 8:482–563. German translation of *De abroganda missa privata.* 1521. In *WA* 8:411–76. English translation, *The Misuse of the Mass.* In *LW* 36:[129], 133–230.

———. *De votis monasticis Martini Lutheri iudicium.* 1521. In *WA* 8:573–669. Translated as *The Judgment of Martin Luther on Monastic Vows.* In *LW* 44:[245], 251–400.

———. *Von beider Gestalt des Sakraments zu nehmen.* 1522. In *WA* 10/2:11–41. Translated as *Receiving Both Kinds in the Sacrament.* In *LW* 36:[221], 237–67.

———. *Von Menschenlehre zu meiden, und Antwort auf Sprüche, so man führet, menschen lehre zu stärken.* 1522. In *WA* 10/2:72–92. Translated as *Avoiding the Doctrines of Men.* In *LW* 35:[125], 131–53.

———. *Sermon von der Geburt Mariä.* 1522. In *WA* 10/3:312–31.

———. *Sermon von den Heiltumen.* 1522. In *WA* 10/3:332–41.

———. *Contra Henricum regem Angliae Martinus Luther Wittenbergae.* 1522. In *WA* 10/2:180–222.

———. *Antwort deutsch auf König Heinrichs Buch.* 1522. In *WA* 10/2:223–63.

———. *Adversus armatum virum Coklaeum.* 1523. In *WA* 11:295–306.

———. *Ein päpstlich Breve dem Rat zu Bamberg gesandt wider den Luther.* 1523. In *WA* 11:342–56.

Luxembourg, Bernard, O.P. *Catalogus haereticorum omnium pene, qui a scriptoribus passim literis proditi sunt, nomina, errores, & tempora quibus vixerunt ostendens, a F. Bernardo Lutzenburgo sacrarum literarum professore quatuor libris conscriptus. Quorum quartus Luteri negotium nonnihil attingit.* [?Cologne: E. Cervicornus, 1522.] 4°, ai–miv^v.

Marcello, Christoforus. *De authoritate summi pontificis et his quae ad illam pertinent. Adversus impia Martini Lutherii dogmata.* Florence: Junta, June 1521. Reprint. Farnborough: Gregg, 1969. 4°, vi + 1–145.

Marlianus, Aloysius. *Oratio ad Carolem Caesarem.* N.p., 1521. 4°, Aii–Biv [*Flug.* 948].

Marstaller, Leonhard. *Centum conclusiones de vera libertate christiana.* N.p., 1524. 4°, Aiii–Cii [*Flug.* 816].

Melanchthon, Philipp. Letter to Oecolampadius, 21 July 1519. In Löscher 3:215–21. Also in CR 1:87–96.

———. *Defensio Philippi Melanchthonis, contra Johannem Eckium, Theologiae Professorem*. 1519. In Löscher 3:596-604. Also in CR 1:108–18.

———. *Didymi Faventini adversus Thomam Placentinum oratio pro M. Luthero Theologo*. 1520. In CR 1:287–358.

———. *Schutzrede Phil. Melanchthons wider den Parisische Urteil für D. Luther*. 1521. In WA 8:295–312.

Mensing, Johannes. *Von dem opffer Christi yn der Messe: Allen Christglawbigen / Deutzsche Nation not tzu wissen. Denen tzu Magdeburck ynn sonderheyt / tzu gut geschrieben / unnd aussgangen. Beweret mit Gotlicher schriffte*. N.p., 1526. 4°, Ai^v–Jiv [*Flug*. 3977].

Modestus, Joannes Antonius, *Oratio ad Carolem Caesarem contra Martinum Lutherum*. Strasbourg: [?J. Grüninger], 10 February 1521. 4°, Aii–Eii.

———. *Adhortatoria epistola ad Martinum Luther, ut cesset maledictis bonos persequi, & Ecclesiam Dei turbare*. N.p., 1521. 4°, ai^v–civ^v [*Flug*. 3950, where it is erroneously attributed to Fundling].

Montanus, Johannes. *Encomium Rubii Longipolli apud Lipsim, in errores quos pueriliter commisit, adversus Wittenbergenses Nemo dictavit*. Leipzig: W. Monacensis, 1519. In Löscher 3:786–98.

[More, Thomas]. *Eruditissimi viri Guilielmi Rossei opus elegans, quo refellit Lutheri calumnias quibus Angliae regem Henricium octavium insectatur*. London: R. Pynson, 1523. In J. M. Headley, ed., *The Complete Works of St. Thomas More 5, i: Responsio ad Lutherum*. New Haven and London: Yale University Press, 1967.

Murner, Thomas, O.F.M. *Ein christliche und briederliche ermanung zu dem hochgelerten doctor Martino Luter Augustiner orden zu Wittemburg (Dz er etlichen reden von dem newen testament der heilligen messe gethon) abstande / und wid mit gemeiner christenheit sich vereininge*. Strasbourg: [?J. Grüninger], 11 November 1520. 4°, Aii–Iii [*Flug*. 3871].

———. *An den Grossmechtigsten und Durchlüchtigsten adel tütscher nation das sye den christlichen glauben beschirmen / wyder den zerstorer des glaubens christi / Martinum Luther eine verfierer der einfeltigen christen*. [?Strasbourg]: J. Grüninger, 24 December 1520. 8°, Aii–Kiv [*Flug*. 696].

———. *Von der Babylonischen gefengkuscz der Kirchen*. N.p., 1520.

———. *Von dem babstentum, das ist von der höchsten Obrigkeit des christlichen Glaubens*. Strasbourg: J. Grüninger, 1520. 4°, Ai^v–Cii [*Flug*. 1603].

———. *Wie doctor M. Luter uss falschen ursachen bewegt Dz geistlich recht verbrennet hat*. Strasbourg: J. Grüninger, 1521. 4°, Ai^v–iii^v.

———. *Bekennung der süben Sacramenten wider Martinum Lutherum, gemacht von dem unüberwintlichen Künig zů Engelland und in Frankreich einen herren zů Hiberniem, Heinrico des namens dem achtesten &c. Doctor Murner hat es vertütscht*. Strasbourg: J. Grüninger, 7 September 1522 [*Flug*. 1568].

———. *Ob der künig uss engelland ein lügner sey oder der Luther*. Strasbourg: J. Grüninger, 10 November 1522. 4°, aii–piv.

————. *Von dem grossen Lutherischen Narren.* 1522. In P. Merker, ed., *Thomas Murners deutsche Schriften,* vol. 9. Berlin and Leipzig: de Gruyter, 1918.

Paris University. *Iudicium adversus Martinum Lutherum.* 10 November 1520. In *WA* 8:267–90.

Powell, Edward. *Propugnaculum summi sacerdotii evangelici, ac septenarii sacramentorum, editum per virum eruditum, sacrarumque literatum professorem Edoardum Pouelum, adversus Martinum Lutherum fratrem famosum et Wiclefistam insignem.* London: R. Pynson, 3 December 1523. 4°, 1–185ᵛ.

Prierias [Sylvester Mazzolinus]. *R.P.F. Sylvestri Prieratis O.P. in praesumptuosas Martini Lutheri conclusiones de potestate Papae dialogus.* 1518. In Löscher 2:12–40.

————. *Replica F. Sylvestri Prieratis, sacri Palatii Apostolici Magistri, ad F. Martinum Luther Ordinis Eremitarum.* January 1519. In *WA* 2:50–56.

————. *Epitoma responsionis ad Martinum Lutherum.* 1519. In *WA* 6:328–46.

————. *Errata et argumenta Martini Luteris recitata, detecta, repulsa et copiosissima trita.* Rome, 1520. 4°, I–CCCXVIII.

Revocatio Martini Lutherii Augustiniani ad sanctam sedem. Cremona, 1520. 4°, aii–fiiᵛ.

Rhadinus Tedeschus, Thomas, O.P. *Thome Rhadini Todeschi Placentini ord. pre. ad illustriss. et invictiss. Principes et populos Germanie in Martinum Lutherum Wittenbergensem or. here. Nationis gloriam violantem: Oratio.* Leipzig: M. Lotter, October 1520. 4°, Aii–Iii [*Flug.* 495].

Rubeus Longipollus, Johannes. *Solutiones ac Responsa Wit. Doctorum in publica Disputatione Lipsica contra fulmina Eckiana parum profatura, tumorque adventus & humilitas eorum recessus, per Jo. Ru. Longi. comparata.* 1519. In Löscher 3:252–71.

Schatzgeyer, Caspar O.F.M. *Scrutinium divinae scripturae pro conciliatione dissidentium dogmatum.* 1522. In U. Schmidt, ed., CC 5 (1922).

————. *Von der lieben heiligen Eerung unnd Anrueffung / durch Gasparn Schatzger Barfůsser ordens. Das Erst teütsch Buchlin. Item vil mer materien jnn jm begreyffend / dann das lateinisch vor aussgangen.* Munich: H. Schobsser, 10 December 1523. 4°, Ai–Niiiᵛ [*Flug.* 1811].

————. *Vonn Christlichen satzungen und leeren / am Christförmigs Leben (der werck halben) betreffend / welche anzůnemen oder auss zeschahe seyen / kürtzlich inn syben zehen Christlichen unterweysungen / sambt sybner irrthumben / verfasst / durch Gasparn Schatzger barfůsser ordens / wie dz hernach gedruckt Register anzaygt* (Munich: H. Schobsser, octave of All Saints' Day 1524. 4°, Aii–Giii [*Flug.* 254].

————. *Tractatus de missa tribus distinctus sectionibus. Quarum prima est de Sacramenti sanctissimi Eucharistiae consecratione. Secunda de sacrificatione. Tertia vero de communione. Quibus inserta est de satisfactione et purgatorio materia.* Tübingen: U. Morhart, January 1525. 8°, aiiᵛ–lvii.

————. *Vom hochwirdigsten sacrament des zartten frönleichnams Christi. Widerlegung etlicher Argument wider das Messopfer.* Munich: H. Schobsser, 1525. 4°, Aii–Eivᵛ [*Flug.* 2682].

————. *Von dem hayligsten Opfer der Mess / sampt jren dreyen fürnemlichsten / und wesenlichsten taylenn / Das ist / vonn der Consecrierung / Opfferung / und Empfahung / des hochwirdigstenn fronleychnams Christi / Ob der gemein Christenmensch / under ainer oder bayder gstaltt jn empfahenn soll.* N.p., 1525. 4°, Aii–Riii^v [*Flug.* 2804].

————. *Ainn warhafftige Erklerung wie sich Sathanas Inn diesen hernach geschriben vieren materyenn vergwentet unnd erzaygt unnder der gestalt eynes Enngels des Liechts.* Munich, 1526.

————. *Replica contra periculosa scripta post Scrutinium divinae scripturae iam pridem omissum emanata.* Tübingen, 1527. 8°, Ai^v–Svii.

————. *Von der waren Christlichen und Evangelischen freyheit; De vera libertate evangelica.* Edited by P. Schäfer. CC 40 (1987).

Sichem, Eustachius van der Rivieren. *Errorum Martini Lutheri brevis confutatio simulque cum eorum rationibus, et peculiarem adiungens eloquentiam, per venerabilem S. Theologiae professorem F. Eustachium de Zickenis divi ordinis praedictatorum aedita.* Antwerp: M. Hittorp, 1521. 4°, Ai^v–Kiv. In Pijper 3:197–285.

————. *Sacramentorum brevis elucidatio simulque nonnulla perversa MARTINI Luther dogmata excludens, quibus & sacramenta temerare ausus est, tum ecclesiasticam ierarchiam prorsum abolere. Proinde & hac tempestate quam impie, cum in Romanam sedem, tum in caeteros ecclesiasticos ordines a nonnullos debacchatur, palam faciens, Per venerabilem Sacrae Theologiae professorem, Fratrem EUSTACHIVM de Zichenis, ordinis Praedicatorum edita.* Antwerp: S. Cocus & G. Nicolaus, 29 July 1523. 4°, ai–qii^v.

Slegel, Matthias. *Wass nützung enntspring von den falschen Lutherischen Catzen / Als von Franzen von Sicking und seiner Teuflischer bundenuss / Die das heylig Ewangelium mit Raüben / morden / Prennen wollen verfechten &c. Gemacht durch Mathias Slegel von Trier.* N.p., 1523. 4°, aii–iii^v [*Flug.* 2630].

Sylvius, Petrus Penick von Forst. *Eyne verklerunge des eynigen waren Apostolischen christlichen gloubens und lere zu erkennen und tzu vermeyden allen vertumlichen irthum / tzwytracht / ketzerey / und unglouben der werlt / Eym itzlichen menschen bey bewarunge seiner selen nothafftig tzu wissen / sich darnach tzu halten. Durch sonderliche ermanungen Gottis beschrieben. De Symbolo Apostolico Tractatus articulorum in ordine Tredecimus / Fundamenta omnium scismatum heresumque conquassans.* [?Dresden: H. Emser], 16 May 1525. 4°, Ai^v–Diii^v [*Flug.* 3343].

————. *Eyn Missive ader Sendbrieff an die Christliche Versammlunge und ssonderlich and die oberkeit Deutzscher Nation zu wegern den unthergang irer herschafft / und das iemmerlich verterbnis der Christenheit / Eym iden so durch tzeitlichen und ewigen friden / seyn leib und tzele sucht zu bewaren nutzlich und itzt nothafftig tzu erfarn und zu lesen.* N.p., August 1525. 4°, Ai^v–Civ^v [*Flug.* 2528].

————. *Ein sunderlich nutzlicher Tractat von der eynigen warhafftigen: gemeyne Apostolischer heyligen Christlichen Kirche / und von yhrer zucht lere / warheyt / ordenunge / krafft / glaubwirdigkeyt und heyligkeyt / so yhr durch Got Christum unnd den heyligen geyst / sunderlich und eyniglich ist tzu geeygent Eym yden tzu bewaren seyne seele / und vornemlich der Christlicher Obirgkeyt tzu erkennen und tzu entwenden / allen vertumlichen yrthum / und anligend ferligkeyt und tzu erhalten das Christliche Testament und gerechtigkeyt / dartzu sie verordent ist / gantz notthafftig zu wissen durch Gotliche ermanungen beschriben. De sancta Catholica et Apostolica Ecclesia Tractatus articulorum in ordine Decium quartus. Malleus hereticorum.* N.p., 1525. 4°, Ai^v–Hii^v [*Flug.* 2505].

——. *Die ersten vier bucher. M. petri Sylvii. Aus welchen: Das erst ist von dem Primat und gmeinem regiment Petri und seiner nachkommender Statheldern / . . . Das ander ist von der ordenung / authoritet und glaubwirdickeit der waren Christlichen kirche / . . . / Das dritt ist von den vier grunden sso Luther fur sich wider Silvestrum gesatzt. / . . . / Das vierde ist von dem warhafftigen Euangelio und lehre Christi.* Dresden, New Year's Day 1528. 4°, Ai^v–Hiv^v [*Flug.* 1812].

Tetzel, Johannes, O.P. *Vorlegung gemacht wyder eynen vormessen sermon von twentzig irrigenn artikeln bebstliche ablas und gnade belangende, allen christglaubigen menschen tzu wissen von nothen.* 1518. In Löscher 1:484–503.

——. *Subscriptas positiones* ("Fifty Theses"). 1518. In Löscher 1:517–22.

Tuberinus, Johannes. *Ad Cesaream regiamque maiestates Tuberinus suus cum privilegio Capellanus contra falsas Luteris positiones.* Tübingen: U. Morhart, 1524. 8°, Aii–Iv^v [*Flug.* 898].

Usingen, Bartholomeus Arnoldi von, O.E.S.A. *Sermo de matrimonio sacerdotum et monachorum.* Leipzig, [?1523]. In K. A. Strand, "Arnoldi von Usingen's 'Sermo de matrimonio sacerdotum et monachorum': The Text of a Rare Edition." *ARG* 56 (1965) 145–55.

Villa Sancta, Alphonsus de, O.F.M. *Problema indulgentiarum, quo Lutheri errata dissolvuntur, et theologorum de eisdem opinio hactenus apud eruditos vulgata astruitur.* London: J. Pynson, 1523. 4°, ai^v–gi^v.

Wimpina [Konrad Koch von Buchen, O.P.] *Quo veritas pateat* ("One hundred and six counter-theses"). Frankfurt an der Oder, 20 January 1518. In Löscher 1:504–14.

——. *Sectarum, errorum, hallutinatorum et schismatum ab origine ferme christianae ecclesiae ad haec usque nostra tempora concisioris Anacephaleoseos, una cum aliquantis Pigardicarum, Vuiglefticarum et Lutheranarum haeresum confutationibus librorum partes tres.* Frankfurt an der Oder, 1528. Folio, I–CLXII.

Wulffer, Wolfgang. *Wider den ketzrischen widerspruch Merten Lutters uff den spruch Petri. Ir seyt eyn koniglich pristerthumb, von uns Wolffgango Wulffer und andern christgleubigen euch tzu Wittenberg tzugeschriben.* Leipzig: [?M. Landsberg], 1522. 4°, Aii–Biii [*Flug.* 322].

——. *Wid' die unselige auffrure Merten Luders von Wolffgango Wulffer und ander christgleubigen euch zw Wittenberg tzugeschribenn.* Leipzig: [?M. Landsberg], 1522. 4°, Ai^v–Biv^v [*Flug.* 323].

SECONDARY
BIBLIOGRAPHY

Albert, P. *Konrad Koch Wimpina von Buchen.* Buchen: Pressverein, 1931.

Albert, R. "Aus welchem Grunde disputirte Johann Eck gegen Luther in Leipzig 1519?" *ZHT* 43 (1873), 382–441.

Althaus, P. *The Theology of Martin Luther.* Philadelphia: Fortress Press, 1966.

Amrhein, A. *Reformationsgeschichtliche Mitteilungen aus dem Bistum Würzburg 1517–1573.* RST 41/42. Münster-Westfalen: Aschendorff, 1923.

Arnold, F. X. "Vorgeschichte und Einfluss des Trienter Messopferdekrets auf die Behandlung des eucharistischen Geheimnisses in der Glaubensverkündigung der Neuzeit." In F. X. Arnold and B. Fischer, eds., *Die Messe in der Glaubenverkündigung,* 114–61. Freiburg im Breisgau: Herder, 1950.

Augustijn, C. "Die Stellung der Humanisten zur Glaubensspaltung 1518–1530." In E. Iserloh and B. Hallensleben, eds., *Confessio Augustana und Confutatio: Der Augsburger Reichstag 1530 und die Einheit der Kirche,* 36–48. RST 118. Münster-Westfalen: Aschendorff, 1980.

Bagchi, D.V.N. "'Eyn mercklich underscheyd': Catholic Reactions to Luther's Doctrine of the Priesthood of All Believers, 1520–25." In W. J. Sheils and D. Wood, eds., *The Ministry: Clerical and Lay,* 155–65. Studies in Church History 26. Oxford: Basil Blackwell, 1989.

Bátori, I. ed. *Städtische Gesellschaft und Reformation.* Spätmittelalter und Frühe Neuzeit 12. Stuttgart: Klett-Cotta, 1980.

Bäumer, R. *Martin Luther und der Papst.* KLK 30. Münster-Westfalen: Aschendorff, 1971.

―――. "Die Konstanzer Dekrete *Haec sancta* und *Frequens* in Urteil katholischer Kontroverstheologen der 16. Jahrhunderts." In R. Bäumer, ed., *Von Konstanz nach Trient,* 547–74. Paderborn: Schöningh, 1972.

―――. "Die Erforschung der kirchlichen Reformationsgeschichte seit 1931: Reformation, katholische Reform und Gegenreformation in der neueren katholischen Reformationsgeschichtsschreibung in Deutschland." *Erträge der Forschung* 34. 39–127. Darmstadt: Wissenschaftliche Buchgesellschaft, 1975.

―――. "Silvester Prierias und seine Ansichten über das ökumenische Konzil," In R. Bäumer, ed., *Konzil und Papst: Festgabe für Hermanns Tüchle,* 277–301. Paderborn: Schöningh, 1975.

―――. "Lehramt und Theologie in der Sicht katholischer Theologen des 16. Jahrhunderts." In R. Bäumer, ed., *Lehramt und Theologie im 16. Jahrhundert,* 34–61. KLK 36. Münster-Westfalen: Aschendorff, 1976.

————. "Vorgeschichte der Bibliographischen Erfassung von Schriften katholischer Kontroverstheologen und Reformer des 16. Jahrhunderts." vii–xxiii. In *Katholische Kontroversen*, ed. W. Klaiber. Münster-Westfalen: Aschendorff, 1978.

————. "Johannes Cochlaeus und die Reform der Kirche." In R. Bäumer, ed., *Reformatio Ecclesiae: Beiträge zu kirchlichen Reformbemühungen von der Alten Kirche bis zur Neuzeit: Festgabe für Erwin Iserloh*, 333–54. Paderborn: Schöningh, 1980.

————. *Johannes Cochlaeus (1479–1552): Leben und Werk im Dienst der katholischen Reform*. KLK 40. Münster-Westfalen: Aschendorff, 1980.

————, ed. *Reformatio Ecclesiae: Beiträge zu kirchlichen Reformbemühungen von der Alten Kirche bis zur Neuzeit: Festgabe für Erwin Iserloh*. Paderborn: Schöningh, 1980.

Becker, H. "Herzog Georg von Sachsen als kirchlicher und theologischer Schriftsteller." *ARG* 24 (1927), 161–269.

Berger, A. E. *Satirische Feldzüge wider die Reformation: Thomas Murner, Daniel von Soest*. Leipzig: Reclam, 1933.

Beumer, J. "Die Opposition gegen das lutherische Schriftprinzip in der Assertio septem sacramentorum Heinrichs VIII. von England." *Gregorianum* 42 (1961), 97–106.

————. "Eine Beispiel katholischer Zusammenarbeit während der Reformationszeit." *FStud* 49 (1967), 373–83.

————. "Der Minorit Thomas Murner und seine Polemik gegen die deutsche Messe Luther." *FStud* 54 (1974), 192–96.

Bezold, F. von. "Die 'armen Leute' und die deutsche Literatur des späten Mittelalters." *Historische Zeitschrift* 41 (1878), 1–37.

Bietenholz, P. G. "Erasmus, Luther und die Stillen im Lande." *BHR* 47 (1985), 27–46.

Blockx, K. *De veroordeling van Maarten Luther door de theologische faculteit te Leuven in 1519*. Brussels: Paleis der Academien, 1958.

————. "The Faculty of Theology in Conflict with Erasmus and Luther." *Louvain Studies* 5 (1975), 252–63.

Bockmann, P. "Der gemeine Mann in den Flugschriften der Reformationszeit." In P. Bockmann, ed., *Formensprache Studien zur Literaturästhetik und Dichtungsinterpretation* 11–44. Hamburg: Hoffmann & Campe, 1966.

Borth, W. *Die Luthersache (Causa Lutheri)*. Lübeck and Hamburg: Matthiesen, 1970.

Bos, F. T. *Luther in het oordeel van de Sorbonne: Een onderzoek naar ontstaan, inhoud en werking van de "Determinatio" (1521) en naar haar verhouding tot de vroegere verordelingen van Luther*. Amsterdam: Graduate Press, 1974.

Boyle, M. O. *Rhetoric and Reform: Erasmus's Civil Dispute with Luther*. Cambridge: Harvard University Press, 1983.

————. "Erasmus and the 'Modern' Question: Was He Semi-Pelagian?" *ARG* 75 (1984), 59–77.

Brecht, M. *Martin Luther: His Road to Reformation, 1483–1521*. Philadelphia: Fortress Press, 1985.

Brooks, P. N., ed. *Reformation Principle and Practice: Essays in Honour of A. G. Dickens.* London: Scolar Press, 1980.

————, ed. *Seven-Headed Luther: Essays in Commemoration of a Quincentenary 1483–1983.* Oxford: Clarendon Press, 1983.

Bruch, R. "Gesetz und Evangelium in der katholischer Kontroverstheologie des XVI. Jahrhunderts." *Catholica* 23 (1969), 16–37.

Chantraine, G. *Erasme et Luther, libre et serf arbitre: Etude historique et theologique.* Paris: Editions Lethielleux and Naumur; Presses Universitaires, 1981.

Chrisman, M. U. "Lay Response to the Protestant Reformation in Germany, 1520–1528." In P. N. Brooks, ed., *Reformation Principle and Practice: Essays in Honour of A. G. Dickens,* 35–52. London: Scolar Press, 1980.

————. "From Polemic to Propaganda: The Development of Mass Persuasion in the Late Sixteenth Century." *ARG* 73 (1982), 175–95.

————. *Lay Culture, Learned Culture: Books and Social Change in Strasbourg 1480–1599.* New Haven and London: Yale University Press, 1982.

Clark, F. *Eucharistic Sacrifice and the Reformation.* Oxford: Basil Blackwell, 1960. Reprint. Chulmleigh: Augustine Publishing Co., 1980.

Clemen, O., ed. *Briefe von Hieronymus Emser, Johannes Cochlaeus, Johannes Mensing und Petrus Rauch an die Fürstin Maragarethe und die Fürsten Johann und Georg von Anhalt.* RST 3. Münster-Westfalen: Aschendorff, 1907.

Cole, R. G. "The Dynamics of Printing in the Sixteenth Century." In L. P. Buck and J. W. Zophy, eds., *The Social History of the Reformation: Festschrift for H. J. Grimm,* 93–105. Columbus: Ohio State University Press, 1972.

————. "The Reformation in Print: German Pamphlets and Propaganda." *ARG* 66 (1975), 93–102.

————. "The Reformation Pamphlet and Communication Processes." In H.-J. Köhler, ed., *Flugschriften als Massenmedium der Reformation,* 139–61. Spätmittelalter und Frühe Neuzeit 13. Stuttgart: Klett-Cotta, 1981.

Crofts, R. A. "Books, Reform and the Reformation." *ARG* 71 (1980), 21–36.

————. "Printing, Reform and the Catholic Reformation in Germany (1521–1545)." *SCJ* 16 (1985), 369–81.

D'Amico, J. *Renaissance Humanism in Papal Rome.* Baltimore and London: Johns Hopkins University Press, 1983.

Deyon, P. "Sur certaines formes de la propaganda religieuse au XVIe siècle." *Annales Economies-Sociétés-Civilisations* 36 (1981), 16–25.

Dickens, A. G. *The German Nation and Martin Luther.* (London: Edward Arnold, 1974.

Doernberg, E. *Henry VIII and Luther: An Account of Their Personal Relations.* London: Barrie & Rockliff, 1961.

Dolan, J. P. "Liturgical Reform among the Irenicists." *Sixteenth Century Essays and Studies* 2 (1971), 72–94.

————. "The Catholic Literary Opponents of Luther and the Reformation." In E. Iserloh, ed., *Reformation and Counter-Reformation,* 191–207. History of the Church 5. London: Burns & Oates, 1980.

Edwards, M. U., Jr. *Luther and the False Brethren.* Stanford: Stanford University Press, 1975.

———. *Luther's Last Battles: Politics and Polemics 1531–46*. Leiden: E. J. Brill (for Cornell University Press), 1983.

———. "Luther's Own Fanatics." In P. N. Brooks, ed., *Seven-Headed Luther: Essays in Commemoration of a Quincentenary 1483–1983*, 124–46. Oxford: Clarendon Press, 1983.

———. "Catholic Controversial Literature, 1518–1555: Some Statistics." *ARG* 79 (1988), 189–204.

———. "Statistics on Sixteenth-Century Printing." In P. N. Bebb and S. Marshall, eds., *The Process of Change in Early Modern Europe: Essays in Honor of Miriam Usher Chrisman*, 149–63. Athens: Ohio University Press, 1989.

———. "*Lutherschmähung*? Catholics on Luther's Responsibility for the Peasants' War." *CHR* 76 (1990), 461–80.

Ehses, S. "Ein Vorschlag des Bischofs von Breslau an Papst Klemens VII. (1524)." *HJ* 14 (1893), 834–36.

Eisenstein, E. L. *The Printing Press as an Agent of Change: Communications and Cultural Transformations in Early Modern Europe*. 2 vols. Cambridge: Cambridge University Press, 1979.

Engelsing, R. *Der Bürger als Leser: Lesergeschichte in Deutschland 1500–1800*. Stuttgart: Metzler, 1974.

Epiney-Burgard, G. "Jean Eck et le commentaire de la 'Théologie mystique' du Pseudo-Denys." *BHR* 34 (1972), 7–29.

Falk, F. "Das Corpus Catholicorum." *Der Katholik* 71/1 (1891), 440–63.

Fraenkel, P. "John Eck's Enchiridion of 1525 and Luther's Earliest Arguments against Papal Primacy." *StTh* 21 (1967), 110–63.

———. "Johann Eck und Sir Thomas More 1525–1526: Zugleich ein Beitrag zur Geschichte des 'Enchiridion locorum communium' und der vortridentinischen Kontroverstheologie." In R. Bäumer, ed., *Von Konstanz nach Trient*, 481–95. Paderborn: Schöningh, 1972.

———. "An der Grenze vor Luthers Einfluss: Aversion gegen Umwertung." *ZKG* 89 (1978), 21–30.

———. "Le schema, l'image et la cible: Luther vu par ses adversaires romains." in *Luther et la réforme allemande dans une perspective oecuménique*, 339–63. Etudes théologiques 3. Chambésy-Geneva: Centre orthodoxe du Patriarcat oecuménique, 1983.

Franzen, A. *Zölibat und Priesterehe in der Auseinandersetzung der Reformationszeit und der katholischen Reform des 16. Jahrhunderts*. KLK 29. Münster-Westfalen: Aschendorff, 1971.

Freudenberger, T. *Hieronymus Dungersheim von Ochsenfurt am Main, 1465–1540. Leben und Schriften*. RST 126. Münster-Westfalen: Aschendorff, 1988.

Friedensburg, W. "Beiträge zum Briefwechsel der katholischen Gelehrten Deutschlands im Reformationszeitalter (aus italienischen Archiven und Bibliotheken)." *ZKG* 16 (1896), 470–99; 18 (1898), 106–131, 233–97, 420–63, 596–636; 19 (1899), 211–64, 473–85; 20 (1900), 59–94, 242–60.

———, ed. *Nuntiaturberichte aus Deutschland*. Erste Abteilung. 12 vols. Gotha: F. A. Perthes 1892–99.

Gleason, E. G. "Sixteenth-Century Italian Interpretations of Luther." *ARG* 60 (1969), 160–73.

Gogan, B. *The Common Corps of Christendom: Ecclesiological Themes in the Writings of Sir Thomas More.* Leiden: E. J. Brill, 1982.

Gravier, M. *Luther et l'opinion publique.* Paris: Aubier, 1942.

Greving, J. *Johann Eck als junger Gelehrter: Eine literar- und dogmengeschichtliche Untersuchung über seinem "Chrysopassus Praedestinationis" aus dem Jahre 1514.* RST 1. Münster-Westfalen: Aschendorff, 1906.

———. *Johann Ecks Pfarrbuch für U. L. Frau in Ingolstadt: Ein Beitrag zur Kenntnis der pfarrkirchlichen Verhältnisse im sechszehnten Jahrhundert.* RST 4/5. Münster-Westfalen: Aschendorff, 1908.

Grimm, H. J. "Luthers Ablassthesen und die Gegenthesen von Tetzel-Wimpina in der Sicht der Druck- und Buchgeschichte." *Gutenberg Jahrbuch* (1968), 139–50.

Grossman, M. "Wittenberg Printing: Early Sixteenth Century." *Sixteenth Century Essays and Studies* 1 (1970), 53–74.

Haering, N. *Die Theologie des Erfurter Augustiner-Eremiten Bartholomäus Arnoldi von Usingen.* Limbourg: Palotiner, 1939.

Hallman, B. M. "Italian 'National Superiority' and the Lutheran Question, 1517–1546." *ARG* 71 (1980), 134–47.

Headley, J. M. "The Reformation as Crisis in the Understanding of Tradition." *ARG* 78 (1987), 5–22.

Helbling, L. *Dr Johann Fabri, Generalvikar von Konstanz und Bischof von Wien 1478–1541: Beiträge zu seiner Lebensgeschichte.* RST 67/68. Münster-Westfalen: Aschendorff, 1941.

Hendrix, S. H. *Luther and the Papacy: Stages in a Reformation Conflict.* Philadelphia: Fortress Press, 1981.

Hennig, G. *Cajetan und Luther: Ein historischer Beitrag zur Begegnung von Thomismus und Reformation.* Stuttgart: Calwer Verlag, 1966.

Herte, A. *Das katholische Lutherbild im Bann der Lutherkommentare des Cochläus.* 3 vols. Münster-Westfalen: Aschendorff, 1943.

Heynck, V. "Zur Rechtfertigungslehre des Kontroverstheologen Kaspar Schatzgeyer OFM." *FStud* 28 (1941), 129–151.

Hiltbrunner, O. "Der Titel der ersten Streitschriften zwischen Eck und Luther." *ZKG* 64 (1952–53), 312–20.

Hirsch, R. "Printing and the Spread of Humanism in Germany: The Example of Albrecht von Eyb." In R. H. Schwoebel, ed., *Renaissance Men and Ideas,* 24–37. New York: 1971.

———. *Printing, Selling and Reading 1450–1550.* 2d ed. Wiesbaden: Harrassowitz, 1974.

Hoar, G. A. "Early Evidences of Catholic Reform in the Thought and Actions of Bartholomeus Arnoldi von Usingen." *ARG* 56 (1965), 155–65.

Holborn, L. "Printing and the Growth of a Protestant Movement in Germany from 1517–1524." *Church History* 11 (1942), 1–15.

Honselmann, K. *Urfassung und Drucke der Ablassthesen Martin Luthers und ihre Veröffentlichung.* Paderborn: Bonifatius, 1966.

Horst, U. "Das Verhältnis von Schrift und Kirche nach Johannes Dietenberger." *Theologie und Philosophie* 46 (1971), 223–47.

———. *Zwischen Konziliarismus und Reformation: Studien zur Ekklesiologie im Dominikanerorden.* Rome: Istituto storico domenico, 1985.

Hoyer, S. "Jan Hus und der Hussitismus in der Flugschriften des ersten Jahrzehnts der Reformation." In H.-J. Köhler, ed., *Flugschriften als Massenmedium der Reformation,* 291–307. Spätmittelalter und Frühe Neuzeit 13. Stuttgart: Klett-Cotta, 1981.

Hurter, H. *Nomenclator literarius theologiae Catholicae: ab exordiis theologiae scholasticae usque ad celebratum concilium Tridentinum: theologos exhibens aetate, natione, disciplinis distinctos.* Vol. 2, 1109–1568. 3d ed. Innsbruck: Libraria Academica Wagneriana, 1906.

Ickert, S. "Defending and Defining the *ordo salutis*: Jakob van Hoogstraten vs. Martin Luther." *ARG* 87 (1987), 81–97.

———. "Catholic Controversialist Theology and *sola scriptura*: The Case of Jakob van Hoogstraten." *CHR* 74 (1988), 13–33.

Immenkötter, H. *Die Confutatio der Confessio Augustana vom 3. August 1530.* CC 33. Münster-Westfalen: Aschendorff, 1979.

Iserloh, E. *Die Eucharistie in der Darstellung des Johannes Eck.* RST 73/74. Münster-Westfalen: Aschendorff,1950.

———. *Der Kampf um die Messe in den ersten Jahren der Auseinandersetzung mit Luther.* KLK 10. Münster-Westfalen: Aschendorff, 1950.

———. "Der Wert der Messe in den Diskussionen der Theologen vom Mittelalter bis zum 16. Jahrhundert." *ZKTh* 83 (1961), 44–79.

———. *The Theses Were Not Posted.* London: Geoffrey Chapman, 1968.

———. *Reformation and Counter-Reformation.* History of the Church 5. London: Burns & Oates, 1980.

———. *Johannes Eck 1486–1543: Scholastiker, Humanist, Kontroverstheologe.* KLK 41. Münster-Westfalen: Aschendorff, 1981.

———. *Kaspar Schatzgeyer OFM: Schriften zur Verteidigung der Messe.* CC 37. Münster-Westfalen: Aschendorff, 1984.

———, ed. *Johannes Eck Enchiridion; Handbüchlein gemeiner stelund Artikel der jetzt schwebenden Neuwen leeren. Faksimile-druck der Ausgabe Augsburg 1533.* CC 35. Münster-Westfalen: Aschendorff, 1980.

———, ed. *Katholische Theologen der Reformationszeit.* 5 vols. KLK 44–48 Münster-Westfalen: Aschendorff, 1984–88.

———, ed. *Johannes Eck (1486–1543) im Streit der Jahrhunderte.* RST 127. Münster-Westfalen: Aschendorff, 1988.

Iserloh, E., and B. Hallensleben, eds. *Confessio Augustana und Confutatio: Der Augsburger Reichstag 1530 und die Einheit der Kirche.* RST 118. Münster-Westfalen: Aschendorff, 1980.

Jedin, H. "Die geschichtliche Bedeutung der katholische Kontroversliteratur im Zeitalter der Glaubensspaltung." *HJ* 53 (1933), 70–97.

———. *A History of the Council of Trent.* 2 vols. (London: Thomas Nelson & Sons, 1957–61.)

――――. "Die Erforschung der kirchlichen Reformationsgeschichte seit 1876: Leistungen und Aufgabe der deutschen Katholiken." In *Erträge der Forschung* 34. Darmstadt: Wissenschaftliche Buchgesellschaft, 1975.

――――. "Kirchengeschichtliches in der älteren Kontroverstheologie." In R. Bäumer, ed., *Reformatio Ecclesiae: Beiträge zu kirchlichen Reformbemühungen von der Alten Kirche bis zur Neuzeit: Festgabe für Erwin Iserloh*, 273–80. Paderborn: Schöningh, 1980.

Junghans, H. "Der Laie als Richter im Glaubensstreit der Reformationszeit." *LJ* 39 (1972), 31–54.

Kalkoff, P. "Zu Luthers Römischem Prozess" *ZKG* 31 (1910), 368–414; 32 (1911), 218ff.

――――. "Kleine Beiträge zur Geschichte Hadrians VI." *HJ* 39 (1919), 31–72.

――――, ed., *Die Depeschen des Nuntius Aleander vom Wormser Reichstag 1521.* Halle, 1886.

Kawerau, G. *Hieronymus Emser. Ein Lebensbild aus der Reformationszeit.* SVR 61. Halle: Verein für Reformationsgeschichte, 1903.

Kawerau, W. *Thomas Murner und die Kirche des Mittelalters.* SVR 30. Halle: Verein für Reformationsgeschichte, 1890.

――――. *Thomas Murner und die deutsche Reformation.* SVR 32. Halle: Verein für Reformationsgeschichte, 1891.

Kieckhefer, R. *Repression of Heresy in Medieval Germany.* Liverpool: Liverpool University Press; Philadelphia: University of Pennsylvania Press, 1979.

Klaiber, W. *Ecclesia militans: Studien zu den Festtagspredigten des Johannes Eck.* RST 120. Münster-Westfalen: Aschendorff, 1982.

――――, ed., *Katholische Kontroverstheologen und Reformer des 16. Jahrhunderts. Ein Werkverzeichnis.* RST 116. Münster-Westfalen: Aschendorff, 1978.

Klomps, H. *Kirche, Freiheit und Gesetz bei dem Franziskanertheologen Kaspar Schatzgeyer.* RST 84. Münster-Westfalen: Aschendorff, 1954.

Koenneker, B. *Die deutsche Literatur der Reformationszeit: Kommentar zu einer Epoche.* Munich: Winkler, 1975.

Köhler, H.-J. "Die Flugschriften: Versuch der Präzisierung eines geläufigen Begriffs." In H. Rabe, H. Molitor, and H.-C. Rublack, eds., *Festgabe für Ernst Walter Zeeden zum 60. Geburtstag*, 36–61. Münster-Westfalen: Aschendorff, 1976. RST Supplement 2.

――――. "Fragestellungen und Methoden zur Interpretation frühneuzeitlicher Flugschriften." In H.-J. Köhler, ed., *Flugschriften als Massenmedium der Reformationszeit*, 1–27. Spätmittelalter und Frühe Neuzeit 13. Stuttgart: Klett-Cotta, 1981.

――――. "The Flugschriften and Their Importance in Religious Debate: A Quantitative Approach." In P. Zambelli, ed., *Astrologi hallucinati: Stars and the End of the World in Luther's Time*, 153–75. Berlin and New York: Walter de Gruyter, 1986.

――――, ed. *Flugschriften als Massenmedium der Reformationszeit.* Spätmittelalter und Frühe Neuzeit 13. Stuttgart: Klett-Cotta, 1981.

Kolodziej, I. "Die Flugschriften aus den ersten Jahren der Reformation (1517–1525)." Dissertation. Freie-Universität, Berlin, 1956.

Kortepeter, M. "German Zeitung Literature in the Sixteenth Century." In R. J. Schoeck, ed., *Editing Sixteenth-Century Texts*, 113–29. Toronto: University of Toronto Press, 1966.

Krabbel, G. *Caritas Pirckheimer: Ein Leben aus der Zeit der Reformation.* 5th ed. KLK 7. Münster-Westfalen: Aschendorff, 1982.

Kurze, D. *Johannes Lichtenberger: Eine Studie zur Geschichte der Prophetie und Astrologie.* Historische Studien 379. Lübeck and Hamburg: Matthiesen, 1960.

Lämmer, H. *Die vortridentinisch-katholische Theologie des Reformationszeitalters aud den Quellen dargestellt.* Berlin, 1858.

Lamping, A. J. *Ulrichus Velenus (Olrich Velensky) and His Treatise against the Papacy.* Studies in Medieval and Reformation Thought 19. Leiden: E. J. Brill, 1976.

Lauchert, F. *Die italienischen literarischen Gegner Luther.* EEJ 8. Freiburg im Breisgau, 1912.

Legge, T. *Flug- und Streitschriften der Reformationszeit in Westfalen.* RST 58/59. Münster-Westfalen: Aschendorff, 1933.

Leinhard, M. "Held oder Ungeheuer? Luthers Gestalt und Tat im Lichte der zeitgenössischen Flugschriftenliteratur." *LJ* 45 (1978), 109–34.

Lemmens, L. *Pater Augustin von Alveld: Ein Franziskaner aus den ersten Jahren der Glaubensspaltung in Deutschland.* EEJ 1, iv. Freiburg im Breisgau: Herder, 1899.

———. *Aus ungedruckten Franziskanerbriefen des XVI. Jahrhunderts.* RST 20. Münster-Westfalen: Aschendorff, 1911.

Lindberg, C. "Prierias and His Significance for Luther's Development." *SCJ* 3 (1972), 45–64.

Looss, S. "Katholische Polemik zur Haltung Luthers im Bauernkrieg." In G. Brendler and A. Laube, eds., *Der deutsche Bauernkrieg 1524/25: Geschichte-Traditionen-Lehren*, 145–51. Berlin: Akademie-Verlag, 1977.

Lortz, J. *The Reformation in Germany.* 2 vols. London: Darton, Longman & Todd; New York: Herder & Herder, 1968.

———. "Wert und Grenzen der katholischen Kontroverstheologie in der ersten Hälfte des 16. Jahrhunderts." In A. Franzen, ed., *Um Reform und Reformation*, 9–32. KLK 27/28 Münster-Westfalen: Aschendorff, 1968.

Lortz, J. and E. Iserloh. *Kleine Reformationsgeschichte: Ursachen, Verlauf, Wirkung.* Freiburg im Breisgau: Herder, 1969.

Ludolphy, I. "Die Ursachen der Gegnerschaft zwischen Luther und Herzog Georg von Sachsen." *LJ* 32 (1965), 28–44.

Lytle, G. F. "John Wyclif, Martin Luther and Edward Powell: Heresy and the Oxford Theology Faculty at the Beginning of the Reformation." In A. Hudson and M. Wilks, eds., *From Ockham to Wyclif*, 465–79. Studies in Church History: Subsidia 5. Oxford: Basil Blackwell, 1987.

Mandonnet, P. *Jean Tetzel et sa Prédication des Indulgences.* Paris: Bureaux de la Revue Thomiste, 1901. Reprinted from *Revue Thomiste* 7 (1899), 481–96; 8 (1900), 178–93.

Manns, P. "Luther und die Heiligen." In R. Bäumer, ed., *Reformatio Ecclesiae: Beiträge zu kirchlichen Reformbemühungen von der Alten Kirche bis zur Neuzeit: Festgabe für Erwin Iserloh*, 535–80. Paderborn: Schöningh, 1980.

Massaut, J.-P. *Josse Clichtove, l'Humanisme et la Réforme de la Clergé.* Paris: Les Belles Lettres, 1968.

Maxcey, C. E. "Why Do Good? Dietenberger's Reply to Luther." *ARG* 75 (1984), 93–112.

May, G. *Die deutschen Bischöfe angesichts der Glaubensspaltung des 16. Jahrhunderts.* Vienna: Mediatrix, 1983.

Merker, P. *Der Verfasser des Eccius Dedolatus.* Halle: Niemeyer, 1923.

Meyer, H. B. *Luther und die Messe.* Paderborn: Bonifacius, 1965.

Moeller, B. "Stadt und Buch: Bermerkungen zur Struktur der reformatorischen Bewegung in Deutschland." In W. Mommsen, ed., *Stadtbürgertum und Adel in der Reformation*, 25–39. Stuttgart: Klett-Cotta, 1979.

Möhler, J. A. *Symbolism, or Doctrinal Differences between Catholics and Protestants.* Translated by J. S. Robertson. 5th ed. London: Gibbings, 1906.

Mosen, P. *Emser: der Vorkämpfer Roms gegen die Reformation.* Halle: C. A. Kämmerer, 1890.

Mueller, G. *Die römische Kurie und die Reformation 1523–1534: Kirche und Politik während des Pontifikates Clemens VII.* Gütersloh: Gerd Mohn, 1969.

Mueller, K. O. *Aktenstücke zur Geschichte der Reformation in Ravensburg von 1523 bis 1577.* RST 32. Münster-Westfalen: Aschendorff, 1914.

Müller, O. *Rechtfertigungslehre nominalistischer Reformationsgegner: Bartholomäus Arnoldi von Usingen OESA und Kaspar Schatzgeyer OFM über Erbsünde, erste Rechtfertigung und Taufe.* Breslau: Müller & Seiffert, 1940.

Nauert, C. H. "The Clash of Humanists and Scholastics: An Approach to Pre-Reformation Controversies." *SCJ* 4 (1973), 1–18.

Negwer, J. *Konrad Wimpina.* Breslau, 1909.

Newald, R. "Wandlungen des Murnerbildes." In H. Gumbel, ed., *Beiträge zur Geistes- und Kulturgeschichte der Oberrheinlande: Festschrift für Franz Schultz*, 40–78. Frankfurt am Main: Diesterweg, 1938.

Nyhus, P. L. "Caspar Schatzgeyer and Conrad Pellican: The Triumph of Dissension in the Early Sixteenth Century." *ARG* 61 (1970), 179–204.

Oberman, H. A. "Wittenbergs Zweifrontenkreig gegen Prierias und Eck: Hintergrund und Entscheidungen des Jahres 1518." *ZKG* 80 (1969), 331–58.

———. *Masters of the Reformation.* Cambridge: Cambridge University Press, 1981.

———. "Zwischen Agitation und Reformation: Die Flugschriften als 'Judenspiegel.'" In H.-J. Köhler, ed., *Flugschriften als Massenmedium der Reformation*, 269–89. Spätmittelalter und Frühe Neuzeit 13. Stuttgart: Klett-Cotta, 1981.

Overfield, J. H. *Humanism and Scholasticism in Late Medieval Germany.* Princeton: Princeton University Press, 1984.

Ozment, S. E. *The Reformation in the Cities: The Appeal of Protestantism to Sixteenth-Century Germany and Switzerland*. New Haven and London: Yale University Press, 1975.

Paulus, N. "Katholische Schriftsteller aus der Reformationszeit." *Der Katholik* 72/1 (1892), 544–64; 73/2 (1893), 213–23.

———. *Der Augustiner Bartholomäus Arnoldi von Usingen: Luthers Lehrer und Gegner*. Freiburg: Herder, 1893.

———. *Die deutschen Dominikaner im Kampfe gegen Luther (1518–63)*. EEJ 4, i–ii. Freiburg im Breisgau: Herder, 1903.

———. "Konrad Wimpina und Johann Fabri: Zwei angebliche Dominikaner." *ZKG* 49 (1925), 467–74.

Pelikan, J. *Reformation and Dogma of the Church 1300–1600*. Vol. 4 of *The Christian Tradition: A History of the Development of Christian Doctrine*. Chicago: University of Chicago Press, 1984.

Polman, P. *L'Elément Historique dans la Controverse Religieuse du XVIᵉ Siècle*. Gembloux, 1932.

———. "La méthode polémique des premiers adversaires de la Réforme." In J.A.H. Bots et al., eds., *Adversaria Pontiani: Verspreide Geschriften van P. Pontianus Polman*, 1–33. Amsterdam: Holland Universiteits Pers, 1976.

Reid, K. *Moritz von Hutten Fürstbischof von Eichstätt und die Glaubensspaltung*. RST 43/44. Münster-Westfalen: Aschendorff, 1925.

Rex, R.A.W. "The English Campaign against Luther in the 1520s." *Transactions of the Royal Historical Society* 5/39 (1989), 85–106.

———. "The Polemical Theologian." In B. Bradshaw and E. Duffy, eds., *Humanism, Reform and the Reformation: The Career of Bishop John Fisher*, 109–30. Cambridge: Cambridge University Press, 1989.

Rischar, K. *Johann Eck auf dem Reichstag zu Augsburg 1530*. RST 97. Münster-Westfalen: Aschendorff, 1968.

Rochler, W. *Martin Luther und die Reformation als Laienbewegung*. Institut für Europäische Geschichte Mainz Vorträge 75. Wiesbaden: Steiner, 1981.

Rupp, E. G. "Luther's Ninety-Five Theses and the Theology of the Cross." In C. S. Meyer, ed., *Luther for an Ecumenical Age*, 67–80. St. Louis: Concordia, 1967.

———. "The Battle of the Books: The Ferment of Ideas and the Beginning of the Reformation." In P. N. Brooks, ed., *Reformation Principle and Practice: Essays in Honour of A. G. Dickens*, 1–19. London: Scolar, 1980.

Sabisch, A. *Die Bischöfe von Breslau und die Reformation in Schlesien: Jakob von Salza (gest. 1539) und Balthasar von Promnitz (gest. 1562) in ihrer glaubensmässigen und kirchenpolitischen Auseinandersetzung mit den Anhängern der Reformation*. KLK 35. Münster-Westfalen: Aschendorff, 1975.

Schade, O. *Satiren und Pasquille aus der Reformationszeit*. 3 vols. Hanover: C. Rumpler, 1856–58.

Schauerte, H. *Die Busslehre des Johann Eck*. RST 38/39. Münster-Westfalen: Aschendorff, 1929.

————. "Johannes Eck und das Konzil." In *Unio Christianorum: Festschrift für Erzbischof Dr Lorenz Jaeger,* ed. O. Schilling and H. Zimmerman, 267–77. Paderborn: Bonifacius, 1962.

Schüssler, H. *Der Primat der heiligen Schrifft als theologisches und kanonistisches Problem im Spätmittelalter.* Wiesbaden: F. Steiner, 1977.

Schottenloher, K. "Buchdrücker und Buchführer in Dienste der Reformation." In *Realencyclopädie für protestantische Theologie und Kirche* (1913) 23:270–74.

————. *Tagebuchaufzeichnungen des Regensburger Weihbischofs Dr Peter Krafft.* RST 37. Münster-Westfalen: Aschendorff, 1920.

Schütte, J. *"Schympf red": Frühformen bürgerlicher Agitation in Thomas Murners "Grossen Lutherischen Narren" (1522).* Germanistische Abhandlungen 41. Stuttgart: Metzler, 1973.

Schweitzer, J. *Ambrosius Catharinus Politus (1484–1553), ein Theologe des Reformationszeitalters.* RST 11/12. Münster-Westfalen: Aschendorff, 1910.

Schwitalla, J. *Deutsche Flugschriften, 1460–1525.* Textsortengeschichte Studien Reihe Germanistische Linguistik 45. Tübingen: Niemeyer, 1983.

Scribner, R. W. "Reformation, Carnival and the World Turned Upside-Down." In I. Bátori, ed., *Städtische Gesellschaft und Reformation,* 234–64. Spätmittelalter und Frühe Neuzeit 12. Stuttgart: Klett-Cotta, 1980.

————. "Practice and Principle in the German Towns: Preachers and People." In P. N. Brooks, ed., *Reformation Principle and Practice: Essays in Honour of A. G. Dickens,* 97–117. London: Scolar, 1980.

————. "Flugblatt und Analphabetentum: Wie kam der gemeine Mann zu reformatorischen Ideen?" In H.-J. Köhler, ed., *Flugschriften als Massenmedium der Reformationszeit,* 65–76. Spatmittelalter Frühe Neuzeit 13. Stuttgart: Klett-Cotta, 1981.

————. *For the Sake of Simple Folk: Popular Propaganda for the German Reformation.* Cambridge: Cambridge University Press, 1981.

Seidemann, J. K. *Die Leipziger Disputation im Jahre 1519.* Dresden and Leipzig: Arnold, 1843.

————. "M. Petrus Sylvius, ein Dominicaner der Reformationszeit." *Archiv für Literaturgeschichte* 4 (1875), 117–158.

————. "Die Schriften des Petrus Sylvius." *Archiv für Literaturgeschichte* 5 (1876), 6–32, 287–310.

Seitz, R. O. *Der authentische Text der Leipziger Disputation.* Berlin: Schwetschke, 1903.

Selge, K.-V. "Die Leipziger Disputation zwischen Luther und Eck." *ZKG* 86 (1975), 26–40.

————. "Das Autoritätsgefüge der westlichen Christenheit im Lutherkonflikt 1517 bis 1521." *Historische Zeitschrift* 223 (1976), 591–617.

Smolinsky, H. "Reformationsgeschichte als Geschichte der Kirche. Katholische Kontroverstheologie und katholische Reform." *HJ* 103 (1983), 372–94.

————. *Augustin von Alveldt und Hieronymus Emser. Eine Untersuchung zur Kontroverstheologie der frühen Reformationszeit im Herzogtum Sachsen.* RST 122. Münster-Westfalen: Aschendorff, 1983.

Spahn, M. *Johannes Cochläus: Ein Lebensbild aus der Zeit der Kirchenspaltung.* Berlin, 1898. Reprint. Nieuwkoop: De Graaf, 1964.

Strand, K. A. *Reformation Bibles in the Crossfire: The Story of Jerome Emser, His Anti-Lutheran Critique and His Catholic Bible Version.* Ann Arbor, Mich.: Ann Arbor Publishers, 1961.

————. "Arnoldi von Usingen's 'Sermo de matrimonio sacerdotum et monachorum': The Text of a Rare Edition." *ARG* 56 (1965), 145–55.

Strauss, G. "The Religious Policies of Dukes Wilhelm and Ludwig of Bavaria in the First Decade of the Protestant Era." *Church History* 23 (1959), 350–73.

Stupperich, R. "Melanchthon und Radini." *ZKG* 100 (1989), 340–52.

Tavard, G. H. *Holy Writ or Holy Church? The Crisis of the Protestant Reformation.* London: Burns & Oates, 1959.

Tompert, E., "Die Flugschriften als Medium religiöser Publizistik: Aspekte der gegenwärtigen Forschung." In J. Nolte, H. Tompert, and C. Windhorst, eds., *Kontinuität und Umbruch: Theologie und Frömmigkeit in Flugschriften und Kleinliteratur an der Wende vom 15. zum 16. Jahrhundert,* 211–21. Stuttgart: Klett-Cotta, 1978.

Tracy, J. D. "Two Erasmuses, Two Luthers: Erasmus' Strategy in Defense of *De libero arbitrio.*" *ARG* 78 (1987), 37–59.

Vercruysse, J. E. "Jacobus Latomus und Martin Luther: Einführendes zu einer Kontroverse." *Gregorianum* 64 (1983), 515–38.

Wedewer, H. *Johannes Dietenberger 1475–1537: Sein Leben und Wirken.* Freiburg, 1888. Reprint. Nieuwkoop: De Graaf, 1967.

Werl, E. "Herzog Georg von Sachsen, Bischof Adolf von Merseberg und Luthers 95 Thesen." *ARG* 61 (1970), 66–69.

Werner, K. *Geschichte der apologetischen und polemischen Literatur der christliche Theologie.* 5 vols. Regensburg: G. J. Manz, 1862–89.

Wicks, J. *Cajetan und die Anfänge der Reformation.* KLK 43. Münster-Westfalen: Aschendorff, 1983.

————. "Roman Reactions to Luther: The First Year (1518)." *The Catholic Historical Review* 69 (1983), 521–62.

Wiedemann, T. *Dr Johann Eck, Professor der Theologie an der Universität Ingolstadt—eine Monographie.* Regensburg: F. Pustet, 1865.

Wiedermann, G. "Cochlaeus as a Polemicist." In P. N. Brooks, ed., *Seven-Headed Luther: Essays in Commemoration of a Quincentenary 1483–1983,* 196–205. Oxford: Clarendon Press, 1983.

Willburger, A. *Die Konstanzer Bischöfe Hugo von Landenberg, Balthasar Merklin, Johann von Lupfen (1496–1537) und die Glaubensspaltung.* RST 34/35. Münster-Westfalen: Aschendorff, 1917.

Wohlfeil, R. *Einführung in die Geschichte der deutschen Reformation.* Munich: Beck, 1982.

Wolf, G. "Die katholische Gegner der Reformation vor dem Tridentinum und Jesuitenorden." *Quellenkunde der deutsche Reformationsgeschichte* 212 (1922), 206–62.

Ziegelbauer, M. *Johannes Eck: Mann der Kirche im Zeitalter der Glaubensspaltung.* St. Ottilien: EOS Verlag, 1987.

Zoepfl, F., *Johannes Altenstaig: Ein Gelehrtenleben aus der Zeit des Humanismus und der Reformation.* RST 36. Münster-Westfalen: Aschendorff, 1918.

INDEX